# Foundations
# of Educational
# Research

# Foundations of Educational Research

## Gilbert Sax

*University of Washington*

Prentice-Hall, Inc. Englewood Cliffs, New Jersey 07632

*Library of Congress Cataloging in Publication Data*

Sax, Gilbert.
    Foundations of educational research.

    Includes bibliographies and index.
    1.  Educational research.    I.  Title.
LB1028.S233       370'.78      78-14596
ISBN 0-13-329300-9

Printed in the United States of America

10  9  8  7  6  5  4  3  2  1

Editorial/production supervision:  *Cathie Mick Mahar*
Interior and Cover design:  *Chris Gadekar*
Manufacturing buyer:  *John Hall*

This is the second edition of a book formerly titled
EMPIRICAL FOUNDATIONS OF EDUCATIONAL RESEARCH

Prentice-Hall International, Inc., *London*
Prentice-Hall of Australia Pty. Limited, *Sydney*
Prentice-Hall of Canada, Ltd., *Totonto*
Prentice-Hall of India Private Limited, *New Delhi*
Prentice-Hall of Japan, Inc., *Tokyo*
Prentice-Hall of Southeast Asia Pte. Ltd., *Singapore*
Whitehall Books Limited, *Wellington, New Zealand*

to Lois,
for whom I am systemically biased;
to our children and grandchildren,
who bring meaning and joy to our lives;
and to our parents,
who made all of this possible

# contents

preface

The application of empirical research methods to education goes back little more than half a century. Since then, the schools have been called upon to fulfill roles and obligations largely unconceived of by nineteenth-century educators. Unfortunately, it has not always been possible to justify modern educational practices or innovations. Like their predecessors, today's educators are often forced into making decisions without knowledge derived from empirical research findings to guide or help justify their actions.

Current knowledge about education has come from many sources, ranging in validity from the biased pronouncements of the grossly mis-informed to highly dependable statements originating with those who have gone to the trouble to test their expectations empirically. Research methods are devised to provide investigators with the techniques, procedures, and knowledge needed to verify or reject these expectations, not with the hope of "proving" one's own point or in finding fault with others', but to study problems within a scientific framework that encourages the resolution of problems by rational and empirical means.

This text is designed to provide readers with the foundations of educational research. It is deliberately not a textbook in statistics, measurement, or historical methodology, although all of these subject areas are, of course, related to empirical research methods.

I am convinced that to try to explain research design to students who have not had at least an introductory course in statistics is to do them a great disservice. They are likely, in a one-semester course in research methods, to learn neither statistics nor research design and to dislike both. The failure to provide graduate students in education with training in statistics and research design contributes to the unhappy precedent of preparing students who are unable to read professional journals or evaluate their own practices.

Nor does this text pretend to cover historical or philosophical research methods. Historiography is in itself a highly complex subject deserving of study on its own by those planning to specialize in the history or philosophy of education. The few pages on historical research methods typically included in texts on research do justice neither to history nor to empiricism.

This text has the following purposes:

*1.* To introduce students to the excitement and interest that accompany the discovery and creation of new knowledge

*2.* To acquaint graduate students in education with the potentials and limitations of empirical research

*3.* To provide students with an understanding of the contributions that empirical research methods have made to educational practices

*4.* To show the relationships between empiricism and the philosophical and theoretical assumptions underlying empirical research procedures

*5.* To describe the tools and methods used in empirical investigations

*6.* To help students become intelligent consumers of and contributors to educational theory and practice

To accomplish these objectives, this text has incorporated a number of special features:

*1.* Chapters are arranged sequentially, taking the student from the point of selecting a research project to the analysis and presentation of findings.

*2.* A detailed summary is provided at the end of each chapter to introduce the student to the content of the chapter and to help in reviewing.

*3.* Every chapter contains a list of annotated supplementary readings. These can take the curious reader into greater depth than can be presented in this text.

*4.* Practice exercises accompany each chapter. Some exercises can easily be converted to objectively scored examinations; others are designed as projects or for class discussion. Difficulty levels range widely. The majority of the exercises are designed to test how well the student can apply and understand the concepts presented in the text.

5. The text is specifically designed for master's degree candidates in education, although it may also be used with more advanced students if the supplementary readings are used extensively.

6. It is assumed that the student has studied and understands basic elements of descriptive and inferential statistics. If this assumption cannot be met, it is suggested that the instructor discuss these topics as early in the course as possible. An appendix on statistical reasoning has been included to help students review these topics.

7. The text is suitable for a one-semester, quarter, or year course in research methods. For a one-semester or quarter course, students can read one to two chapters per week and perhaps design a study of their own; for a more extended course, each chapter can be enriched with supplementary readings. Students might also be asked to conduct their own study if the course can be carried out over a year's time.

This text the Foundations of Educational Research differs from the first edition Empirical Foundations of Educational Research in a number of ways:

1. References, research studies, and topics have been updated to reflect the current literature in educational research.

2. The writing style has been modified to eliminate possible sex stereotyping; similarly, references to various ethnic and racial groups use terms that are currently accepted by these groups.

3. A glossary of important terms has been included both as a study aid for students and to allow instructors to change the order of chapter presentations should they care to do so.

4. Six appendices have been added:

a. A test analysis form has been included to help the student evaluate and select appropriate educational and psychological measures.

b. Ethical considerations in conducting research point out the student's ethical and legal responsibilities and provide additional criteria for evaluating research.

c. The elements of statistical reasoning should be of value to students who need a review of statistical inference or an introduction to statistical reasoning. The emphasis is on understanding statistical reasoning and not on computational routines.

d. A detailed outline of the research paper has been included so that students can better understand the elements that go into a thesis, dissertation, or published research study.

e. An appendix on writing a research report summarizes the stylistic and organizational principles needed to write and evaluate research.

f. A list of library sources useful in educational research has been included to aid the student in locating research literature.

5. Chapter 3 (Selecting the Research Problem) includes a section on using the library in educational research. The combination of these two topics points out the relationship between reviewing the literature and selecting a research problem.

6. The organization of chapters within the text has been improved.

7. New chapters have been added. The original chapter on experimental design, for example, has been divided into factors affecting internal and external validity and types of experimental designs. A chapter on unobtrusive measures has also been added.

8. The discussion of reliability has included a greater emphasis on classical test theory and on the research conditions that call for different types of reliability coefficients.

9. The chapter on data processing has been revised to reflect the many changes that have occurred in the past ten years. The electromechanical calculator, for example, has almost entirely given way to electronic calculators.

I am indebted to a number of persons who were extremely helpful in the preparation of this revision. Mrs. Mary Todd and Mrs. Ruth Natividad typed parts of the manuscript; my wife, Lois, checked all bibliographical references, read the manuscript, had me revise passages until they were clear, typed and prepared the final manuscript for printing, performed all the many tasks required to revise a text, and did so in her charming and patient ways as she worked on an advanced degree and kept our family functioning. It is to her that I especially dedicate this text.

I am also indebted to Dr. Alan Klockars, who read the statistical appendix; to Dr. Percy Peckham, whose review of the earlier manuscript and detailed comments on the revision helped guide my thinking; and to the many students who provided me with their suggestions for improving the text. Mrs. Claire Marston, Research Librarian, University of Washington, provided invaluable assistance in reviewing Chapter 3. I am also indebted to the Literary Executor of the late Sir Ronald A. Fisher, F.R.S., Cambridge, and to Oliver & Boyd, Ltd. for their permission to reprint from their book *The Design of Experiments.* To all of these persons I owe a debt of gratitude and appreciation. They are not, of course, responsible for any errors of omission or commission.

GILBERT SAX
*University of Washington*

the
scientific
basis
of
education

1

## SOURCES OF KNOWLEDGE

The need for reliable knowledge concerning education has never been as keenly felt as it is today. The schools, at one time agencies dedicated to the education of the elite, have been changing their functions, curricula, and methods to accommodate increasing demands from a society that has insisted upon quality education.

It is not surprising, considering the many changes in education over the past half century, that educators have often lacked the knowledge needed to justify these modifications in educational practice. Instead, many justifications were based, at least in part, on the biases of individual educational reformers, on appeals to authority, or, perhaps even worse, on dogmatic assertion. Under such conditions it was easy for subjectivity and bias to override objective and empirical methods of studying educational problems.

This lack of valid knowledge and the concomitant dependence on prescientific ways of thinking not only allowed unexamined and inefficient practices to continue but also prevented a number of worthwhile educational experiments from being conducted. In 1897, for example, J. M. Rice asked the participants at the annual meeting of the Department of Superintendence how it would be possible to determine if students who are given 10 minutes of spelling each day learn any less than those who are given 40 minutes each day. He discovered that some educators did not even believe an answer to this question was possible. Rice stated, ". . . to my great surprise, the question threw consternation into the camp. The first to respond was a very popular professor of psychology engaged in training teachers in the West. He said, in effect, that the question was one which could never be answered; and he gave me a rather severe drubbing for taking up the time of such an important body of educators in asking them silly questions."[1]

Dependable knowledge about education has come from many different sources. At the beginning of the twentieth century educators could not easily imagine that scientific methods could provide answers to questions that had interested teachers for the preceding two thousand years, and it was little wonder that Rice had difficulty persuading the members of the Department of Superintendence to accept these methods. The prevailing attitude was that educational problems could be resolved through appeals to five sources: common sense, authority, intuition, revelation, or logic.

## The Appeal to Common Sense

The appeal to common sense can be considered from two points of view: as (1) a means for "justifying" preconceived beliefs, or (2) as a way of referring to knowledge that has been previously verified. When used to justify preconceived ideas, the appeal to common sense stifles communication and prevents or discourages experimentation. Thus, as long as common sense dictated that the study of difficult subjects such as Latin, Greek, or mathematics would "exercise the mind," there were few demands for experimental investigation of the matter. Indeed, in 1892, when President Eliot of Harvard was appointed chairman of the Committee of Ten on Secondary School Studies by the National Educational Association, the Committee recommended that only difficult subjects be counted on to "exercise the mind." The implementation of the Committee's recommendations led to a sterile, difficult, and impractical curriculum which did much to eliminate many of the less able students from the public schools. These "common sense" beliefs were not modified until the first quarter of the twentieth century, when experimental evidence had been accumulated to discredit them.

The second meaning of *common sense* refers to generally accepted

[1] J. M. Rice, *Scientific Management in Education* (New York: Hinds, Noble & Eldredge, 1913), pp. 17–18.

and empirically verified knowledge. With this definition, information derived through common sense represents a body of already investigated beliefs which may be modified as additional evidence is obtained. Thus, the present-day educator may "take it for granted" that quiet children are not always the best-adjusted ones, a position that was not always accepted. Nonetheless, these common sense beliefs can be reexamined and reformulated as new information is accumulated.

## The Appeal to Authority

The uncritical acceptance of someone else's beliefs has retarded knowledge about education just as in other disciplines. Throughout history, there have been individuals who were castigated because they refused to accept the word of some "authority." In the Middle Ages, the teachings of Aristotle and the Church were used as a means of coercing people into "accepting" current religious practices. In more modern times, references to educational "authorities" in education have been used to justify one's own position and to stifle communication and inquiry. When an argument is started with "Dewey said . . . ," it is assumed too often that there is little need to discuss the matter further.

The appeal to authority is not always an unreasonable way of dealing with certain kinds of information. Knowledge has grown too rapidly for anyone to be equally competent in all subjects. Thus, it may be necessary to accept someone's word if it is not possible, either by aptitude or inclination, to obtain the evidence for oneself.

Mander[2] has proposed four criteria for judging whether or not a person may be considered an authority. First, *the individual who is being judged as an authority should be identifiable.* That is, it should be possible to discover the name of the person being recommended as an authority. Statements such as "Many educators believe . . ." or "Specialists in education claim . . ." are imprecise unless the educators or specialists are identified.

A second criterion suggested by Mander is that *the authority should be recognized as such by members of the profession in which competency is claimed.* Membership in professional societies and reputation among colleagues may be used as a rough but useful measure of the extent to which the authority's statements have the sanctions of that professional group. To be sure, the danger always exists that personal prejudices or unpopular beliefs may unfairly discredit an otherwise accurate opinion. Nonetheless, failure to apply this criterion can lead to an intellectual anarchy in which the persons most knowledgeable are denied the opportunity to evaluate their peers.

A third criterion is that *the cited authority should be living.* In ancient Greece, Aristotle could reasonably have been considered an "expert" in sci-

[2]A. E. Mander, *Logic for the Millions* (New York: Philosophical Library, 1947), pp. 57–60.

ence and logic; however, he could only be considered an expert in science today if no important or contradictory facts or arguments had come to light after his death.

The fourth criterion is that *an authority should not be biased.* That is, it is necessary to judge whether or not prejudices, biases, and stereotypes are interfering with the ability of a person to make a clear and rational judgment. Admittedly, such evaluation is difficult, but difficulty should not prevent one from trying to make these judgments.

## The Appeal to Intuition and Revelation

Revelations are direct and immediate insights concerning "truth" or "reality"; they are often presumed to originate from God. If these hunches or experiences are believed to have "natural" origins, they are called intuitions.

At one time or another everyone has probably experienced intuitions or hunches suggesting, for example, that a particular stranger should not be trusted, or that taking a particular fork in the road when lost would lead to one's destination. These intuitions, derived from past experiences with similar phenomena, may or may not provide dependable knowledge concerning the expected or predicted consequences of every decision. The distrusted stranger may, if given the opportunity, turn out to be a loyal and good friend; the unselected road may be quicker and safer than the one chosen by intuition. Intuitive beliefs cannot always be trusted without empirically verifying their consequences.

Revelations are more difficult to analyze than are intuitions, since their source is presumed to originate outside of human experience. Because the belief in a supernatural existence rests upon faith, the scientist has no way to validate or invalidate revelations unless they contradict empirical experiences. Proclamations that the world will end on a certain day are invalid when that day has passed safely. If there is a conflict between a private "revealed truth" and empirically derived knowledge, the strength of the argument will favor empiricism. Even though there is nothing final or absolute about scientific knowledge, the methods employed by scientists involve a set of rigorous criteria for evaluating "truth." Scientific findings can be examined by anyone with a willingness and ability to do so. The private nature of a revelation makes it impossible to examine it openly or to duplicate it for further consideration. Thus, while the revelation may have tremendous importance for the person experiencing it, its private nature does not provide a very convincing argument for others.

## The Appeal to Logic

Rationalism is the philosophic position that places reason over both revelation and experience. In general, rationalists take the position that concepts such as God, causality, or mathematical "proofs" do not depend upon either experience or revelation but can be proven through rational processes, especially deduction.

Deduction is the process of drawing specific conclusions from premises in a form known as a syllogism. The most common type is the categorical syllogism, which takes the form

*All A is B* (or, for example, All humans are mortal)
*C is A* (Socrates is a human)
*Therefore, C is B* (Therefore, Socrates is mortal)

The conclusion that Socrates is mortal is a logical deduction from the major premise that "All humans are mortal" and from the minor premise, "Socrates is a human." Since equalities equal to each other are being compared, the conclusion is valid.

Deduction is not an unreasonable way of deriving knowledge. Mathematical reasoning, for example, is dependent upon rules of logic which specify the definitions of various terms and their interrelationships. The scientist employs these rules and definitions to help derive relationships and specific conclusions. For example, it is a simple matter to demonstrate mathematically that adding a constant to a series of scores will augment the mean of the original series by the value of the constant. This can be done by defining each term needed and performing operations in accordance with rules and procedures that do not violate logical principles.

Although deduction is useful, it is quite another matter to believe that it is the primary method for deriving all "truth." In deductive reasoning, the conclusions may reveal nothing about "reality," since major or minor premises may not correspond with the "real" world. Thus, it is safe to state that "All humans are mortal," since "mortal" and "humans" are semantic equivalents. But nothing prevents anyone from stating, "All humans are elephants" and "Socrates is a human." The conclusion must then be drawn that "Socrates is an elephant." Note that the rules of logic do not specify what the empirical relationships must be among humans, elephants, and Socrates. Conclusions may be logically correct even though premises are not.

## SCIENCE AS A SOURCE OF KNOWLEDGE

This text characterizes science as a method and attitude rather than as an absolute body of knowledge or as an attempt to lend authority or prestige to one's proclamations (as in the expression, "Science has proven . . ."). As a method, empirical science relies on observation to develop and to validate explanatory systems called *theories*; as an attitude, science consists of a willingness to examine and, if need be, to modify or repudiate one's own beliefs, ideas, or methods as new or more reliable evidence is obtained.

# CHARACTERISTICS OF SCIENCE

## Reduction and Control of Bias

Scientists, like other human beings, are not without prejudices, biases, and misinformation. Emotional sterility characterizes neither the scientist nor the scientific attitude. Research requires a compelling curiosity and a willingness to modify personal beliefs when the evidence so demands. The very selection of a research topic is a value judgment made by the scientist. Nonetheless, the scientific attitude is violated when the scientist disregards evidence contrary to personal beliefs or arranges conditions so that only the favored or desired outcome is likely to occur.

## The Quest for Precision

Although science does demand as much rigor and precision as is possible, this demand should not be confused with a search for absolute or irrefutable truth. Human beings can depend only upon themselves, their methods, and their instruments to understand their environment. There is no appeal to higher authorities to validate methods or conclusions. Findings and conclusions are always tentative and subject to modification as new knowledge and methods are created.

## Verification

The scientist reports observations so that other investigators can confirm or reject them. Science does not, or at least should not, have secret or privileged information. Research depends upon this self-corrective function in which all scientists have the right to question findings and conclusions that cannot be verified.

## Empiricism

Empiricism is the position that observation and experience are the prime means of obtaining knowledge and that other approaches (intuition and common sense, for example) are relegated a lower priority should they be in conflict with empirically obtained data.

The basic form of reasoning used by empiricists is *induction*, which draws a general conclusion from specific observations. Unless observations are accurately obtained and recorded, the conclusions drawn may well be fallacious. Research techniques are devised to prevent, reduce, or control errors of observation. Tests are used to observe how students will respond under some specified and uniform condition; experiments are performed to control (eliminate or hold constant) certain observations; and records are kept so that other interested persons can check independently on the researcher's observations. Mechanical or electronic equipment may aid in observation.

## Theory Construction

Some persons erroneously believe that theory is the result of useless contemplation and as such deserves little, if any, consideration. Others are more willing to concede that theory may have value, but that it is not as important as "practical" knowledge.

Raw observations do not form a science no matter how accurate they may be. Even organized observations do not necessarily constitute a science. A telephone directory or a teacher's roll book may be both accurate and organized, and yet they are not sciences. *A scientific theory is a unified system of principles, definitions, postulates, and observations organized to most simply explain the relationships among variables.* This explanatory function of theory and its derivation from empirical data differentiate the scientific theory from mere contemplation or from uselessness.

To demonstrate how theories are developed, suppose that the following "facts" have been verified, reconfirmed under various conditions, and are universally agreed upon:

*1.* Forgetting increases with time.

*2.* The beginning and end of a memorized list will be retained to a greater extent than will material in its center.

*3.* After sleeping, pupils can recall data they could not recall the night before (the "reminiscence" effect).

*4.* Forgetting increases as more material is learned.

The scientist attempts to develop or induce from particular observations a theory or generalization that will explain all four facts. Suppose that the following statements are considered as possible explanations:

a. *Theory of disuse:* Forgetting occurs because material degenerates unless practiced.

b. *Psychoanalytic theory:* Forgetting occurs because unpleasant memories are repressed.

c. *Interference theory:* Forgetting occurs because material learned early in a sequence interferes with the learning of later material (*proactive inhibition*), and material learned later in a sequence interferes with previously learned material (*retroactive inhibition*).

To what extent does each of the three theories explain all of the facts?[3] The theory of disuse can account for the apparent decay of memory

---

[3]As used here, a *fact* is an observation of some physical datum or event.

over time, but it does not explain facts two or four and is in direct contradiction to fact three.

The psychoanalytic theory may partially account for the so-called reminiscence effect, but it does not explain the other facts. The only theory which seems to account for all of the facts is the interference theory. It explains fact one by asserting that more interference is likely over long periods of time than over shorter intervals. It explains fact two on the grounds that the terminal part of any sequence to be memorized can only be interfered with by preceding parts (i.e., affected proactively), while the beginning of the sequence can only be affected by material which is learned later on (affected retroactively). However, the material in the center of the sequence is affected by preceding as well as by following events and thus becomes most interfered with (affected both proactively and retroactively). The interference theory only partially explains fact three by postulating that during sleep there is little chance for interference to occur. Fact four is explained by the greater amount of interference possible with a larger amount of material to be learned.[4] In the process of induction, one ordinarily tries to account for as many facts as possible by developing the fewest number of theories or explanatory generalizations. The most useful theories are those which most adequately and simply explain the greatest number of relevant facts.

## The Relationship between Theories and Facts

The researcher developing a theory must be willing to modify it to account for discrepant facts; the opposite process, modifying facts to conform to a pet theory, has been called "Maier's Law."[5] It facetiously states: "If the facts do not conform to the theory, they must be disposed of."[6] Maier has suggested a number of ways facts have been ignored to perpetuate a poor theory. One way is to give the facts a new name.

> Giving disturbing facts a name is almost as good as explaining them because a name supplies a useful answer to inquisitive people. For example, a lecturer in describing the habits of people living near the North Pole told his audience how children ate blubber as if it were a delicacy. Later a questioner asked the speaker why these children liked a food that would not be attractive to children living here. The lecturer replied that this was so because the children were Eskimos. The questioner replied "Oh, I see" and was satisfied. In a similar manner the word "catharsis" explains why we feel better after expressing pentup feelings.[7]

[4]These "facts" and "theories" have been oversimplified to make the process of induction clear. The example should be considered illustrative only.
[5]N. R. F. Maier, "Maier's Law," *American Psychologist*, 15, no. 3 (1960), pp. 208–12.
[6]Maier, "Maier's Law," p. 208.
[7]Maier, "Maier's Law," p. 209.

Facts may also be disregarded in another way. According to Maier, the most efficient way of eliminating facts that do not correspond with theory is to fail to report them.

> Naturally it takes a critical individual to determine what is worth reporting and what is irrelevant. For example, one researcher reported that his experiment on delayed reaction was conducted on the third floor of the building but did not tell how many tests he ran in a day. Later it was found that the number of tests per day determined the length of a delay, while the floor used was not important. Since selection is always with us, what better aid is there for the selecting of facts than a good theory.[8]

The relationship of fact to theory has not always been well understood by many researchers. The student should keep in mind how theory may be used to clarify facts and how facts may be used to validate theory. Van Dalen[9] has indicated a number of ways in which theory and facts are interrelated:

> 1. *Theory defines the relevancy of facts.* Not all facts are of equal value. Some facts, although highly dependable, may not be related to anything of immediate importance. Thus a researcher could collect data about the sizes of foreheads of elementary school children or try to determine the number of songs seniors can learn over a given period of time. But these facts, once obtained, have limited applicability. Having a theoretical structure helps determine which kinds of facts are needed to validate or invalidate a given theory.
>
> 2. *Theory develops systems of classification and a structure of concepts.* Since nature does not provide a ready-made system of classifying objects, events, or methods, it is up to the researcher to organize facts in such a way that they become useful. A theoretical structure helps the scientist organize facts by relating them to a broader concept of theory.
>
> 3. *Theory summarizes facts.* It may be difficult for the scientist to retain large numbers of seemingly unrelated facts. However, as a theory is developed which explains these facts, it becomes easier to summarize large masses of data by subsuming them into a meaningful structure. Thus, one theory may explain a large number of facts.
>
> 4. *Theory predicts facts.* One purpose of theory is to predict events. A novice teacher, for example, may have rather specific questions concerning the behavior of a given child, such as why the child continually hits others. Without the benefit of theory, it would be necessary to investigate the characteristics of every child before it would be possible to discuss aggressiveness in general. Once a theory has been established and confirmed in a number of different

---

[8] Maier, p. 210.

[9] D. B. Van Dalen, "The Relationship of Fact and Theory in Research," *Educational Administration and Supervision*, 45, no. 5 (1959), pp. 271–74.

situations, it enables the teacher to predict within the limits of probability what will happen when certain events occur. Thus, a psychoanalytic theory might suggest that aggression is displaced hostility; another theory may suggest that aggression is related to the amount of frustration experienced. No matter what the specific form of the theory, it allows the teacher or researcher to predict and perhaps explain the child's behavior.

5. *Theory points out needs for further research.* A fruitful source of research topics can be found in attempts to confirm or refute theories already proposed. All theories are tentative formulations and can be modified to conform to known facts. By examining the implications of theory, the investigator may find useful research ideas.

An example may clarify this process. Suppose one does accept the interference theory of forgetting (see page 7). One way of selecting a research topic is to test the implications of this theory. For example, the interference theory states that retention is a function of the amount of interference. Suppose that this theory is tentatively accepted. What should the researcher then be able to predict concerning forgetting? Any of the "facts" listed on page 7 would help support that theory. These facts then become a possible topic for investigation. Each theory should be capable of generating hypotheses which can be experimentally tested to clarify, expand upon, and delimit various aspects of the theory itself.

Theories not only contribute to knowledge, but it is also true that facts contribute to theory.[10] First, facts stimulate theory construction. As more and more data are added to any body of knowledge, the need to organize and explain these facts increases. This organizational process continues and forms the nucleus for the development of theory. Thus, it is quite reasonable to select research topics to obtain facts to help develop some body of theory.

## Simplicity

The so-called *law of parsimony* states that of several equally suitable theories, science will tentatively "accept" the simplest. The law of parsimony does not state that only simple theories can be accepted or that complex explanations are inappropriate. It simply assumes a hierarchy of tentative explanations, each of which must be tested in greater detail. Researchers accept an explanation only in the sense that they plan to investigate the simpler explanation before looking into more complex ones.

## Models

In addition to constructing theories, scientists often use *models* or abstract representations of phenomena to help explain the relationships among variables. A model airplane and a map are abstractions of their

[10]Van Dalen, pp. 273–74.

prototypes; similarly, mathematical models can represent many empirical relations. Models help to explain phenomena by pointing out the essential similarities and differences between the model and its prototype. For example, electronic computers may be used to form a model of the human brain or to simulate large-scale management problems involving the deployment of personnel. Essentially, the model can be used to test hypotheses and to save time, effort, and funds.

## SUMMARY

1. Five methods of obtaining knowledge were discussed:

**a.** Common sense may refer to "generally accepted but incorrect information," or to "generally accepted and empirically verified knowledge." The first definition is used to avoid presenting evidence for beliefs; the second use of the term is more defensible.

**b.** The appeal to authority is an attempt to "take someone else's word for it," rather than to investigate matters as carefully as possible for oneself. Criteria for judging authorities are that the authority 1) must be identifiable; 2) must be recognized as such by members of the profession in which competency is claimed; 3) must be living, or no new and relevant facts should have come to light after the authority's death; and 4) must not be biased.

**c.** Intuitive beliefs are "hunches" or "insights" into the relationships between variables which suggest a course of action and which are derived from one's past experiences with similar phenomena. If put to the empirical test, intuitions can be verified or disproved, providing a check upon one's beliefs. If intuitive beliefs or feelings are not verified or disproved empirically, they provide no justifiable basis for action but that of convenience.

Revelations are beliefs or feelings claimed to be derived "supernaturally." The validity of private revelations is open to question, especially if they conflict with empirical observations.

**d.** Rationalism is the belief that reason yields more reliable knowledge than does revelation or experience. Rationalists emphasize *deductive* reasoning as a primary means of gaining knowledge. Thus, they would argue that mathematics and logic provide more reliable information than does empiricism. Unfortunately, the conclusions derived depend only on the logical process, not on the validity of the premises.

2. Science is defined in this book as a method or attitude with the following characteristics:

**a.** *Reduction and control of bias.* Scientists recognize their fallibility and make their observations in as objective a manner as possible. They are not, however, without personal values, principles, prejudices, or interests.

**b.** *The quest for precision.* A distinction was made between the scientist's desire for precision and accuracy and the quest for absolute or irrefutable knowledge. The scientist depends upon tools, techniques, and methods to provide knowledge but recognizes that this knowledge is not perfect.

**c.** *Verification.* Because scientists are fallible, they must allow others to verify or disprove their conclusions. In turn, they examine evidence provided by other investigators.

**d.** *Empiricism.* Empiricism stresses observation and experience and employs inductive reasoning as the prime means for establishing principles and generalizations.

**e.** *Theory construction.* A theory is a set of principles, definitions, postulates, and facts organized so as to explain the interrelationships among variables. Theories attempt to explain these interrelationships as simply as possible, according to unifying principles.

1) *The relationship between theories and facts.* In developing a theory, the scientist examines observations and tries to discover the general statement that will most completely account for them. The following ways to dispose of facts and perpetuate an inadequate theory are naming relationships instead of explaining them, and failing to report those facts which do not agree with the theory.

2) *The relationship between facts and theories.* Theory defines the relevancy of facts, helps classify them, summarizes them, predicts them, and suggests research needed to confirm or reject a given theory.

3) *Simplicity, or the law of parsimony.* The law of parsimony reminds the scientist that theoretical explanations should be kept as simple as possible. This avoids the necessity of testing the consequences of superfluous postulates.

**3.** *Models.* One way of explaining phenomena is to relate observations to a body of theory. Another way is to develop a model to show the relevance of the observation to the model. Models can be used to simulate empirical relationships and to reduce time, effort, and expenditure of funds.

## PRACTICE EXERCISES

**1.** Each of the following statements might be considered by some persons as "perfectly obvious," and therefore not in need of investigation. Indicate how certain you are that each statement is "correct." If you are uncertain that it is correct, indicate what evidence you would need to determine the correct answer. If you are certain the statement is correct, indicate the reasons for your belief.

**a.** All boys become men. Albert became a man. Therefore, Albert at one time was a boy.

**b.** When the pupil–teacher ratio is lowered, teachers *will be able* to do a better job of teaching than they are now *able* to do.

**c.** Kindergarten teachers should have had children of their own to raise before they enter the teaching profession.

**d.** Teachers should be model citizens so the childrens will emulate them.

**e.** Some children love their teachers.

**f.** Schools are either elementary, junior high, high schools, or colleges.

**2.** Indicate the difficulty (if any) in accepting each of the following persons or statements as authoritative. If further information is needed, indicate what type of information you would require before you could evaluate the statement or person.

**a.** Judge Jones, a member of the Supreme Court, states that the poor relationship between parents and children is the cause of juvenile delinquency.

**b.** The author of this textbook says that education can be studied scientifically.

**c.** Admiral Rickover states that the schools in Europe are better than the schools in the United States.

**d.** John Dewey says that values depend upon their consequences.

**e.** Most educational psychologists agree that motivation is important in learning.

**3.** For each of the following examples, indicate the methods you could employ to verify or reject the statement or question. Which statements or questions cannot be investigated? Why?

**a.** How high is up?

**b.** The principal of a school is responsible for its program.

**c.** Teachers should be equally prepared in knowledge of subject matter and in methods of teaching.

**d.** The kindergarten teacher should receive the same pay as the high school teacher if they are both equally well trained to do their jobs.

**e.** These questions are not difficult.

**4.** What theory could you develop that would help explain each of the following sets of facts? Assume that each of the facts is "true." What other information is needed to further verify your theory?

*Facts for Set I*

**a.** At 6:00 A.M., John is awakened by a person talking to him very softly from the window of his room.

**b.** The voice is so low that he cannot make out what the person is saying.

**c.** There is no one in his room but himself.

**d.** He runs outside but there is no one there.

**e.** Each time he returns to the room he hears the voice again.

*Facts for Set II*

**a.** Of 20 cats isolated from birth from all other animals, 9 were known to kill rodents.

**b.** Of 21 cats who saw rodents being killed, 18 were known to kill.

**c.** Of 18 cats reared with rodents, only 3 were known to kill.

**d.** The cats' diet (vegetarian or nonvegetarian) was unrelated to whether they killed or not.[11]

*Facts for Set III*

**a.** Most of the world's best-known persons have been males.

**b.** More men than women have been in homes for the retarded.

**c.** More men than women have been identified as gifted.

*Facts for Set IV*

**a.** Blacks who migrate to the North do as well on standardized tests as those who remain in the South.

**b.** The average tested IQ for the black is 9 to 10 points lower than the average Caucasian's.

**c.** Some black children have IQ's as high as 200.

**d.** Northerners consistently score higher than Southerners of the same racial extraction.

**e.** Caucasians score consistently higher than blacks living in the same region.

**5.** For each of the following theoretical positions, indicate what facts you would need to give credence to the theory. How could such facts be obtained?

**a.** *Theoretical Position I:* Frustration leads to aggression. (frustration–aggression theory)

**b.** *Theoretical Position II.* Reinforcement is necessary for learning. (theory of reinforcement)

**c.** *Theoretical Position III:* Much significant human behavior is unconsciously motivated. (theory of subconscious motivation)

**d.** *Theoretical Position IV:* Children are born bad. (theory of innate depravity)

## Selected Supplementary Readings

1. BJORK, ROBERT A. "Why Mathematical Models?" *American Psychologist*, 28, no. 5 (May 1973), pp. 426–33. An excellent account of the need for and meaning of mathematical models in understanding human behavior. Written specifically for students with minimum mathematical backgrounds.

2. BROUDY, HARRY S.; ROBERT H., ENNIS, and LEONARD I. KRIMERMAN, *Philosophy of Educational Research*. New York: John Wiley & Sons, 1973, 942 pp.

---

[11]Z. Y. Kuo, "The Genesis of the Cat's Response to the Rat," *Journal of Comparative Psychology*, 11, no. 1 (1930), pp. 1–35.

A book of readings containing 60 articles organized into 12 chapters: "Educational Research as Science"; "Nature, Scope, and Strategy of Educational Research"; "Research Ethics"; "Observation"; "Inference"; "Testability"; "Causation"; "Models"; "Value Judgments in Science"; "Concepts and their Delineation"; "Behaviorism"; and "Programmed Instruction."

3. FEIGL, HERBERT, and MAY. BRODBECK, *Readings in the Philosophy of Science.* New York: Appleton-Century-Crofts, 1953, 811 pp. A collection of readings ranging widely in level of difficulty. Students will find the following selections most helpful in extending their knowledge of the meaning and assumptions underlying science. Pages 8–18 contain an excellent critique of misconceptions of science; advanced students may find selections on pages 47–102 concerning the meaning of verifiability to be of interest. The meaning of *explanation* in the sciences can be found on pages 319–352 and 688–743; concepts of causality and determinism are treated on pages 387–407. Of special importance to students of educational psychology is Section V, "Philosophical Problems of Biology and Psychology," pages 523–659. Pages 757–780 contain some excellent articles: "The Limits of Science"; "Causality and the Science of Human Behavior," and "The Laws of Science and the Laws of Ethics."

4. KAPLAN, ABRAHAM. *The Conduct of Inquiry.* San Francisco: Chandler Publishing Co., 1964, 428 pp. Written by a philosopher, this text examines the philosophical assumptions underlying research in the behavioral sciences.

5. LARRABEE, HAROLD A. *Reliable Knowledge.* Scientific Methods in the Social Studies rev. ed. Boston: Houghton Mifflin Co., 1964, 409 pp. An excellent introduction to the problems of obtaining and evaluating reliable knowledge. Especially relevant material can be found in Chapter 2, "Man as Knower: From the Inside"; Chapter 3, "Formal Logic: What Follows from Premises"; and Chapter 4, "Toward Scientific Method: Observation—'Get the Facts'".

6. NAGEL, ERNEST. *The Structure of Science: Problems in the Logic of Scientific Explanation.* New York: Harcourt, Brace & World, 1961, 618 pp. Students will find the introduction, titled "Science and Common Sense," to be of interest. In addition, Chapter 2, "Patterns of Scientific Explanation," discusses the role and meaning of *explanation* in the sciences.

7. ROSS, MINA. "The Scientist in Society: Inspiration and Obligation." *American Psychologist*, 63, no. 2 (March–April 1975), 144–49. An illuminating account of the changing roles and obligations of science and scientists.

8. SUPPES, PATRICK. "The Place of Theory in Educational Research." *Educational Researcher*, 3, no. 6 (June 1974), 3–10. Suppes discusses five arguments showing the relevance of theory to research (the contributions of theory in the natural sciences, the value of theory in differentiating between the important and the trivial, the search for explanations, the need to go beyond problem solving, and the need to avoid the "triviality of bare empiricism.") Suppes then provides some excellent examples of theory in educational research (statistical theory and economic models). The last part of the article is titled "Sources of Theory."

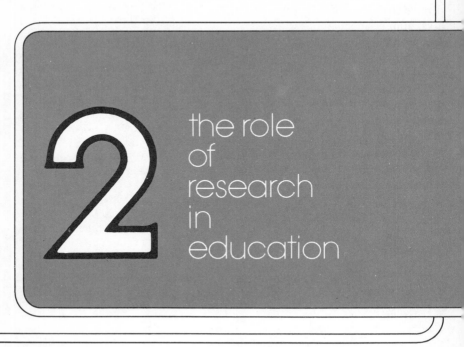

# 2 the role of research in education

Discussion among educators often centers around the promise of research in general and the lack of accomplishment of educational research in particular. This paradox of extolling the promise of research while criticizing its accomplishments is based upon a misunderstanding of the nature of educational research. Although Americans have long considered "Progress . . . to be the first law of nature,"[1] they have, at the same time, refused to state explicitly the direction that progress ought to take. Inherent in this plea for progress is the belief that research can, or at least should, provide the knowledge needed to contribute to educational reforms and improvements. What has not been understood is that research alone is unable to transform the schools into utopias.

[1] Vernon L. Parrington, *The Romantic Revolution in America*, Vol. II of *Main Currents in American Thought* (New York: Harcourt, Brace & World, 1954), p. ix.

Changes in education have resulted from and contributed to many diverse social, economic, and political conditions. Research does not exist in a vacuum unaffected by the hopes, aspirations, and limitations of the rest of society. Considering the fallibility of research findings and remembering that these findings must be evaluated by considering local economic, political, social, and aesthetic beliefs and practices, it should be clear that any given research finding cannot expect universal, immediate acceptance and implementation. What may be a reasonable way of solving a problem in one community may not be desirable or feasible in another. Thus, although research may provide knowledge about empirical relationships, educators may very well refuse to implement these findings if, for example, the implementation might lead to economic or social injustice.

## TYPES OF RESEARCH

Reliable knowledge about education can be derived from the application of various research methods: analytic, descriptive, and experimental (see Table 2-1).

TABLE 2-1

Types of Research and Their Relationship to Educational Practice

|  | Analytic | Descriptive | Experimental |
|---|---|---|---|
| Purpose | To derive relationships within a deductive system | To describe existing conditions | To test causal relationships |
| Methods | Deductive, mathematical, historical, philosophical, legal, linguistic | Correlations, surveys, case studies, direct observation, cross-cultural, growth studies | Comparison of experimental and non-experimental groups by systematically varying conditions |
| Relation to practice | Points out assumptions and possible consequences of proposed changes; useful in establishing criteria | Describes currently existing conditions so that they can be modified later | Shows the effects of a proposed innovation |

## Analytic Research

Analytic research includes mathematical, linguistic, historical, and philosophical analyses, as well as any deductive system that can be used to derive relationships not necessarily of an empirical nature. Examples of analytic research include the development of new statistical procedures, the analysis of language through grammar and linguistics, and the analysis of assumptions and implications through logical and philosophical procedures.

Analytic research helps point out the assumptions and possible consequences of proposed innovations. The historian, for example, may be in a position to show how a proposed change is related to some historical event that has already been tried and evaluated. Analysis may also be used to help establish criteria for the evaluation of an innovation.

One form of analytic research is *data retrieval*. Its purpose is to gather information from both primary and secondary sources. A primary source is one that has direct access to an original observation. For example, an original manuscript or a report from an eyewitness are primary sources of information. In contrast, a secondary source is removed one or more times from the original observation. A report from a secondhand witness or a book that summarizes the contents of original reports are secondary sources.

By searching the literature, the investigator concerned with innovation can take advantage of the experiences of others engaged in related pursuits. Data retrieval may point out weaknesses in an approach or help the researcher relate a proposed study to those that have been conducted previously (see Chapter 3 for a more thorough discussion of data retrieval methods and goals).

## Descriptive Research

The purpose of *descriptive research* is to describe current conditions without their being influenced by the investigator. Descriptive research includes correlational analyses, case studies, surveys, and interviews, as well as direct observation. These techniques will be discussed in greater detail in later chapters.

Descriptive research is often of greatest value during the initial stages of an investigation. If the current status of a problem is described, steps may be taken later to remedy it. If, for example, educators are concerned about the effects that high school dropouts are likely to have on the economy, a first step might be a study to determine how many students leave high school before graduating, what occupations they move into, their salaries, etc. Descriptive research may also help point out the extent of a problem and indicate how serious and widespread it is. Once this information is available, educators can consider methods of resolving the problem.

## Experimental Research

The purpose of *experimental research* is to study "causal" relationships. It may be used, for example, to study the effects rewards have on learning or to evaluate the advantages of one incentive over another. The investigator tries to control (i.e., eliminate or hold constant) the effects of irrelevant conditions to study the effect of one or more variables on another.

The role of the experiment in solving the school dropout problem might be to determine which of various proposals for retaining students leads to the largest number graduated. These proposals might include the establishment of a work–study program where the student works half day and attends school half day; or they might involve an evaluation of the "job corps," the use of volunteers to help motivate students planning to drop out of school, etc. Before deciding which proposals will be evaluated, answers are needed to such questions as: "What is the relationship between social class and opportunity for success in the public schools?" "How does the reward structure in schools affect achievement?" "Under what conditions and at what ages do negative attitudes toward school begin?" "What factors are most responsible for motivating students to remain in and enjoy school?" Unless these and other related questions are investigated, an experimental program designed to test one method of reducing dropouts against another is not likely to be very successful.

# THE RELATIONSHIP BETWEEN
# RESEARCH AND EVALUATION

The purpose of research is to explain empirical relationships among variables. This knowledge may concern itself with theory development or it may have the more immediate goal of studying current educational practices. Research conducted to contribute to theory is called *basic research*; research designed to study problems of more immediate application is called *applied research*. The distinction between the two involves differences in emphasis rather than any fundamental dissimilarity.

Evaluation differs from research in that it serves a different purpose, namely, to make *decisions* about the adequacy of a program, a learning medium, a teacher's effectiveness, or a special curriculum. The decision can be to maintain, modify, eliminate, or improve upon whatever is being evaluated.[2] Research and evaluation differ with regard to the nature of the deci-

---

[2]The differences between research and evaluation are by no means agreed upon by all researchers or evaluators. See, for example, John K. Hemphill, "The Relationships Between Research and Evaluation Studies," in Ralph W. Tyler, ed., *Educational Evaluation: New Roles, New Means*. The Sixty-eighth Yearbook of the National Society for the Study of Education, Part II (Chicago: University of Chicago Press, 1969), pp. 189–220 for one view on this distinction. See also Chapters 1–3 of W. James Popham, ed., *Evaluation in Education: Current Applications* (Berkeley, Calif.: McCutchan Publishing Corp., 1974), pp. 3–199, for a somewhat different approach. For example, the term "evaluation research" is currently being used for a study that "produces as a conclusion . . . a judgment of value, worth, or merit" (Popham, p. 4).

sions made, the extent to which outcome commitments are formed, and perhaps to a lesser extent, the nature of the treatment variables.

## Nature of Decisions

Different decisions are made in research and in evaluation studies. The researcher is usually interested in knowing whether a given set of conditions "makes a difference." Statistical tests of significance are meaningful because they indicate the probability that two or more samples are derived from the same or different populations. For example, if immediate and delayed reinforcement have different and consistent effects on learners, the researcher could conclude that these variables make a difference. But making a difference does not necessarily mean that sufficient evidence has been presented to *recommend* one treatment over another.

Evaluation studies may also use statistical tests of significance. One teaching method may be superior to another in a statistical sense, but it is quite possible that neither would be recommended if costs or undesirable side effects were considered. Statistical tests alone involve no necessary moral imperatives or prescriptions for making decisions to implement a new program. Additional evidence is needed that students are attaining objectives and that benefits outweigh costs.

Another difference between research and evaluation concerns the immediacy of the decisions that are made. For the researcher who is trying to *understand* the psychological mechanisms of learning and instruction, no immediate decision is necessary from research except perhaps to reject or "accept" the null hypothesis. The evaluator, however, must recommend a course of action. Any delay in evaluating a program simply means that current programs, whether effective or not, are likely to be continued.

## Commitment to Improvement

As pointed out in Chapter 1, the researcher tries not to allow value judgments and expectations to interfere with the methods used in an investigation. The researcher is committed to using methods that are not biased for or against any preconceived notions concerning what the outcomes "should" be. Results that consistently fail to confirm research expectations may be disappointing personally, but they can still contribute to knowledge.

Evaluators also avoid bias in selecting methods of studying a program, but they are committed to producing the best possible *results*. The desired outcomes are specified in advance, and every effort is made to attain them. Methods and materials are modified until the desired effects are realized. A new arithmetic unit, for example, might be designed to "increase learning" and to "reduce learning time." Each term in quotation marks would have to be defined behaviorally. An increase in learning might be defined to mean that no student would obtain a score of less than 85 percent on a specified arithmetic test; a reduction in learning time might mean that all students would reach the specified criterion on the arithmetic test in no more than one-half the time currently spent in learning the same content.

Suppose the evaluator discovers that the unit increases learning but fails to do so within specified time constraints. Unlike the researcher who can report *but not modify* findings, the evaluator has an obligation to modify the unit until the specified criterion is met.[3] Modifications may be suggested from studying previously conducted research and evaluation studies, from analyses of the test performance and classroom behavior of those students who failed to complete the unit in time, or from the observations and attitudes of teachers, students, and parents.

## The Nature of the Treatment Variables

An experimental "treatment" is any condition the researcher selects for observation of its effects on a given group of individuals. Unlike the purpose of a medical treatment, which does imply improvement or cure, subjects exposed to an experimental treatment or condition are expected only to *change* as a result of that exposure, but not necessarily to *improve*. For example, no improvement is expected when subjects are given increasing amounts of alcohol to study changes in driving ability; nonetheless, amount of alcohol is a treatment variable when its effects are being studied.

Experimental treatments vary considerably in standardization and therefore in the degree to which they can be reproduced and their effects isolated by other experimenters. Alcohol, for example, can be described chemically and quantitatively, and the mode of administration (orally or by injection) can be controlled and its effects measured. Investigators can systemically vary alcohol type (scotch, vodka, etc.), amount, speed of intake, mode of administration, and any number of variables regarding subjects (age, sex, weight, previous experience with alcohol). If contradictory results are reported by different researchers, it would be possible to identify those factors that produced these differences.

Now consider a study designed to compare the achievement of students in an "open classroom" with those attending a "traditional," self-contained class. One difficulty is in describing and defining the differences in the experimental treatments being compared. These treatments may be defined so vaguely that it is impossible to conduct any studies. The decision to compare programs assumes that the teachers are equally competent and

---

[3]The decision could also be to eliminate innovative but unnecessary programs or to "accept" a lower standard of student performance.

effective, that the teacher-pupil ratio and instructional materials are the same, that the students are equally intelligent, and so forth. Even if these assumptions were valid, the treatment variable would still be vague, and it would be difficult to know which variables made a difference.

If treatment variables are imprecise, findings may not be applicable to any other groups or situations. Findings that apply to only one situation or one set of conditions contribute little to a science of education or to practical changes in the operations of schools. If the goal of science is to *understand* empirical relationships, the failure to define treatment variables perpetuates ambiguity and is counterproductive to the development of generalizable knowledge.

Evaluation studies, however, may well be of some value in decision making even though treatments are highly complex. The evaluation of an "open classroom," for example, might be carried out in a district to help decide on the future of that program. The intent might not be to determine which specific aspects of the program (such as the teachers, textbooks, school plant, or parent attitudes) were responsible for changes in student achievement, although that information would be highly desirable. The study would reveal whether or not the overall effects warranted the continuance of the program, but it might be impossible to determine which aspects of the program were effective and which were not.

## RESEARCH, EVALUATION, AND EDUCATIONAL CHANGE

Because theory suggests which facts are relevant to the understanding of a problem, researchers and evaluators who disregard theory may lack a guide in selecting important variables to investigate. Little is gained by trying to implement every suggestion that might be proposed to improve education.

Many innovations are implemented at great cost and with little benefit to students. Indeed, some have had serious negative effects that remained undiscovered for years. The so-called new math is a case in point. In 1951, the University of Illinois Committee on School Mathematics (UICSM) began working on the secondary mathematics curriculum to make it more understandable, less laden with unexplained rules, and of greater interest to students. Almost fifteen years later, Harold Hand made the following comments:[4]

[4]Harold C. Hand, "Integrity and Instructional Innovation," *The Educational Forum*, 30, no. 1 (1965), pp. 9–10. By permission of Kappa Delta Pi, an Honor Society in Education, owners of the copyright.

Without exception all of the news items in the press and all the comments in the popular magazines concerning the new mathematics programs that I have encountered have been laudatory to some degree. . . . About three years ago, however, the distinguished head of the mathematics department in a large eastern university made a blistering attack on the new mathematics courses. . . . His attack was largely based on the grounds that the new courses neglected aspects of mathematics which youngsters need to learn. This was followed by a three page statement, also critical of the new mathematics programs . . . which was signed by professors of mathematics at 32 institutions.

Neither school board members nor the public at large has been told that there are competent scholars in mathematics who seriously question the soundness of the highly touted mathematics courses. *Nor have they been told that the experimental validation of a belief on which the new programs in science as well as those in mathematics are banking is lacking.* [italics added]

Even earlier, however, the late Max Beberman was reported to be troubled by the new math although he was a leader in the UICSM movement. Beberman's concern was that younger students' computational skills were being neglected in the UICSM program. Beberman's suggestions were to move more slowly, to prepare teachers more adequately, and to introduce the new math gradually and experimentally.[5] This admission of program failure is not only rare, but it is also a tribute to a man with the humility and courage to admit error publicly.

Behind the statement that innovations should be based on tested principles is the realization that some innovations have had serious negative effects. Any far-reaching, costly, or potentially damaging innovation should not only have a strong theoretical and empirical justification, but it should also be implemented with a small group of students whose parents can be assured that adequate remediation will be available should the program be ineffective. As one researcher put it:

Ideas spring from the innovator's mind into direct application to children and teachers with no intermediate steps. If medicine did things the way we do, the Salk vaccine would have been administered to everyone merely because Jonas Salk thought it should be, and was persuasive enough to get us to do it. . . . *We should adopt the point of view that ideas should not be tried on children until there is some large amount of evidence that the ideas are workable and the results will be beneficial.* [italics added][6]

[5]Francis J. Mueller, "The Public Image of 'New Mathematics,' " *The Mathematics Teacher* (November 1966), p. 621.

[6]Daniel E. Griffiths, *Research in Educational Administration: An Appraisal and a Plan* (New York: Bureau of Publications, Teachers College, Columbia University, 1959), p. 31.

Although proposed innovations should be supported by research, evaluation studies are also needed to determine their benefits and undesirable effects. These undesirable effects are not necessarily limited to students participating in a program; they can also affect other students, parents, teachers, and the community in general. A no-failure grading policy, for example, might be justified on "humanitarian" principles, but one wonders how this policy would affect those students who observe their classmates being promoted without putting forth much effort. Or one could ask how such a policy among high school students would affect university admission requirements. How many students, for example, might be encouraged by a guaranteed promotion policy to take advanced classes for which they have little preparation, and how will these changes in enrollments affect teachers and other students? Will parents support a no-failure policy, or will it create antagonism among parents and between parents and the school administration? A recommendation to implement such a policy obviously requires long-term research and evaluation studies.

## Development as an Impetus to Educational Change

Development contributes to educational change by lowering costs and increasing the efficiency of products, practices, or conditions in order to promote their greater use. In industry, for example, the responsibility of

TABLE 2-2

Development, Demonstration, and Dissemination and Their Relationship to Educational Practice

|  | Development | Demonstration | Dissemination |
|---|---|---|---|
| Purpose | Build a more efficient product | To show use of innovations | To make innovations known |
| Methods | Lower costs, make palatable, eliminate problems | Use in classrooms with teachers | Publication |
| Relation to practice | Makes innovations possible | Shows value of innovation | Increased use of innovation |

development is to take a product *which has been shown to have value* and produce it efficiently and inexpensively. Development is a continuing process which contributes to as well as benefits from research and evaluation.

However, development should not proceed without evidence that the proposed change is worthwhile and that negative effects are minimal. One ordinarily does not waste time lowering costs for a product or idea that has little value.

### Demonstration as an Impetus to Educational Change

Once a product or idea has been developed, it is necessary to *demonstrate* how it works. The purpose of the demonstration is to persuade others to accept the innovation. Development may indicate that a new approach to teaching mathematics is both efficient and inexpensive, but the demonstration will show teachers and administrators that the approach is operationally useful and desirable; unless it has some demonstrated appeal, it is unlikely to find its way into very many classrooms.

### Dissemination as an Impetus to Educational Change

The dissemination of knowledge, an important impetus for modifying educational practice, carries with it a responsibility for prudence, caution, and restraint. The purpose of dissemination is to inform, and not to persuade or cajole readers into accepting an innovative idea or product. Unfortunately, many journal articles in education have recommended changes in the curriculum, in teaching, and in methods that are contradictory to one another and that offer little or no evidence to support their claims.

Dissemination of information can be of value at all stages of research or evaluation and need not be delayed until a "final verdict" has been rendered regarding the efficacy of some proposed innovation. Educators have the right to know what evidence supports and argues against a proposed change.

# FACTORS HINDERING EDUCATIONAL RESEARCH

Although research has made valuable contributions to knowledge about education, it has nevertheless been unable to make the type of contribution many educators have felt it should. In part, this is due to the lack of cooperation between researchers and evaluators. Other conditions, however, have also hindered the progress of educational research. These include the lack of funds for research, the general lack of skill among educators in the methodology of research, the difficulties in bridging the gap between theory and practice in the schools, and the willingness of some educators to accept unreliable or undependable research findings.

## Lack of Funds for Educational Research

Research cannot make much progress unless funding is available for equipment, personnel, and supplies. To be sure, even if sufficient funds were provided, research would still be hampered by inadequately trained researchers and the use of inefficient research designs. Nonetheless, without adequate expenditures for research, the best designs and the best researchers are likely to fail.

Industry and business have been estimated to contribute between 5 and 15 percent of their funds to research. By carefully explaining the values of research to stockholders and governing boards, industries have been able to appropriate rather large sums of money for both basic and applied problems. Unfortunately, it has not been as easy for educational administrators to urge school boards to expend larger proportions of their budgets for research and evaluation.

The years between 1969 and 1975 represented a serious decline in federal support of educational research, although there was an increase in aid to low-income students, which is included as part of the research and development budget. Apart from aid to low-income students, the federal government in 1969 contributed about 1.0 percent of the federal R&D budget to education; in 1976 that value is expected to increase to 1.5 percent, but in 1975, federal R&D expenditures were at about the same level of funding as in 1969 ($150 million) despite the effects of inflation.[7]

Compared with these rather small appropriations, industry, business, and private foundations have been more generous in providing research funds for education. In 1962, the Ford Foundation was estimated to be granting more money to improve education than was the federal government.[8]

The federal government alone cannot provide the full support needed if research is going to live up to the demands of educators and the public. Other agencies (both public and private) should share the responsibility for funding research adequately. For example, the federal government contributes 53 percent of all R&D support nationwide; another 43 percent is contributed by industry, although the amount for educational

[7]National Science Foundation, *An Analysis of Federal R&D Funding by Function, 1969–1976*. NSF Document 75–330 (Washington, D.C.: Superintendent of Documents: U.S. Government Printing Office, August 1975), p. 47.

[8]Lindley J. Stiles, "The Cooperative Research Program: Contributions and Next Steps," *Phi Delta Kappan*, 43, no. 6 (1962), pp. 231–236.

research is unknown; the remaining 4 percent comes from universities, colleges, and nonprofit institutions.[9]

## Lack of Training in Educational Research

One important reason that educational research has not made the contribution educators have demanded lies in the training of researchers themselves. Competent researchers must be selected with care and allowed to work and study in an atmosphere which respects intellect and scholarship.

However, even assuming that professors of education are able to attract the most able students to work on advanced degrees, methods of teaching research methodology will have to be upgraded. By no means do all doctoral-granting institutions require work in measurement and research for a doctorate in education. One would expect an even smaller number of institutions to require work in research at the master's degree level.

Considering the need for research in education, it might be expected that professors of education would be devoting relatively large amounts of time to research. But college professors, like their counterparts in the public schools, are occupied with myriad administrative and teaching assignments that cut rather heavily into research time. The result is that ". . . even in the institutions selected because of their research activities, most of the faculty members are officially assigned little or no time for research."[10]

Adequate research requires time to think about methods of attacking important problems. In an attempt to be objective as well as to encourage research among faculty members, many universities place a heavy priority on the *number* of research papers published by faculty members rather than on the *quality* of each project. The result is that the reward system encourages much publication which duplicates well-established research or at best makes a trivial contribution. Thus, rather than devoting valuable time to planning for an important investigation, many researchers find the need to publish so strong that the quality of their research suffers.

Teachers, too, are unprepared to read and understand educational research studies. In one survey,[11] for example, the investigators found that elementary teachers typically read nontechnical journals subscribed to by their schools. Most articles in these journals were of the "how-to-do-it" vari-

[9]National Science Foundation, 1975, p. iii.

[10]Nicholas A. Fattu, "A Survey of Educational Research at Selected Universities," in Frank W. Banghart, ed., *First Annual Phi Delta Kappa Symposium on Educational Research* (Bloomington, Ind.: Phi Delta Kappa, 1960), pp. 1–21.

[11]John J. Cogan, "Elementary Teachers as Nonreaders," *Phi Delta Kappan*, 56, no. 7 (March 1975), pp. 495–496.

ety and provided suggestions that were largely unsupported by evidence. If one criterion for a profession is that its practioners be able to read and understand the pertinent research literature, training in educational research methods should be a part of teacher-training programs.

## Bridging the Gap between Theory and Practice

Americans are pragmatic in the sense that they expect research to be judged by its products. Unfortunately, some persons have considered "products" rather narrowly and have thus been concerned only with the immediate and practical utility of research findings. Unless educational research leads directly to educational reform, they become disillusioned.

Teachers are often annoyed by having to increase knowledge about education as well as to provide for educational reform. These two objectives, although by no means incompatible, have attracted their own advocates.

The differences between "practical" and "theoretical" may tend to obscure their interrelationships. For example, the history of the physical sciences shows that what begins as a problem in theoretical research may, some years later, be of great practical importance. Thus, early workers in atomic theory did not realize how their work would contribute to the use of radiation to combat cancer. The practioners of science—the applied scientist and the technologist—have taken science's principles and have put its products to work to satisfy human needs and desires. The basic sciences have, in turn, benefited from applied science and technology. Many industries employ large numbers of scientists to do basic research, in the hope, of course, that the knowledge obtained can ultimately be profitable.

Unwillingness to recognize the practicality of theory or the contributions to theory that applied research can make has led to an unfortunate split among educators. One may hear "practical administrators" attacking "ivory-tower" professors for their lack of understanding of practical administrative problems. And, conversely, educational theoreticians may look with disdain upon administrators for their "anti-intellectual" bias. Practical and theoretical matters should be considered as parts of a continuum with which all should be concerned, rather than as separate, mutually exclusive entities.

*Action* or *cooperative research* is an attempt to implement research and evaluation studies in the schools by applying group dynamics to facilitate change. At one extreme are those who claim that action research is a new methodology original to and arising from educational problems;[12] at the

---

[12]Norton L. Beach, "Research Goes into Action," *Journal of Educational Research*, 47, no. 5 (1954), pp. 351–358.

other are those who contend that action research and scientific research are incompatible.[13] Instead of joining the debate, it may be more instructive to consider the characteristics of action research in greater detail.

Action research in education developed in response to the need for implementing educational theory into workable classroom practices. Its intent, if not always its accomplishment, was to help teachers solve some of their problems by involving them in research. It recognized that the translation of theory into practice requires the cooperation and personal involvement of teachers working closely with research specialists.

An example may help to clarify the methods, strengths, and weaknesses of action research. In one study reported by Corey,[14] the investigators were social studies teachers who, before the investigation was begun, tentatively accepted the hypothesis that there is positive correlation between the knowledge pupils have of famous characters in American history and the extent to which pupils admire these characters. The teachers stated, "This prediction is based on our belief that we should give more emphasis to the biographical method." A second hypothesis was that admiration for characters in American history will increase as a result of a one-semester course in American history. A third and final hypothesis was that there is some relationship between the degree of admiration students feel for characters in American history and the extent to which these pupils are judged to behave in accordance with traits similar to those found in historical personages.

To obtain knowledge of the extent to which historical persons were admired, a list of 28 names was passed out to students in three classes, who were asked to check every historical character for whom some degree of admiration was felt. Students were also asked to indicate on a 5-point scale the extent of their admiration (5 points for "Admire very much" and 1 point for "Admire merely because others do"). Each student received a "Degree of admiration score," obtained by summing the number of points given for each person admired and dividing by the number of persons admired. A sociometric measure was used to evaluate peer group relationships, and a matching test of 10 items was used to measure pupils' recognition of historical personages.

For the three classes combined, the teachers found that the correlation between the amount of information about historical characters and the degree of admiration was only $+0.05$. The mean "Degree of admiration score" at the beginning of the semester was 3.70 and at the end, 3.79; the

---

[13]Robert M. W. Travers, *An Introduction to Educational Research*, 2d ed. (New York: Macmillan Co., 1964), pp. 54–56.

[14]Stephen M. Corey, *Action Research to Improve School Practices* (New York: Bureau of Publications, Teachers College, Columbia University, 1953), pp. 61–70.

correlation between student reputations with classmates and admiration scores was +0.07.

A few comments are in order concerning the execution of this study. In the first place, there is a great need for teachers to evaluate empirically their own beliefs and practices. As its proponents readily admit, action research cannot be used to develop general theoretical positions or to test beliefs and practices involving large numbers of persons. However, if the results of such investigations are going to be useful to the teachers themselves, they should be aware of the extent to which currently obtained research findings are applicable to their future students. In the present investigation, this factor was not evaluated.

Second, if the teachers were interested in whether or not they should give more emphasis to the biographical method, a correlation was not the appropriate statistic to use since it does not imply causality. What is needed to test the hypothesis is an experimental comparison between the effects of the biographical method and other methods which might produce important effects.

Third, action research in general suffers from a naïve empiricism which refuses to examine what previous research has found. Even a casual search[15,16] through the literature would have pointed out that: 1) only about half of children's favorite characters are historical; 2) fewer than 10 percent of children select characters of the opposite sex; and 3) children do not always identify with historical characters who have personality traits in common with their own, but may identify with those having quite divergent traits. Perhaps even more important, one investigation had already been published which showed that knowledge about historical characters and students' attitudes were largely unrelated.[17] Had these teachers gone to the trouble to review the literature *before* developing their hypotheses, they might not have used a list of 28 historical characters that contained the name of only one woman (Harriet B. Stowe), they might have included contemporary heroes along with historical characters, and they would almost certainly have used some measure of "character" other than a sociometric device.

Fourth, the tests administered may have been unreliable, as the teachers themselves suggested. This is likely since the maximum "Degree of admiration score" was only 5 points. But, since the teachers did not bother to test the reliability of their instruments, there is no way of telling if the negative results were a consequence of unreliable measures, particular teach-

[15]M. Louise Stoughton and Alice M. Ray, "A Study of Children's Heroes and Ideals," *Journal of Experimental Education*, 15, no. 2 (1946), pp. 156–160.

[16]David Spence Hill, "Personification of Ideals by Urban Children," *The Journal of Social Psychology*, 1, no. 3 (1930), pp. 379–392.

[17]John R. Rackley, "The Relationship of the Study of History to Student Attitudes," *Journal of Experimental Education*, 9 (Sept. 1940), pp. 34–36.

ing methods employed, textbooks, teacher personality, etc. These factors were left uncontrolled.

Action research may help to reduce the lag between the discovery of knowledge and its application in the classroom. As such, it will demand more knowledge of research methods among its practitioners, and will require greater care in the dissemination and application of theoretical information by the academician.

## Uncritical Acceptance of
## Research Findings and Methods

The uncritical acceptance of research findings is another factor that has hindered educational progress. The willingness to unquestioningly accept any conclusion that is part of a research paper has been the source of much difficulty in education. This uncritical acceptance of research information results in educators' blindly refusing to question existing beliefs and practices; they will not investigate what are, at least to them, well-established principles.

Once accepted as a part of "knowledge," these beliefs are remarkably resistant to change. One author has gone so far as to call the uncritical acceptance of research findings the "standardization of error."[18] That is, after an idea has been circulated and generally accepted, it is almost impossible to change the attitudes of those who originally agreed with it. A celebrated case in point is the purposeful hoax perpetrated by H. L. Mencken in 1917. Writing in the New York *Evening Mail*, Mencken admonished his readers for failing to recognize ". . . one of the most important profane anniversaries in American history, to wit, the seventy-fifth anniversary of the introduction of the bathtub into These States." Mencken facetiously went on to describe some of the difficulties early bathtub users faced, such as attacks against the use of the bathtub by the medical profession, legislation restricting its use to certain months of the year, and the bathtub tax.

Mencken was so successful in fooling the public that in May of 1926 he felt that the hoax had gone far enough, and he admitted publicly the inconsistencies, errors, and deceptions which he had employed. But by this time the hoax had been too well accepted. It had been reported as fact in professional journals, articles, and newspapers, and the error had been completely standardized. One newspaper went so far as to print Mencken's admission only to reprint his original false article three weeks later!

In education, the uncritical acceptance of research findings is altogether too common. Studies and investigations are reported which may take

[18]Vilhjalmur Stefansson, *Adventures in Error* (New York: Robert M. McBride and Co., 1936).

years to discount. As an example, it is often cited as "fact" that a mental age of 6-5 is the minimum necessary to begin a reading program. Others have dogmatically asserted that the minimum mental age is 6-0. Neither of these conclusions can be justified. They are based upon a 1931 study by Morphett and Washburne[19] on the achievement of first-grade children in learning to read. These investigators found that almost half of the children studied who had mental ages of 6-0 or less failed to read up to the criteria established for satisfactory reading, and that the majority of children having mental ages of 6-6 or higher were able to meet these same criteria.

However, an examination of the materials required for reading in 1931 indicates that they would be considered too difficult for many of the children attending school today. In addition, the criteria for satisfactory reading were set at a higher level than most teachers today would require. The implication, of course, is that with better materials and improved instruction, mental ages need not reach some magic level before reading instruction may begin, and that what constitutes failure at one period of time is not necessarily a constant for all periods.

Reading is not the only area in which incorrect conclusions have been perpetuated. In a widely read book, Rosenthal and Jacobson[20] provided "evidence" which they interpreted as supporting their position that teachers' expectations affect student intellectual performance. Twenty percent of elementary school children in grades 1 to 6 were singled out by the experimenters as those who could be expected to demonstrate "unusual potential for intellectual growth." Unknown to the teachers, however, these students were selected purely by chance and should have gained no more than would the children not selected. According to the researchers:

> Eight months later these unusual or "magic" children showed significantly greater gains in IQ than did the remaining children who had not been singled out for the teacher's attention. The change in the teachers' expectations regarding the intellectual performance of these allegedly "special" children had led to an actual change in the intellectual performance of these randomly selected children.[21]

Because teachers do have expectations of student performance, this study has broad implications for teaching—provided, of course, that it

[19]Mabel V. Morphett and C. Washburne, "When Should Children Begin to Read?" *The Elementary School Journal*, 31, no. 7 (1931), pp. 496–503.
[20]Robert Rosenthal and Lenore Jacobson, *Pygmalion in the Classroom: Teacher Expectation and Pupils' Intellectual Development* (New York: Holt, Rinehart and Winston, 1968), 240 pp.
[21]Rosenthal and Jacobson, pp. vii–viii.

was methodologically sound. However, in November 1968, Thorndike[22] had some harsh words regarding the adequacy of data gathering and analysis.

> The enterprise which represents the core of [*Pygmalion in the Classroom*], and presumably the excuse for its publication, has received widespread advance publicity. In spite of anything I can say, I am sure it will become a classic—widely referred to and rarely examined critically. Alas, it is so defective technically that one can only regret that it ever got beyond the eyes of the original investigators! Though the volume may be an effective addition to educational propagandizing, it does nothing to raise the standards of educational research.[23]

The essence of Thorndike's criticism concerns the use of the Tests of General Ability (TOGA) for the students in this study. These tests were administered in May 1964, and the results reported to teachers in September of that year. The crucial analysis involves all students tested in May 1964 and again one year later.

The only apparent differences in "intellectual performance" between experimental students (those whose teachers were told they would "spurt") and control students occurred in grades 1 and 2 for 19 students. The pretest scores yielded IQ's that varied between means of 30.79 and 119.47 for six classrooms. As Thorndike put it, some children in a rather average elementary school "barely appear to make the grade as imbeciles!"

Thorndike also raises the question of how it is possible for the mean IQ of the first graders to be as low as 58.0. Because Rosenthal and Jacobson do not report raw scores on the TOGA, Thorndike attempted to estimate these values by assuming that a mental age of 3-6 would be reasonable for an IQ of 58.0. In Thorndike's words:

> Alas, the norms do not go down that far! It is not possible to tell what the authors did, but finding that a raw score of 8 corresponds to an "M. A." of 5.3, we can take a shot at extrapolating downward. We come out with a raw score of approximately 2! Random marking would give 5 or 6 right![24]

A similar problem occurs with the six experimental students who had a posttest mean IQ of 150.17. An IQ of 150 for students at the end of the second grade yields a reasonable estimate of 11-3 as a mental age. The prob-

[22]Robert L. Thorndike, "Review of Rosenthal and Jacobson's 'Pygmalion in the Classroom,'" *American Educational Research Journal*, 5, no. 4 (November 1968), pp. 708–711.

[23]Thorndike, p. 708.

[24]Thorndike, p. 710.

lem is that the TOGA manual goes no higher than a mental age of 10-0 for a score of 26. To get a mental age of 11-3 requires that students obtain scores of 28+. That represents a perfect score on this test which could only occur if everyone obtained the same score. Unfortunately, this could not have happened since the standard deviation is reported by Rosenthal and Jacobson as 40.17 points.

Delving into the Pygmalion study in detail points out the necessity of being critical about research findings. Conclusions can be no better than the adequacy of the methods used to generate data. (At the end of this chapter the interested student can find the references for Rosenthal and Jacobson's analysis of Thorndike's review and Thorndike's rejoinder. They make exciting reading.)

What are the conditions that lead to the standardization of error? At least four factors seem to contribute, according to Cartwright,[25] who presented an excellent case history of the "risky shift" phenomena, so named because of the unexpected finding that groups tend to take greater chances than do individuals (as measured by an instrument titled the CDQ, or Choice Dilemmas Questionnaire). About 200 studies were published between 1961 and 1971 on the risky shift phenomenon. As it turned out, a major flaw in these studies was their dependence on a single score to summarize the amount of shift on the 12 CDQ items. Cartwright's four contributing factors are:

> *1. Labeling.* A more neutral term such as "group discussion effect" hardly compares in impact with a catchy and easily remembered term like *risky shift.*
>
> *2. Motivation.* The researchers' motivation to explain the risky shift led them away from the analysis of the CDQ itself; few persons were motivated to examine the CDQ as the source of the problem.
>
> *3. Methodology.* Most researchers thought of the CDQ as *a* test rather than as 12 separate items, each having its own unique characteristics. Thus, researchers assumed that the risky shift was a characteristic of the individuals and groups but not of the methods (tests) used in the experiments.
>
> *4. Media of communication.* Most of the information about the risky shift was published in articles and books, implying a time lag of about 3 years between completion of a piece of research and its publication. Thus, over a period of 10 years, there could be only a few study–publication cycles. A more effective communication system might have discouraged the standardization of error.

[25]Dorwin Cartwright, "Determinants of Scientific Progress: The Case of Research on the Risky Shift," *American Psychologist,* 28, no. 3 (March 1973), pp. 222–231.

## SUMMARY

**1.** Educators often believe that research is capable of transforming the public schools into future utopias in spite of the past disappointments of research. What has not been understood is that research provides reliable information and not necessarily a prescription for change.

**2.** Three types of research were described:

**a.** *Analytic research* studies nonempirical relationships deductively.

**b.** *Descriptive research* studies current conditions.

**c.** *Experimental research* investigates causal relationships.

**3.** Both basic (theoretical) and applied research attempt to explain empirical relationships among variables. Evaluation, in contrast, attempts to help educators make decisions regarding the adequacy of a program. The differences between research and evaluation include the following:

**a.** The nature of the decision. Statistical decisions provide the researcher with a statement of probability or likelihood; evaluation decisions must consider the moral and economic effects of the proposed program on the lives of students and the broader community.

**b.** Differences in commitment. Researchers are less committed to meeting prespecified objectives than are evaluators who are morally obligated to help students reach these objectives. The researcher's obligation is to avoid bias and to use the most effective procedures for studying a given problem, but there is less of a commitment to modify educational practice.

**c.** The nature of the treatment variable. Research studies usually try to isolate experimental treatments so that their effects, both individual and in combination with one another, can be understood. Some evaluation studies may be carried out even though specific treatment effects cannot be isolated.

**4.** Educational changes have not always been of benefit to students. Costly, far-reaching, or potentially damaging modifications should have strong theoretical bases and empirical trials with a small sample of students who can be helped should the program be ineffective.

**a.** *Development* can help to improve educational practice by lowering costs and increasing the efficiency of products, practice, or conditions.

**b.** *Demonstrations* are used to persuade teachers, parents, and school administration that a proposed innovation is workable in the local situation.

**c.** *Dissemination* informs educators and the public about the values and limitations of a proposed innovation.

**5.** A number of conditions have hampered educational research:

**a.** Federal funds for educational research have actually declined in buying power between the years 1969 and 1975.

**b.** More emphasis is placed on the quantity of research published by faculty members in education than on the quality of that research. Some colleges and universities require few if any research courses for advanced students. Most teacher training programs do not prepare teachers to read and understand research studies.

**c.** Failure to recognize and accept the contributions of both theory and practice has led to fruitless debate and to dissipation of energy. Theory can guide practice which, in turn, can help to modify theory. Action research has the potential of helping to bridge the gap between theory and practice; often, however, it has failed to exercise the control of variables that is expected in research.

**d.** Too often research findings are disseminated and accepted as proven by educators without their having read the evidence critically. The study of *Pygmalion in the Classroom* was cited as a case in point. The acceptance of research findings from inadequately designed studies seems to occur especially if 1) the phenomenon being studied is given a catchy title; 2) researchers are motivated to study one aspect of a phenomenon and to disregard other less interesting but important considerations; 3) the methods used fail to examine crucial elements of experimental design; and 4) there is a long delay in the publication of articles that are critical of the research.

## PRACTICE EXERCISES

**1.** Suppose that you are the superintendent of a small city school district and that you have a number of research findings and recommendations on your desk. Indicate which of these recommendations you would be willing to implement in your schools, assuming, of course, that the findings are reliable. Indicate which factors led to your decision.

| *Findings* | *Recommendations* |
|---|---|
| **a.** Girls are more mature than boys at comparable chronological ages. | **a.** Girls should enter school a year earlier than boys. |
| **b.** High school students who take courses in driver education have fewer accidents than those who are not given such training. | **b.** Schools should provide courses in driver education. |
| **c.** Students who retake courses after failing them do less well when they retake the course | **c.** Students should not be failed. |

than do their counterparts who were passed.

d. The correlation between teaching "success" and the amount of knowledge obtained in college courses is low but positive.

e. In communities where playgrounds are available, there is less juvenile delinquency than in communities without playgrounds.

d. Administrators should select teachers more on their personality and character than on their achievement.

e. Administrators should allow students to use school playgrounds after school.

**2.** Classify each of the following examples into the type of research or research activity it calls for (analytic, descriptive, experimental, development, demonstration, or dissemination):

a. Two sets of data are correlated.

b. A teacher looks up the research on the teaching of reading.

c. A teacher tries to show parents the advantages of a new textbook in mathematics.

d. A course of study is being redone to make it simpler and more palatable to students.

e. A student is interested in knowing the number of seniors who attended summer school during the previous summer session.

f. A teacher believes that stuttering is caused by neurological problems.

g. An experimenter reviews the literature to find evidence for some position.

h. A business teacher installs a time clock in the classroom to see if this improves the attitudes of students toward being efficient.

**3.** Examine in detail any of the following new programs. What assumptions does the method make about human learning? What evidence is there that the assumptions are correct? What other methods could be used that might bring about the same objectives?

a. Team teaching

b. Open classrooms

c. Invididualized reading programs

d. Chemical Bond Approach

e. UICSM math program

## Selected Supplementary Readings

1. On the distinctions between research and evaluation and on methodological issues of evaluation, see Tyler, Ralph W., ed. *Educational Evaluation: New Roles, New Means.* The Sixty-eighth Yearbook of the National Society for

the Study of Education, Part II. Chicago: University of Chicago Press, 1969, 409 pp.; Wortman, Paul M. "Evaluation Research: A Psychological Perspective." *American Psychologist*, 30, no. 5 (May 1975), pp. 562–575; Thomas, Lawrence G., ed. *Philosophical Redirection of Educational Research.* The Seventy-first Yearbook of the National Society for the Study of Education, Part I. Chicago: University of Chicago Press, 1972, 374 pp.; Popham, W. James, ed. *Evaluation in Education: Current Applications.* Berkeley, Calif.: McCutchan Publishing Corp., 1975, 585 pp.; Anderson, Scarvia B., et al. *Encyclopedia of Educational Evaluation.* San Francisco: Jossey-Bass, Publishers, 1975, 515 pp.; Struening, Elmer L., and Guttentag, Marcia, eds. *Handbook of Evaluation Research,* 2 vols. Beverly Hills: Sage Publications, 1975.

2. See Miles, Matthew B. *Innovation in Education.* New York: Bureau of Publications, Teachers College, Columbia University, 1964, 689 pp., for a comprehensive analysis of the factors that retard and advance educational progress. See also Pincus, John. "Incentives for Innovation in the Public Schools." *Review of Educational Research,* 44, no. 1 (Winter 1974), pp. 113–144.

3. A number of excellent articles have appeared in the *Educational Researcher* that relate to the role of research and researchers in education. See, for example, Worthen, Blaine R. "Competencies for Educational Research and Evaluation." 4, no. 1 (January 1975), pp. 13–16; Reicken, Henry W., et al. "The Purpose of Social Experimentation." 3, no. 11, (December 1974), pp. 5–9; Carroll, John B., and Suppes, Patrick. "The Committee on Basic Research in Education: A Four-Year Tryout of Basic Science Funding Procedures." 3, No. 2 (February 1974), pp. 7–10. Another article which is critical of basic research appears after Carroll and Suppes' article: Fincher, Cameron. "COBRE and the Dilemmas of Basic Research in Education." (pp. 11–13). See also Evans, John W. "Evaluating Educational Programs—Are We Getting Anywhere?" 3, no. 8 (September 1974), pp. 7–12.

4. On the role of basic and applied research, see Ebel, Robert L. "Some Limitations of Basic Research in Education." *Phi Delta Kappan,* 49, no. 2 (October 1967), pp. 81–84. Contrast this article with Cronbach, Lee J. "The Role of the University in Improving Education." *Phi Delta Kappan,* 47, no. 10 (June 1966), pp. 539–545; and with Hilgard, Ernest R. "The Translation of Educational Research and Development into Action." *Educational Researcher,* 1, no. 7 (July 1972), pp. 18–21.

5. Krathwohl, David R. "An Analysis of Perceived Ineffectiveness of Educational Research and Some Recommendations." *Educational Psychologist,* 11, no. 2 (1974), pp. 73–86. The author argues that educational research has served mainly as a "legitimizer of change" rather than as a leader of change. Ornstein, Allan C. "The Limitations of Research." *American Psychologist,* 30, no. 4 (April 1975), pp. 511–513, believes that controversial research has been overregulated by universities and the federal government.

See also Shulman, Lee S. "Reconstruction of Educational Research." *Review of Educational Research*, 40, no. 3 (June 1970), pp. 371–396.

6. Rosenthal's reply to Thorndike's criticism of *Pygmalion in the Classroom* appears in the *American Educational Research Journal*, 6, no. 4 (November 1969), pp. 689–691. Thorndike's rejoinder is on page 692 of the same issue. For other analyses of teacher expectancy effects, see Barber, Theodore Xenephon, et al. "Five Attempts to Replicate the Experimenter Bias Effect." *Journal of Consulting and Clinical Psychology*, 33, no. 1 (1969), pp. 1–6; Gephart, William J. "Will the Real Pygmalion Please Stand Up?" *American Educational Research Journal*, 7, no. 3 (May 1970), pp. 473–475. Rosenthal's reply to Barber's article appears on pages 7–10 and Barber's rejoinder is on pages 11–14 of the same issue. A particularly illuminating article is by Finn, Jeremy D. "Expectations and the Educational Environment." *Review of Educational Research*, 42, no. 3 (Summer 1972), pp. 387–410.

7. An interesting analysis of the quality of educational research can be found in Ward, Annie W., Hall, Bruce W., and Schramm, Charles F. "Evaluation of Published Educational Research: A National Survey." *American Educational Research Journal*, 12, no. 2 (Spring 1975), pp. 109–128. Unfortunately, the authors found that most educational research was "of mediocre quality" but had improved since the early 1960s.

8. On the influence between research and educational practice, see Kerlinger, Fred N. "The Influence of Research on Education Practice." *Educational Researcher*, 6 (September 1977), pp. 5–11, which was the presidential address at the Annual Meeting of the American Educational Research Association, New York City, April 1977. In the same issue, also see Jackson, Philip, and Kieslar, Sara B. "Fundamental Research and Education." (pp. 13–18).

# 3 selecting the research problem

A familiarity with previous investigations is an essential preparation for the selection of a research problem. Without it, students may be unable to justify the need for a proposed investigation, they may select a hypothesis to test that has already been confirmed or disconfirmed, or they may use techniques shown to be invalid. A review of the literature should point out the value of a study and suggest the most useful methods.

One reason students find it difficult to select a research problem is that they often confuse a *problem* with the *purpose* and methods used by the investigator. A problem is "a perplexing situation . . . translated into a question or series of questions that help determine the direction of subsequent inquiry."[1] A perplexing situation may exist because of apparent contradic-

[1]Carter V. Good, ed., *Dictionary of Education*, 3d. ed. (New York: McGraw-Hill Book Co., 1973), pp. 438–439.

tions in the literature or because reported findings were derived from questionable procedures. In contrast to a *problem*, the *purpose* of the study is to resolve the perplexing situation by certain specified *methods*. Without a clear statement of the problem, the purpose and methods used will be meaningless.

## TYPES OF RESEARCH PROBLEMS

### Research to Clarify or Validate Theory

Theory can aid in the selection of a research problem by clarifying, limiting, and defining theoretical formulations. Consider, for example, the interference theory of forgetting described in Chapter 1. Somewhat oversimplified, it states that forgetting occurs because newly acquired information is interfered with by both previous and subsequent learning. The theory, however, leaves many questions unanswered. For example, what is the relationship between number of previous (or subsequent) learning activities and amount of forgetting? Do previously learned activities interfere with newly acquired information or can some activities facilitate retention? Each of these questions forms the basis of a research problem that can be justified on the grounds that the proposed research will help to clarify the meaning of the interference theory.

In addition, the consequences of theory can be used to test indirectly the validity of the theory itself. The interference theory, for example, *implies* that: 1) there should be a positive correlation between amount learned and amount of forgetting; 2) material located at the ends of lists to be learned should be retained better than material located at the center of the list; and 3) not all activities interfere with retention since, for example, previous knowledge of how to play the violin may facilitate learning the viola. Each of these implications provides a basis for a research problem.

The relationship between empirical investigations and theory can be seen by examining Figure 3-1, where the *EI's* represent *empirical investigations* designed to help develop a body of theory. Each empirical investigation adds

**Figure 3-1**
THE RELATIONSHIP BETWEEN EMPIRICAL INVESTIGATIONS
AND THEORY DEVELOPMENT.

further knowledge to the development of a theory. In turn, the theory implies certain consequences (*C*), whose validation lends credence to the theory. In the beginning stages of theory development, the empirical investigations provide information about the theory; once the theory is better understood, its consequences are tested to determine whether they are in accord with those predicted by the theory. In the selection of a research problem, investigations may be chosen at either the *EI* level or the *C* level. In either case, the student should be familiar with the major empirical investigations leading to the formulation of the theory and to studies which have tested the consequences of the theory.

## Research to Clarify Contradictory Findings

Investigators should examine research *methods* for possible discrepancies if there are contradictory conclusions from research investigations. Where experimental designs have been weak, conclusions based upon these designs are open to serious question.

An example will help demonstrate the point. In discussing *under-achievement*, Peterson has indicated a number of research findings which seem to contradict each other:

> Consider these conclusions, for example. It has been observed that the father of the low achiever has less education and ranks lower in occupational status than the father of the high achiever. Yet, another study states the opposite—*more* education and *higher* occupational levels among the fathers of low achievers. And a third study finds no difference in educational or occupational level between the two groups.
>
> Helpful? Let's look further: The home of the underachieving student is more likely to be broken by death or divorce, or, the loss of one or both parents has no effect on achievement. Take your choice.
>
> Is birth order important? One author states that the achievement of the only child or the oldest sibling is poorest. Another reports no significant differences between older and younger siblings in intelligence or achievement.[2]

In the example just cited, an apparent contradiction in findings could lead a researcher to design studies which might provide more definitive answers concerning the characteristics of the underachiever. In the first place, the definitions of "underachievement" were different in each of these studies. Peterson himself has indicated that the use of four different criteria for determining what shall be considered underachieving behavior probably contrib-

---

[2]John Peterson, "The Researcher and the Underachiever: Never the Twain Shall Meet," *Phi Delta Kappan*, 44, no. 8 (1963), p. 379.

uted to the apparent discrepancies among reported findings. In some studies, underachievers may be from widely different types of schools or from different communities, and may vary considerably in age and grade. In addition, the estimation that the child is able to do better work may come from different sources. In some instances, the source may be the teacher's judgment; in other cases, it may be standardized test results. Because the characteristics of underachievers are determined by such diverse sources, each having different criteria as to what constitutes underachievement, studies are likely to show contradictory findings.

Just how could one select a problem that attempts to clarify contradictory findings? Using studies on underachievement as an example, the researcher could repeat earlier contradictory investigations, selecting a number of different types of schools in different communities, using elementary and high school children of both sexes, and specifying the criteria for determining underachievement. To be sure, this would lead to a rather complex study, but it would help to clarify findings which now appear to be inconsistent.

## Research to Correct Faulty Methodology

Another source for selecting a research topic may be found in generally accepted conclusions based on faulty research designs. In educational and psychological measurement, for example, it is generally well accepted that scores corrected for guessing tend to correlate very highly with uncorrected test scores. This conclusion is based upon the following type of research design:

*1.* One group of students takes a test.
*2.* The papers are scored twice, once by correcting for guessing and once without the correction.
*3.* The correlation between corrected and uncorrected scores is computed.

The results invariably indicate a very high correlation, and this evidence is used to argue against correcting examination papers for guessing. The reason given is that since the scores are highly correlated, they must be measuring the same factors. However, Davis has indicated that the research design is faulty:

> The writer discounts statements that the correlations between sets of test scores obtained with and without correction for chance are exceedingly high. In the first place, the correlations cited are usually spuriously high because they are obtained by scoring the same set of test papers in two ways. In this situation, the directions for administering the tests are

the same and thus can be appropriate only to *one* of the two scoring procedures. It would be desirable to obtain the correlation between two comparable forms of the same test administered successively to the same sample with two sets of directions—one appropriate to scoring without correction for chance success and one to scoring with it. This correlation should be compared with a parallel-forms reliability coefficient [see Chapter 8] for the same test based on the same sample. An exact test of the significance of the difference between the two coefficients would permit inferences to be drawn regarding the point at issue.[3]

This statement by Davis encouraged Sax and Collet[4] to conduct a study "to compare the effects on reliability and validity of the conventional correction for guessing formula

$$\left[ S = R - \frac{W}{K - 1} \right]$$

under an instruction which permits guessing with the effects under an instruction designed to discourage guessing."[5] The authors found that "The correlation obtained by scoring the same test two different ways (by counting the number right and by using the conventional correction formula) had a minimum value of 0.98, while the correlation between the number-right scores on one test with the corrected scores on a parallel form was 0.71. This difference is significant at the 0.01 level ($t = 29.75$)."[6] Davis' contention that the correlations between corrected and uncorrected test scores is spuriously high gained empirical support in this study.

In general, many research topics suggest themselves after a careful analysis and critique of previously conducted studies. The attitude to guard against is being overly critical on minor or unimportant details. To criticize and replicate a study because of some unimportant detail adds little to knowledge.

## Research to Correct Inappropriate Use of Statistics

Often an important study yields questionable results because the statistics used are not applicable. These studies may be replicated using more appropriate statistical methods.

[3]Frederick B. Davis, "Item Selection Techniques," in E. F. Lindquist, ed., *Educational Measurement* (Washington, D.C.: American Council on Education, 1951), p. 277.

[4]Gilbert Sax and LeVerne S. Collet, "The Effects of Differing Instructions and Guessing Formulas on Reliability and Validity," *Educational and Psychological Measurement*, 28, no. 4 (Winter 1968), pp. 1127–1136.

[5]Sax and Collet, p. 1128.

[6]Sax and Collet, p. 1132.

An example or two may be helpful at this point. In early investigations involving the relationship between cigarette smoking and the prevalence of lung cancer, researchers computed correlations between the number of cigarettes smoked per day and the prevalence of cancer. What the researchers really wanted was evidence as to whether or not smoking *caused* lung cancer; what they actually obtained was the correlation, or degree of relationship, between smoking and cancer. This information, while useful, could not be used as decisive evidence showing a causal relationship. The researchers failed to recognize that correlations do not necessarily imply causality.

On a much broader level, the million-dollar PROJECT TALENT research sponsored by the Cooperative Research Branch of the U.S. Office of Education has been criticized on essentially the same grounds. As Stanley has stated:

> I admire the testing operation itself. The American Institute for Research and the University of Pittsburgh have good cause to be proud of it, despite a few inevitable flaws in design and execution. It is the promised attempt to tease out "causation" from essentially correlational data that gives me pause. . . .
>
> Viewed narrowly, all ten questions [asked by the PROJECT TALENT staff] deal only with association, not causation, but straightway they have causal implications that might be misleading. Take No. 3, for example: "Are small classes more effective than large classes?" One can compute quite readily the correlation of class size as it occurs "naturally" in PROJECT TALENT schools with various test scores, but it is a far more difficult task to prove that class size helps "cause" the differences among means of classes and that therefore classes "should" be of a certain size or sizes in order to maximize desired outcomes of instruction.[7]

If the research or article is judged to have some theoretical or practical importance, then it could very well be replicated using a more appropriate statistical technique.

## Research to Resolve Conflicting Opinion

One very useful source of research problems is the examination of contradictory opinions of authorities. In one study, for example, Sax and Collet[8] reported that although tests can affect learning,

---

[7]Julian C. Stanley (Book Review), *Teachers College Record*, 64, no. 5 (1963), pp. 433–434.

[8]Gilbert Sax and LeVerne S. Collet, "An Empirical Comparison of the Effects of Recall and Multiple-Choice Tests in Student Achievement," *Journal of Educational Measurement*, 5, no. 2 (Summer 1968), pp. 169–173.

The literature is not clear ... concerning the relative advantages of using recall or multiple-choice examinations as teaching devices. Adams (1964) and Green (1963) take the *a priori* position that recall-type examinations "promote the use of superior study methods." In contrast, Gerberich, Greene, and Jorgansen (1962) and Ebel (1965) argue that both types of examinations are "probably" equally effective as motivators.

Little empirical evidence is available to support either of these contentions. ... What empirical evidence is available does not directly compare the achievement of individuals trained to take either multiple-choice or recall examinations who *expect* to take the same form of final examination under actual classroom conditions. ...

The student contemplating a research study would do well to look for disparate opinions in textbooks, published research studies, and sources that review the literature on various topics.

## Research to Resolve Practical Field Problems

Many important research projects develop out of attempts to solve practical problems faced by classroom teachers and administrators. These problems are called practical, not because they lack theoretical bases, but because the intent of the investigator is to study a pressing and immediate problem. Thus, for example, a classroom teacher might be concerned about the number of spelling words or arithmetic problems students can effectively learn during an hour. Similarly, an administrator may want to make the most effective staffing decisions to improve extracurricular activities. Although research findings might apply to other schools and other administrators, the primary intent is to solve a local problem.

In a sense, the problems faced by the administrator and the classroom teacher have implications that extend beyond the immediate ones. The teacher will no doubt apply current findings on spelling and arithmetic to next year's classes. The administrator who finds that the staff was most effective when allowed to choose its own extracurricular activities to supervise will probably encourage new staff members to select their own supervisory functions in future years. The assumption which both make is that future classes and future members of the staff will act in the same way as the subjects did when the study was undertaken. However, this conclusion is valid only if the characteristics of the students or teachers remain constant over time. The teacher and administrator might have to repeat their investigations every year to be sure that the characteristics of their subjects are not changing.

Would it not be of greater value, then, for the teacher to know the minimum periods of time required for spelling at various levels of student abilities and aptitudes than it would be to know that this year's students require only 10 minutes of spelling instruction per day? And once having this information, would it not be of use to other teachers? The more comprehensive the research is, the more useful it may be. Research highly restricted to one given condition (i.e., spelling) in one given classroom is not only unlikely to arouse wide interest, but may not actually be of great value to the researcher.

Somehow many persons have the attitude that if the research is to solve a practical problem it need not be well controlled or involve statistical analyses of data. Nothing could be farther from the truth. As Massialas and Smith point out:

> At the fingertips of the classroom teacher lie innumerable opportunities for research which may be the source of additional insight into many of the problems of understanding the teaching-learning process. . . . A systematic, thoughtful, and vigorous approach to the investigation is necessary if we are to expect a clear design and valid strategy of attack. Only when tight and organized frames of reference are consciously employed will the field of education move toward quality research.[9]

# CRITERIA USED TO SELECT A RESEARCH PROBLEM

## The Criterion of Interest

The criterion of *interest* is a necessary but not sufficient reason for selecting a particular research problem. Without interest in a topic, the effort and care characteristic of well-designed research studies are likely to be lacking. Interest is not, however, a *sufficient* criterion since it can lead researchers to investigate trivial problems. The nature of scientific research demands that findings be communicated, but this does not mean that the researcher has to select a problem of concern to everyone or even to most persons. However, to qualify as a *problem*, there must be a perplexing situation which, when resolved, contributes to a better understanding of some educational phenomena.

## The Economic Criterion

Another criterion for selecting a research topic is *economic*. The realities of life may force the researcher to reject an investigation because of cost estimates; costs also may limit the breadth or complexity of a proposed

[9]Byron G. Massialas and Frederick R. Smith, "Quality Research: A Goal for Every Teacher," *Phi Delta Kappan*, 43, no. 6 (1962), p. 256.

study. Costs related to the hiring of personnel, the use of computers, the construction or purchase of equipment and materials, and overhead must be considered, especially in evaluation studies, where some ratio of cost per yield is often required. When the researcher expects an economic return for expenditures (as, for example, in industry), then costs can be computed. In "pure" or basic research, where the contribution is primarily theoretical, the yield may be impossible to estimate.

There is, of course, no justification whatsoever for undertaking a project simply because it is inexpensive or easy to execute.

## The Investigator's Ability and Training

Another factor to be considered in the selection of a research problem is the *investigator's ability and training*. Every person embarking on a research study has limitations in experience and capacity which should be recognized if unnecessary frustration is to be avoided. It is at this point that intellectual honesty is essential; it is a sign of maturity to be able to recognize one's own limitations.

Even if researchers are *potentially* capable of undertaking elaborate research, there remain the matters of training and the amount of time they may be willing or able to devote to the project. The design of some studies requires investigators to have competence in areas where they have not had formal training. In some instances, this may be remedied rather quickly by background reading or by asking someone competent to advise the project. Students should remember that to wait until the research project has begun before evaluating their strengths and weaknesses is to invite needless delay at best and an incomplete or meaningless project at worst.

## The Criterion of Uniqueness

The criterion of *uniqueness* assumes that research projects have some originality in either purpose or method. Some studies, for example, may be justified because they attempt to extend research findings to groups not previously investigated; other studies are of value because they investigate a highly unique set of conditions unlikely to occur again. An investigator could reasonably take a study originally limited in scope and try to make it more comprehensive and, ultimately, more widely applicable.

However, not every study which involves some event needs to be *replicated*, or repeated, using various groups, if the conditions which underlie the event are made explicit. Thus, fairly unique events may be investigated if the underlying theoretical conditions are specified. For example, on October 30, 1938, the originally scheduled radio program on the Mercury Theatre was "interrupted" by the announcement that Martians had invaded the United States. Almost immediately, panic broke out among the program listeners, many of whom believed the story of the invasion to be true. As one investigator reported:

> Long before the broadcast had ended, people all over the United States were praying, crying, fleeing frantically to escape death from the Martians. ... Such rare occurrences provide opportunities for the social scientist to study mass behavior. ... The situation created by the broadcast was one which shows us how the common man reacts in a time of stress and strain. ... The panic situation we have investigated had all the flavor of everyday life and, at the same time, provided a semi-experimental condition for research. In spite of the unique conditions giving rise to this particular panic, *the writer has attempted to indicate throughout the study the pattern of the circumstances which, from a psychological point of view, might make this the prototype of any panic.*[10]

In the study of education, occasions arise when nonreplicable, unique events may be investigated. The process of school integration, for example, would be difficult, if not impossible, to study in other contexts or under other conditions. Thus, a unique event may be studied as long as the conditions are stated which make it a model for other related and similar events.

But uniqueness as a criterion for the selection of a research problem does not require that every event be studied in every context. This relates to the problem of just how far research findings can be generalized. Usually, the most useful investigations are those which allow the researcher to make the broadest and most inclusive generalizations concerning any given topic; conversely, investigations of limited applicability, either theoretically or practically, are of less value. Thus, a hierarchy of problems can be formed, with the most inclusive one having the highest priority. In practice this would mean that, given a choice of possible problems to be studied, the student would be making the greatest contribution by selecting the problem that has the greatest probability of yielding results which lead to general theories and laws.

## USING THE LIBRARY
## IN EDUCATIONAL RESEARCH

### Document Analysis

As a noun, a *document* refers to any source that provides evidence or information; as a verb, it refers to the process of providing evidence (e.g., to document the need for increases in federal aid to education). The two mean-

---

[10]Hadley Cantril, "The Invasion from Mars," in Eleanor E. Maccoby, Theodore M. Newcomb, and Eugene L. Hartley, eds., *Readings in Social Psychology*, 3d ed. (New York: Henry Holt and Co., 1958), pp. 291–300. Italics added. Reprinted by permission of Princeton University Press.

ings of *document* are usually complementary but not always so. A document used to provide evidence may or may not turn out to be a very convincing source.

As a written or printed source, the document is not evidence *per se*. The researcher's responsibility is to examine the document and to verify not only its authenticity but also to demonstrate its relevance to the problem at hand. The document provides little if any information that should escape *interpretation* by the researcher.

Documents must, therefore, be analyzed. Nothing is gained in writing a review of the literature that contains purposeless "facts." And since the purpose of a literature review is to explain the relationship of a proposed study to previous works on the same topic, it follows that the review must be analytic and critical.

Documents may be classified in the following manner:[11] manuscript or printed, private or public, and intentional or unpremeditated. The *Congressional Record*, for example, is printed, public, and intentional (i.e., designed to provide a record of lasting value). Unpremeditated documents consist of diaries, business transactions, teacher roll books—in short, written records that serve an immediate and functional purpose. Webb et al.[12] have pointed out the problem with such documents—namely, the document is no guarantee of accuracy. Any member of Congress, for example, is given the opportunity to alter any statement that is to appear in the *Congressional Record*. The researcher will have to make the judgment of accuracy.

Diaries are usually in manuscript form, private, and unpremeditated, but not always so. Some diaries are printed, public, and intentional. Any statement selected from a diary requires care in interpretation since the intent of a diarist's statements may be unclear and may need to be checked against other sources. Perhaps the best way to evaluate a diary or other document is to apply criteria for an authority as described in Chapter 1. Is the document writer known, living, and unbiased? If the writer is identified but deceased, any statement attributed to that person should be consistent with other evidence written by the same author.

Document analysis has two major shortcomings that the researcher must consider:[13] selective deposit and selective survival. For a document to be analyzed it must be available. To the extent that not everyone privy to an event produces a document, selective deposit becomes a problem. Those who chose to prepare a document probably viewed the event in a different manner than those who chose not to do so. Selective survival refers to the fact that not

[11]Jacques Barzun and Henry F. Graff, *The Modern Researcher*, rev. ed. (New York: Harcourt, Brace & World, 1970), p. 147.

[12]Eugene Webb, Donald T. Campbell, Richard D. Schwartz, and Lee Sechrest, *Unobtrusive Measures: Nonreactive Research in the Social Sciences* (Chicago: Rand McNally & Co., 1966), p. 56.

[13]Webb et al., p. 85.

all documents produced are available for analysis. Which documents are available and which ones have been destroyed, burned, or otherwise made unavailable can produce strong bias which the researcher should attempt to analyze.

Private documents[14] include military reports, suicide notes, case history notes kept by psychiatrists, sales records, industrial and institutional records, and other printed and written documents. Galton's IQ, for example, was estimated as being close to 200 by Terman[15] who examined one of Galton's letters to his sister in which he describes his own accomplishments:

MY DEAR ADÈLE,

I am 4 years old and I can read any English book. I can say all the Latin Substantives and Adjectives and active verbs besides 52 lines of Latin poetry. I can cast up any sum in addition and can multiply by 2, 3, 4, 5, 6, 7, 8, [9], 10, [11].

I can also say the pence table. I read French a little and I know the clock.

FRANCIS GALTON
Febuary [sic] 15, 1827

Galton's early sense of humility surfaced when he pasted over the 9 and 11, believing perhaps that he might have claimed too much even for himself. Even more telling is the fact that Galton wrote the letter *the day before* his *fifth* birthday although he claims he is only four years old!

# SOURCES OF INFORMATION USEFUL IN DEVELOPING A REVIEW OF THE LITERATURE

So many sources of information are currently available in education that it is impossible to list them here. Instead, the student is referred to the extremely helpful research librarians available at university and college libraries. The suggestion here is for the student to begin with the general sources and then proceed to the more specific and detailed indexes and abstracts.

## Textbooks

Textbooks are unusually good sources with which to begin. Authors of texts attempt to discuss as simply as possible the most important topics.

---

[14]Webb et al., pp. 88–111.

[15]Lewis M. Terman, "The Intelligence Quotient of Francis Galton in Childhood," *American Journal of Psychology*, 28 (1917), pp. 209–215.

Most textbooks will also provide a bibliography, although it may not be extensive or as current as those in journal articles.

## Encyclopedias

Another excellent source is the *Encyclopedia of Educational Research*. Each edition is published about every 10 years and summarizes research on many different topics. The student might also consider the 10-volume set of the *Encyclopedia of Education*, the current *Education Yearbooks*, or the 17 volumes of the *International Encyclopedia of the Social Sciences*, each with excellent selected bibliographies. Be sure not to overlook *The Handbook of Research on Teaching* edited by N. L. Gage in 1963 and R. M. W. Travers in 1973.

## Indexes, Abstracts, and Computer Searches

Once the student understands the general literature on a given topic, more specific information can be found in indexes and abstracts. ERIC (Educational Resources Information Center), for example, is a system of compiling information about education. It includes *Resources in Education* (RIE), which indexes unpublished reports, and the *Current Index to Journals in Education* (CIJE) which indexes periodical literature. The system can be used manually or computer searches can be requested.

Documents included in RIE have been indexed and abstracted by a number of ERIC Clearinghouses established by the federal government in June of 1964. Each clearinghouse is responsible for a given topic: counseling and personnel services, reading and communication skills, etc. As each new and unpublished report is received, the appropriate clearinghouse categorizes it into subject categories or descriptors prescribed by the *Thesaurus of ERIC Descriptors*. When using the *Thesaurus*, look for the major descriptors first (the most important and relevant terms) and then for the minor descriptors (those more peripheral to the topic). RIE began publication in 1966 and is published monthly.

CIJE began publication in 1969 and indexes approximately 700 periodicals. Although CIJE does not abstract journals, it does give frequent annotations when the title of the article is not indicative of its subject. Use the *Education Index* rather than CIJE if the article you are searching for was published prior to 1969. Appendix VI of this text provides detailed information on other sources that can be useful in reviewing the literature.

## WRITING THE REVIEW OF THE LITERATURE

The *Review of the Literature* is included in a research study to show its relation to other investigations on the same topic. If the study is being conducted to clarify contradictory findings that have appeared in the literature, the reader will want to know what these contradictions are and how the proposed investigation will help to clarify matters.

The *Review of the Literature* is not designed to be an exhaustive listing of all studies having even the remotest relevance to the proposed investigation. Rather, it is an attempt to describe the *problem* or perplexing situation and the current state of knowledge on the topic to be investigated.

## Selection of Studies to Be Included in the Review of the Literature

The following suggestions are designed to help the student select the most relevant sources of information.

*1.* Many more references can be included in the review of the literature in a thesis or dissertation than can be reported if the research is to be published in a journal. Journal space is usually quite limited, making it necessary to include only the most relevant information. In addition, journals are addressed to specialists, who presumably are familiar with previous research studies; therefore, the review can be curtailed.

*2.* Of two similar and equally valuable articles on the same subject, select the more recent for detailed analysis. The older article may be referred to thus: "Similar results were found by Jones (1927)." In this way, the review is kept as up to date as possible, but credit is still given to earlier relevant works.

*3.* Some reason should be given for the inclusion of each reference in the review of the literature. Some articles may be included because of their historical interest. Thus, the reviewer might state: "Although Pavlov (10) appears to have been the first investigator to employ the differential effect of partial versus continuous reinforcement, it was Skinner (12, 46) who recognized the theoretical and practical importance of Pavlov's discoveries."

*4.* Some articles might be included in the review because the writer wishes to discriminate between various theoretical positions or between findings that are ostensibly contradictory. Where this is the case, the writer can describe the major points of view for each position, and then simply provide a reference to the advocates of each. Thus, the review of the literature might state, "Whereas Skinner (1958) has advocated the use of many small steps in preparing material suitable for programmed instruction, Crowder (1960) has suggested that some students may skip materials which are simple for them. In partial support of Skinner's contention, Coulson and Silberman (1960) found that the use of small steps led to significantly higher scores on examinations than did the use of larger steps."

*5.* Where there is disagreement in opinion or methodology in the published literature, the student can select articles for inclusion in the review which seem to be representative of various points of view or which have used different techniques.

## Organizing the Review of the Literature

The review of the literature should never be a listing of various studies vaguely related to the proposed topic for investigation. Each review should have a clear organization. One method of organization gives a historical development of the topic and its current status; another approach provides evidence for and against a given position and then demonstrates how the proposed study will help resolve the issue or some aspect of it; still another approach describes the current status of a given topic and shows how the proposed study will contribute to a better understanding of that topic. Although no one approach is best under all conditions, the review should always be selective, organized, and clearly related to the *problem*.

# DEVELOPING NOTE-TAKING SKILLS

The ability to take meaningful and relevant notes on a selected topic is sometimes acquired—if at all—only after the student has wasted much valuable time and energy. No one is capable of retaining all that has been read, nor is it possible for the student to have readily available all sources and references that may be needed. A number of suggestions for taking notes follow.

## Use a Uniform Bibliographical Card System

Perhaps the most useful way to take notes is to develop a uniform manner of treating all information. This is most simply accomplished by using five-by-eight-inch cards. Cards are not only durable, being somewhat sturdier than notebook paper, but they can also be added to or removed from a file without tearing pages, and they are all of uniform size and shape. The card shown in Figure 3-2 is a useful prototype.

The student will find certain advantages in using this type of card:

*1.* The library call number simplifies the locating of a specific source.

*2.* The "Type of Reference" provides headings for organizing the bibliography, as:

    a. Books

    b. Books: parts of series (e.g., encyclopedias)

    c. Periodicals

    d. Unpublished materials (e.g., theses)

    e. Government documents

    f. Newspapers

The items numbered 1 through 11 indicate the parts of the bibliographic reference which need to be completed. For example, it is necessary to record

| Library Call no. | Type of reference | File heading | Card no. |
| --- | --- | --- | --- |

Author (s)

Name of Journal

| Volume No. | Month of Publication | Year of copyright |
| --- | --- | --- |

Total no. of pages

| City of Publication | Name of publisher |
| --- | --- |

| Possible Uses of Articles or Book | Type of Information Provided |
| --- | --- |
| (Check appropriate categories) | (Check appropriate categories) |
| General background | Correlational |
| Provides confirming evidence | Developmental |
| Provides contradictory evidence | Experimental |
| Quote (specify exact pages quoted) | Historical |
| Example of poor methodology | Personal opinion |
| Example of useful methodology | Philosophical |
| Other (specify) | Other (specify) |

**Figure 3-2**
EXAMPLE OF A NOTE-TAKING CARD: FRONT SIDE.

the following information for a periodical: author (1), journal title (3), volume (7), issue number (8), date (9), specific pages of the article or quote (11), and the title of the article itself (12).

*3.* The "Topic" is to help the student organize the cards by subject. It should be short and specific (e.g., the Wechsler Adult Intelligence Scale: Predictive Validity of).

*4.* The card number can be useful if there is more than one card relating to a given reference. For example, a long quote may have to be written on the backs of two cards. All the pertinent bibliographical information can be on card one; the same source can continue on the second card.

*5.* The source location can refer to a specific library, a person who possesses the document, or perhaps to the specific location of the source (NE corner, 3rd floor, Undergraduate Library).

*6.* Print the names of all authors to avoid later transcription errors, and keep authors' names in the order in which they were listed.

*7.* Titles of articles and chapters are ordinarily enclosed within quotation marks.

*8.* Names of journals and titles of books are underlined.

*9.* The section of the card titled "Uses of Source(s)" serves two purposes: 1) it forces the student to read critically; and 2) it allows the student to organize notes by placing articles and books having similar information together.

*10.* By checking the appropriate categories in "Type of Information Provided," the student will be reminded of the methods the author used.

*11.* The back of the card may be used for notes.

## Notes Should Be Written for a Specific Purpose

Notes are only as good as they are useful. Illegible, incorrect, or inaccurate notes are a hindrance rather than an aid. The following suggestions on note taking may be helpful:

*1.* Of two equally useful references, the more recent should be used because it is not only the most up to date, but it also probably includes references to older articles or texts.

*2.* Do not spend time copying pages of data, especially long tables or statistical information. Not only does copying take much time, but it also may lead to errors. Instead, use duplicating equipment (i.e., Xerox, Thermofax, etc.) which is available at nominal cost in most university libraries.

*3.* It is to the student's advantage to rephrase all notes before writing them from an original source. This can prevent both plagiarism and copying information not well understood. In addition, by rephrasing the material to be put on note cards, the student selects only the most relevant information.

*4.* If the article is to be used for background information, indicate on the

**Figure 3-3**
AN EXAMPLE OF A NOTE-TAKING CARD SHOWING THE AUTHOR'S PURPOSES, METHODS, AND FINDINGS.

Purpose: To study differences and interactions between Ss under different schedules and delays of reinforcement in the learning of concepts.
Hypotheses: The greater the delay of reinforcement, the greater number of acquisition trials will be required to learn concepts to mastery; 100% reinforcement will lead to more rapid acquisition of concepts than will 50% aperiodic reinforcement; interactions should not be significant.
Design: N = 120; H.S. students matched on CTMM-IQ, sex, and CA under following conditions:

| Schedule of reinforcement | | Delay periods | | | |
|---|---|---|---|---|---|
| | | zero | 10 min. | 20 min. | 40 min. |
| | 100% | | | | |
| | 50% | | | | |

Reinforcement was a green light. One acquisition trial per day. Criterion for mastery was no. of days required to associate correctly 3 nonsense syllables with 5 examples of each concept in form of Chinese characters.

Findings: Hypothesis 1 confirmed; hypothesis 2, insignificant results; 3, confirmed.

back of the card the author's purpose, methods, and conclusions. A study could be summarized[16] as shown in Figure 3-3.

5. Before writing notes, decide the reason for remembering these particular materials. Read the entire article to determine which parts, if any, are worth retaining. Today, an exhaustive bibliography is seldom required. A carefully selected bibliography is more meaningful than a longer one containing superfluous information.

6. Beauty is not the prime requisite in taking notes. Retyping notes or taking notes in shorthand to be written or typed later are wasteful procedures.

## SUMMARY

1. Six types of research problems were described:

   **a.** Research may be conducted to clarify or to validate some aspect of educational theory.

   **b.** Research may help to clarify contradictory findings in previously conducted research.

   **c.** Research may be instigated to correct methodological faults.

   **d.** Research may be conducted to correct the faulty use of statistics.

   **e.** Research may help to resolve conflicting opinions.

   **f.** Research may be used to resolve practical problems faced by teachers or administrators.

2. Four criteria for the selection of a research problem were discussed:

   **a.** *Interest.* Researchers have the obligation to select problems which not only interest them but also have some probability of concerning other researchers.

   **b.** *Economics.* Some proposed projects may not be feasible because of the expense involved. Convenience and low costs are not justifications for selecting a research problem.

   **c.** *Ability and training.* Researchers should consider their own training before committing themselves to a particular investigation. Time needed to gain competency should also be considered.

   **d.** *Uniqueness.* Research projects should potentially be capable of adding new information to education.

3. Documents may be classified as manuscript or printed, private or public, and intentional or unpremeditated. Document analysis may suffer from "selective deposit" and from "selective survival."

4. Various sources of information useful in developing a review of the literature were described. Among them are textbooks, encyclopedias,

---

[16]Gilbert Sax, "Concept Acquisition as a Function of Differing Schedules and Delays of Reinforcement," *Journal of Educational Psychology*, 51, no. 1 (1960), pp. 32–36.

and the ERIC system which includes RIE (Resources in Education) and CIJE (Current Index to Journals in Education).

**5.** The review of the literature is designed to show the relevance and importance of a proposed study to previously conducted investigations. The review is selective and organized around the research problem.

**6.** A uniform bibliographical card system was described and recommended. The front of the card contains source data; the reverse side contains information on the topic itself.

## PRACTICE EXERCISES

**1.** Classify the following documents as being (a) manuscript or printed, (b) private or public, or (c) intentional or unpremeditated.

  **a.** The Magna Carta

  **b.** A new federal law

  **c.** A journal article

  **d.** A mimeographed paper circulated by a researcher for comments from colleagues

  **e.** Research notes maintained by an investigator

**2.** Indicate which source or sources you would examine to locate the following information.

  **a.** A document on exceptional children circulated (but never published) in 1973

  **b.** An article published in 1955

  **c.** An article in a state educational journal published in 1974

  **d.** An exhaustive bibliography on all studies related to school dropouts in the past 10 years

**3.** If you could select any five journals, which would be most related to research being conducted in your field of specialization or interest? In what ways do these journals differ from one another? What kind of information does each contain?

**4.** Prepare a review of the literature on a topic of your choice. Use note cards as depicted on pages 55 to 56.

## Selected Supplementary Readings

1. One of the best general references on sources of information in the social sciences is White, Carl M., and associates. *Sources of Information in the Social Sciences: A Guide to the Literature.* 2d ed. Chicago: American Library Association, 1973, 702 pp. The chapter on education (pp. 425–491) contains a section on classics in education, introductory works, educational history,

philosophy, educational psychology including measurement and guidance, curriculum and instruction, preschool and elementary education, secondary education, higher education, teacher education, adult education, special education, educational research, administration and supervision, and criticism and controversy. The last 40 pages provide a list of guides to educational literature, sources of reviews, current guides to research, current books, abstracts and summaries (general and specialized), bibliographies, directories, educational personnel, associations, scholarships, dictionaries, encyclopedias, handbooks, yearbooks, statistical sources, and journals.

2. A good source of psychological information is Bell, James Edward. *A Guide to Library Research in Psychology*. Dubuque, Iowa: Wm. C. Brown Co., 1971, 211 pp.

3. Although written especially for historians, Barzun, Jacques, and Graff, Henry F. *The Modern Researcher*. rev. ed. New York: Harcourt, Brace & World, 1970, 430 pp., is also relevant for other disciplines. Principles of historiography are discussed in Chapters 1–10; Chapters 11–16 contain excellent suggestions on the art of writing that are crucial for all researchers.

# 4 the research hypothesis

In 1843, John Couch Adams, a baccalaureate candidate at St. John's College, Cambridge, began to investigate the reasons why the planet Uranus failed to follow faithfully its mathematically predicted orbital path. According to Newton's law of gravitation, the planet should have been at one point in its orbit, while observation clearly demonstrated that it was elsewhere. Adams recognized that either Uranus did not operate as did the other planets or there was an unknown outer planet whose gravitational attraction produced perturbations in Uranus' orbital path. Three years later, in 1846, Adams and Leverrier, independently, calculated the size and location of the planet later named Neptune, even before it was discovered by the use of the telescope.

Almost a half-century later, Percival Lowell began his search for a planet which he hypothesized could be found beyond Neptune. He used essentially the same reasoning that led Adams and Leverrier to the discovery of Neptune. Lowell published his final calculations in 1915; in 1930, the planet Pluto was observed on a photographic plate for the first time.

Why were Adams, Leverrier, and Lowell so certain that unknown planets were responsible for these orbital perturbations? In part, the answer is to be found in the role that hypotheses play in scientific research. *Hypotheses are statements of the expected relationships between two or more variables.* Hypotheses are used to explain and predict occurrences and events. Adams, for example, could have "explained" the aberrant motions of Uranus by postulating any or all of the following conditions:

*1.* The premise of the concept of the uniformity of nature should be reevaluated and reformulated to incorporate apparent exceptions to astronomical laws.

*2.* Newton's law of gravitation does not hold for planets so distant from the sun.

*3.* Uranus has a satellite which affects its motions.

*4.* The passage of a comet was responsible for the unpredictable motions of Uranus.

*5.* A planet closer to the sun than Uranus was pulling it out of its predicted orbit.

*6.* A planet farther from the sun than Uranus was pulling it out of its orbit.

It would, of course, be quite possible to put some of these hypotheses to an empirical test. However, this would require much wasted time. Consider, for example, just how much time would be needed to continually search the skies for unseen comets or planets without having some knowledge of where to begin the search.

What then can be done? Here is where reasoning and deduction play a most important part in the scientific enterprise by reducing the number of tentative explanations or hypotheses to those which seem most reasonable. Examine in greater detail each of the hypotheses just presented to see why only the last hypothesis was considered worthy of investigation.

*1.* To question the uniformity of nature would require an entirely new set of assumptions and beliefs that could not be substantiated except for the apparent lack of predictability concerning the orbit of Uranus. The principle of parsimony requires a simpler solution than one which holds only for a given planet but for no other physical event. Thus, this hypothesis was not seriously considered, except by a very small number of nineteenth-century astronomers.

*2.* Similarly, most astronomers were unwilling to deny Newton's law of gravitation, which had been confirmed previously in many different circumstances. The law of parsimony was again invoked, and Newtonian laws were considered adequate to explain orbital eccentricities if some other body could be found whose gravitational attraction could account for the perturbations.

*3.* The existence of a satellite revolving around Uranus and causing the orbital eccentricities was also denied by most astronomers. A satellite which could affect the orbit of Uranus would have to be large enough to be seen with a telescope. All attempts to find such a satellite were unsuccessful.

*4.* Could collision with a comet produce the perturbations? Leverrier himself denied the possibility. Whatever the causal agent was, it had to have a steady and continual effect if it were to account for the known facts. A comet could not sustain such an effect over long periods of time.

*5.* The existence of a planet closer to the sun than Uranus was also ruled out. It could be demonstrated mathematically that the perturbations had to come from beyond Uranus' orbit.

*6.* The presence of a planet outside of Uranus' orbit was the most likely explanation for its known eccentricities. Such a planet would have been difficult to observe because of its distance from the sun, but it could account for the steady and continual perturbations; in addition, its presence could be tested and verified without the necessity of changing basic assumptions concerning the uniformity of nature or the law of gravitation.

Logic, however, is not always a substitute for direct observation. By ruling out the first five hypotheses, one does not automatically have to accept the sixth unless there is some assurance that there are only six possibilities. Scientists are not ordinarily in possession of this degree of certainty; thus, "proof" by the method of elimination only establishes which possibilities are likely. Eliminating seemingly unproductive hypotheses establishes a hierarchy or priority which allows the researcher to investigate the most fruitful approaches first.

## CRITERIA FOR EVALUATING HYPOTHESES

### Deduction of Consequences

The *sine qua non* of a research hypothesis is that it must allow investigators to confirm or deny it. Any hypothesis that cannot be tested is useless. Thus, if it is argued that a particular subtance is weightless, odorless, and invisible, and that it neither affects nor is affected by any other substance, there would be no way to investigate that hypothesis since there are no consequences which can be treated.

An indefensible position is to state hypotheses in question form rather than as statements of expectations. Questions may be useful in defining a research "problem," but they fail to specify an expectation that can be confirmed or rejected.

## Consistency with Known Facts

The researcher has an obligation to develop hypotheses that are consistent with known facts. At first thought, it may appear that the questioning of well-established facts and principles is in opposition to this criterion, and that development of hypotheses consistent with known facts might prevent the investigation of some research topics. It must be admitted at the outset that the latter is a possibility and should be guarded against continually. Science should contain no beliefs so sacred that they cannot be questioned. Nonetheless, the criterion of having hypotheses conform to known principles is designed not to retard knowledge but to guard against the pursuit of unproductive hypotheses.

## Development of Multiple Hypotheses[1]

A single hypothesis allows for only one implication to be confirmed or disconfirmed. Few *problems* in education, however, are so simple that they can be resolved by testing a single hypothesis. What the researcher has to do is to consider a multiplicity of plausible explanations for a given event and to test these explanations empirically.

As an example, consider the *problem* or perplexing question, "What is the effect, if any, of noise on students?" Even a cursory review of the literature will demonstrate just how complex this question is. Noise can be meaningful or meaningless, loud or soft, continuous or intermittent, prolonged or temporary, necessary or unnecessary, controllable or uncontrollable—to mention just a few dimensions. Student effects may involve errors on a myriad of tasks, annoyance, adaptation, cooperation, etc. Any theory regarding the effect of noise on students will have to consider these various conditions. Rival explanations for the same or similar events will need to be tested and incorporated into the theory, which will have to be modified to account for discrepant findings.

The complexity of problems in education is one reason for establishing and testing multiple hypotheses. Another reason is that it is often desirable to develop hypotheses which, if confirmed, would force the researcher to modify, eliminate, or at least reconsider some favored position. This might be accomplished by deliberately setting up conditions to demonstrate that one's own position is fallacious.

[1] T. C. Chamberlin, "The Method of Multiple Working Hypotheses," *The Scientific Monthly*, 59 (November 1944), pp. 357–362.

## Parsimony

A fourth criterion for a good hypothesis, as for a good theory, is that it be as simple as possible while still accounting for the known facts. The law of parsimony argues that testing the simpler hypotheses first is more advantageous and economical in time and effort.

# SOME OBJECTIONS TO HYPOTHESIS CONSTRUCTION

A number of objections to the use of hypotheses have been raised. Newton's famous quote, *"Hypothesis non fingo"* ("I do not make hypotheses"), has been used out of context to justify all sorts of beliefs, ranging from the assertion that constructing hypotheses is tantamount to biasing the investigator to the statement that they prevent the researcher from trying other and more fruitful approaches. These beliefs will be examined in greater detail.

### The Belief That the Hypothesis Will Bias the Investigator

One of the first formally to reject the hypothesis was Sir Francis Bacon. A thoroughgoing empiricist, Bacon denied the use of the syllogism and even went so far as to deny the extensive use of mathematics in solving empirical problems. One can sympathize with his desire to rid science of superstition and an overdependence upon Aristotelian logic, but scientists do need some way to plan observations. Hypotheses help do this by specifying which variables to observe.

Certainly, hypotheses can be misused when investigators become so enthralled by their own beliefs that they refuse to accept contrary evidence. The hypothesis is a statement that predicts what a particular relationship will be. Those who use hypotheses solely to support their own views and who refuse to modify their beliefs as new evidence is accumulated are not using hypotheses to predict but to avoid careful investigation. Those who do not state hypotheses, of course, may be equally biased.

Another argument should be considered. If an investigator does develop an attachment to a favorite hypothesis to the extent that others are dismissed, the problem is not that there are too many hypotheses but that too few have been considered. By constructing multiple hypotheses, the investigator admits at the outset that there are many possible explanations for events and that each relevant hypothesis should be tested empirically. This procedure increases the probability that a researcher will consider alternative explanations.

## The Case for Serendipity

According to Cannon,[2] Horace Walpole first coined the word *serendipity*, after reading the fairy tale *The Three Princes of Serendip*. The fairy tale describes the wanderings of the princes who, instead of finding what they were searching for, accidentally came across other discoveries. In a more modern sense, *serendipity* has been used to refer to unforeseen or accidental discoveries. More specifically, it has been used by some authors[3] to refer to the ability of the researcher to successfully put aside what was a primary interest when a more important and more interesting possibility shows itself by accident. As Sidman has stated:

> Unless the experimenter's attitude is one of interest in anything that turns up, he is likely to overlook a chance finding. When a hypothesis-bound investigator, after carefully designing his apparatus and experimental procedure to answer a specific question, finds that his equipment has broken down in the midst of the investigation, he is likely to consider the experiment a failure. He may shed a few tears of frustration, but will probably roll up his sleeves, rebuild the apparatus, and start all over again, knowing that science is made by martyrs like himself. On the other hand, the simple-minded curiosity tester is likely to look closely at the data produced by the apparatus breakdown. Since he has little personal investment in his own guesswork, he may find the accidental experiment more interesting than the one he started to do—and without tears he is off on a new track.[4]

The case for serendipity cannot be denied. Many of the greatest discoveries have been made purely by accident. But this should not blind the student to the fact that the great majority of discoveries were found by those who were "hypothesis-bound," i.e., in the process of testing hypotheses.

There is a clear danger in carrying serendipity too far. If researchers were to drop every research project to investigate data produced by each apparatus failure, little research would ever get done. If hypotheses are carefully thought out, they are probably of sufficient importance to be tested empirically. The investigator has to weigh giving up the empirical testing of hypotheses against the odds that by accident a new and more important discovery will be made. There is, of course, nothing that rules against the researcher temporarily putting aside original hypotheses to investigate some more interesting discovery.

[2]Walter Bradford Cannon, *The Way of an Investigator* (New York: W. W. Norton & Co., 1945), pp. 68–78.
[3]Cannon, pp. 68–78; Arthur J. Bachrach, *Psychological Research: An Introduction* (New York: Random House, 1962).
[4]Murray Sidman, *Tactics of Scientific Research* (New York: Basic Books, 1960), p. 10.

# WRITING THE RESEARCH HYPOTHESIS

Hypotheses should be developed after the review of the literature has been written (see Chapter 3). Without knowing what has already been done, it is impossible to determine what remains to be accomplished.

An example of how hypotheses are developed out of the review of the literature appears in an article by Samuels and Dahl,[5] who attempted to determine whether readers do, in fact, change reading rates according to the purpose of reading:

> Flexibility in reading (Tinker & McCullough, 1962) refers to the ability of an individual to adjust his reading rate according to the difficulty of the material and the purpose. Current conceptualizations of the proficient reader suggest that he has a high degree of flexibility. Developing reading rate flexibility is a goal in most elementary school reading programs as well as advanced programs for adult readers.
>
> With this goal in mind a number of researchers have investigated the degree to which readers do alter their reading rate according to material and purpose. Studies in which various age groups, materials, and purposes were used have found little flexibility in reading (Boyd, 1966; Herculane, 1961; Hill, 1964; Letson, 1959; McDonald, 1963; Rankin & Hess, 1970; Theophemia, 1962). In a detailed review of the literature on this topic Miller . . . concluded, "most studies suggest that students, by and large, are not flexible readers" (p. 23). . . .
>
> A careful review of the literature on reading flexibility suggests that the lack of flexibility found in readers may be the result of failure of the tests used in these studies to inform the subject clearly as to the exact purpose for which he is to read. Many of the tests commonly used to determine flexibility present the reader with ambiguous directions and unclear goals. . . .
>
> When the student is given no directions or contradictory directions such as "Read quickly but carefully," he is faced with the dilemma of not knowing how quickly and how carefully he is to read. . . .
>
> The purpose of this study was two-fold: (a) to test the hypothesis that despite previous negative findings, readers do alter their reading rate according to their purpose and (b) to establish test conditions under which this competence can be exhibited.

This review of the literature demonstrated that most investigators found pupils did not adjust reading rates for different kinds of materials and

[5]S. Jay Samuels and Patricia R. Dahl, "Establishing Appropriate Purpose for Reading and Its Effect on Flexibility of Reading Rate," *Journal of Educational Psychology*, 67, no. 1 (February 1975), pp. 38–43.

this failure resulted from the researchers' failure to clarify the students' task. Because of these methodological problems, the authors argued that the common-sense notion that students do alter reading rates is correct.

## Specific Suggestions for Writing the Research Hypothesis

Vague or unclear hypotheses are of little value either to the researcher or to the research report reader. A number of suggestions for writing the research hypothesis follow, although some of these principles have been referred to earlier.

*1.* Write hypotheses after a thorough review of the literature. The review may point out what earlier investigators have found, what techniques were used, which were useful, and which were of little value. To test hypotheses before a thorough review leads to much wasted time.

*2.* Research hypotheses are usually placed in the first chapter of a thesis or dissertation. In published reports, research hypotheses usually follow a brief review of the literature.

*3.* Research hypotheses should be written in statement form rather than as questions, unless, of course, a thorough review of the literature fails to provide any direction. These expectations should be derived from the review of the literature.

*4.* Usually, the researcher should plan on having more than one research hypothesis to test. The review of the literature should provide evidence as to whether or not a contemplated hypothesis is likely to yield important results.

*5.* Research hypotheses should not be worded in null form (see Appendix III.). Research hypotheses should predict significant differences or significant relationships. The null form of the research hypothesis is usually presented in the chapter on "Procedures" and again in the chapter on "Findings."

*6.* Every term in the hypothesis should be clearly defined in the research paper. If a large number of terms need to be defined, they may appear in a section titled "Definitions of Terms," immediately following the statement of the hypotheses.

*7.* Each hypothesis should be testable.

Take, for example a paper by Neel,[6] who attempted to study the following hypotheses:

*1.* The more authoritarian a person is, the more likely he is to have difficulty learning material which (a) deals with humanitarian philosophy or (b) is ambiguous. . . .

---

[6]Ann Filinger Neel, "The Relationship of Authoritarian Personality to Learning: *F* Scale Scores Combined to Classroom Performance," *Journal of Educational Psychology*, 50, no. 5 (1959), pp. 195–199.

2. The more authoritarian a person is, the more dislike he should manifest for materials involving ambiguous or humanitarian materials.[7]

Suppose these statements are given to a researcher who is asked to replicate Neel's experiment. Given only those two hypotheses, it would be difficult to answer the following questions:

*1.* How will authoritarianism be measured?

*2.* What will be the characteristics of the subjects used in this study? Will they be elementary school, secondary school, or college students? Of what sex? From what socioeconomic backgrounds? How bright must they be?

*3.* How does one measure the amount of difficulty a person has in learning?

*4.* Just what constitutes a "humanitarian" philosophy? How can this be measured?

*5.* How will ambiguity be measured?

*6.* How will the amount of dislike which a person manifests for "ambiguous or humanitarian materials" be measured?

Although one cannot provide answers to each of these questions in the research hypotheses themselves, they must be answered somewhere in the thesis or research paper. One possibility is to define terms immediately following the presentation of the hypotheses. (The characteristics of well-defined terms will be examined in more detail shortly.) In addition, a section titled "Limitations" or "Delimitations" may state that the experimenter plans to delimit the study to include only college students, or perhaps that one particular test will be used to measure authoritarianism.

Neel does provide her readers with specific answers to the above questions. In the major heading of her paper, "Subjects and Procedure," she indicates that her subjects ". . . were 30 male senior medical students taking a required class in psychiatry." Authoritarian personality was measured by the *F* scale, given to each student during a regular class period. Neel indicated that students ". . . were told this was a study by psychologists investigating social attitudes among medical students with reference to the kind of specialty they intended to enter."[8]

Humanitarianism was measured on a 1- to 5-point scale determined from each student's reaction to a test item concerning an indigent person. The ambiguous material consisted of two items asking what the student would do under different conditions where there was no predetermined correct or right answer. At the end of the semester, the students were asked to

[7]Neel, pp. 195–196.
[8]Neel, p. 196.

evaluate the course, and their remarks were taken as a measure of the degree to which they enjoyed or disliked it. The chi-square test was used to determine whether differences were significant or not.

In complete form, then, Neel's first hypothesis ("The more authoritarian a person is, the more likely he is to have difficulty learning material which deals with humanitarian philosophy") could have read, "Male senior medical students taking a required class in psychiatry and scoring above the median on the $F$ scale will subsequently attain significantly lower scores on a humanitarian scale than will those who are below the median on the $F$ scale."

## DEFINITION OF TERMS

All vague, ambiguous, or unusual terms used in hypotheses should be defined in the research report. Terms that are commonly understood by specialists within a given subject might be defined as an aid to the nonspecialist.

### Lexical Definitions

Lexical definitions, those found in dictionaries, explain a given term *as it is used by most persons*. As long as a definition contains words understood by the reader, lexical definitions are of value.

Lexical definitions provide both a *genus* and *differentia*. The genus, as in biology, is the major category containing subordinate species. A *zariba*, for example, is a type of stockade (the genus) constructed in some parts of Africa (the differentia).

A number of rules have been established for defining terms by means of genus and differentia.

*1. Convertibility.* The word to be defined and the definition should be interchangeable. Thus, to define a cat as an animal violates this principle since cats are animals but not all animals are cats.

*2. Avoidance of Circularity.* A circular definition contains the word to be defined. To define a researcher as someone who conducts research is to invite confusion. Try also to avoid replacing one ambiguous term in a definition with another equally confusing one.

*3. Affirmation.* Definitions should state what the meaning of a term is, not what it is not. It does little good, for example, to list all of the things a zariba is not.

*4. Clarity.* Above all, definitions must be clear, and to be so, they must avoid ambiguity and vagueness. An ambiguous term has more than one meaning within a given context; a vague term has no specific referent.

5. *Structure.* Children sometimes define words by saying, "Beauty is when . . ." or "Latitude is where. . . ." The principle violated here is that if the term to be defined is an abstract noun (e.g., beauty), the genus should also be an abstract noun (a "quality" or a "state," for example). Failure to abide by this rule leads to awkward expression.

## Operational Definitions

In 1927, the Harvard physicist P. W. Bridgman published *The Logic of Modern Physics.*[9] The book was written to clarify some of Einstein's work on the theory of relativity, but it did much more. Bridgman helped found the philosophical school of thought variously called *operationalism*, or *operationism*, which is closely related to the philosophical position called *logical positivism*, or *logical empiricism*. At first, scientists seized upon operationalism as a means of defining terms and as a way of separating scientific problems from pseudoscientific problems. However, under the influence of Schlick, Carnap, and Feigl, operationalism became a school of thought having its own advocates and disbelievers. What is operationalism? It is no more than good scientific methodology, coupled with an unwillingness to talk about nonverifiable propositions. Operationalists attempt to define words by the operations that it takes to produce them. In defining the concept of length, for example, Bridgman has stated:

> . . . what do we mean by the length of an object? We evidently know what we mean by length if we can tell what the length of any and every object is, and for the physicist nothing more is required. To find the length of an object, we have to perform certain physical operations. The concept of length is therefore fixed when the operations by which length is measured is fixed: that is, the concept of length involves as much as and nothing more than the set of operations by which length is determined. In general, we mean by any concept nothing more than a set of operations; the concept is synonymous with the corresponding set of operations.[10]

Consider the definition of intelligence. If intelligence is defined as a capacity, then the definition has already lost one major requirement needed for an operational definition: a capacity, at least as yet, cannot be measured. In defining the concept of intelligence, the question to ask is how to go about measuring it. What operations are needed to state that John has an IQ of 127? If one set of operations involves the administration of the 1972 edition of the Stanford–Binet test and another involves administering the Wechsler Adult Intelligence Scale, then two different concepts of intelligence are being

[9]P. W. Bridgman, *The Logic of Modern Physics* (New York: The Macmillan Co., 1927).

[10]Bridgman, p. 5.

used. In other words, there are as many different concepts of intelligence as there are measures of it.

Operational definitions are stipulative. That is, the definer stipulates what is meant by a given term and in so doing indicates the process of measuring the term itself. Thus, authoritarianism could be defined as a set of scores on the *F* test; personality could be defined as the score obtained by a person on any test or rating scale one wishes to specify.

What then happens to terms that cannot at present be measured? Either they are artifacts of the language, or they will somehow have to be related to observables. Thus, nonobservables such as drive, motivation, intelligence, and personality will be considered as *intervening variables*. An *intervening variable* is one that expresses the relationship between stimulus and response variables, and that is not necessarily presumed to actually exist. A researcher may, for example, give a test to students (a stimulus situation) and observe how they respond. The researcher may *infer* that some intellectual activity went on between the time the students read the question and the time they responded and may be willing to call this activity intelligence. Note that although intelligence is not seen, heard, tasted, smelled, or touched, the concept is tied both to an observable stimulus situation and to the students' responses to that situation.

Education contains many examples of intervening variables. Such concepts as motivation or drive may be considered to be intervening variables. John is told to pay attention; he then sits up and begins reading his book. If someone were asked to *state* why John sat up, the answer might be that he was motivated to do so. As used in this example, motivation has been inferred and is not an explanation of why this behavior occurred. To understand how motivation manifests itself, it will be necessary to define it operationally and to hypothesize and test the relationship between the teacher's behavior, for example, and the behavior of the student who has been "motivated."

## SUMMARY

**1.** Hypotheses are statements of the expected relationships between two or more variables. Hypotheses are of value if they can help the researcher eliminate unproductive approaches to a problem and if they can help to focus the direction of research.

**2.** Four criteria for evaluating hypotheses were described:

**a.** *Deduction of consequences.* Hypotheses must either be confirmed or disconfirmed. Any hypothesis having a nontestable effect serves no purpose.

**b.** *Consistency with known facts.* Hypotheses should be consistent with previously verified information or data.

**c.** *Development of multiple hypotheses.* Educational problems are too complex to be solved by a single hypothesis. Multiple hypotheses provide a better understanding of the problem.

**d.** *Parsimony.* Hypotheses should be as simple as possible while still accounting for known facts.

3. Some objections to hypothesis construction were noted and analyzed:

   **a.** The hypothesis may bias the researcher. Hypotheses are always tentative expectations and thus amenable to modification. Hypotheses contrary to one's bias should also be tested empirically.

   **b.** Serendipity. The principle of serendipity states that scientific advancements occur primarily by chance and not by hypothesis testing. Although many scientific advancements have occurred because scientists were willing to postpone their original investigations in deference to the study of some chance event, the likelihood is not great that these findings will be of importance.

4. A number of specific suggestions were made for writing hypotheses:

   **a.** Hypotheses should be developed after the review of the literature has been written to take advantage of the works of previous investigators.

   **b.** Hypotheses are usually included in the first chapter of a thesis or dissertation; ordinarily they follow a brief review of the literature in published journal articles.

   **c.** Hypotheses should be stated as expectations of what will occur, and not in question form, unless there is no available evidence to guide the investigator.

   **d.** Usually more than one hypothesis should be tested.

   **e.** Research hypotheses should be stated positively and not in null form.

   **f.** Each unclear, vague, or ambiguous term in the hypothesis should be clearly defined in the research paper.

   **g.** Each hypothesis should be testable.

5. Definitions may be *lexical* or *operational.*

   **a.** A *lexical* definition attempts to define a word by specifying the *genus* and *differentia,* or major category and subcategory. A number of rules for the lexical definition were presented:

      1) *Convertibility.* The principle of convertibility is designed to make the term to be defined interchangeable with the explanatory words.

      2) *Circularity.* The definition should not contain the word to be defined.

      3) *Affirmation.* Definitions should state the essential characteristics of the terms to be defined.

      4) *Clarity.* Definitions should avoid vague, ambiguous, and figurative language if they are to achieve maximal clarity.

      5) *Structure.* The genus and the term being defined should be stated at the same degree of abstraction.

**b.** *Operational* definitions are those in which a concept is defined by the operations used to measure it. Operational definitions have an advantage over lexical definitions in that they indicate the processes necessary to measure the concept, whereas lexical definitions ordinarily do not.

Operationalism has become associated with the philosophical position called *logical empiricism*, or *logical positivism*, which attempts to analyze the meaning of words so that they are capable of verifying empirical referents; the validity of concepts which do not have empirical referents (i.e., metaphysical propositions) is denied.

**6.** Intervening variables are those which intervene between stimulus and response situations but which are not accorded actual or physical properties. They are used primarily as a convenient way of summarizing the relationship between stimuli and responses. As long as stimulus and response variables are operationally defined, nothing more is required for intervening variables.

## PRACTICE EXERCISES

**1.** From your review of the literature on a given topic (see Chapter 3), establish four or five research hypotheses that conform to the criteria of good hypotheses as indicated in this chapter.

**2.** Translate *each* of the following questions into multiple research hypotheses. Define operationally each of the terms in italics.

    **a.** Are girls *better readers* than boys?

    **b.** Do older teachers have more *discipline problems* than *younger* ones?

    **c.** Do students who have *friendly teachers appreciate* music more than those who have teachers who are *hostile*?

    **d.** Does a *democratic* teacher *motivate students* more than does a *laissez-faire* teacher?

    **e.** *Can children learn* to *read before* they are *mentally ready*?

**3.** A teacher hypothesizes that a student is not reading for one or more or the following reasons:

    **a.** Poor motivation

    **b.** Emotional problems

    **c.** Visual or hearing problems

Indicate what processes the teacher could follow to test each of these hypotheses? Which ones would be suggested first? Why?

**4.** Criticize each of the following definitions:

    **a.** Research is no more than investigation.

    **b.** Research is not just perspiration or inspiration.

    **c.** Intelligence is the ability to see relationships.

**d.** Educational research is doing the best you can to find out about education.

**e.** A concept is a symbol.

## Selected Supplementary Readings

1. To gain a better understanding of the operational definition and of operationalism, the following sources are recommended: Bridgman, Percy William. *The Logic of Modern Physics.* New York: Macmillan Co., 1927, especially Chapters 1 and 2. Ellis, Albert. "An Operational Reformulation of Some of the Basic Principles of Psychoanalysis." Herbert Feigl and Michael Scriven, eds. *The Foundations of Science and the Concepts of Psychology and Psychoanalysis.* Minnesota Studies in the Philosophy of Science, Vol. I. Minneapolis: University of Minnesota Press, 1956, pp. 131–154. See also article in same source by Feigl, Herbert. "Some Major Issues and Developments in the Philosophy of Science of Logical Empiricism," pp. 3–37. In "Symposium on Operationism." *Psychological Review*, 52, no. 5 (September 1945), pp. 241–294, Professors Boring, Bridgman, Feigl, Israel, Pratt, and Skinner each attempt to answer basic questions concerning operationalism.

2. CANNON, WALTER BRADFORD. *The Way of an Investigator.* New York: W. W. Norton & Co., 1945, 229 pp. See especially Chapters 5 and 6, "The Role of Hunches" and "Gains from Serendipity." The author emphasizes the role that unconscious processes play in developing ideas worthy of investigation. He also indicates the necessity for having a "prepared mind" if one is to take advantage of accidental discoveries. See also Bachrach, Arthur J. *Psychological Research: An Introduction.* New York: Random House, 1962, Chapters 1 and 3, for other examples of serendipity and what Bachrach called "hypothesis myopia."

3. CHAMBERLIN, T. C. "The Method of Multiple Working Hypotheses." *Scientific Monthly*, 59 (November 1944), pp. 357–362. An excellent account of the need for multiple- rather than single-hypothesis construction. Although Chamberlin was a geologist, the article is still relevant to researchers in other disciplines.

4. Most textbooks in logic contain an analysis of the formal definition. The following texts will provide information concerning the definition: Larrabee, Harold A. *Reliable Knowledge: Scientific Methods in the Social Studies.* rev. ed. Boston: Houghton Mifflin Co., 1964, especially Chapters 5–8. See also Leonard, Henry S. *An Introduction to Principles of Right Reason.* New York: Holt, Rinehart and Winston, 1957, especially pp. 271–404. See also Scriven, Michael. "Definitions, Explanations, and Theories." Herbert Feigl, Michael Scriven, and Grover Maxwell, eds, *Concepts, Theories, and the Mind-Body Problem.* Minnesota Studies in the Philosophy of Science, Vol. II. Minneapolis: University of Minnesota Press, 1958, pp. 99–195.

5. See PLATT, JOHN R. "Strong Inference." *Science*, 146 (October 16, 1966), pp. 347–353. In addition to supporting the development of multiple hypotheses, Platt argues that hypotheses must be capable of being *disproved* since the *support* of a hypothesis does not *establish* its validity (i.e., a random selection of marbles from a bin may all be white, but this finding cannot "prove" that the remaining marbles will also be white. A single black marble, however, is sufficient to demonstrate the induction is untrue).

6. WILLOWER, DONALD J. "Some Illustrated Comments on Hypothesis Construction and Research." *Journal of Educational Research*, 56, no. 4 (December 1962), pp. 210–213. The author indicates ways in which hypotheses may be derived from theory, especially in educational administration.

# 5

## research design: descriptive approaches

Most investigators wisely study the current status of a problem before they attempt to modify educational practices. Many early studies in education tried to do little more than describe existing educational practices in much the same way that the U.S. Office of Education has provided descriptive statistics and information to keep educators and the public abreast of the current status of education. Unfortunately, these descriptions do not always point out the most efficient ways to improve educational practices, nor do they necessarily indicate causal relationships, which must be known in any science. Research involving the collection of data for the purpose of describing existing conditions is called *descriptive research*, in contrast to studies which attempt to manipulate or control the environment (primarily to investigate causal relationships), called *experimental research*.

# THE CASE STUDY

The clinical case study used to investigate the problems faced by an individual is generally familiar. Physicians can learn about patients not only by studying present symptoms but also by investigating previous illnesses, diseases, operations, etc., that might clarify and help diagnose current complaints. Similarly, teachers may wish to discover the attitudes, abilities, and interests of students to understand their individual problems.

In research, the definition of the case study is extended to include *any relatively detailed description and analysis of a single person, event, institution, or community.* The researcher may analyze the counseling services of a particular high school or study minority group attitudes in an elementary school. Or the concern may be with understanding a particular child from a severely culturally deprived or highly unusual environment.

In clinical work, the benefits of the case study accrue primarily to the patient. In this sense, the case study is said to be *idiographic*; that is, it attempts to understand the behavior and attitudes of the individual without attempting to generalize these findings to other persons or groups. In contrast, most research studies attempt to develop principles or theories having wider applicability. The attempt in research is to develop *nomothetic* knowledge, or knowledge that relates to larger numbers of persons, institutions, or events.

The differences between idiographic and nomothetic approaches are differences in emphasis. Each approach can be used to complement the other. Piaget, for example, has developed a theory of child development from detailed observations of a few children. His intent was to develop knowledge of a nomothetic nature. But teachers can also use Piaget's findings to help them understand individual behavior. Thus, the relationships between idiographic and nomothetic approaches tend to be complementary and reciprocal.

## The Uses of Case Studies in Research

One purpose of the case study in research is to provide the investigator with hypotheses that might be difficult to study in other contexts. In the preliminary stages of inquiry, determining which variables are relevant to a particular problem can be difficult. Instead of studying large numbers of persons, events, or institutions, it is often less expensive and simpler to investigate a limited number of cases. If, for example, the intelligence of a child who has been isolated from most normal stimulation is found to be extremely low, it could be *hypothesized* that low intelligence is one consequence of understimulated environments. The case study provides hypotheses that can be tested later with larger numbers of subjects.

Second, the investigator may find in the case study unique situations that can be used to test hypotheses. In one investigation,[1] the researcher was interested in studying emotional development. She was able to find a ten-year-old child who was born blind and deaf, but who nonetheless showed normal emotional responses to various stimuli (such as laughing when tickled), even though these could not possibly have been imitated. Evidently, the way in which emotional responses exhibit themselves is largely unlearned. It is important to realize that the type of behavior studied would probably remain fairly constant among other blind-deaf children. In addition, there was no possibility for the child to learn emotional responses. In most case studies, these conditions are not nearly so well controlled.

Third, the case study may be interesting in and of itself. It may provide new insights, help modify preexisting beliefs, and point out gaps in knowledge. A study of an isolated culture, for example, might extend knowledge of childrearing practices and educational beliefs. A study of a child reared in an orphanage from birth might show a later inability to identify with a mother or father. A study of the social structure of a small frontier town might help define the social structure of the community, and how this structure affects public education.

Fourth, the case study may also be useful in demonstrating how a theoretical model can be exhibited in a concrete example. Thus, in their study of the authoritarian personality, Adorno et al.[2] hypothesized that ethnocentrism is characteristic of persons who are aggressive and repressed, and who displace their hostilities onto minorities. In contrast, those who are tolerant of others have insight into their own problems, more realistic ways of resolving them, and can accept unconventional ways of behaving. To point out the dramatic differences between high and low ethnocentric persons, the case histories of Mack and Larry were described in detail as examples of different behavior patterns.

## Conducting a Case Study

One of the first steps in conducting a case study is to select those cases which typify the major dimensions of the problem. The search is not for a random sample from some specified population, but for a case that is

---

[1]Florence L. Goodenough, "Expression of the Emotions in a Deaf-Blind Child," *Journal of Abnormal and Social Psychology*, 27, no. 3 (1932), pp. 328–333.

[2]T. W. Adorno et al., *The Authoritarian Personality* (New York: Harper & Row, 1950).

a relatively pure example of the phenomenon under investigation. In a study of extreme environmental deprivation, the researcher will want to find a case of deprivation unencumbered with irrelevant variables. Unfortunately, it is not always easy to determine at the outset of an investigation just which variables are irrelevant and which are not. Perhaps the best course is to select cases that are as simple as possible and that exhibit the phenomenon being studied. Often the most useful cases in helping to generate or test hypotheses are those that clearly represent some extreme position. A comparison of a right-wing Republican and a left-wing Democrat is likely to yield more fruitful hypotheses than would a study of moderate Republicans and Democrats.

Once the cases are selected, information is gathered from as many relevant sources as are needed to validate the hypotheses. These sources may include interviews, educational and psychological tests, or other means of collecting data. The purpose of the investigation determines which data are relevant. In a study of the effects of extreme overprotection, the researcher may wish to interview or administer various psychological tests to the parents and child. The methods used must allow the investigator to confirm, reject, or at least to generate hypotheses that lead to or are derived from theory. Little is gained by compiling information that is unrelated to the testing of hypotheses derived from or contributing to some theoretical position.

## Some Limitations and Difficulties in Conducting Case Studies

One limitation of the case study in research is that it is difficult to determine which factors, historical or contemporary, are relevant to the phenomenon under investigation. If a child has been overprotected by one parent and rejected by the other, is the rejection the cause, effect, or an irrelevant circumstance of overprotection? Simply because some behavior preceded another is no assurance that one is the cause and the other is the effect.

Second, there has been a tendency in using the case study to select convenient cases rather than those which can either yield or test hypotheses. A remedial reading teacher may want to write a case study on a child having difficulty in reading, simply because data (IQ scores, achievement scores, etc.) are available on this child and it would be convenient to use these data for a thesis. Or a researcher may want to describe the guidance services in a particular high school without considering the potential contributions of the study. Neither convenience nor simplicity is sufficient to justify conducting a case study.

# THE SAMPLE SURVEY

Because Chapters 8 and 10 will consider problems of sampling and questionnaire development—the two essential components of the sample survey—it is necessary here only to remind the student that the sample survey is a type of descriptive research in which survey data are obtained from respondents to test hypotheses concerning the status of some educational problem. An example might be an administrator's interest in knowing the attitudes of school board members throughout the United States toward, for example, teacher tenure. A review of the literature should provide specific hypotheses that will suggest appropriate survey questions.

# CORRELATIONAL STUDIES

An examination of the history of educational research depicts a clear movement away from what Meehl[3] has called the *discriminative* use of statistics toward a *structural* use. The discriminative use of statistics involves descriptions of relationships with no concern about underlying theories of behavior. Consider the following questions: "What is the relationship between intelligence and achievement test scores?" "Are experienced teachers better able to maintain discipline than new teachers?" "To what extent are teachers able to estimate which children are in need of remedial reading?" In each of these examples, the investigator is not particularly concerned with educational or psychological theories relating to intelligence, achievement testing, discipline, or reading. Rather, the emphasis is on answering a specific question of minor theoretical importance.

The relative simplicity of this discriminative approach has appealed to many graduate students who, once they have mastered the technique of computing correlations or other statistics, have used these methods without due regard for the value of their research proposals. Correlational analyses are important tools in research, but not all problems employing these techniques are worthwhile.

As indicated earlier, the current tendency in educational research is to move away from simple descriptions toward an analysis of behavior related to some theoretical system. Examples of questions which emphasize the structural use of statistics are: "What are the basic psychological factors that constitute intelligence?" or "What types of reinforcements or rewards are most effective in maintaining motivation?" Answers to questions of these

[3]Paul E. Meehl, *Clinical Versus Statistical Prediction: A Theoretical Analysis and Review of the Evidence* (Minneapolis: University of Minnesota Press, 1954), pp. 10–18.

types are important insofar as they constitute a body of educational theory related to intelligence or motivation.

Factor analysis, relationship, and prediction studies are types of correlational studies.

## Factor Analysis

*Purpose.* The purpose of factor analysis is to simplify and organize large numbers of correlations.[4] Suppose, for example, that a researcher is interested in knowing the number of *factors* (traits or attributes) that underlie a battery of tests, a large number of items within a single test, or perhaps the number of factors being measured by any number of different tasks. Factor analysis is designed to measure and identify the factors common to all of the measurements under investigation.

*An Example of a Factor Analysis Problem.* Consider a study conducted by Czirr[5] who asked subjects to rate 12 concepts along 16 dimensions such as BAD–GOOD, HARMFUL–HELPFUL, PASSIVE–ACTIVE, etc. The 12 concepts were 1) thermometer, 2) computer, 3) mosquito, 4) pollution, 5) Edison, 6) earthquake, 7) research, 8) virus, 9) Pasteur, 10) biology, 11) volcano, and 12) lightning. The question being analyzed is how many *different* factors or traits are being measured by these concepts? Without the benefit of the factor analysis, there may appear to be numerous ways these concepts can be organized: animate vs. inanimate (2 factors); instruments vs. noninstruments (2 factors); concepts vs. instruments vs. persons (3 factors); or perhaps just one factor, which might be labeled a "survival" factor. Indeed, without the benefit of a factor analysis one might conceivably consider each of the 12 concepts to be a separate and independent factor. The number of factors depends upon the correlations among the 12 rated concepts. That is, if all 12 concepts are highly correlated with each other, they are all measuring a factor in common; 3 factors would be extracted from the analysis if, for example, thermometer, computer, research, and biology were highly intercorrelated (perhaps forming a "science" factor) as were Edison and Pasteur (this factor might be labeled a "famous men" factor); the remaining concepts might form a "natural disaster" factor. As will be seen later, the actual labeling of the factors is often rather arbitrary.

Factor analyses are most readily accomplished by use of electronic

[4]See J. P. Guilford, *Psychometric Methods*, 2d ed. (New York: McGraw-Hill Book Co., 1954), pp. 470–471. Many of the ideas presented in this section have been described in greater detail by Guilford.

[5]John E. Czirr, "Factor Analysis and Scoring Techniques for a Science Related Semantic Differential Instrument" (Paper presented at the 1970 Annual Meeting of the American Educational Research Association, Minneapolis, Minn., March 6, 1970), 9 pp.

data processing equipment. Although this text cannot go into the various types of factor analyses in detail, interpreting the results of the factor analysis performed on the 12 concepts is of value.

Table 5-1 shows the correlation of each of Czirr's 12 concepts with

**TABLE 5-1**

A Factor Matrix Showing the Correlation between Each of 12 Concepts and 2 Factors (*A* and *B*), the Common-Factor Variances, and Communalities ($h^2$)

| CONCEPTS | Factors | | Common-Factor Variances | | Communalities ($h^2$) |
|---|---|---|---|---|---|
| | *A* | *B* | *A* | *B* | $h^2$ |
| Thermometer | 0.59 | 0.02 | 0.3481 | 0.0004 | 0.3485 |
| Computer | 0.74 | 0.20 | 0.5476 | 0.0400 | 0.5876 |
| Mosquito | 0.09 | 0.62 | 0.0081 | 0.3844 | 0.3925 |
| Pollution | 0.08 | 0.54 | 0.0064 | 0.2916 | 0.2980 |
| Edison | 0.63 | 0.18 | 0.3969 | 0.0324 | 0.4293 |
| Earthquake | 0.07 | 0.72 | 0.0049 | 0.5184 | 0.5233 |
| Research | 0.80 | 0.12 | 0.6400 | 0.0144 | 0.6544 |
| Virus | 0.19 | 0.67 | 0.0361 | 0.4489 | 0.4850 |
| Pasteur | 0.78 | 0.12 | 0.6084 | 0.0144 | 0.6228 |
| Biology | 0.80 | 0.14 | 0.6400 | 0.0196 | 0.6596 |
| Volcano | 0.21 | 0.68 | 0.0441 | 0.4624 | 0.5065 |
| Lightning | 0.32 | 0.56 | 0.1024 | 0.3136 | 0.4160 |

$$\Sigma A = 3.3830 \quad \Sigma B = 2.5405$$
$$\bar{X}_A = 0.28 \quad \bar{X}_B = 0.21$$

*Source:* Factor loadings are from Czirr, p. 2.

each of 2 factors labeled, for convenience, Factors *A* and *B*. The correlation of the concept or test with each factor is known as a *factor loading*. Thermometer, for example, correlates or loads 0.59 with Factor *A* and 0.02 with Factor *B*. It therefore is a better measure of Factor *A* than of Factor *B*. Table 5-2 demonstrates those concepts that load on Factor *A* and those that load on Factor *B*. Just what these factors will be labeled is somewhat arbitrary (Czirr labeled them "positive" and "negative" factors, but any term that reasonably identifies the factor will do).

Table 5-1 provides information in addition to the factor loadings and the number of factors extracted. The square of the factor loading yields what is called *common-factor variance*. The square of any correlation coefficient yields the proportion of variance held in common between the two

TABLE 5-2

Concepts That Load with Factors *A* and *B*

| | *A* | | *B* |
|---|---|---|---|
| Research | (0.80) | Earthquake | (0.72) |
| Biology | (0.80) | Volcano | (0.68) |
| Pasteur | (0.78) | Virus | (0.67) |
| Computer | (0.74) | Mosquito | (0.62) |
| Edison | (0.63) | Lightning | (0.56) |
| Thermometer | (0.59) | Pollution | (0.54) |

*Source:* Czirr, p. 2.

variables correlated. For example, if height and weight correlate 0.50 with one another, 25 percent of the variance associated with height is also associated with weight. Because thermometer loads or correlates 0.59 with Factor *A*, there is an overlap in variance of 34.81 percent between the concept and that factor ($0.59^2 = .3481$). When the factor variances for each concept are added, the last column of Table 5-1 is formed. The *communality* (symbolized by $h^2$) is simply the sum of each common-factor variance and is that portion of variance responsible for allowing variables to correlate with one another. If a test or concept has a communality of zero, it cannot correlate with any other variable.

*Ideally*, a concept or test should correlate highly with one factor and zero with all others. In this regard, the factor analysis of the 12 concepts is by no means perfect. Lightning, in particular, loads too heavily on Factor *A*. Some factor analyses may yield rather ambiguous results should a test correlate or load equally on two or more factors. The Czirr study was selected for discussion here partly because it yielded two relatively clear factors.

Note that the sums of the common-factor variances have been provided in Table 5-1. These sums are called *eigenvalues*, or *latent roots*. When divided by the number of concepts, they estimate the total proportion of variance explained by or accounted for by that factor. Factor *A* explains 28 percent of the variance while Factor *B* explains 21 percent. The proportion of variance accounted for by the 2 factors is 49. Perhaps if more factors could have been extracted, a greater proportion of variance might have been accounted for. In this example, however, a third factor would have contributed little since one criterion commonly used to determine when to stop extracting factors is when the eigenvalues fall below 1.0. The eigenvalues for a third factor were, in fact, much lower than 1.0.

The factor matrix in Table 5-1 was computed from the data in Table 5-3 which shows the correlations among the 12 concepts. Note that certain

# TABLE 5-3
## A Table of Intercorrelations among 12 Concepts

| | 1 | 2 | 3 | 4 | 5 | 6 | 7 | 8 | 9 | 10 | 11 |
|---|---|---|---|---|---|---|---|---|---|---|---|
| 1. Thermometer | | | | | | | | | | | |
| 2. Computer | 0.44 | | | | | | | | | | |
| 3. Mosquito | 0.07 | 0.19 | | | | | | | | | |
| 4. Pollution | 0.06 | 0.17 | 0.34 | | | | | | | | |
| 5. Edison | 0.38 | 0.50 | 0.17 | 0.15 | | | | | | | |
| 6. Earthquake | 0.06 | 0.20 | 0.45 | 0.39 | 0.17 | | | | | | |
| 7. Research | 0.47 | 0.62 | 0.15 | 0.13 | 0.53 | 0.14 | | | | | |
| 8. Virus | 0.13 | 0.27 | 0.43 | 0.38 | 0.24 | 0.50 | 0.23 | | | | |
| 9. Pasteur | 0.46 | 0.60 | 0.14 | 0.13 | 0.51 | 0.14 | 0.64 | 0.23 | | | |
| 10. Biology | 0.47 | 0.62 | 0.16 | 0.14 | 0.53 | 0.16 | 0.66 | 0.25 | 0.64 | | |
| 11. Volcano | 0.14 | 0.29 | 0.44 | 0.38 | 0.25 | 0.50 | 0.25 | 0.50 | 0.25 | 0.26 | |
| 12. Lightning | 0.20 | 0.35 | 0.38 | 0.33 | 0.30 | 0.43 | 0.32 | 0.44 | 0.32 | 0.33 | 0.45 |

*Source:* The data in this table were reconstructed from information provided by Czirr. Correlations were rounded to two places.

concepts correlate moderately with one another but much lower with other groups of concepts. Thermometer, computer, Edison, research, Pasteur, and biology—in short, those concepts that form Factor *A*—correlate from 0.38 to 0.66. Those concepts that form Factor *B* correlate between 0.34 and 0.50. But the correlations tend to be much lower when comparing any concept in Factor *A* with any in Factor *B*. This is exactly what one would expect since these factors are assumed to be independent.

## Some Applications of Factor Analysis

*Interpreting Intelligence.* The first application of factor analysis was by Charles Spearman,[6] who postulated that intelligence consisted of two factors: *g* (or the general ability to educe relationships) and *s*, specific factors unique to a given test. British psychologists have retained Spearman's concept of intelligence, whereas American psychologists have accepted Thurstone's idea that intelligence is too complex to be described by *g* alone. Guilford has postulated that intelligence is composed of some 120 different factors and has constructed numerous tests and items to measure these factors.

*Test Revision.* Factor analysis of tests can help to improve them in a number of ways. First, factor analysis can verify their underlying structure as a measure of construct validity (see Chapter 9). If a test is designed to measure one particular trait, it should yield only a single factor. The presence of a single factor would help to establish the construct validity of the test.

Second, sometimes a test is constructed that is designed to measure a single factor such as attitudes toward drugs. A series of items could be written and tried out on some specified population. A factor analysis might demonstrate the presence of three or four factors. Instead of having a meaningful total score, a factorially complex test measuring more than one attribute should be divided into a number of different tests, each of which measures a single factor. If there are only a few items that load on a given factor, the investigator can construct additional items of the same type to increase reliability; nonfunctional items (those that fail to load significantly on any factor) can be eliminated.

Third, factor analysis can simplify test interpretation and bring order to what initially might appear to be an overwhelming amount of information. The example of the 12 concepts described earlier is a case in point. Another example concerns factor analyzing tests that have been scored in different ways (e.g., "rights" and "rights minus wrongs"). Such seemingly minor changes can substantially modify the factorial structure of the test. But it is

[6]Charles Spearman, " 'General Intelligence': Objectively Determined and Measured," *American Journal of Psychology*, 15, no. 2 (April 1904), pp. 201–293.

obviously better to know how the factor structure changes under different conditions than it is to retain erroneous beliefs.

*Hypothesis Testing in Experimentation.* In an experiment, the researcher wants to measure the effect produced by some deliberately planned intervention. In one study, for example, the researchers[7] were interested in the nature of the changes in factor structure on a number of tests as individuals became more adept in learning to fly an airplane. At the initial stages of learning, the highest loadings were with pencil-and-paper tasks. But as learning progressed, motor functions became more important.

*Determining the Structure of Nonhuman Factors.* Factor analysis can also be used to good advantage in studying the structure on nonhuman factors such as organizations. Adkins,[8] for example, has provided a witty and interesting analysis of the structure of the American Psychological Association which, at the time of writing, had 17 divisions (military, industrial, educational, etc.). The question posed by Adkins was whether or not membership in one division was correlated with membership in other similar divisions. If so, the total number of divisions might be reduced to a more meaningful and useful number. The factor analysis suggested that the 17 divisions could be reduced to 7: quantitative, theoretical, experimental, personnel, clinical, social, and developmental. Interestingly enough, despite the implications of Adkins' study, the number of divisions in the American Psychological Association actually increased from 17 to 35 in the years between 1954 and 1975. Factor analysis may provide information, but evidently no one is required to act in accordance with this knowledge.

## Relationship Studies

One purpose of correlational studies is to show how two or more variables are related to each other. The basic principle behind all relationship studies follows from John Stuart Mill's canon of concomitant variation:

> Whatever phenomenon varies in any manner whenever another phenomenon varies in some particular manner, is either a cause or an effect of that phenomenon, or is connected with it through some fact of causation.[9]

Suppose that an investigator is interested in studying the relationship between the number of cigarettes smoked per day and the grade point average

---

[7]E. A. Fleishman and W. E. Hempel, "Changes in Factor Structure of a Complex Psychomotor Test as a Function of Practice," *Psychometrika*, 19 (1954), pp. 239–252.

[8]Dorothy C. Adkins, "The Simple Structure of the American Psychological Association," *The American Psychologist*, 9, no. 5 (May 1964), pp. 175–180.

[9]John Stuart Mill, *A System of Logic*, 8th ed. (London: Longmans, Green & Company, 1930), p. 263.

(GPA) of high school students. Mill's canon of concomitant variation states that if the investigator should find that cigarette consumption varies inversely with GPA (i.e., those who smoke a great deal have low GPA's, and those who do not smoke have high GPA's), then cigarette smoking is the cause of GPA, the effect of GPA, or related to GPA through some third factor. In other words, correlations demonstrate only that a relationship exists or does not exist, but they cannot indicate whether or not the relationship is causal. Thus, a reliable correlation of $-0.85$ between number of cigarettes smoked per day and GPA could be interpreted in one of three ways:

1. Cigarette smoking lowers GPA.
2. Low GPA's are responsible for producing students who smoke.
3. A third factor (such as emotional maladjustment) produces both low GPA's and the tendency to smoke.

Even under circumstances where the correlation between two variables is $+1.0$, it is impossible to infer causation. For example, the measurement of length in inches and centimeters correlates perfectly, but it is nonsense to talk about inches causing centimeters or centimeters causing inches. They are simply two different ways of measuring the same entity.

Relationship studies are often useful in exploratory research where other types of information are not available. These exploratory investigations are useful because they may help to point out relevant and irrelevant variables that can later be used in experiments to test causal hypotheses. The point to keep in mind is this: while correlations do not necessarily imply causation, a correlation of zero does eliminate the possibility that there is a causal relationship between the two variables under consideration. Considering the expense, time, and effort that go into many experimental studies, the exploratory relationship study is useful to help eliminate those variables whose correlation is zero. A higher priority can then be assigned to those variables which correlate more highly.

*Spurious Correlations.* A correlation is "spurious" to the extent that it either over- or underestimates the "true" correlation between two variables. Spuriously high correlations are likely to occur when ratios, gains, or events occurring over long periods of time are correlated.

As an example of a spuriously high correlation, take the correlation between the ratio IQ and chronological age. Since IQ is a ratio of mental age (MA) to chronological age (CA), MA/CA is being correlated with CA. Because CA is involved in both variables, the correlations are likely to be spuriously high. The result of correlating ratios having common but variable denominators is called *spurious index correlation*. This effect is eliminated if denominators can be held constant. Thus, in correlating IQ (or MA/CA) with EQ (educational quotient, or the ratio of educational age to CA), the CA in the denominator will increase the correlation between the two ratios unless students are selected who have equal CA's. If CA's are equal they will cancel out, leaving the correlation between MA and EA (educational age).

Another type of spurious correlation occurs whenever initial or final scores are correlated with individual gains. Assume for a moment that students are tested at the beginning of an experiment and again at the end. By subtracting the initial scores from the final scores, a measure of gain is computed. Since both the initial and final scores are a part of the gain, any correlation between either score and the gain is likely to be spuriously high.

The presence of a third factor can also spuriously increase the correlation between two variables. A third factor such as age can increase the correlation between the measures of height and weight, since age affects both. Similarly, one would expect a correlation between vocabulary test scores and height, if only for the reason that both are related to maturity, or chronological age. In this instance, it may be useful to partial out the effects of age. In other words, the researcher may want to show the relationship ($r$) of vocabulary scores ($x$) and height ($y$), with age ($a$) held constant or partialed out. This relationship can be shown using a *partial correlation coefficient*:

$$r_{(xy)a} = \frac{r_{xy} - r_{xa}r_{ya}}{\sqrt{1 - r_{xa}^2}\sqrt{1 - r_{ya}^2}}$$

where $r_{(xy)a}$ is the correlation between vocabulary scores and height, with age held constant; $r_{xy}$ is the correlation between vocabulary scores and height; $r_{xa}$ is the correlation between vocabulary scores and age; and $r_{ya}$ is the correlation between height and age.

Letting $r_{xy} = 0.50$, $r_{xa} = 0.80$, and $r_{ya} = 0.60$, then

$$r_{(xy)a} = \frac{0.50 - (0.80)(0.60)}{\sqrt{1 - 0.80^2}\sqrt{1 - 0.60^2}}$$

$$r_{(xy)a} = \frac{0.50 - 0.48}{\sqrt{0.36}\sqrt{0.64}}$$

$$r_{(xy)a} = \frac{0.02}{0.48}$$

$$r_{(xy)a} = 0.04$$

In other words, if chronological age is partialed out, the correlation between vocabulary scores and height is reduced from 0.50 to 0.04. The original correlation of +0.80 was spuriously high because of the presence of chronological age that correlated with both measures.

Correlations are also likely to be spuriously high if the events to be correlated occur over some time span. It can be expected, for example, that the amount of beer consumed and the number of auto accidents from 1900 to 1975 correlate highly. The presence of a third factor, the increase in population between 1900 and 1975, might account for the increase of both beer consumption and number of accidents.

*Linearity of Regression.* A major assumption underlying $r$ is that of linearity of regression. This can be most readily checked by developing a table with the $x$ variable on the horizontal axis and the $y$ variable along the vertical axis. Find the mean for each row and each column. A line drawn through the column means and one drawn through the row means should form two straight or reasonably straight lines.[10] If the lines curve or bend, then linearity of regression cannot be assumed. In this case, either scores will have to be normalized[11] or the correlation ratio, eta,[12] will have to be used instead of $r$. Computing $r$ when data are curvilinear seriously lowers the linear correlation coefficients between the two variables in question.

## Prediction Studies

The ability to predict is as important to education as it is to medicine, economics, or meteorology. Superintendents must predict trends in school enrollment, principals should know how the PTA will respond to a proposed curriculum change, guidance counselors need to know what Johnny's chances are for completing college, and teachers must be able to predict how their classes will respond to new teaching methods.

*Single-Variable Prediction.* Single-variable prediction means that only one predictor is used to predict a criterion. In contrast, multiple prediction means that two or more variables (called *independent variables*) will be used to predict a criterion (called a *dependent variable*). In single-variable prediction the researcher may want to predict height (the dependent variable) from weight (the independent variable), achievement test scores from intelligence test scores, or marital adjustment from degree of security in childhood. The value to be predicted is called the dependent variable, because its value depends upon the prediction; predictors are called independent variables because they are under the independent control of the investigator.

[10]A more precise approach in testing for linearity of regression is to use an $F$ test; see George A. Ferguson, *Statistical Analysis in Psychology and Education*, 4th ed. (New York: McGraw-Hill Book Co., 1976), p. 237.

[11]The process of normalizing a distribution of scores is described in J. P. Guilford and Benjamin Fruchter, *Fundamental Statistics in Psychology and Education*, 6th ed. (New York: McGraw-Hill Book Co., 1978), pp. 478–484.

[12]Eta, the correlation ratio, is described in detail in Ferguson, pp. 236–238.

Regression equations can be used to predict the most likely value in a dependent variable. Consider the following scores obtained by 5 students (in practice at least 20 pairs of scores would probably be used).

TABLE 5-4

Hypothetical Distribution of Scores for Each of Five
Persons on Variables $X$ and $Y$

| Students | Variable $X$ | Variable $Y$ |
|:---:|:---:|:---:|
| A | 1 | 2 |
| B | 2 | 1 |
| C | 3 | 3 |
| D | 4 | 5 |
| E | 5 | 4 |
| | $\Sigma X = 15$ | $\Sigma Y = 15$ |
| | $\bar{X} = 3.0$ | $\bar{Y} = 3.0$ |
| | $s_x = 1.58$ | $s_y = 1.58$ |
| | $r_{xy} = 0.80$ | |

Let all $X$ values be plotted against a horizontal axis and all $Y$ values against a vertical axis (see Figure 5-1 below). Because there are no negative values, only the upper right quadrant is used. The problem in prediction is to fit a straight line through the various dots so that the sum of the squared

Figure 5-1
PLOT OF THE PAIRED $X$ AND $Y$ SCORES.

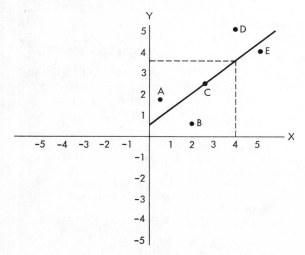

distances between each dot and the line (called a *regression line*)[13] is at a minimum value. A minimum value is desirable since all future predictions will be based on that regression line. An individual with an $X$ value of 4 (see Figure 5-1) would be predicted to have a $Y$ value close to 4 since the correlation between $X$ and $Y$ is relatively large.

Two attributes entirely determine the characteristics of the regression line—its slope and its intercept. The slope of a regression line is the vertical/horizontal ratio. Examine the dashed lines in Figure 5-2. An increase of 2

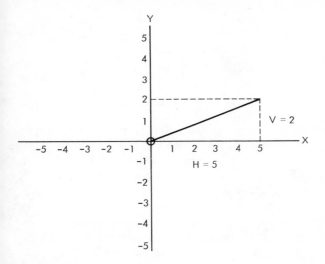

**Figure 5-2**
SHOWING THE VERTICAL AND HORIZONTAL VALUES (2 TO 5)
AND AN INTERCEPT OF ZERO.

units on the vertical, or $Y$, axis is accompanied by 5 units of $X$. The ratio 2/5 or 0.40 is the slope of the regression line. The other attribute is the intercept, or the point on $Y$ where the regression line crosses it. Since the regression line crosses the $Y$ axis at 0.00, the intercept is 0.00. A line parallel to the regression line that crosses the $Y$ axis at 3.0 would give a slope of 0.40 and an intercept of 3.0.

Suppose that all of the $X$ and $Y$ values were converted to $z$-scores having a mean of 0.00 and a standard deviation of 1.0. This conversion is important since it can be shown that $r_{xy}$ is equal to the slope of the regression line when all scores are converted to $z$-scores. The formula for a $z$-score is

$$z_x = \frac{X - \bar{X}}{s_x} \quad \text{and} \quad z_y = \frac{Y - \bar{Y}}{s_y}$$

---

[13]The regression line is like a mean. If the difference between each point and the regression line were summed, the resulting sum would always equal zero. By squaring every difference, negatives would be eliminated.

Since the means and standard deviations are identical for variables $X$ and $Y$ in Table 5-4, the conversion from raw scores to $z$-scores is a relatively simple matter (see Table 5-5).

TABLE 5-5

A Conversion of Raw Scores to $z$-Scores for Five Persons

| Student | Score on Variable $X$ | Score on Variable $Y$ | $z_x$ | $z_y$ |
|---------|------------------------|------------------------|---------|---------|
| A | 1 | 2 | −1.27 | −0.63 |
| B | 2 | 1 | −0.63 | −1.27 |
| C | 3 | 3 | 0.00 | 0.00 |
| D | 4 | 5 | +0.63 | +1.27 |
| E | 5 | 4 | +1.27 | +0.63 |

The $z$-score for student $A$ on variable $X$ is given by the formula $(1 - 3)/1.58 = -1.27$ (rounded). All other $z$-values are found in the same way. A $z$-score of $-1.27$ simply means that the student scored 1.27 standard deviations *below* the mean. By converting to $z$-scores, a set of standard scores having a constant mean (zero) and standard deviation (1.0) has been produced. Whatever the original units might be (pounds, inches, IQ scores), they can be correlated since the $z$-score provides a common basis for comparison, namely, the number of standard deviations above and below the mean.

Earlier it was stated that any line (including a regression line) could be described completely by its slope and intercept. Raw score slopes can be greater than 1.0, and the intercept could be anywhere along the $Y$ axis. The general formula for a straight line is: $Y' = a + bX$ where $Y'$ is a predicted value along the $Y$ axis, $a$ is the point where the regression line crosses the $Y$ axis, $b$ is the slope of the line (vertical/horizontal ratio), and $X$ is any predictor value.

When all raw scores have been converted to $z$-scores, the slope of the regression line ($b$) is equivalent to the correlation between $X$ and $Y$. Hence, it can be shown that

$$Y' = r_{xy}\frac{s_y}{s_x}(X - \bar{X}) + \bar{Y}$$

Suppose someone obtained a score of 4.5 on variable $X$. What is the most likely value that person will attain on variable $Y$? Using the data in Table 5-5, the best predictor would be:

$$Y' = 0.80\frac{1.58}{1.58}(4.5 - 3.0) + 3.0 = 4.20$$

The regression equation points out some interesting relationships. First, if $X$ and $\bar{X}$ are equal, $X - \bar{X}$ will be zero and $Y'$ will equal $\bar{Y}$. In other words, if a person is at the mean of a predictor value, the best estimate of $Y'$ will be the mean of $Y$, the variable being predicted. Also, if the correlation between $X$ and $Y$ is zero, $Y' = \bar{Y}$. This means that even if there is zero correlation between $X$ and $Y$, there is still a value that can be predicted, namely, the mean of the $Y$ variable. One other point should be clarified since it appears so often in research studies. The term "regression of $Y$ on $X$" is interpreted to mean the prediction of variable $Y$ from a given value of $X$. Simply change "regression" to "prediction" and the word "on" to "from." This, then, will mean "the *prediction* of $Y$ *from* $X$."

The amount of error in predicting can be estimated by using the formula for the standard error of estimate ($SE_{est}$):

$$SE_{est} = s_y\sqrt{1 - r_{xy}^2}$$

The $SE_{est}$ provides a measure of the extent to which the paired scores fall on the regression line and thus make predictions perfect. If $r_{xy} = 1.0$, there will be zero errors of estimate. As the paired scores fall off the regression line, the $SE_{est}$ will equal the amount of variability of scores along the vertical axis. In other words, if $r_{xy}$ is 0.00, the standard deviation of the errors in prediction will equal the standard deviation of the $Y$, or predicted, scores. For the previous example,

$$SE_{est} = 1.58\sqrt{1 - 0.80^2} = 1.58\sqrt{0.36} = 0.95 \text{ (rounded)}[14]$$

What this 0.95 means is that for any predicted value such as 4.2, approximately 68 percent of persons will obtain scores $\pm 0.95$ points around that value.

*Multiple-Variable Prediction.* The simplest prediction problem involves one predictor variable and one criterion. In such instances, single-variable prediction is the appropriate model. In multiple-variable prediction there are two or more predictors to be combined for increased accuracy.

In the example of single-variable prediction, a regression equation was used to predict one variable from knowledge of another. However, there are many other variables that could also have been used in an attempt to predict more accurately. The researcher may want to employ two or more

[14]The appropriate formula to use in predicting $X$ from $Y$ is:

$$X' = r_{xy}\frac{s_x}{s_y}(Y - \bar{Y}) + \bar{X}$$

The $SE_{est}$ becomes $s_x\sqrt{1 - r_{xy}^2}$ if $X$ is the value to be predicted and is not the predictor.

predictors to help maximize prediction. Considering the computational work involved with three or more predicted variables, the student would do well to explore the possibility of using electronic data processing methods. We will not describe here the formulas used in multiple-regression problems. The reader is referred to Guilford and Fruchter[15] and Ferguson[16] for these formulas.

The problem in multiple regressions is to find a procedure that permits the researcher to combine any number of predictors so that they will correlate maximally with a criterion. The method that will combine multiple predictors optimally depends on the weights assigned to each predictor. These weights are called *beta weights* and are symbolized by $\beta$. $\beta_1$ is the beta weight for the first predictor, $\beta_2$ for the second, and so on. Although any number of predictors can be combined to predict some criterion $Y'$, little is gained after three or four predictors have been used. Any additional predictors will increase the complexity and tediousness of calculation (unless, of course, electronic computers can be used) and, perhaps more seriously, not contribute much to the prediction of the criterion.

The beta weights used in multiple-regression problems involve the correlation of the criterion with the various predictors and the correlations among the predictors. Unless the beta weights are used, predictors will not reach maximum accuracy. Sometimes students erroneously believe that prediction is bound to increase if the various predictors are summed, averaged, and then correlated against the criterion. The difficulty with that procedure is that each predictor in a composite is weighted proportionally to its standard deviation. If a particular variable has a large standard deviation, it is already weighted more heavily than would be a variable having a smaller standard deviation. Unfortunately, the standard deviations and beta weights do not necessarily yield comparable weights.

A worked-out multiple-regression equation would appear in the following form (data are fictitious):

$$Y' = 0.026X_1 + 0.044X_2 - 2.31$$

This can be interpreted to mean that for every point increase in predictor variable $X_1$, there will be an increase of 0.026 points in the criterion $Y'$; also, for every point increase in predictor variable $X_2$, the criterion will increase 0.044 points. The negative value 2.31 is a constant analogous to *a* in the formula for a straight line for two variables (see page 94), but since

[15]J. P. Guilford and Benjamin Fruchter, *Fundamental Statistics in Psychology and Education*, 6th ed. (New York: McGraw-Hill Book Co., 1978), Chapter 16.

[16]George A. Ferguson, *Statistical Analysis in Psychology and Education*, 4th ed. (New York: McGraw-Hill Book Co., 1976), Chapter 27.

there are at least three variables in a multiple-regression problem (two predictors and a criterion), their relationship has to be expressed in three dimensions (e.g., like a closed box), and a plane surface within the box takes the
place of a regression line. The value of the constant, $\alpha$, depends on where that
plane coincides with one side of the box representing the criterion.

The multiple-regression equation can be used to predict $Y'$ (e.g.,
grade in algebra) for any given student. If predictor variable $X_1$ is an IQ of
150 and $X_2$ is the student's score on a math test ($X_2 = 40$ points), the multiple regression becomes

$$Y' = 0.026(150) + 0.044(40) - 2.31 = 3.35$$

The best prediction of the student's grade in algebra would be 3.35.

*Multiple Correlation.* Suppose that the correlation between a predictor and criterion was 0.76 and that a second predictor, $X_2$, was added to
increase the prediction of $Y'$, the dependent variable. The multiple-correlation coefficient $R$ can be computed to provide an indication of the gains made
by adding the second variable. If the beta weights are known,[17]

$$R = \sqrt{\beta_1 r_{Y1} + \beta_2 r_{Y2}}$$
$$R = \sqrt{0.595(0.76) + 0.412(0.65)}$$
$$R = \sqrt{0.72}$$
$$R = 0.848 \text{ or } 0.85 \text{ (rounded)}$$

The addition of the second predictor increased prediction from 0.76
to 0.85. This coefficient, 0.85, can be interpreted in the same manner as any
other correlation involving two variables. Perhaps the most useful interpretation is to convert $R$ to $R^2$, which is called a *coefficient of multiple determination.* $R^2$ gives an estimate of the proportion of variance in $Y'$ that is determined by the combination of predictors $X_1$ and $X_2$. If $R$ is 1.0, then $R^2$ is also
unity and prediction is perfect. In that case the combination of $X_1$ and $X_2$
would contain all of the variance in $Y'$. If $R = 0.85$, $R^2 = 0.72$; thus, 72
percent of the variance in $Y'$ is being determined by the combination of $X_1$
and $X_2$. In the single-variable problem, where $r = 0.76$, the coefficient of
determination $r^2$ is equal to 0.58. This means that 58 percent of the variance
related to algebra grades is also related to the test scores derived from $X_1$.

*Methods of Increasing Accuracy of Prediction.* One major principle
used to increase the accuracy of predictions is to select predictors that have

---

[17] Assume $\beta_1 = 0.595$, $r_{Y1} = 0.76$, $\beta_2 = 0.412$, and $r_{Y2} = 0.65$. Remember that $r_{Y1}$
is the correlation between a criterion and a predictor and $r_{Y2}$ is the correlation between the
same criterion but a second predictor.

high correlations with the criterion but low correlations with each other. This relationship can be most easily seen by examining the general formula for a three-variable multiple correlation problem:

$$R^2 = \frac{r_{Y1}^2 + r_{Y2}^2 - 2r_{Y1}r_{Y2}r_{12}}{1 - r_{12}^2}$$

Note that this formula may be used when beta weights are unknown and that the formula concerns $R^2$ and not $R$. To obtain $R$, extract the square root of $R^2$.

In the first place, it can be seen that in the extreme case where $r_{12} = 0$, the third term in the numerator $(-2r_{Y1} r_{Y2} r_{12})$ will also become zero, thus increasing $R^2$. Also, where $r_{12} = 0$, the denominator becomes unity. Thus, if the predictors do not correlate with each other, $R^2$ will be equal to $r_{Y1}^2 + r_{Y2}^2$. In other words, the multiple correlation will be a function of the extent to which predictors correlate with the criterion.

Second, notice that there is some advantage in having $r_{12}$ as high as possible. If, for example, $r_{12} = 0.99$, the denominator becomes 0.01. This will raise the value of $R^2$.

Table 5-6, developed by Guilford and Fruchter,[18] shows what happens to $R^2$ and $R$ when $r_{Y2}$ and $r_{12}$ are allowed to vary.

In the first example, $r_{12}$ (the correlation between two predictors)

TABLE 5-6

Examples of Multiple Correlations in a Three-Variable Problem
When Intercorrelations Vary

| Example | $r_{Y1}$ | $r_{Y2}$ | $r_{12}$ | $R^2$ | $R$ |
|---------|----------|----------|----------|-------|-----|
| 1 | 0.4 | 0.4 | 0.0 | 0.3200 | 0.57 |
| 2 | 0.4 | 0.4 | 0.4 | 0.2286 | 0.48 |
| 3 | 0.4 | 0.4 | 0.9 | 0.1684 | 0.41 |
| 4 | 0.4 | 0.2 | 0.0 | 0.2000 | 0.45 |
| 5 | 0.4 | 0.2 | 0.4 | 0.1619 | 0.40 |
| 6 | 0.4 | 0.2 | 0.9 | 0.2947 | 0.54 |
| 7 | 0.4 | 0.0 | 0.0 | 0.1600 | 0.40 |
| 8 | 0.4 | 0.0 | 0.4 | 0.1905 | 0.44 |
| 9 | 0.4 | 0.0 | 0.9 | 0.8421 | 0.92 |
| 10 | 0.4 | 0.2 | -0.4 | 0.3143 | 0.56 |
| 11 | 0.4 | -0.4 | -0.4 | 0.2286 | 0.48 |

[18] J. P. Guilford and Benjamin Fruchter, *Fundamental Statistics in Psychology and Education*, 6th ed. (New York: McGraw-Hill Book Co., 1978), p. 380.

$= 0.0$, which yields a relatively high $R$. In the second example, $r_{12}$ is increased to 0.4 and $R$ drops, as predicted. In the third example, $r_{12}$ is high and $R$ drops because little is to be gained by combining $r_{Y1}$ and $r_{Y2}$ if the two predictors are highly correlated.

Compare examples 1 and 4. Because the correlation between one of the predictors and the criterion has been reduced in example 4, $R$ also is reduced. Example 5 has an even lower $R$ since $r_{12}$ has increased. The increase in $R$ in example 6 results from the fact that $r_{12}$ is high. Remember that a very high or very low intercorrelation between the two predictors will increase $R$.

In examples 7 to 9, one predictor fails to correlate with the criterion but does correlate (in examples 8 and 9) with the other predictor. As $r_{12}$ increases from 0.0 to 0.9, $R$ also increases. In example 7, all of the prediction is due to $r_{Y1}$; variable $X_2$ plays no part at all in determining $R$. Examples 8 and 9 yield relatively high $R$'s simply because of $r_{12}$. Thus, even though a test fails to correlate with a criterion ($r_{Y2} = 0.0$), it can still help to increase the value of $R$ if it correlates with some other variable that does correlate with the criterion.

Comparing example 10 with example 5, it can be shown the $R$ is higher when $r_{12}$ is negative than when it is positive. As a matter of fact, the $R$ in example 10 is higher than the $R$ in example 6, even though $r_{12}$ is $-0.4$. Guilford and Fruchter have indicated that this situation is not too likely, but it is a possibility. What happens is that $R$ increases as $r_{12}$ approaches zero and will continue to increase as $r_{12}$ becomes negative.

Example 11 is the same as example 2 except that variable $X_2$ has a reversed scale. The $R$'s in both examples are identical.

## DEVELOPMENTAL STUDIES

The professional education of teachers almost universally requires some knowledge of child growth and development. Knowledge of how children grow—whether this growth is biological, cognitive, or emotional—not only has theoretical importance for education as a science but also has applications to curriculum development, teaching methods, determination of educational objectives, and interpersonal relationships.

The most important educational advantages to be gained through the study of child development probably lie in human learning and instruction. Any comprehensive theory of learning or instruction will have to consider the biological and psychological characteristics of children at various ages and maturational levels. Both curriculum and teaching methods can be made more effective if applied with an understanding of developmental trends.

## Longitudinal and Cross-Sectional Methods

Two general methods have evolved in studying human development: the longitudinal and cross-sectional approaches. An individual or a group is studied longitudinally when the researcher follows the same persons over a period of time. In the cross-sectional approach, different persons are selected at each stage of development.

With longitudinal approaches, one person or group is observed over time periods 1, 2, 3, . . . , $N$; with cross-sectional approaches, different groups at different stages of development are observed at approximately the same time. If the researcher is interested in studying the vocabulary development of children from ages one through ten, he or she can select a group of one-year-olds and follow them until they are ten years old (i.e., follow them longitudinally); or it is possible to select a group of one-year-olds and measure their vocabulary, find a different group of two-year-olds and measure their vocabulary, etc., all at about the same time.

The greatest advantage of the cross-sectional over the longitudinal approach is one of economy. Most investigators are understandably reluctant to wait as long as the longitudinal approach demands before their research is ready for dissemination. With the cross-sectional approach researchers can complete their investigations just as rapidly as they can collect and analyze their data. They do not have to wait until a group of children mature but can select individuals at different stages of maturation.

The cross-sectional approach is also economical in a different way. It allows researchers to select a larger number of persons, although the number of variables investigated may have to be reduced. Keeping records and tracking down persons who move from city to city can be quite expensive in longitudinal studies. Thus, researchers using longitudinal designs try to gather as much infomation as possible from each person in the sample. In cross-sectional studies, subject mobility is not a significant problem because each group is studied once. Because of this, researchers using cross-sectional methods can afford to select a larger number of subjects than in longitudinal studies.

The longitudinal approach is a type of "repeated measurements" design.[19] Whereas the cross-sectional approach assumes that groups selected at different ages are comparable, in the longitudinal approach, which employs the same subjects over and over again, groups are not only comparable, they are identical—if the repeated measurements do not lead to either practice effects (increase in test scores as a result of continued practice in taking examinations) or fatigue.

---

[19]A repeated measurements design uses the same persons as experimental and control subjects to ensure their comparability on all variables except those that are deliberately introduced by the experimenter (see Chapter 6, pages 133-138).

An example may help to clarify the problem. Assume that an investigator is interested in studying the language development of children in grades 1 through 5. If a longitudinal approach is used, any variables that correlate with language scores, such as IQ, sex, social adjustment, etc., are easily controlled. This can be seen in Table 5-7.

TABLE 5-7

Increase in Language Scores as a Function of Chronological Age, Holding IQ Constant (data are fictitious)

| Group | Grade Level | Mean IQ | Mean CA | Mean Language Scores |
|-------|-------------|---------|---------|----------------------|
| A | 1 | 100 | 6.4 | 30 |
| A | 2 | 100 | 7.4 | 35 |
| A | 3 | 100 | 8.4 | 40 |
| A | 4 | 100 | 9.4 | 45 |
| A | 5 | 100 | 10.4 | 50 |

Here, the increase in language scores is clearly not attributable to fluctuations in IQ since IQ is held constant by using the same individuals repeatedly.

As indicated earlier, the cross-sectional approach assumes that the different samples are comparable. Note what could happen if this assumption does not hold (see Table 5-8).

TABLE 5-8

Cross-Sectional Model with Language Scores Confounded with IQ (data are fictitious)

| Group | Grade Level | Mean IQ | Mean CA | Mean Language Scores |
|-------|-------------|---------|---------|----------------------|
| A | 1 | 90 | 6.4 | 30 |
| B | 2 | 95 | 7.6 | 35 |
| C | 3 | 100 | 8.5 | 40 |
| D | 4 | 105 | 9.6 | 45 |
| E | 5 | 110 | 10.4 | 50 |

Since groups *A*, *B*, *C*, *D*, and *E* vary on mean IQ, differences in language scores do not necessarily represent *only* differences in chronological age. Group *E* may have attained the highest score on the language test not simply because it was more mature but because it contained the brightest individuals of all five groups.

Another advantage of the longitudinal approach is that it is sensitive to the measurement of individual differences over time. This approach is especially important where rate changes are involved.[20] In studying adolescent growth patterns, a cross-sectional approach will combine data from both early and late maturing subjects and cancel out whatever individual differences arise out of variable maturation rates.[21] Only if the data are collected longitudinally can these individual differences be noted.

Still another advantage may be claimed for the longitudinal approach. Take, for example, a study involving the measurement of attitude changes toward education between the ages of twenty and seventy. With the cross-sectional approach, it is possible to find relatively large samples of subjects at each pertinent age level. However, the survivors at any given age are likely to differ systematically from those who died. These differences can be found in those variables which relate to survival, such as intelligence and good health. In the longitudinal approach, it is possible to estimate the characteristics of those who survived as well as those who died, because previous information has been obtained on both.

## Naturalistic Observation

Most of the research performed with preschool children has attempted to observe how these children behave when uninfluenced by the researcher.[22] Although many of the problems concerning observation in general (see Chapter 11) are also relevant to developmental studies, a number of specialized techniques have also been developed.

1. *The diary* is a day-to-day written record of new or novel aspects of infant behavior written by adults having access to a child who can be observed. Usually the adults are parents who have some training in observational techniques, although degree of competency varies widely. At one extreme are the often overzealous and biased diaries kept by many parents as reminders of their offspring's accomplishments; at the other extreme are care-

[20]William Kessen, "Research Design in the Study of Developmental Problems," in Paul H. Mussen, ed., *Handbook of Research Methods in Child Development* (New York: John Wiley & Sons, 1960), p. 47.

[21]Frank K. Shuttleworth, "The Physical and Mental Growth of Girls and Boys Aged Six to Nineteen in Relation to Age at Maximum Growth," *Monograph of the Society for Research in Child Development*, 4, no. 3 (1939).

[22]Herbert F. Wright, "Observational Child Study," in Paul H. Mussen, ed., *Handbook of Research Methods in Child Development* (New York: John Wiley & Sons, 1960), pp. 75–76.

fully controlled observations of child development such as those by Darwin,[23] Preyer,[24] Shinn,[25] and Piaget.[26]

As a research technique, the diary has greater potential value than accomplishment. First, the longitudinal nature of the data collected by diaries requires that records be kept over relatively long periods of time. This is likely to discourage those most prone to do research—professors who wish to publish and graduate students working on degrees. Second, diaries are particularly susceptible to unreliable and invalid reporting. Nonetheless, few other techniques can supply such a continuous and rich record of child development.

2. *Episode sampling* derives its name from its purpose and method. Essentially, observers attempt to study systematically a given episode or event as it naturally occurs without influencing it unduly by their presence. The responsibility of the investigators is to describe as accurately as possible the inception, progress, and termination of the phenomenon being studied.

An example of how episode sampling works is provided by Dawe,[27] who was interested in studying quarreling behavior among preschool children. Each time a quarrel occurred, Dawe recorded the duration of the quarrel, the names and sexes of the participants, the reasons for the quarrel, and the conditions leading to its termination.

Upon completion of the investigation, Dawe had obtained information concerning the average rate of quarreling per hour, duration of quarrels, intra- and intersex relationships, etc.

Almost any type of behavior can be studied in episode sampling, for instance, sleeping, aggression, laughing, crying, and misconduct. Not only do the data obtained from episode sampling provide norms for the interpretation of child behavior, but they also supply information that can be useful in understanding and controlling deviant forms of behavior. For example, if it is known that the number of quarrels decreases with the age of the child, it may be possible to tolerate more quarrels from younger than from older children.

3. *Time sampling* is another approach to the study of child development. Instead of restricting a study to a given episode or event, it is possible to describe all that a child does within some definite, predetermined, and representative period of time. A child may behave quite differently in the morning

23Charles Darwin, "A Biographical Sketch of an Infant," *Mind*, 2 (1877), pp. 285–294.

24William Preyer, *The Mind of the Child*, trans. H. W. Brown (New York: Appleton-Century-Crofts, 1888–1889).

25Milicent W. Shinn, *The Biography of a Baby* (Boston: Houghton Mifflin Co., 1900).

26*La Naissance de l'Intelligence chez l'Enfant* (Neuchâtel: Delachaux & Niestlé, 1936); *The Origins of Intelligence in Children*, trans. M. Cook (New York: International University Press, 1952).

27Helen C. Dawe, "An Analysis of Two Hundred Quarrels of Preschool Children," *Child Development*, 5, no. 2 (1934), pp. 139–157.

than in the afternoon, on Mondays than on Tuesdays, and before vacations than after vacations. By taking random samples of the child's behavior at different times, observational bias can be reduced. In general, one is better off taking a large number of short observations than a few longer ones.

In time sampling, investigators have to determine the number of observations, their frequency and length, the number of persons and the behaviors that will be observed, the methods used to record what subjects do or say, and the manner in which data will be analyzed.

If time samples are recorded narratively, content analysis is the appropriate means for analyzing the data. In general, one can either count the frequency with which various events occur, or use time as a base. If frequency is the method of choice, one can determine: 1) the total number of times a given behavior occurred; 2) the mean number of times the behavior occurred per subject; or 3) the ratio of the number of times a given behavior occurred to the total of all behaviors recorded. If, on the other hand, time is used as the base, then one can determine: 1) the number of times a given behavior occurred per unit of time; 2) the total amount of time spent on some activity; or 3) the percentage of total time spent on the behavior under consideration. More than one method of analyzing data can be used.

*4. Situational observations* control the setting in which the observations will take place, but no other restrictions or conditions are imposed.

One of the most ambitious situational observations was undertaken by Hartshorne and May[28] in the *Character Education Inquiry*. Over 10,000 students, of various economic, social, ethnic, and intellectual backgrounds participated in the inquiry, whose purpose was to determine which children would lie, cheat, or steal if presented with the opportunity. This study, now a classic, is also discussed in Chapter 11.

The greatest advantage of the situational test is the lack of artificiality in the tasks imposed on subjects. Instead of depending upon a person's willingness and ability to discuss his or her attitudes toward stealing, lying, or cheating, those behaviors can be observed when subjects are given the opportunity to engage in them.

What a person does in a specific situation can be thought of as one sample of behavior that is likely to have low reliability, since a single response may or may not represent typical behavior. The test-retest correlations over a period of six months averaged about 0.50 for various tasks in the Character Education Inquiry. This is not particularly high.

Validity presents a difficult problem for situational measurements. Few criteria are available other than the behavior being observed. The correlation of observational measures of honesty with the ratings of honesty by teachers averages about 0.35 in the Hartshorne-May studies.

One other point deserves comment. The intercorrelations of the various observational tests were, in most instances, positive but low, the median being 0.20. Thus, for example, one type of classroom cheating had

[28]Hugh Hartshorne and Mark A. May, *Studies in Deceit* (New York: The Macmillan Co., 1928).

only a 0.10 correlation with cheating in an athletic contest. Clearly, cheating is not a general trait but manifests itself differently depending upon circumstances. Since each observational test requires elaborate preparation, the expense and time might well be prohibitive.

## Difficulties in Doing Research with Young Children

One difficulty in studying young children is that they lack sophistication in language development. Thus, pencil-and-paper tests are usually out of the question unless responses are limited to checkmarks placed on pictures. Similarly, instructions have to be so worded that they are simple, clear, and unambiguous. More important is that every opportunity be given for each child to understand exactly what is expected. This may require much time and patience on the part of the investigator.

Another problem faced by those doing research with young children involves motivation. One simply cannot expect five- or six-year-olds to be overjoyed with the prospect of having their regular activities interrupted to participate in some research project unless they are familiar with the investigator and are at ease in his or her presence. A week or two with the group as an informal assistant to the regular teacher can do much to gain the confidence and respect of the children.

One other point should be emphasized. Investigators have a moral obligation not to penalize or harm a child in any way simply for the purpose of doing research, no matter how important that research is considered to be. If there is a possibility that the child can be hurt (physically or emotionally), this should be conveyed to the school authorities and the child's parents before the research is undertaken. The researcher is obligated not to minimize the possibility of risk.

## CROSS-CULTURAL STUDIES

Few students of education have concerned themselves with the study of conditions in cultures other than their own, but by studying various phenomena in different cultures and contexts, eduational researchers can clarify the meaning of these phenomena in their own culture.

A distinction should be made between cross-cultural and comparative studies. Cross-cultural studies test hypotheses designed to contribute to theory. Comparative studies, in contrast, accept the validity of a theory but show how it is applied in different cultures.[29]

[29]George W. Goethals and John W. M. Whiting, "Research Methods: The Cross-Cultural Method," *Review of Educational Research*, 27, no. 5 (1957), pp. 441–442.

## Steps in Conducting a Cross-Cultural Study

1. *Determining the theory to be investigated* is usually the first step in conducting a cross-cultural study.

One of the first cross-cultural studies was conducted by Tylor,[30] who was interested in studying various aspects of the theory of evolution as it applied to laws of marriage and descent. It was not until over half a century later that these methods were used to test behavior theory.[31] At that time (1943), Horton[32] studied the relationship between the drinking of alcohol and anxiety and found that alcohol reduced inhibition in all cultures studied.

Because cross-cultural studies assume that behavior can be compared from one culture to another, it is not surprising to find that the topics selected for investigation have been both broad and fundamental. In studying child development, for example, Mead[33] was able to demonstrate that the problems accompanying adolescence among American girls were culturally determined. Similarly, Hullian learning theory was applied by Whiting[34] in his study of the Kwoma, and various psychoanalytic concepts (weaning, oral fixations, etc.) were investigated by Whiting and Child.[35]

2. *Selecting the sample* is somewhat more complex in cross-cultural studies than in the study of one's own culture. Not only are there the usual problems facing any researcher in selecting samples within a culture, but there is the additional problem of selecting the culture itself.

Certainly, one's hypotheses provide a limiting factor in selecting an appropriate culture. Margaret Mead,[36] for example, selected the Samoans because

> In complicated civilisations like those of Europe, or the higher civilisations of the East, years of study are necessary before the student can begin to understand the forces at work within them. . . . A primitive people without a written language present a much less elaborate problem and a trained student can master the fundamental structure of a primitive society in a few months.

[30]Edward B. Tylor, "On a Method of Investigating the Development of Institutions; Applied to Laws of Marriage and Descent," *Journal of Anthropological Institutes of Great Britain and Ireland*, 18 (1889), pp. 245–269.

[31]Goethals and Whiting, pp. 442–443.

[32]Donald Horton, "The Functions of Alcohol in Primitive Societies: A Cross-Cultural Study," *Quarterly Journal of Studies on Alcohol*, 4 (1943), pp. 199–320.

[33]Margaret Mead, *Coming of Age in Samoa* (New York: Blue Ribbon Books, 1928).

[34]John W. M. Whiting, *Becoming a Kwoma: Teaching and Learning in a New Guinea Tribe* (New Haven, Conn.: Yale University Press, 1941).

[35]John W. M. Whiting and Irvin L. Child, *Child Training and Personality: A Cross-Cultural Study* (New Haven, Conn.: Yale University Press, 1953).

[36]Mead, p. 8.

Furthermore, we do not choose a simple peasant community in Europe or an isolated group of mountain whites in the American South, for these people's ways of life, though simple, belong essentially to the historical tradition to which the complex parts of European or American civilisation belong. Instead, we choose primitive groups who have had thousands of years of historical development along completely different lines from our own, whose language does not possess our Indo-European categories, whose religious ideas are of a different nature, whose social organisation is not only simpler but very different from our own.

Once the culture is selected, informants within the culture must be chosen. It takes time to discover who the reliable informants are, what their limitations might be, and how more reliable reports might be obtained. Generally, the greater the number of informants that can be reached, the better; then it may be discovered whether reports given by men differ from those given by women, and whether information supplied by children differs from that supplied by adults.

3. *Selecting the variables* to study is the next step in a cross-cultural study. Again, cross-cultural studies involve problems not faced by those doing research in their own culture. A study of adolescent behavior in one's own culture could be done without delving into too many other aspects of culture. In studying a completely unknown group, however, information on customs and values may not be as readily available.

One very useful source of information on the types of data which may be collected was provided by Murdock et al.[37] in conjunction with the Human Relations Area Files (HRAF). These files contain, on five-by-eight-inch paper slips or microfilm cards, as much information about a given culture as can be obtained from books, periodicals, and journals, although excerpts rather than an entire work may be included. Each file has been annotated and analyzed according to 710 different categories of cultural and natural information. Each paper slip or microfilm card contains the name of the group investigated, the information source, cross listings of relevant information, and the excerpt itself. Murdock's outline contains many categories of information the investigator may wish to study. By using these files, the investigator can obtain information on many cultures without having to travel to these places personally.

4. *Collecting the data* is the next step. Direct observation and the interview are the two methods employed most often in crosss-cultural studies. Especially useful are many of the projective techniques, case studies, observational rating scales, and sociometric methods.

5. *Analyzing and interpreting the data* is the last step in conducting

---

[37]George P. Murdock et al., *Outline of Cultural Materials*, 4th rev. ed. (New Haven, Conn.: Human Relations Area Files, 1971).

a cross-cultural study. The type of analysis will depend upon such factors as the purpose of the study and the methods used to collect data. Field notes and information obtained through interviews can probably be handled best through content analysis (see Chapter 12). The design of the study should allow for the determination of the reliability and validity of as many instruments and techniques as possible. Once this information is available, the researcher can determine the amount of error and, consequently, the amount of confidence that can be placed in the obtained data.

Because cross-cultural studies allow for little control or manipulation of variables, the investigator generally has to work within some type of correlational analysis. Thus, for example, Whiting and Child[38] have shown that there is a negative correlation between age of socialization and strength of guilt feelings in various cultures. As with any correlational analysis, what is not known is the direction of the causal relationships or even if the relationships are causal. The examination of alternative explanations may help to clarify the meaning and interpretation of the relationships obtained.

## SUMMARY

**1.** In descriptive research an account of the current status of some person or problem is obtained without the investigator's influencing or controlling the participating subjects, events, institutions, or communities.

**2.** The case study is one type of descriptive research in which a detailed investigation of a person, institution, event, or community is conducted.

**a.** The case study places emphasis upon the individual and thus stresses an *idiographic* rather than a *nomothetic* approach to the study of behavior.

**b.** Clinically, the case study is most often used for diagnosis and remediation. For research purposes, the case study can be helpful in four general ways: 1) as a means of showing how some theoretical model can be applied to the individual case; 2) as a means of generating hypotheses which later can be verified for larger numbers of subjects; 3) as a means of providing new ideas; and 4) as a means of testing hypotheses.

**c.** The selection of subjects for detailed analysis involves the finding of atypical cases that exemplify some relevant trait. Random sampling methods are, therefore, inappropriate.

**d.** Case study materials are collected from as many sources as possible and employ as many different techniques as are needed.

**e.** One difficulty with the case study is that causal relationships are difficult to determine. Another difficulty is that cases may be selected

[38]Whiting and Child, pp. 256–257.

because of convenience rather than for their contribution to a body of theory.

**3.** The sample survey is a nomothetic technique (concerned with generalities and not with the individual case) which attempts to describe some aspect of a population by selecting unbiased samples of individuals who are asked to complete questionnaires, interviews, or tests.

**4.** Factor analysis is a type of descriptive research that is designed to aid in the interpretation of correlation matrixes by extracting those factors that account for or explain those intercorrelations. An intuitive example of how factors may be identified was provided.

    **a.** The proportion of common-factor variance contributed by each factor is called the test's *communality* ($h^2$). Two measures correlate to the extent that their common-factor variances overlap.

    **b.** The problem in factor analysis is to go from a correlation matrix to a factor matrix that shows the correlation of each variable with the extracted factors. The square of these correlations can be summed for each variable to provide $h^2$.

    **c.** By examining the variables that correlate or load most highly with each factor, the nature of each factor can be examined and the extracted factor labeled by a descriptive term.

    **d.** The use of factor analysis was described in relationship to the interpretation of psychological constructs such as intelligence, to its use in test construction and revision, as a means of hypothesis testing, and in determining the structure of nonhuman factors such as those present in organizations.

**5.** Correlational studies do not indicate whether variable $X$ caused $Y$, whether $Y$ caused $X$, or whether some third condition ($Z$) is related to $X$ and $Y$. A correlation of zero does mean that no relationship—including a causal relationship—is present.

    **a.** Spurious correlations may occur when ratios, gains, or events occurring over long periods of time are correlated. In correlating beer consumption with automobile deaths from 1910 to 1976, for example, a high and positive correlation would be expected if for no other reason than that population increases affect both variables being correlated.

    **b.** A partial correlation coefficient can be used to eliminate the effects of some extraneous variables from influencing the correlation between two variables.

    **c.** Correlations assume linearity of regression (i.e., when $X$ and $Y$ variables are plotted, the plot should approximate a straight line). If this assumption cannot be met, the value of $r$ will be spuriously low.

**6.** One purpose of research is to maximize predictions.

    **a.** The simplest prediction problem involves a single predictor and criterion. Regression equations are used to predict criterion values. Criteria are predicted most accurately when plotted values lie close to the regression line. The characteristics of the regression line are described by its slope and intercept. A regression equation was developed from knowledge of the regression line's slope and intercept. The standard error of estimate was described as a measure of prediction error.

**b.** Multiple-variable prediction involves two or more predictors. Beta weights are applied to each predictor to maximize predictability. Although computational routines were omitted in the text, references were provided for the interested student. The computed multiple regression equation indicates the number of points the criterion can be expected to change for every point increase in each of the predictors.

**c.** Multiple correlations, symbolized $R$, can be used to indicate the amount of gain realized by adding additional variables to increase the accuracy of prediction.

**d.** The accuracy of predictions can be increased by using predictors that correlate highly with the criterion and low with one another. If the correlation between predictors is extremely high, this can also be used to increase $R$. Even if a test fails to correlate with a criterion, $R$ may increase if the test correlates with another variable that does correlate with the criterion.

**7.** Developmental studies concern themselves with cognitive, affective, and psychomotor changes occurring over time. Such studies not only have theoretical importance but also are important in curriculum development and teacher education.

**a.** The longitudinal approach to the study of development requires that the investigator follow the same subjects over a period of time. Because the same individuals are used, comparability of subjects is assured. The design also allows for analyses of rate changes and individual differences, and for analyses over the life span. The difficulty with the longitudinal approach is that the investigator has to wait until subjects grow older to complete the study.

**b.** The cross-sectional approach makes it possible to collect developmental data in much shorter periods of time than with the longitudinal method and is, therefore, economical. Instead of studying the same group of subjects, the cross-sectional approach studies different groups at different stages of development. The use of the technique assumes that groups are comparable.

**c.** The diary is a form of naturalistic observation used to study and analyze child behavior. A daily record is kept of important or significant changes occurring from infancy through childhood. The method is only as useful as reporters are qualified to observe and record data.

**d.** Episode sampling is an attempt to study the inception, progress, and termination of some significant aspect of behavior such as crying, quarreling, sleeping, or laughing. The investigator keeps a record of those events leading to the behavior in question, the duration of the episode, and the factors leading to its termination.

**e.** In time sampling, the investigator apportions observations among a number of predetermined time intervals to reduce biases produced by selecting convenient but unrepresentative times for observation. Analyses can proceed by counting the frequency with which various events occur, or time can be used as the base.

**f.** Situational observations involve the placement of subjects into different circumstances to see how they will respond. The situation is the only variable manipulated. The investigator keeps a record of the subjects' behavior.

**g.** There are a number of difficulties involved in doing research with young children. Because they lack sophistication in the use of written language, directions usually must be given orally. Responses may have to be limited either to oral replies or to simple checkmarks placed on or by pictures. Another difficulty in working with young children is that motivation may be hard to establish. Ethical considerations require that the child's welfare be placed above other considerations.

**8.** The cross-cultural study was described as another example of descriptive research. By testing hypotheses in cultures other than one's own, a greater degree of generality can be obtained than if a study is limited to one's native culture.

**a.** A distinction was made between cross-cultural and comparative research. Cross-cultural investigations attempt to study theoretical issues by correlating events or occurrences in different cultures. In contrast, the comparative study takes the validity of some theory for granted but demonstrates how the theory applies in different cultural contexts.

**b.** Determining the theory to be investigated is the first step in conducting a cross-cultural study.

**c.** The second step is to select an appropriate culture and subjects within the culture. Generally, the problem is to find a culture that is simple, distinctive, and accessible. The selection of informants within the culture is not the relatively simple matter found in studying one's own culture. Time is required to become familiar with the language, customs, and prestige systems which must be understood before informants can be obtained.

**d.** The types of information to be collected in a cross-cultural study are more complex than those found in studying one's own culture. The outline provided by the Human Relations Area Files was described as one source of suggestions concerning the variables that are important to note.

**e.** Although direct observation and the interview are the two most important techniques used in cross-cultural research, other methods may also be used. These include but are not limited to projective techniques, observational rating scales, and sociometric methods.

**f.** The final step in conducting a cross-cultural study is analyzing and interpreting the data. Data analysis is a function of the methods used. Field notes, for example, best lend themselves to a content analysis.

## PRACTICE EXERCISES

**1.** Indicate the type of research each of the following examples calls for (case study, factor analysis, sample survey, relationship study, prediction study, developmental study, or cross-cultural methods):

**a.** A teacher is interested in knowing why John stutters.

**b.** A student is interested in knowing whether the Oedipus complex is a universal problem.

**c.** A superintendent is interested in knowing if most people in the school district will vote for a new bond proposal.

**d.** A parent wants to know if guilt feelings are associated with harsh toilet training procedures.

**e.** A student in a history of education class wants to write a paper on the history of the Schlockville School District.

**f.** Billy wants to know if he has the ability to get into college.

**g.** A new teacher wants to investigate the connection between size of district and beginning salaries paid to teachers.

**h.** A counselor is interested in finding out if student attitudes may be measured along a single dimension.

**i.** A psychologist is interested in studying identification problems among adolescents.

**2.** Since events in the life of any given individual cannot be reproduced or controlled, is the case history a scientific method? Defend your answer.

**3.** One use of the case study in research is to show how a theoretical formulation can be translated into an actual example. In the Adorno study referred to in the text, a high-ethnocentric person and a low-ethnocentric person were selected. Is this sample biased? Explain your answer.

**4.** Suppose that all correlations in a five-by-five matrix are 0.90 or higher. How many factors would you expect there to be? Why?

**a.** If a researcher comes up with six factors in a five-by-five matrix, what might this suggest?

**b.** What is the maximum number of factors that could be derived from the correlation matrix in Table 5-3, page 84.

**5.** Complete and interpret the following factor matrix.

| TESTS | Factors | | | Factor Variances | | | COMMUNALITIES |
| | A | B | C | A | B | C | ($h^2$) |
|---|---|---|---|---|---|---|---|
| 1 | .80 | .20 | .03 | ___ | ___ | ___ | ___ |
| 2 | .02 | .05 | .60 | ___ | ___ | ___ | ___ |
| 3 | .20 | .20 | .20 | ___ | ___ | ___ | ___ |

   **a.** Which test is the best measure of Factor $A$? $B$? $C$?

   **b.** Which factor is least well defined by the factor analysis?

   **c.** Should test 3 be retained or eliminated? Why?

   **d.** Compute and interpret the eigenvalues. What proportion of variance is accounted for by each of the three factors?

   **e.** What is the factor loading of test 2 with Factor $B$?

**6.** Suppose that an "unbiased and independent research organization" finds that there is a perfect positive correlation between the number of cigarettes smoked and the likelihood of lung cancer. What could it legitimately conclude?

**7.** Indicate what difficulties will be encountered if the following procedures are followed (in some cases, there may be no difficulty):

   **a.** An investigator correlates the scores on subtest $X$ with the corresponding total scores of the same test.

   **b.** Two sets of numbers are selected by means of a table of random numbers. The first pair of numbers is divided by 2, the second pair by 3, the third pair by 4, etc. An investigator then correlates the divided scores in the first set with those in the second.

   **c.** A teacher correlates students' mean scores in arithmetic with their mean scores in social studies.

   **d.** A teacher is interested in knowing whether or not class improvement correlates with intelligence test scores.

**8.** It is generally agreed that there is a relatively high correlation between income and amount of education. Suppose, however, that someone suggests that the correlation is spurious because it fails to take intelligence into effect. Given the following correlations between amount of education ($X$), income ($Y$), and intelligence ($Z$), partial out the effects of intelligence and draw a conclusion from your results: $r_{xy} = 0.60$; $r_{xz} = 0.80$; $r_{yz} = 0.40$.

**9.** In which of the following situations would you predict a curvilinear relationship?

    **a.** Scores on a code-substitution task are correlated with chronological age. Chronological age varies from 7–0 to late adulthood.

    **b.** Amount of hair is correlated with chronological age from birth to death.

    **c.** Height and weight are correlated for children between the ages of one and ten.

**10.** An investigator is interested in predicting amount of income ($Y$) from knowledge of amount of education ($X$). Given $r_{xy} = 0.60$, $s_x = 3$ years, $s_y = \$2500$, $M_x = 15$ years, and $M_y = \$12,000$, work out a regression equation and interpret its meaning. Also, compute the standard error of estimate and interpret its meaning.

**11.** Indicate what effects you would expect each of the following conditions to have on the multiple-correlation coefficient. Indicate what additional information you would want if the effects are indeterminate.

    **a.** The correlation between independent variables is reduced.

    **b.** The correlation between independent variables is increased to 0.95.

    **c.** The independent variables correlate highly with each other but not with the criterion.

    **d.** An independent variable is made to correlate negatively with both the other independent variable and the criterion.

**12.** Indicate whether a longitudinal or cross-sectional approach is referred to or called for in each of the following examples:

    **a.** An investigator is interested in studying the average age at which children begin to walk.

    **b.** This method is likely to obscure individual differences.

    **c.** Economy is the primary objective (assume the longitudinal and cross-sectional methods are equally useful and valid).

    **d.** Other things being equal, this method is preferable if subjects are known to be highly mobile.

    **e.** The researcher needs a large number of measurements from a few subjects.

    **f.** This method reduces practice effects.

    **g.** This method assumes that samples are comparable although, in practice, they may not be.

    **h.** Other things being equal, this method is preferable if it is expected that subjects cannot be retested in the future.

**13.** For each of the following examples, indicate whether the example refers to or calls for the use of the diary, episode sampling, time sampling, or a situational observation.

    **a.** Two individuals competing for a position as superintendent of schools are each allowed to spend two days performing those duties. Members of the school board evaluate their behavior.

**b.** An investigator studies competitive behavior by going from school to school each time there is a student body election.

**c.** Albert is seen fighting an average of 3 times per day.

**d.** Albert fights on the average of 3 times per day, smiles 15 times, cries once, and complains 4 times.

**e.** This method is idiographic, longitudinal, and subject to the most bias.

**14.** A professor of secondary education describes the similarities and differences in education in the United States and in England. Is this a cross-cultural study or a comparative study? Why?

**15.** Design a cross-cultural study. Specify the topic to be investigated, the culture to be studied, the relevant variables, the methods to be used for data collection, and the method of data analysis.

## Selected Supplementary Readings

1. For a defense and description of the case study method, see Allport, Gordon W. *Personality: A Psychological Interpretation.* New York: Henry Holt and Co., 1937. See also Allport, G. W. *Personality and Social Encounter.* Boston: Beacon Press, 1960; Murray, Henry A., et al. *Explorations in Personality.* New York: Oxford University Press, 1938; Allport, G. W. "The Use of Personal Documents in Psychological Science." *Social Science Research Council, Bulletin 49* (1942). For an attack against a completely idiographic approach, see Lundberg, A. G. "Case-Studies vs. Statistical Methods: An Issue Based on Misunderstanding." *Sociometry,* 4, no. 4 (1941), pp. 379–383. Even more vitriolic is the work of Sarbin. See, for example, Sarbin, T. R. "The Logic of Prediction in Psychology." *Psychological Review,* 51, no. 4 (1944), pp. 210–228; and Sarbin, T. R. "Clinical Psychology: Art or Science?" *Psychometrika,* 6, no. 6 (1941), pp. 391–400. For a discussion of the general topic, see Meehl, Paul E. *Clinical vs. Statistical Prediction: A Theoretical Analysis and a Review of the Evidence.* Minneapolis, Minn.: University of Minnesota Press, 1954.

2. The following sources on factor analysis can be recommended although they differ greatly in the degree of mathematical sophistication required of students. Some of the easier sources include: Guilford, J. P. *Psychometric Methods,* 2d ed. New York: McGraw-Hill Book Co., 1954, pp. 470–538; Child, Dennis. *The Essentials of Factor Analysis* (New York: Holt, Rinehart and Winston, 1970, 107 pp.; Ferguson, George A. *Statistical Analysis in Psychology and Education,* 3d ed. New York: McGraw-Hill Book Co., 1971, pp. 404–426. Ferguson's chapter on factor analysis does not appear in the fourth edition of his text; Adcock, C. J. *Factor Analysis for Non-Mathematicians.* Melbourne: Melbourne University Press, 1954, 88 pp. More advanced texts include the following: Comrey, Andrew L. *A First Course in Factor*

*Analysis*. New York: Academic Press, 1973; Cattell, Raymond B. *Factor Analysis*. New York: Harper & Brothers, 1952, 462 pp.; Fruchter, Benjamin. *Introduction to Factor Analysis*. New York: Van Nostrand Reinhold Co., 1954, 280 pp.; Harman, Harry H. *Modern Factor Analysis*, 2d ed. Chicago: University of Chicago Press, 1967, 474 pp.; Horst, Paul. *Factor Analysis of Data Matrices*. New York: Holt, Rinehart and Winston, 1965, 730 pp.

3. For methods of correlational analysis, see Ezekiel, Mordecai. *Methods of Correlational Analysis*. New York: John Wiley & Sons, 1959. See also Chapters 8–12 in McNemar, Quinn. *Psychological Statistics*. New York: John Wiley & Sons, 1962.

4. Multiple correlations with more than four variables become rather time-consuming and complex. Perhaps the simplest numerical solution is given in McNemar, Quinn. *Psychological Statistics*, 3d ed. New York: John Wiley & Sons, 1962, pp. 180–184; but see also Cornell, Francis G. *The Essentials of Educational Statistics*. New York: John Wiley & Sons, 1956, pp. 329–333. If there are more than three or four variables, the problem is best handled by electronic computers. The rationale behind these procedures is based upon the Doolittle method. See Doolittle, M. H. "Method Employed in the Solution of Normal Equations and the Adjustment of a Triangulation." *U.S. Coast and Geodetic Survey Report*, no. 3 (1878), pp. 115–120. A modification used rather often is found in Appendix V of Stead, William H., et al. *Occupational Counseling Techniques: Their Development and Application*. New York: American Book Co., 1940. The use of multiple regression is best described in Kerlinger, Fred N., and Pedhazur, Elazar J. *Multiple Regression in Behavioral Research*. New York: Holt, Rinehart and Winston, 1973, 534 pp. See also Wainer, Howard. "Estimating Coefficients in Linear Models: It Don't Make No Nevermind." *Psychological Bulletin*, 83, no. 2 (March 1976), pp. 213–217.

5. On developmental studies, see Mussen, Paul H., ed. *Handbook of Research Methods in Child Development*. New York: John Wiley & Sons, 1960. The *Handbook* contains 22 chapters divided into five major sections: General Research Methodology in Child Development, The Study of Biological Growth and Development, The Study of Cognitive Processes, The Study of Personality Development, and The Study of the Child's Social Behavior and Environment.

6. An excellent book of readings showing the relationship of education to anthropology is Spindler, George D. *Education and Culture: Anthropological Approaches*. New York: Holt, Rinehart and Winston, 1963. It is not, however, a textbook on methodology. See also Minturn, Leigh, and Lambert, William W. *Mothers of Six Cultures: Antecedents of Child Rearing*. New York: John Wiley & Sons, 1964. The first half of the text describes the use of factor analysis in the interpretation of interview data of mothers in six cultures. This is based upon data obtained in another text, Whiting, Beatrice B., ed. *Six Cultures: Studies of Child Rearing*. New York: John Wiley & Sons,

1963. Both of these works will provide the student with a feeling for and an appreciation of cross-cultural methods.

7. For three excellent sources of observational techniques along with extensive bibliographies, see: Medley, Donald M., and Mitzel, Harold E. "Measuring Classroom Behavior by Systematic Observation." N. L. Gage, ed., *Handbook of Research on Teaching.* Chicago: Rand McNally & Co., 1963, pp. 247–328; Rosenshine, Barak, and Furst, Norma. "The Use of Direct Observation to Study Teaching." Robert M. W. Travers, ed., *Second Handbook of Research on Teaching.* Chicago: Rand McNally & Co., 1973, pp. 122–183; and Gordon, Ira J., and Jester, R. Emile. Chapter 6 in the Travers *Handbook*, pp. 184–217. To determine whether or not observers are aware of (and perhaps responding subconsciously to) treatment conditions, see Beatty, Williams W. "How Blind Is Blind? A Simple Procedure for Estimating Observer Naiveté." *Psychological Bulletin*, 78, no. 1 (July 1972), pp. 70–71. On the criteria for evaluating observation systems and manuals, see Herbert, John, and Attridge, Carol. "A Guide for Developers and Users of Observation Systems and Manuals." *American Educational Research Journal*, 12, no. 1 (Winter 1975), pp. 1–20.

8. Unfortunately, there is a paucity of information concerning methodological issues in cross-cultural research. See, however, Whiting, John W. M. "The Cross-Cultural Method." Chapter 14 in Lindzey, Gardner, ed., *Handbook of Social Psychology.* Cambridge, Mass.: Addison-Wesley Publishing Co., 1954, pp. 523–531. A briefer but more up-to-date approach can be found in Goethals, George W., and Whiting, John W. M. "Research Methods: The Cross-Cultural Method." *Review of Educational Research*, 27, no. 5 (1957), pp. 441–448 (Chapter 2). Sindell, Peter S. "Anthropological Approaches to the Study of Education." *Review of Educational Research*, 39, no. 5 (December 1969), pp. 593–605, is also worth studying. Two issues of the *American Anthropologist* bear consideration. See Romney, A. Kimball, and D'Andrade, Roy Goodwin, eds. "Transcultural Studies in Cognition." *American Anthropologist*, 66, no. 3, part 2 (June 1964); and "Selected Papers in Method and Technique." Special issue of *American Anthropologist*, 65, no. 5 (1963). Part II, "Field Research Techniques," in a book of readings by Adams and Preiss is also valuable: Adams, Richard N., and Preiss, Jack J., eds. *Human Organization Research.* Homewood, Ill.: Dorsey Press, 1960.

research design:
factors affecting
internal
and external
validity

The question "What would happen if . . ." can best and sometimes only be answered if the investigator can impose different treatments on various groups. Responses to these treatments or experimental conditions are observed by the experimenter to determine their differential effects. This ability to arrange for the conditions of observation and to impose different amounts or kinds of a treatment on subjects is what characterizes experimental methods.

## VARIABLES IN EXPERIMENTAL RESEARCH

Treatments vary from study to study, their specific characteristics being determined by the hypotheses under investigation. For example, in a study involving the effects of various amounts of drug $X$ on ability to add columns of figures, the investigator has the responsibility of deciding how much of the drug subjects (*Ss*) will be given. One group, for example, might be given 0.5 mg. of drug *X*, another 0.10 mg., etc. In a different study involving the effects of two reading methods on student achievement, the experimenter (*E*) can manipulate both the type and the amount of training subjects will receive.

In experimentation, the manipulated variable is called an *independent variable*.[1] It is under the direct control of *E*, who may vary it in any way desired. In the examples given above, the amounts of drug *X* and teaching methods are both independent variables because they can be manipulated by *E*. Note that independent variables are described by amount as well as by kind.

Although *E* manipulates independent variables, *Ss* have to respond to some task fixed by *E*. In the drug experiment, *Ss* were given the task of adding columns of figures; in the reading methods study, *Ss* may be asked to respond to an achievement test on reading. The variable to which *Ss* will be asked to respond is called a *dependent variable*; its effect depends upon the presence, absence, or amount of the independent variable. Dependent variables often consist of test scores, although rating scales, interview responses, questionnaires, or direct observation of student behavior are also possible.

Some variables cannot be manipulated but must be accepted by the experimenter in their unmodified form. These *organismic, or classification, variables* are usually attributes of subjects, such as different levels of intelligence, sex, grade levels, and the like. Individuals can be classified by sex, for example, but a person's sex cannot be modified to suit the experimenter. Should a study attempt to compare males and females on some learning task, any differences found might be attributable to sex differences but not necessarily so. Any differences found between boys and girls could be due to differences in intelligence, training, motivation, or a myriad of other conditions present in all human beings, and not necessarily to biological differences between sexes. What this means is that the experimenter who is trying to demonstrate causal relationships should be able to *manipulate* experimental conditions and observe their effects. Organismic variables cannot be manipulated and cannot, by themselves, point out causal relations.

In the hypothetical drug study, many conditions other than drug *X* might be responsible for *Ss* learning to add. Anything that correlates with the dependent variable *could* affect it. These conditions include age, previous experience with arithmetic or drugs, intelligence, sex, socioeconomic level, motivation, physical health, and emotional problems. All of these factors, and more, must be controlled if *E* wants to conclude that drug *X* and not one

---

[1] Some synonyms for independent variable include treatment variable and experimental variable.

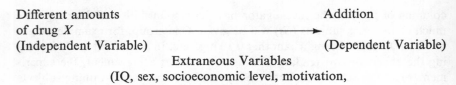

Different amounts                              Addition
of drug $X$
(Independent Variable)                 (Dependent Variable)
Extraneous Variables
(IQ, sex, socioeconomic level, motivation,
physical and emotional health, etc.)

**Figure 6-1**
RELATIONSHIP BETWEEN INDEPENDENT AND DEPENDENT VARIABLES WITH THE PRESENCE OF EXTRANEOUS VARIABLES.

of these *extraneous variables* increased addition skills. This situation is diagrammed in Figure 6-1. The presence of extraneous factors makes it difficult or impossible to determine if drug $X$ or some extraneous variable is responsible for changes in the dependent variable.

## SOME CRITERIA FOR EVALUATING EXPERIMENTAL DESIGNS

### Randomization As a Means of Reducing Systematic Error

One of the most important contributions of modern experimental design concerns the use of randomization to reduce systematic error.[2] Systematic error refers to those differences between obtained and true effects that are all in the same direction and that accumulate as $N$ increases. In contrast, random errors tend to cancel each other as $N$ is increased.

As an example of how systematic error can be generated, consider the following experiment. The hypothesis will be that spelling method $A$ is "superior" to spelling method $B$. To test this hypothesis, $E$ plans to take one group of subjects, teach them spelling by method $A$, and measure the number of words $Ss$ spell correctly. $E$ then plans to teach spelling method $B$ to another group. The spelling test given previously will be used again. The statistical analysis will determine whether $Ss$ performed better under method $A$ or method $B$.

Suppose also that groups $A$ and $B$ both consist of volunteers and that the experimenter assigned the first 30 volunteers to group $A$ and the second to group $B$. Any nonchance differences between $Ss$ in the two groups should be attributable to method, but in this example, $E$ has to consider the equivalence of the two groups. $Ss$ who first volunteer to participate in a study might differ in systematic ways from those who are last to volunteer. The first

[2]R. A. Fisher, *The Design of Experiments* (London: Oliver and Boyd, 1935).

group of volunteers is probably more motivated and perhaps more academically able. Differences in spelling scores cannot be interpreted as reflecting only differences between methods *A* and *B*. The failure to assign all 60 *Ss* randomly to two treatments could produce systematic errors favoring one group over the other. The extent to which systematic error can be reduced is one criterion for evaluating experimental studies.

## Sensitivity

Sensitivity refers to the ability of an experiment to detect true differences between experimental and control groups. Sensitivity can be increased in at least four ways: by reducing the variability of the *Ss*, increasing *N*, improving the experimental design, and providing powerful treatments.

*Reducing the Variability of the Ss.* In teaching spelling by two methods, *E* could select a population of *Ss* and randomly assign half of the group to receive method *A* and the other half to receive method *B*. At the end of the experiment, all *Ss* will take the same spelling test. Table 6-1 illustrates the scores obtained by 10 fictional *Ss*,[3] half of whom are exposed to *A* and half to *B*.

The means for groups *A* and *B* are 5 and 10, respectively. The variance of scores in group *A* is 6.5;[4] for group *B* it is 52.0. Clearly, there is

TABLE 6-1

Hypothetical Scores Obtained by 10 *Ss* Randomly
Assigned to Two Groups

|  | *A* | | *B* | | |
|---|---|---|---|---|---|
|  | 8 | | 10 | | |
|  | 2 | | 20 | | |
|  | 7 | | 0 | | |
|  | 3 | | 8 | | |
|  | 5 | | 12 | | |
|  | | | | | Totals |
| $\Sigma X$ | 25 | + | 50 | = | 75 |
| $(\Sigma X)^2$ | 625 | + | 2500 | = | 3125 |
| $\Sigma X^2$ | 151 | + | 708 | = | 859 |

[3]To simplify the explanation, only 10 cases are used. In practice, more cases would be advantageous.

[4] $s^2 = \dfrac{\Sigma (X - \bar{X})^2}{N - 1}$

variability *within* each of the two groups as well as differences *between* groups. Using these fictitious data, an *F* ratio can be computed as shown in Table 6-2.[5]

## TABLE 6-2

Analysis of Variance Comparing Two Methods
of Teaching Spelling (data are fictitious)

| Source of Variation | Sum of Squares | Degrees of Freedom | Mean Square, or Variance Estimate |
|---|---|---|---|
| Between groups | 62.5 | 1 | 62.5 |
| Within groups | 234.0 | 8 | 29.25 |
| Total | 296.5 | 9 | |

$$F = \frac{62.5}{29.25} = 2.14$$

To be significant at the 0.05 level, *F* has to be at least 5.32. Note that the denominator of the *F* ratio is computed from the variance *within* groups. If this could be made smaller, the *F* ratio would increase, making it more probable that the null hypothesis could be rejected. Table 6-3 shows the effect of reducing the within-group variance while maintaining the same means for groups *A* and *B*.

The analysis of variance for the data in Table 6-3 is summarized in Table 6-4.

When the within-group variance was reduced, the *F* ratio was increased from 2.14 to 250.0. Note also that the between-group sum of squares was unchanged. Random error or within-group variance was, however, reduced substantially by making groups more homogeneous.

In practice, it is difficult to increase the sensitivity of an experiment by selecting *Ss* so as to reduce within-group variability. This variability is a function of one's sampling plan; to reduce it artificially by deliberately select-

---

[5]The student should recall that *F* is the ratio of the between-group variance to the within-group variance. Variances are obtained by dividing the sum of squares by the degrees of freedom. The sum of squares, in turn, can be found by the following formulas:

Total sum of squares: $(SS_T) = \Sigma\,(\Sigma\,X^2) - \frac{(\Sigma\,X^2)}{N} = 859 - \frac{75^2}{10} = 296.5$

Between-group sum of squares: $(SS_B) = \frac{\Sigma\,(\Sigma\,X)^2}{n} - \frac{(\Sigma\,X)^2}{N} = \frac{25^2 + 50^2}{5} - \frac{75^2}{10} = 62.5$

Within-group sum of squares: $(SS_w) = \Sigma\,(\Sigma\,X)^2 - \frac{\Sigma\,(\Sigma\,X)^2}{n} = 859 - \frac{3125}{5} = 234.0$

where *n* is the number of cases in each group; and *N* is the total number of cases in the sample.

TABLE 6-3

Hypothetical Scores Obtained by 10 *Ss*
Randomly Assigned to Two Groups:
Within-Group Variability Reduced

|  | *A* |  | *B* |  | Totals |
|---|---|---|---|---|---|
|  | 4 |  | 10 |  |  |
|  | 5 |  | 10 |  |  |
|  | 5 |  | 10 |  |  |
|  | 5 |  | 10 |  |  |
|  | 6 |  | 10 |  |  |
| $\Sigma X$ | 25 | + | 50 | = | 75 |
| $(\Sigma X)^2$ | 625 | + | 2500 | = | 3125 |
| $\Sigma X^2$ | 127 | + | 500 | = | 627 |

TABLE 6-4

Scores Obtained by 10 *Ss* Randomly Assigned to Two
Groups Keeping Between-Group Variance Constant

| Source of Variation | Sum of Squares | Degrees of Freedom | Mean Square, or Variance Estimate |
|---|---|---|---|
| Between groups | 62.5 | 1 | 62.5 |
| Within groups | 2.0 | 8 | 0.25 |
| Total | 64.5 | 9 | |

$$F = \frac{62.5}{0.25} = 250.0$$

ing homogeneous groups will limit generalization to populations of little interest to *E*. Some experimental designs, however, reduce the error term (i.e., the denominator of the *F* ratio). Within-group variance can also be reduced if reliable tests are used as the dependent variable and if all *Ss* are treated consistently. Treating *Ss* differently will increase the within-group variance and make it less likely to reject the null hypothesis.

Consider the following hypothetical grade point averages obtained by *Ss* participating in an experiment on the effectiveness of a new drug. Assume *Ss* were assigned randomly to the two groups.

The *F* ratio between the two original means of 3.80 and 2.80 is highly significant ($F_1 = 1050$). To see what happens when reliability is decreased,

## 0.5 mg Drug X

| ORIGINAL GPA | ± | RANDOM FACTORS | = | NEW GPA |
|---|---|---|---|---|
| 3.7 | + | 0.5 | = | 4.2 |
| 3.8 | − | 0.1 | = | 3.7 |
| 3.9 | + | 0.8 | = | 4.7 |
| 3.7 | − | 0.6 | = | 3.1 |
| 3.8 | + | 0.0 | = | 3.8 |
| 3.9 | − | 0.4 | = | 3.5 |
| 3.7 | + | 0.2 | = | 3.9 |
| 3.8 | − | 0.1 | = | 3.7 |
| 3.9 | + | 0.4 | = | 4.3 |
| 3.7 | − | 0.8 | = | 2.9 |
| 3.8 | + | 0.9 | = | 4.7 |
| 3.9 | − | 0.3 | = | 3.6 |
| 3.7 | + | 0.0 | = | 3.7 |
| 3.8 | − | 0.6 | = | 3.2 |
| 3.9 | + | 0.4 | = | 4.3 |

$N =$ 15

Sum = 57.0    56.4

$\bar{X} =$ 3.80    3.76

$s =$ 0.08    0.68

$s^2 =$ 0.0064    0.46

$F_1 = 1050$

## Placebo Group

| ORIGINAL GPA | ± | RANDOM FACTORS | = | NEW GPA |
|---|---|---|---|---|
| 2.7 | + | 0.9 | = | 3.6 |
| 2.8 | − | 0.2 | = | 2.6 |
| 2.9 | + | 0.9 | = | 3.8 |
| 2.7 | − | 0.9 | = | 1.8 |
| 2.8 | + | 0.5 | = | 3.3 |
| 2.9 | − | 0.7 | = | 2.2 |
| 2.7 | + | 0.1 | = | 2.8 |
| 2.8 | − | 0.4 | = | 2.4 |
| 2.9 | + | 0.4 | = | 3.3 |
| 2.7 | − | 0.8 | = | 1.9 |
| 2.8 | + | 0.6 | = | 3.4 |
| 2.9 | − | 0.2 | = | 2.7 |
| 2.7 | + | 0.5 | = | 3.2 |
| 2.8 | − | 0.7 | = | 2.1 |
| 2.9 | + | 0.9 | = | 3.8 |

15

42.0    42.9

2.80    2.86

0.08    0.68

0.0064    0.46

$F_2 = 14.44$

add a random number to each set of GPA's. Random numbers can be found on page 184. Add the first number in the first column of Table 8-1, then subtract the second number in that column, etc. Express each number as a decimal. Every other number is subtracted since, in the long run, the random positive values should cancel the negative ones.

The principle to remember is that the presence of chance or random factors in the dependent variable reduces the probability of rejecting the null hypothesis. The $F$ ratio decreased from $F_1 = 1050$ to $F_2 = 14.44$ because of the greater accumulation of random error. These random, or chance, factors increase the within-group variance (in the example, the increase is from 0.0064 to 0.46) but will not markedly affect the between-group variance. Note that the experimental group means changed $-0.04$, and the placebo group increased by 0.06. In the long run, the expectation would be that random variables would have no effect on the means since positive and negative values would cancel each other out.

*Increasing N.* Another way of increasing the sensitivity of an experiment is to increase the number of $Ss$. The original data yielded an $F$ ratio of 2.14, not large enough to reject the null hypothesis at the 0.05 level. See what happens if $N$ is increased from 10 to 30. As before, the means will be kept constant at 5.0 and 10.00, respectively, for groups $A$ and $B$ (see Table 6-5).

The tabled value of $F$ for 1 and 28 degrees of freedom is 4.20. The $F$ ratio of 7.48 is significant at the 0.05 level. It is clearly advantageous to increase the number of $Ss$ if it is possible to do so.

The student should consider what would happen in the extreme case of $N = 2$. This means that one $S$ would be placed in group $A$ and the other in group $B$. Any difference between the two $Ss$ in treatment effect could not be separated from within-group variance. For example, if one $S$ obtains a spelling score of 5 and the other a score of 10, there is no way to estimate the within-group variance, and therefore, no comparison can be made.

The analysis of variance for the data in Table 6-5 is given in Table 6-6.

*Improving the Experimental Design.* Sensitivity can be increased by increasing the homogeneity of $Ss$, increasing the number of $Ss$, and most important, improving the experimental design. This can be done in a number of ways, such as by using an analysis of covariance design where appropriate (see pages 129-133), or repeated measurements designs (see pages 133-138). The first step is to be sure that some method exists for estimating the sensitivity of an experiment. Too often, as Lindquist has stated, this consideration is postponed until after data are collected, when it is found that no appropriate test of significance is available. By redesigning the experiment, it may be possible to analyze data economically and still obtain a valid estimate of

TABLE 6-5

Hypothetical Scores Obtained by 30 *Ss* Randomly Assigned
to Two Groups: *N* Increased from 10 to 30

|  | *A* |  |  | *B* |  |  |
|---|---|---|---|---|---|---|
|  | 8 | 8 | 8 | 10 | 10 | 10 |
|  | 2 | 2 | 2 | 20 | 20 | 20 |
|  | 7 | 7 | 7 | 0 | 0 | 0 |
|  | 3 | 3 | 3 | 8 | 8 | 8 |
|  | 5 | 5 | 5 | 12 | 12 | 12 |

|  |  |  |  |  | Totals |
|---|---|---|---|---|---|
| $\Sigma X$ | 75 | + | 150 | = | 225 |
| $(\Sigma X)^2$ | 5625 | + | 22,500 | = | 28,125 |
| $\Sigma X^2$ | 453 | + | 2,124 | = | 2,577 |

TABLE 6-6

Analysis of Variance Comparing Two Methods
of Teaching Spelling: *N* Increased to 30

| Source of Variation | Sum of Squares | Degrees of Freedom | Mean Square, or Variance Estimate |
|---|---|---|---|
| Between groups | 187.5 | 1 | 187.50 |
| Within groups | 702.0 | 28 | 25.07 |
| Total | 889.5 | 29 | |

$$F = \frac{187.50}{25.07} = 7.48$$

treatment effects. Unless this estimate is available at the beginning of an experiment, a good deal of labor may be expended for nothing.

Experiments should be designed so that the total variance can be partitioned into components to determine what proportion is responsible for treatment effects and what proportion is responsible for error. Lindquist has made the following point:

> Sometimes . . . the mistake is made of failing to isolate that part of the total variance which is due to *controlled* sources, and an "error" variance is employed which is really a composite due both to controlled and uncontrolled sources. In matched group experiments . . . , for example, the mistake has been made of failing to "take out" of the error variance that part of the total variance due to the controlled (matched) variable, and of

still using the error estimate appropriate for independent (unmatched) random samples. The result, of course, is to make the so-called "error" variance unduly large and to make the experiment seem less precise than it really is.[6]

*Providing Powerful Treatments.* Sometimes experimenters fail to select powerful treatments (i.e., those that do make an important and measurable difference), and sometimes the effects of potentially powerful treatments are not given a chance to show up. Any treatments selected because of their potential importance should be given in sufficiently strong and prolonged "doses" to be measurable. For example, the experimenter who plans to study the effects of a new counseling program or method over just a few weeks' time is not giving this program the advantages it may deserve.

## INTERNAL VALIDITY

### Control of Extraneous Variables

One purpose of designing experiments is to eliminate or account for the presence of extraneous variables. An experiment is said to possess *internal validity* if the relationships between the independent and dependent variables are unambiguous and uncomplicated by the presence of extraneous variables. Campbell and Stanley[7] have identified a number of conditions that detract from internal validity.

*Selection.* In the formation of treatment and nontreatment groups, an attempt is made (through procedures to be discussed later) to keep them as equivalent as possible prior to the administration of the experimental treatment. However, if there are systematic differences between groups as they are initially selected, then there is no way to tell if differences between groups on the dependent variable are attributable to treatment effects or to these initial selection differences. Methods used to avoid selection threats are described on pages 127-140.

*History.* In experiments conducted over long periods of time, many uncontrolled factors may intervene to produce changes in the dependent variable other than those produced by the experimental treatment. Suppose, for example, that *E* is trying to measure the effects of a deliberately planned propaganda campaign to increase the social status of teachers. To do this, specially prepared films are developed and shown on television for six months.

---

[6]E. F. Lindquist, *Design and Analysis of Experiments in Psychology and Education.* (Boston: Houghton Mifflin Co., 1953), p. 4.

[7]Donald T. Campbell and Julian Stanley, "Experimental and Quasi-Experimental Designs for Research on Teaching," Chapter 5 in N. L. Gage, ed., *Handbook of Research on Teaching* (Chicago: Rand McNally & Co., 1963), pp. 171–246.

Before the experiment is begun, $E$ selects a random sample of television viewers and determines their attitude toward public school teachers; six months later, $E$ retests the same sample of viewers. Suppose that $E$ finds that there was a dramatic shift in attitudes in the direction hypothesized. Could $E$ then conclude that the films were responsible for the shift? The answer is partially dependent on the presence or absence of extraneous variables. If the newspapers were simultaneously carrying on a campaign to elevate the role of teachers or if some historic event intervened to increase teaching prestige, attitude changes could reflect these extraneous events and not the effects of the film campaign.

*Maturation.* With the passage of time, not only is there a greater chance for uncontrolled events to occur, but $Ss$ may also change. $Ss$ get older, reaction times slow down, vision is decreased, etc. If the investigation is going to be carried out over long periods of time, the fact that $Ss$ change in important ways will have to be considered as part of the research design. Otherwise, $E$ may erroneously conclude that the experimental treatment produced changes in the dependent variable when these changes might reflect only the effects of increased maturation.

*Testing.* Sometimes an experimental design calls for a pretest and posttest to be administered to the same group of $Ss$. If taking the pretest has any measurable effect on posttest scores, then this extraneous factor, testing, must be accounted for. In some studies, for example, administering a pretest may provide for practice effects and an increase in scores on the dependent variable. In this case, it may be difficult to tell if the pretest or the experimental treatment produced differences in the dependent variable.

*Instrumentation.* In educational research, dependent variables require the use of tests or observers. In many instances, dependent variables are affected by changes occurring in the efficiency of the scorers or raters. For example, much time and effort may be expended to correct the first papers read. As fatigue, boredom, and the pressure of other activities increase, scoring accuracy may decrease. If the experimental papers are read first, they might be rated more stringently than control papers. Differences between experimental and control groups would then be difficult to separate from the effects produced by differential scoring of the instrument.

*Statistical Regression.* If $Ss$ are selected to participate in an experiment because they are atypical in some trait, a retest score will increase if the $Ss$ were originally below average and decrease if $Ss$ originally were above average. Suppose in the drug study that $E$ were interested only in the effects that the drug has on gifted and retarded students. The first thing $E$ might do is go through the school records and select the brightest and the slowest students for inclusion in the study. Scores at these extremes of the distribution usually contain more error than the more moderate scores. In part, this is because many chance factors place students at the top or bottom of a distribution. These same chance factors are not likely to be present again in the posttest. Even in the absence of an experimental treatment, posttest scores for those $Ss$ selected because they are bright will be lower than their initial scores; posttest scores for students at or near the bottom of the distribution will increase over initial scores, not because they have become brighter, but simply because the laws of chance refuse to keep the low-scoring persons continually at the bottom of the distribution. Atypical $Ss$ are said to regress toward the mean on a repeated measure.

*Experimental Mortality.* Unless pretest and posttest measures are based on the same persons, posttest comparisons of experimental and control groups are likely to be invalid. Take, for example, a study concerned with determining the attitudes of students toward school. Suppose that the research design calls for studying children in grades 8 through 12. Assuming that most compulsory school attendance laws will keep all $Ss$ in school until they are about sixteen, $E$ can be reasonably certain, at least for those sixteen years of age or younger, that some attitudes toward school will be fairly negative since the sample will contain a number of $Ss$ who will drop out of school when they can. However, if $E$ continues to sample $Ss$ over sixteen years of age who are still in school, their attitudes toward school will appear to have miraculously improved! The explanation, of course, is that there are systematic differences between $Ss$ who drop out of school and those who remain. When individuals systematically drop out of a study, experimental mortality has occurred.

## METHODS OF EQUATING EXPERIMENTAL AND CONTROL GROUPS

A meaningful experiment must compare treatment effects, and any comparison, of course, must consist of two or more conditions. All groups are selected initially (by means described in this section) to be as similar to one another as possible. At the end of the experiment, $E$ wants to know that any nonchance differences found in the dependent variable between experimental and control groups were not due to initial differences.

Although all experiments require comparisons to be made on the dependent variable, a control group[8] that receives no conditions may not be necessary or even desirable. Whether or not to employ a control group

---

[8]The meaning of *control group* is sometimes ambiguous. It may refer to a group given a placebo "treatment," or it may refer to a group with no treatment at all. Ideally, control $Ss$ should receive a placebo treatment.

depends upon the hypotheses under investigation. The now classic example of a faulty experimental design employing an unnecessary control group is the Lanarkshire Milk Experiment reported by "Student" in 1931.[9] The purpose of the investigation was to determine the effects of raw and pasteurized milk on the height and weight of students over a four-month period. One experimental group consisted of 5,000 students who were given three-quarters of a pint of raw milk daily, another experimental group received the same amount of pasteurized milk, and a control group received no milk during the experiment. For some reason, the sizes of the control and experimental groups were made equal, making the total $N = 20,000$ $Ss$. However, the hypothesis simply required a comparison between two groups, one receiving raw milk and the other pasteurized milk. The inclusion of a control group allowed an additional comparison between $Ss$ who had milk and those who did not, though this comparison was not required by the hypothesis.

## Randomization

In the drug experiment, it was noted that a number of extraneous variables were present that could confound the relationship between the drug and scores on an addition test. These extraneous variables included intelligence, socioeconomic level, and motivation. To make sense out of experimental comparisons, it is necessary to make certain that groups are comparable in all relevant characteristics before the independent variable (drug $X$) is introduced.

One way to equate groups is to assign $Ss$ by some random procedure to experimental and comparison groups. The easiest way is to use a table of random numbers as described in Chapter 8. Each $S$ is given a number, and $E$ enters a table of random numbers and reads off as many as are needed for the experimental group. The remaining $Ss$ are placed in the control groups.

Another possible way of assigning $Ss$ to groups randomly is by tossing a coin or die. $Ss$ can be placed in the experimental group if the coin comes up "heads" or in the control group if it comes up "tails." If a die is used, $Ss$ can be assigned to multiple groups.

It may seem strange that randomization is recommended as one of the best ways to equate groups. How can $E$ be sure that the groups are really equated? Wouldn't it be better to equalize groups by matching $Ss$ in the experimental and control groups on the extraneous variables that correlate most highly with the dependent variable?

Although there are some advantages to matching which will be considered later, one does not have to match to equate groups. The procedure of randomly assigning $Ss$ to experimental and control groups is the best guaran-

[9]Student, "The Lanarkshire Milk Experiment," *Biometrika*, 23 (1931), pp. 398–406.

tee of random distribution of all characteristics associated with *Ss*. *Assuming that E has a large enough sample*, there is every reason to believe that extraneous variables will be equalized for all groups.

Another advantage to randomization is that in many experiments *E* may be uncertain or unaware of what the extraneous factors are. In the drug experiment, for example, there may be an infinite number of conditions other than drug *X* that could affect achievement. Clearly, *E* cannot match *Ss* on all possible conditions. However, by randomly assigning *Ss*, *E* not only is able to equate groups on known factors (IQ, motivation, etc.) but also on all unknown factors.

Randomization also helps to avoid much of the artificiality characteristic of investigations which use matched groups representing no important population. By assigning *Ss* at random, *E* can make use of all available persons, not just those for whom a match can be found.

Still another advantage of randomization is that it is the simplest procedure for assigning *Ss* to different treatment groups. It takes less time and effort than any other method. Thus, it is possible to increase the number of *Ss* without increasing administrative costs prohibitively.

In general, the subjective assignment of *Ss* to experimental or control groups should be avoided. In the Lanarkshire Milk Experiment, not only was the control group unnecessary, but the means of selecting *Ss* were biased. Initially, schools and experimental treatments were to be selected at random with *Ss* within each school to receive the same treatment. Unfortunately, teachers were then allowed to reassign *Ss* in the mistaken belief that this would make experimental and control groups more equal in the number of well-nourished and undernourished children. In reassigning *Ss*, however, the teachers subconsciously took pity on the undernourished children and assigned them to the experimental groups so they could receive milk. Thus, the control groups contained a larger proportion of well-nourished children than would be expected by chance. One can imagine the surprise of the experimenters when they reweighed and remeasured the children four months later only to find that the control group which received no milk had gained more and was taller than the experimental groups that were given milk!

## The Analysis of Covariance[10]

Another extremely useful procedure for "equating" is the analysis of covariance technique. The word *equating* has been placed in quotation marks to show that groups are matched on data obtained prior to the imposition of

[10]It is beyond the scope of this text to delve very far into the rationale behind the analysis of covariance. See Allen L. Edwards, *Experimental Design in Psychological Research*, 4th ed. (New York: Holt, Rinehart and Winston, 1972), pp. 369–393.

the experimental treatment. These measurements are obtained for each $S$ and should correlate with the dependent variable. These measurements are called *covariates*, or *adjusting variables*.

The analysis of covariance adjusts the means on the dependent variable to account for any initial differences among groups. The analysis of covariance (ANCOVA) tests the significance of the differences between two or more groups after initial differences are statistically eliminated. The advantage of the analysis of covariance is that $E$ has all of the benefits of random assignment of $Ss$ to experimental and control groups while being able to eliminate the effects of any initial and known differences between groups. The ANCOVA increases the sensitivity of the experimental design.

One assumption underlying the ANCOVA is that the covariate is linearly related to the dependent variable. That is, the relationship between the pretest and posttest scores in Table 6-7 must be best represented by a straight line. If not, modifications in procedure will need to be considered.

Second, the correlation between pretest and posttest scores must be relatively high but not necessarily positive. As the correlation increases in magnitude, the experiment will increase in precision or sensitivity. If the correlation is 0.0 or close to zero, there is some *disadvantage* in using an ANCOVA design.

Third, the initial differences among groups on the covariate should be random. If groups could not be randomly assigned, there should be good reason for believing that there are no systematic differences among them. The ANCOVA cannot eliminate the effects of large initial differences among intact groups, for example.

Fourth, it is assumed that the covariate is obtained prior to the introduction of the experimental treatment and therefore cannot be affected by the treatment. Pretests, of course, cannot be affected by the experiment. One would not, however, introduce a test to be used as a covariate once the experiment has been underway.

Finally, the ANCOVA is not restricted to the use of a single covariate or to a one-way analysis of variance design. The use of up to three or four covariates will often help to eliminate initial differences between groups. After that, the amount of gain will be negligible. Since every covariate used means a loss of 1 degree of freedom, too many covariates could lead to a loss in precision or sensitivity. The ANCOVA can also be used to eliminate initial differences among groups in factorial designs.

*The Nature of Covariance Adjustments.* The ANCOVA adjusts or modifies the between- and within-groups variance in certain predictable ways. Consider the following possibilities and the effects of the ANCOVA adjustments ($\bar{X}$ is the covariate mean; $\bar{Y}$ is the mean of the dependent variable).

*1. Covariates equal: dependent variables equal*

|  | $\bar{X}$ | $\bar{Y}$ |
|---|---|---|
| Experimental group | 10 | 20 |
| Control group | 10 | 20 |

In this example, the covariate means are identical as are the dependent variable means. The ANCOVA adjustment will reduce the denominator of the $F$ ratio, but the between-group variance on the dependent variable will still be zero. This is because the means on the dependent variable are identical. The differences between the dependent variable means resulting from the ANCOVA will still be zero since there is no initial difference in the means for the two groups to adjust. In practice, having *identical* means on either $X$ or $Y$ variables will be extremely rare.

*2. Covariates equal; dependent variables unequal*

|  | $\bar{X}$ | $\bar{Y}$ |
|---|---|---|
| Experimental group | 10 | 25 |
| Control group | 10 | 20 |

Here, the two groups are identical on the covariate, but one group is superior to the other in the dependent variable. The adjustment will involve reducing the denominator of the $F$ ratio, making it more likely to reject the null hypothesis than if no adjustment were made. Again, it is most unlikely that the covariate means will be identical.

*3. Covariates unequal; dependent variables equal*

|  | $\bar{X}$ | $\bar{Y}$ |
|---|---|---|
| Experimental group | 10 | 20 |
| Control group | 8 | 20 |

In this example, the dependent variables are the same, but there is a difference between the covariate means. Should an analysis of variance be used to test the significance of the difference between the two $Y$ means, there could be no difference. But if an ANCOVA adjustment is made, the experimental group's $\bar{Y}$ would be decreased to compensate for the initial high value on the covariate, and the control group's $\bar{Y}$ would increase. In addition to the adjustment in the dependent variable, there would be an adjustment to reduce the within-group variance. Thus, the numerator of the $F$ ratio would increase, and the denominator would decrease, making the rejection of $H_0$ more likely.

*4. Covariates and dependent variables differ in same direction*

|  | $\bar{X}$ | $\bar{Y}$ |
|---|---|---|
| Experimental group | 10 | 25 |
| Control group | 8 | 20 |

In example 4, the covariate and dependent variable means are both higher in the experimental group than in the control group. Part of the reason for the difference in the two $Y$ means could be due to the initial advantage of the experimental group on the covariate. The adjustment will involve *reducing* the difference between the two $\bar{Y}$ measures. The experimental group's mean on $Y$ will decrease while the control group's $\bar{Y}$ will increase. Because the ANCOVA will reduce the *numerator* of the $F$ ratio in this example, it *may* be more difficult to reject the null hypothesis using the ANCOVA than if a simple analysis of variance had been used on the $Y$ measures. But keep in mind that the ANCOVA will also reduce the *denominator* of the $F$ ratio. This reduction in the $F$ ratio denominator depends on the correlation between $X$ and $Y$. The higher the correlation is, the smaller will be the denominator. Whether or not $F$ will be significant depends on the extent to which the ANCOVA reduces the between- and within-group variances.

*5. Covariates and dependent variables differ, but in opposite directions*

|  | $\bar{X}$ | $\bar{Y}$ |
|---|---|---|
| Experimental group | 10 | 20 |
| Control group | 8 | 25 |

The covariate mean for the experimental group is higher than the control mean, but the dependent variable mean is lower. Despite the initial advantage on the covariate, the experimental group had a lower mean on $Y$. The ANCOVA adjustment will increase the difference between the two dependent variable measures by lowering the $\bar{Y}$ for the experimental group and increasing $\bar{Y}$ for the control. Because the difference between groups has been increased, the researcher has also increased the probability of rejecting the null hypothesis. A second advantage of the covariance adjustment is to reduce the within-group variance. This further increases the likelihood of finding a significant difference between the means of the dependent variable.

Table 6-7 presents the pretest and posttest scores of 10 *Ss* (5 in each group) and Table 6-8 summarizes the ANCOVA.

Compare the data in Table 6-8 with that of Table 6-1. The unadjusted sum of squares was 62.5; the adjusted sum of squares was increased to 168.62, almost tripling in value. In addition, the within-groups sum of squares de-

TABLE 6-7

Pretest and Posttest Scores Obtained by 10 Ss Assigned
Randomly to Two Treatments, A and B

| A | | B | |
|---|---|---|---|
| X (PRETEST) | Y (POSTTEST) | X (PRETEST) | Y (POSTTEST) |
| 6 | 8 | 3 | 10 |
| 2 | 2 | 6 | 20 |
| 5 | 7 | 0 | 0 |
| 3 | 3 | 2 | 8 |
| 4 | 5 | 4 | 12 |
| $\Sigma X_A = 20$ | $\Sigma Y_A = 25$ | $\Sigma X_B = 15$ | $\Sigma Y_B = 50$ |
| $\bar{X}_A = 4.0$ | $\bar{Y}_A = 5.0$ | $\bar{X}_B = 3$ | $\bar{Y}_B = 10$ |
| $\Sigma X_A^2 = 90$ | $\Sigma Y_A^2 = 151$ | $\Sigma X_B^2 = 65$ | $\Sigma Y_B^2 = 708$ |

TABLE 6-8

Analysis of Covariance for Two Groups of 5 Ss Each

| Source of Variation | Sum of Squares for Errors of Estimate | Degrees of Freedom | Mean Square, or Variance Estimate | F |
|---|---|---|---|---|
| Adjusted means | 168.62 | 1 | 168.62 | 57.16 |
| Within groups | 20.67 | 7 | 2.95 | |
| Total | 189.29 | 8 | | |

creased from 234.0 to only 20.67. These two adjustments led to a highly significant $F$ ratio of 57.16 from the nonsignificant value of 2.14, even though 1 degree of freedom was lost in calculating the regression coefficient needed to adjust posttest scores. Obviously, in this example it was well worthwhile to use the ANCOVA adjustment.

### Repeated Measurements

One of the most effective ways to reduce differences between Ss is to use a repeated measurements design. In the simplest example of a repeated measurements design (a one-way ANOVA with repeated measurements), each S is tested or observed under two conditions (such as an experimental and a control condition). Since the same Ss are involved in both conditions, it would be possible to compare the differences between the means of the two conditions to determine whether or not the difference is statistically significant. Unlike experiments where *Ss* are assigned randomly to *either* a treatment or control group, the repeated measurements design attempts to eliminate the effects of extraneous variables by using each *S* as his or her own control. Thus, each subject is asked to respond to experimental *and* to control tasks. Ostensibly, the advantage of this design is to use the same *Ss* under all conditions to make sure that extraneous variables are equal.

Nothing requires that repeated measurements designs be restricted to just two groups. Any number of treatment and control conditions can be imposed on each *S*. Nor is there any need to restrict oneself to just treatment and control conditions; any number of different independent variables may be involved in the experiment. It is possible, for example, to analyze the responses of *Ss* who are divided into different methods groups *and* who are tested any number of times to yield a two-way analysis of variance with repeated measurements. Each *S* could, for example, be placed into one of three reading groups and be tested any number of times on information they had read (this repeated testing might provide information regarding retention of facts). This experiment could be described as a two-way analysis of variance with repeated measurements on the various occasions. It is even possible in some situations to use the same *Ss* in all comparisons (that is, there may be repeated measurements over more than one independent variable).

Consider a simple one-way ANOVA with repeated measurements in which 5 *Ss* are tested under two conditions, *A* and *B* (see Table 6-9). First, note that one advantage to this type of design is that *Ss* act as their own comparison groups. Albert takes a test following instruction in the two spelling methods, *A* and *B*, as do the other four *Ss*. The data in Table 6-1, in contrast, came about by assigning 5 *Ss* to method *A* and another 5 to method *B*. The repeated measurements design is economical since fewer *Ss* can be used, though there are still ten observations.

TABLE 6-9

Scores Obtained by 5 *Ss*, Each Exposed
to Two Experimental Procedures

| Subjects | Method *A* | Method *B* |
|----------|-----------|-----------|
| Albert | 8 | 10 |
| Betty | 2 | 20 |
| Carl | 7 | 0 |
| Delbert | 3 | 8 |
| Elaine | 5 | 12 |

A second advantage is that the analysis of variance for the repeated measurements design allows $E$ to reduce the denominator of the $F$ ratio by subtracting the sum of squares attributable to individual differences. By reducing the denominator of the $F$ ratio, $E$ can increase the probability that the null hypothesis will be rejected. However, *this advantage accrues only if there is a high positive correlation between the pairs of scores.*

Table 6-10 shows the analysis of variance for the repeated measurements design[11] using the data in Table 6-9.

## TABLE 6-10

Analysis of Variance for a Repeated Measurements Design

| Source of Variation | Sum of Squares | Degrees of Freedom | Mean Square or Variance Estimate |
|---|---|---|---|
| Between groups (columns) | 62.5 | 1 | 62.5 |
| Between subjects (rows) | 71.0 | 4 | 17.75 |
| Interaction | 163.0 | 4 | 40.75 |
| Total | 296.5 | 9 | |

$$F = \frac{62.5}{40.75} = 1.53$$

Using 10 *randomly assigned Ss*, the $F$ ratio (see Table 6-1) was 2.14, with 1 and 8 degrees of freedom associated with the between-group and within-group sums of squares, respectively. Using exactly the same data but assuming repeated measurements on the 5 *Ss*, the $F$ ratio was only 1.53, with 1 and 4 degrees of freedom.[12] Not only did the $F$ ratio diminish, but 4 degrees

---

[11]The computation of the sum of squares is as follows:

Total sum of squares: $(SS_T) = \Sigma X^2 - \frac{(\Sigma X)^2}{N} = 859 - \frac{75^2}{10} = 296.5$

Between-group sum of squares: $(SS_{BG}) = \Sigma (\Sigma Y_{rk})^2 - \frac{(\Sigma X)^2}{N} = \frac{25^2 + 50^2}{5} - \frac{75^2}{10} = 62.5$

Between-subject sum of squares: $(SS_{BS}) = \frac{\Sigma (\Sigma X_r)^2}{k} - \frac{(\Sigma X)^2}{N}$

$$= \frac{18^2 + 22^2 + 7^2 + 11^2 + 17^2}{2} - \frac{75^2}{10} = 71.0$$

Residual sum of squares: $(SS_R) =$ total sum of squares $-$ between-group sum of squares $-$ between-subject sum of squares

Residual sum of squares: $(SS_R) = 296.5 - 62.5 - 71.0 = 163.0$

where all symbols are defined as used previously, and where $r$ is rows and $k$ is columns.

[12]The interaction mean square is used as the denominator of the $F$ ratio for repeated measurements designs.

of freedom were lost. Clearly, for the data at hand, it was a mistake to use a repeated measurements design. The reason is that the correlation between the paired scores in Table 6-10 is negative ($r = -0.63$). *The advantage of the repeated measurements design over randomization occurs only if the correlation between the paired scores is positive and high.*[13] Since the correlation is negative, one would have been better off not using a repeated measurements design.

For instructional purposes, rearrange the scores obtained by the 5 $Ss$ so that the correlations are both positive and high. These changes can be seen in Table 6-11 where $r = +0.92$.

The use of the repeated measurement design when $r$ is both high and positive resulted in a larger $F$ ratio (5.1) than with the randomized group design ($F = 2.14$) or with $r$ negative ($F = 1.53$). A comparison of Tables 6-10 and 6-12 demonstrates that error was reduced from 40.75 to 12.25, but that the total and between-groups sums of squares remained unchanged.

The analysis of variance can then be shown in Table 6-12.

Two further points should be noted. When $Ss$ were assigned at random, the degrees of freedom for the between- and within-group sums of squares were 1 and 8, respectively. The tabled value for $F$ with degrees of freedom equal to 1 and 8 is 5.32 (0.05 level). However, in the repeated measurements design, the degrees of freedom involve the number of *paired* scores minus 1. Thus, it is necessary to enter the $F$ table with 1 and 4 degrees of freedom. The tabled value is 7.71, and the $F$ ratio is still not significant. This illustrates an important consideration: although repeated measurement designs may increase the $F$ ratio, the loss of degrees of freedom may still make it worthwhile to randomly assign $Ss$ to different treatments. This is especially true if the scores are not highly correlated or if they correlate negatively.

---

[13]The rationale behind this rests on the principle that positive correlations reduce the interaction mean square which is used as the denominator of the $F$ ratio. Conversely, negative correlations add to that value. To see why this is true, examine the formula for a $t$-test. The $t$-test can be used instead of the $F$ ratio if only two treatments are being compared. Thus, the $t$-test will yield the same conclusions as will $F$ under the assumption that there are only two comparison groups. The formula for $t$ is:

$$t = \frac{\bar{X}_A - \bar{X}_B}{\sqrt{s_{\bar{X}_A}^2 + s_{\bar{X}_B}^2 - 2r_{AB}(s_{\bar{X}_A})(s_{\bar{X}_B})}}$$

The numerator is simply the difference between the two means, $A$ and $B$. The denominator is the standard error of the difference between correlated means (correlated because two measures are taken on each subject). The first two terms under the radical are the error variances for each mean; the third term involves multiplying the correlation between the paired scores by 2 and multiplying that product by the standard error of the mean for group $A$ and by the standard error of the mean for group $B$. If the groups are uncorrelated, the third term under the radical becomes zero; if $r$ is positive, the effect will be to reduce the numerical value of the denominator and increase the value of $t$; but if the correlation is negative, this has the effect of *increasing* the denominator and will reduce the value of $t$. Small values of $t$, like small $F$ ratios, mean that differences are unlikely to be significant.

TABLE 6-11

Scores Obtained by 5 *Ss*, Each Exposed
to Two Experimental Treatments (scores modified
so that $r_{AB}$ is positive and high)

| Subjects | Method $A$ | Method $B$ |
|---|---|---|
| Albert | 8 | 20 |
| Betty | 2 | 0 |
| Carl | 7 | 12 |
| Delbert | 3 | 8 |
| Elaine | 5 | 10 |

TABLE 6-12

Analysis of Variance after Correlations between
Scores Have Been Increased

| Source of Variation | Sum of Squares | Degrees of Freedom | Mean Squares |
|---|---|---|---|
| Between groups (columns) | 62.5 | 1 | 62.5 |
| Between subjects (rows) | 185.0 | 4 | 46.25 |
| Interaction (treatment $X$ subjects) | 49.0 | 4 | 12.25 |
| Total | 296.5 | 9 | |

$$F = \frac{62.5}{12.25} = 5.1$$

One other problem faces the experimenter interested in or contemplating the use of a repeated measurements design. Sometimes the presentation of one method has an effect on a second or a third method. Thus, it would be possible to run into difficulties if all *Ss* were first given method *A* and then given *B*. Method *B* might be expected to yield a higher mean than would method *A* if only because of practice effects. The best solution to this problem is to *counterbalance* the order of presentation (for example, half of the *Ss* can be presented method *A* preceding method *B*, and the other half can receive method *B* preceding *A*).[14] Other methods of counterbalancing are discussed in Chapter 7.

In investigations not explicitly concerned with the study of transfer

[14]In studies where the effects of transfer of learning need to be known, one would not counterbalance the order of presentation. The repeated measurements design is ideal for that purpose. Counterbalancing is necessary if the order effect is not desirable.

effects, $E$ must be concerned with the use of repeated measurements designs. Suppose, for example, that $Ss$ are given the task of applying a rule (such as "Use $i$ before $e$ except after $c$") under different noise conditions. Once learned, it is unlikely that $E$ will be able to forget the rule and its application simply because of a change in background noise. Keppel[15] notes that counterbalancing will not work in deception studies where $Ss$ are told to expect one condition but are given a different treatment, in studies involving shock or fear (if $Ss$ are electrically shocked for responding incorrectly, it is unlikely they could disregard this effect if they are subsequently told they will no longer be shocked), or if $Ss$ are given a pleasant experience first, it is unlikely that they can be unaffected by subsequently presented unpleasant experiences. In short, avoid repeated measurements designs whenever carryover or transfer effects are irrelevant to the study and cannot be eliminated by counterbalancing.

## Matched Groups

Instead of using the same $Ss$ two or more times, $E$ may match or equate two or more $Ss$ on those variables that correlate with the dependent variable. As in the repeated measurements design, the greatest benefits accrue if the correlations are both positive and high.

The spelling experiment comparing methods $A$ and $B$ involves a number of extraneous variables that have to be controlled. Because intelligence correlates highly with achievement, it is often used as a matching variable. Similarly, chronological age correlates positively with achievement. As a matter of fact, there are literally hundreds of variables that correlate with measures of achievement. It is probably impossible to find two $Ss$ who are alike on all extraneous variables. For all practical purposes, $E$ can select only the few variables that correlate most highly with the dependent variables. To the extent that matching accounts for the differences among $Ss$, error can be substantially reduced; however, perfect matches are virtually impossible.

Perhaps the simplest way to match $Ss$ is to rank them on the extraneous variable that correlates mostly highly with the dependent variable. Suppose that $E$ has 80 $Ss$ to assign to one control and three experimental groups. Furthermore, assume that of all the information $E$ has concerning $Ss$, $E$ believes that intelligence test scores correlate most highly with the dependent variable. IQ scores obtained by $Ss$ are then placed in order, with the highest score at the top of the list and the lowest at the bottom. A line is placed under the fourth, eighth, twelfth . . . eighteenth score. Within each *block*[16] of 4 $Ss$, $E$ has to randomly assign each $S$ to either the control group or one of the three

---

[15]Geoffrey Keppel, *Design and Analysis: A Researcher's Handbook* (Englewood Cliffs, N.J.: Prentice-Hall, 1973), p. 399.

[16]The matched group design is sometimes called a *randomized-block design*, especially in agricultural experiments where blocks correspond to plots of land.

experimental groups. Thus, $Ss$ are randomly assigned within each block of four, but differ systemically from one block to another. From this procedure, $E$ can generally expect means and variances for each of the four groups to be approximately equal. The analysis of variance proceeds in the same manner as if a repeated measurements design were being employed.

Another commonly used matching technique uses $Ss$ who are within $X$ number of points of each other on the matching variable. Generally, $X$ is the standard error of measurement ($S_{meas} = s\sqrt{1 - r_{YY}}$) of the variable used to equate $Ss$, although other more arbitrary limits have been used. If intelligence test scores are being used as a matching variable, the standard error of measurement will be approximately 5 points if $s = 16$ and $r_{YY}$, the reliability coefficient, $= 0.91$. $E$ would then try to match $Ss$ within 5 points of one another.

The difficulty with this procedure is that there are so few high or low scores that extreme scores are not likely to be matched. When extreme scores are systematically avoided, samples are biased. In addition, $E$ may have to eliminate many other $Ss$ for whom a match cannot be found, which again contributes to biased sampling. A more serious difficulty is that $Ss$ who have been matched are equated on just a few of the many possible extraneous variables. To eliminate any systematic differences between groups, $Ss$ should be assigned randomly to groups after being matched.

A third matching procedure involves equating separate intact groups on their means and variances. Because these are intact groups, the means and variances of the matching variable will differ between the two groups. To make groups more similar, $E$ may decide to move some of the $Ss$ from one group to another or to eliminate extreme cases in a group having a higher mean or variance.

There are a number of serious disadvantages to matching by means and variances. In the first place, randomization has been neglected, and the groups have not been equated on all extraneous variables. If $Ss$ were assigned randomly and then moved from one group to another to better equalize the means and variances, $E$ might very well equate $Ss$ on one variable but introduce systematic differences on others. Randomization is the best way to assure that groups are equivalent. This principle holds even if $Ss$ are paired. In that case, randomization determines into which group a given $S$ will be placed.

## Changing the Experimental Unit

What does one do if $Ss$ cannot be randomly assigned? If, for example, $Ss$ attending different schools are to be compared, one possibility would be to use schools as the sampling unit instead of the $Ss$ within schools. For example, $E$ might randomly select 5 schools for group $A$ and 5 for $B$. The mean score of all *Ss* within each school would constitute one score value which, because it is a mean, will be more stable than would the individual scores of *Ss* in each school. Since 10 *schools* were selected, there are essentially 10 *cases* in this type of study although there may be thousands of students involved. Obviously, there will be a severe loss in degrees of freedom if schools are the sampling unit rather than students, but the variability within groups *A* and *B* will also be greatly reduced since the variability of means will be smaller than the variability among subjects. Where individuals cannot be matched, entire classrooms or schools can be used instead.

## EXTERNAL VALIDITY

An experiment possesses *external validity* if findings can be generalized to other persons, conditions, and settings. Internal validity, in contrast, is not concerned with generalizing experimental findings but with stating the relation between independent and dependent variables as unambiguously as possible. Internal validity is a necessary (but not a sufficient) precondition for external validity. One cannot generalize ambiguous findings, and one cannot assume that findings are generalizable simply because threats to internal validity have been eliminated.

In a sense, all internally valid experiments are generalizable to *some* degree. Even if mice are used in highly controlled laboratory conditions (to gain better control of experimental conditions), *E* can generalize findings to similar groups of mice under similar experimental conditions. The problem for the experimenter is to determine just how similar the conditions and mice need to be before results can be generalized to other conditions, other mice, or perhaps other species. As Cronbach[17] has shown, this determination can be extremely difficult. Inconsistent findings at one time were reported by different laboratories studying the effects of hexobarbital on the sleeping behavior of mice. Ordinarily, mice sleep about 35 minutes after the drug is administered, but some labs had reported that the mice awoke after only 16 minutes. Eventually, it was found that the difference was due to the type of bedding on which the mice slept. When red cedar was used, this increased the action of enzymes that metabolized hexobarbital, and the mice awoke early. Without the red cedar bedding, the mice slept longer.

If bedding can affect mice, one can only imagine the number of conditions that can affect the behavior of students in a classroom. Since no

[17]Lee J. Cronbach, "Beyond the Two Disciplines of Scientific Psychology," *American Psychologist*, 30, no. 2 (February 1975), p. 121.

two classrooms are identical, which aspects are likely to affect generalizability and which are not? No simple answer to that question is possible, but a number of threats to external validity have been identified.[18]

## Population Validity

Population validity refers to generalizations from an accessible population to a population of ultimate interest to the researcher (called the *target* population). The accessible population is immediately available to the researcher, and it is from that group that $E$ randomly draws a sample. For example, $E$ may be interested in the behavior of all third graders but has to be satisfied with studying third graders in nearby school districts. Only if $Ss$ in the local districts are similar to $Ss$ nationally can $E$ generalize results to the more extensive group. Since this similarity is unlikely, $E$ would be better off explicitly defining the accessible population and drawing a random sample of $Ss$ from this more restricted group. If $Ss$ are not drawn randomly from any specified population, generalization to that population or to any other population will be hazardous.

## Selection by Treatment Interaction

Sometimes generalization is thwarted because results hold only for a given sample of $Ss$. For example, if all $Ss$ are volunteers this presents no particular threat to internal validity, but it could affect the ability to generalize to nonvolunteers.

## Maturation by Treatment Interaction

The effects of some treatments depend upon the maturational level of $Ss$. A treatment effective with older children may have no effect or a completely different effect on younger $Ss$. $E$ may want to include $Ss$ of different ages in a study to determine if experimental results can be generalized over a number of age or grade levels. Similarly, there has been a concerted effort in recent years to study *aptitude by treatment interactions* related to teaching.[19] $Ss$ with high aptitudes might well benefit from a different approach to teaching than would $Ss$ of more limited academic background.

[18]See Cronbach, pp. 116–127. Also, Campbell and Stanley, "Experimental and Quasi-Experimental Designs"; Glenn H. Bracht, "Experimental Factors Related to Aptitude–Treatment Interactions," *Review of Educational Research*, 40, no. 5 (December 1970), pp. 627–645; and Glenn H. Bracht and Gene V Glass, "The External Validity of Experiments," *American Educational Research Association Journal*, 5, no. 4 (November 1968), pp. 437–474.

[19]Richard E. Snow, "Representative and Quasi-Representative Designs for Research on Teaching," *Review of Educational Research*, 44, no. 3 (Summer 1974), pp. 265–291.

## Reactive Arrangements

Reactive arrangements refer to situations in which Ss realize they are part of an experiment. They may be more cooperative than other Ss and behave in other, nontypical ways. The use of nonreactive (unobtrusive) measures would eliminate this threat to external validity.[20]

The so-called Hawthorne effect[21] is an example of a reactive arrangement. The effect was so named because it was noted in an experiment carried out at the Hawthorne plant of Western Electric Corporation. The investigators wished to study the effect on production of varying physical conditions among a small group of women given the task of wiring relays. They found that production increased each time working conditions were improved. They then began to systematically eliminate each improvement. Contrary to their expectations, production continued to increase. After they interviewed the workers, it became clear what had happened. The women enjoyed the prestige of being set apart from their fellow workers so much that, to remain in the experiment, they worked harder regardless of the nature of the treatment afforded them. This threat to external validity could be reduced by de-emphasizing the fact that Ss were participating in a research study. Experimental attempts to deliberately produce the Hawthorne effect have been conducted by Cook[22] who concluded that the effect is not nearly as pervasive as originally believed. Nonetheless, it is a *threat* to external validity and should be guarded against.

## Describing the Independent Variable Explicitly

Unless experimental treatments and settings are described explicitly by the researcher, it may not be possible to determine which aspects of treatments or settings are producing differences and to determine if findings will generalize to other settings.

Consider studies designed to compare open vs. traditional classrooms. If "open" and "traditional" are not described in detail, it may be extremely difficult to determine which aspects of the experimental method produced differences—aspects such as the nature of the curriculum, textbooks, audio-visual materials, organization of instructional units, homework, teacher interest, parent acceptance, number of students in a room, and the

[20]Eugene Webb et al., *Unobtrusive Measures: Nonreactive Research in the Social Sciences* (Chicago: Rand McNally & Co., 1966), 225 pp.

[21]F. J. Roethlisberger and William J. Dickson, *Management and the Worker* (Cambridge, Mass.: Harvard University Press, 1939).

[22]Desmond L. Cook, *The Impact of the Hawthorne Effect in Experimental Designs in Educational Research*, Cooperative Research Project No. 1757, U.S. Office of Education, June 1967, 160 pp.

like. Simply to report that Ss exposed to one method performed better than Ss exposed to another method does not help determine what those methods were or to what conditions they apply.

## Multiple Treatment Interference

This threat to external validity occurs if Ss are exposed to two or more consecutive treatments or experiments. Generalization would be limited to Ss who have had prior experimental experience. Previous experience as an experimental subject could enhance or reduce that person's effectiveness in subsequent studies. Ss who have been deceived in one study, for example, might not be willing to participate in subsequent studies. The repeated use of Ss attending experimental schools could be another example of multiple treatment interference.

## Novelty and Disruption Effects

Innovations in methods, materials, or settings can affect student behavior. For example, students may become fascinated if they are provided with their own typewriter for learning how to read and spell, or Ss could become intrigued with arithmetic if they were given access to a computer terminal. Experimental groups might initially perform at a higher level than control Ss on posttests as a result of some unique or novel treatment. If the experiment were carried out long enough, these unique effects might well dissipate.

Disruption effects can also occur. Teachers or students who are familiar with one treatment may balk when a new treatment is forced on them. These effects may be reduced by allowing sufficient time for novelty and disruption to become ineffective.

## Experimenter Effects

As a threat to external validity, experimenter effects refer to both deliberate and involuntary behaviors or characteristics of experimenters that restrict generalizations to Ss influenced by them. Some Es may help Ss relax, and others may not; some might inadvertently suggest or reinforce desired behaviors; some voices may be annoyingly harsh or too soft; and Ss may attend to such traits as the experimenter's age, sex, clothing, accent, ethnic background, and the like. E may also inadvertently disregard relevant behaviors of Ss that fail to substantiate personal beliefs.

As a minimum, researchers should report the methods used to standardize instructions and presentation of experimental stimuli to Ss. Double blind experiments can be run where neither Ss nor Es are aware of the purpose of the experiment or which persons constitute experimental and control groups.

## Pretest Sensitization

Sometimes pretests are administered in research to measure pre–post gains or (unnecessarily) to check on the adequacy of randomization. If a pretest is used, it may be that experimental findings might then apply only to *Ss* who have been similarly pretested.

Welch and Walberg[23] have summarized the result of ten studies conducted between 1949 and 1967 in which a pretest was used. Four studies showed that pretest had no effect; three showed that the pretest interfered with the experimental treatment; and three showed a positive increase as a result of the pretest. In the positive group, the pre–post delay ranged from one hour to twelve days. Generally, pretest effects were more likely to occur if attitudes or opinions were the criteria rather than cognitive factors. In the study conducted by Welch and Walberg using 2000 *Ss* and 57 physics teachers throughout the United States, the authors found that treatment effects differed significantly ($p < 0.05$) but that the pretest had no significant effect. Evidently, a relatively long pre–post delay (six months or longer) using cognitive pretests is unlikely to make much of a difference. Over shorter periods of time and with affective measures, the pretest might well affect external validity.

## Posttest Sensitization

Because tests are capable of providing instruction, *Ss* may learn concepts on a posttest that they might not have acquired during the experimental sessions. If so, *E* could generalize findings only to posttested groups. The same effect could occur on attitude measures if the posttest helps *Ss* to strengthen or develop their beliefs.

## Interaction of History and Treatment

History can be a threat to internal validity because *E* is not in a position to judge whether the experimental treatment or some historical and extraneous event produced changes in the dependent variable. For external validity, generalization is restricted to a particular occasion or period of time, such as a study of attitudes toward government conducted during the Watergate trials. Conceivably, the attitude might have been different if the questions

[23]Wayne W. Welch and Herbert J. Walberg, "Pretest and Sensitization Effects in Curriculum Evaluation," *American Educational Research Journal*, 7, no. 4 (November 1970), pp. 605–614.

were asked at another time. Similarly, one can question attitude studies toward labor if they were conducted during a strike.

## Measurement of the Dependent Variable

Dependent variables can take many different forms. They may consist of observations, pencil-and-paper tests, unobtrusive measures, anecdotes, and the like. Although tests constitute the most frequently used dependent variable, these can be standardized or locally constructed, be in multiple-choice, essay, or true–false format, be easy or difficult, be long or short, etc. Results obtained from one type of test may or may not be found if a different dependent variable is used. Researchers might do well to include more than one reliable and valid dependent variable in a study to investigate their differential effects.

## Interaction of Treatment with Time

Most *Es* administer the dependent variable as soon after the last experimental treatment as possible. But in some studies, retention checks measured at different time intervals could yield quite different findings. For example, Fig. 6-2 shows the different levels of performance of two treatments, *A* and *B*, at 4 different time periods. If performance is measured at times 1

**Figure 6-2**
SHOWING THE RELATIVE EFFECTIVENESS OF TWO TREATMENTS, *A* AND *B*, AT 4 DIFFERENT TIME PERIODS.

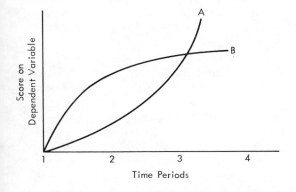

and 3, *E* will conclude that treatments *A* and *B* are equal in their effects. But if tested at time 2, treatment *B* will be superior to *A*; and at time 4, *A* will be superior to *B*. One way to measure these differences is to plan on testing *Ss* at different times.

## SUMMARY

**1.** Four types of variables in experimentation were discussed.

**a.** The *independent variable* is manipulated by $E$ and constitutes the experimental treatment.

**b.** The *dependent variable* is a subject response variable.

**c.** *Organismic variables* are subject classifications (sex, IQ, etc.) that may be studied by $E$ but are not manipulated by $E$.

**d.** *Extraneous variables* correlate with and could affect the dependent variable. Experimental designs are intended to control these extraneous variables and to permit $E$ to observe the relationship between independent and dependent variables.

**2.** Criteria for evaluating experimental designs include the following:

**a.** *Randomization* as a means of reducing systematic error. Any systematic (nonrandom) differences between groups (other than the experimental treatment, of course) should be eliminated by randomization.

**b.** *Sensitivity*, or the precision of an experiment to detect differences between groups, can be increased four ways.

1) Reducing the variability of subjects by decreasing random or chance factors. This can be accomplished by using reliable dependent measures and by treating subjects in a consistent manner.

2) Increasing $N$ is a very effective way to increase sensitivity.

3) Some experimental designs are more sensitive to treatment effects than are others.

4) Treatments should be given every opportunity to make a difference. This can be done by extending the amount of time that subjects are permitted to be in contact with experimental treatments, and if possible, to increase the "strength" or amount of treatment.

**3.** The *internal validity* of an experiment refers to the extent to which there is a clear and unambiguous relationship between independent and dependent variables. A number of threats to internal validity have been identified.

**a.** *Selection.* Unless groups are initially selected so that their comparability can be assured, differences between them might be attributable to these initial differences and not to the effects of the experimental treatment.

**b.** *History.* Any extraneous event occurring throughout the duration of the experiment that is permitted to affect one group but not another could affect the dependent variable.

**c.** *Maturation.* Internal and irrelevant changes within subjects may affect the dependent variable.

**d.** *Testing.* If pretests are used in an experiment, this might affect posttest measures.

**e.** *Instrumentation.* Changes in scoring standards or changes among the raters themselves can affect the dependent variable.

**f.** *Statistical regression.* Whenever $Ss$ are selected who are highly atypical on a trait, a repeated test is likely to increase (if $Ss$ originally were low) or decrease scores (if $Ss$ were initially high on that trait).

**g.** *Experimental mortality.* The failure of all $Ss$ to complete the experiment could affect dependent measures.

**4.** A number of procedures were described to equate experimental and control groups.

**a.** *Randomization.* If $Ss$ are assigned to treatment and control conditions on a purely random basis, this is the best assurance that all extraneous variables have been controlled. Randomization can be accomplished by using a table of random numbers, a coin, die, or any other procedure that permits chance to operate in an unbiased manner.

**b.** *Analysis of covariance (ANCOVA).* The ANCOVA statistically "adjusts" the means of the dependent measures to account for any initial differences among groups. Differences among groups even following randomization can be eliminated if there is a relatively high correlation between the variable used for adjustment (called a *covariate*, or *adjusting variable*) and the dependent variable. In addition, ANCOVA reduces the sum of squares within groups making the rejection of $H_0$ more probable. ANCOVA assumes linearity and that the covariate measure is obtained *before* the presentation of the experimental treatment.

**c.** *Repeated measurements.* In repeated measurements designs, $Ss$ act as their own controls. Because the same $Ss$ are involved in each treatment group, equivalence is assured unless there are carryover or transfer effects that cannot be eliminated by counterbalancing. To be effective, the repeated measurements design requires a high and positive correlation between pretest and posttest scores.

**d.** *Matched groups.* Sometimes it is advantageous to equate $Ss$ on some extraneous variable that correlates with the dependent variable and then to assign $Ss$ to treatment and control conditions.

1) The simplest procedure is to rank order $Ss$ on the extraneous variable and then to *randomly* place one of the two highest scoring $Ss$ into the experimental group and the other $Ss$ into the control group.

2) Another procedure is to match $Ss$ who are within one standard error of measurement from one another and then to assign $Ss$ randomly; this procedure, however, may eliminate some $Ss$ for whom a match cannot be found.

**e.** *Changing the experimental unit.* Matching intact groups by trying to equate their means and variances was *not* recommended. Instead, the classroom or school may become the sampling unit. If this is done, classes or schools are assigned randomly; the mean for each classroom or school unit becomes a "score" value. $N$ is, therefore, the number of such units and not the number of $Ss$ in those units.

**5.** *External validity* refers to the extent to which experimental findings can be generalized to other persons, conditions, and settings. Threats to external validity have been identified.

**a.** *Population validity.* This refers to the hazard in attempting to generalize from an accessible population to a population of ultimate interest to $E$.

**b.** *Selection by treatment interaction.* Some treatments apply to one group of $Ss$ (e.g., volunteers) and other treatments to other $Ss$ (non-volunteers).

**c.** *Maturation by treatment interaction.* Some treatments apply to older and some to younger $Ss$.

**d.** *Reactive arrangements.* Whenever $Ss$ realize that they are participating in a study, their behavior may change accordingly, and this limits generalizations to non-naive $Ss$.

**e.** *Describing the independent variable explicitly.* Generalizations may be limited if $E$ has failed to describe experimental conditions explicitly.

**f.** *Multiple treatment interference.* Whenever $Ss$ are repeatedly exposed to multiple treatments, generalizations may be limited to $Ss$ who have been so treated.

**g.** *Novelty and disruption effects.* $Ss$ who are subjected to some innovation might well lose interest over time. Similarly, disruptions may lead to unique responses.

**h.** *Experimenter effects.* This refers to the effect of the experimenter on the behavior of $Ss$.

**i.** *Pretest sensitization.* The administration of a pretest may limit generalization to those $Ss$ who have been pretested.

**j.** *Posttest sensitization.* The posttest itself may restrict generalizations to $Ss$ who have been posttested.

**k.** *Interaction of history and treatment.* This refers to the inability to generalize research findings beyond some specific occasion or period of time.

**l.** *Measurement of the dependent variable.* Dependent variables can be measured in many different ways. Findings may be restricted in generalization to the specific type of format used in a study.

**m.** *Interaction of treatment with time.* Usually, the measurement of the dependent variable occurs immediately following the presentation of the experimental treatment. But delays in measurement could lead to different results.

## PRACTICE EXERCISES

**1.** Indicate which of the following fictitious research titles are amenable to experimental rather than descriptive research:

  **a.** Attitudes of High School Students toward Science Instruction

  **b.** Reasons for Pupil Dropout during High School

  **c.** Factors Leading to Emotional Maladjustment among Lower Socio-economic Groups

  **d.** Some Effects of Eye Examinations among Poor Readers

  **e.** Systematic Differences between Graduates and Dropouts at the High School Level

**2.** For each of the above studies calling for an experimental design, indicate the independent and dependent variable and any extraneous variables.

**3.** Indicate the most likely effect that each of the following procedures would have on the null hypothesis (state the principles involved):

  **a.** Reducing the number of cases in the experimental group as an economy move

  **b.** Adding additional cases to the control group

  **c.** Gaining additional control of variables by using laboratory type studies

  **d.** Using a statistical design appropriate for independent groups when groups are actually equated

  **e.** Using some nonrandom method of assigning $Ss$ to experimental and control groups

  **f.** Sampling $Ss$ in bright and dull groups instead of using all available $Ss$

  **g.** Employing an analysis of covariance design

**4.** For each of the following experimental problems, indicate what kinds of threats to internal validity (selection, history, etc.) are involved:

  **a.** In a repeated measurement design, the attempt is made to study the effects of a film on racial intolerance. At the time the treatment is presented, a race riot breaks out.

  **b.** A teacher of the mentally retarded argues that a method of teaching increased the IQ's of students.

  **c.** An investigator announces that gifted students are all underachievers.

**d.** In a study designed to measure the effects of sex on school achievement, males are placed in one group and females in another. Males and females are matched on IQ scores during kindergarten and will be followed up for four years.

**e.** Before seeing a motion picture favorable to public education, *Ss* are asked to fill out a lengthy questionnaire on attitudes toward education.

**f.** An investigator reports that follow-up records in a given school indicate that between grades 7 and 12 pupils drop considerably in percentile rank in comparison with national norms.

**5.** An investigator has the possibility of using either a matched group or repeated measurements design. Other conditions being equal, which would you recommend? Why?

**6.** What potential threats to external validity may be involved in each of the following examples?

**a.** Most experiments on the effects of under- and overachievement have not agreed on the meaning of those terms. As a result, findings have been inconclusive.

**b.** Many studies on methods of increasing student reading comprehension seem to yield conflicting results.

**c.** This threat may be realized if retention checks are allowed to vary widely from study to study.

**d.** A pretest uses a word that reminds *Ss* of the discussion in the text.

**e.** A posttest uses a word that reminds *Ss* of the discussion in the text.

**f.** A researcher continues to use the same group of *Ss* for a series of studies.

**g.** Boys are affected in one way and girls in a different way by a particular study.

**7.** Describe some ways that might reduce each of the threats to internal and external validity in the examples above.

## Selected Supplementary Readings

1. Perhaps the best single source of information regarding experimental design is Campbell, Donald T., and Stanley, Julian C. "Experimental and Quasi-Experimental Designs for Research on Teaching." Chapter 5 in N. L. Gage, ed., *Handbook of Research on Teaching*. Chicago: Rand McNally & Co., 1963, pp. 171–246.

2. On the relationship between various experimental designs and sensitivity, see Ray, William S. *An Introduction to Experimental Design*. New York: The Macmillan Co., 1960, pp. 235–242; and Keppel, Geoffrey. *Design and*

*Analysis: A Researcher's Handbook.* Englewood Cliffs, N.J.: Prentice-Hall, 1973, pp. 521–546.

3. On specific types of experimental designs, see Edwards, Allen L. *Experimental Design in Psychological Research*, 4th ed. New York: Holt, Rinehart and Winston, 1972, 488 pp.; Lindquist, E. F. *Design and Analysis of Experiments in Psychology and Education.* Boston: Houghton Mifflin Co., 1953, 393 pp.; Winer, B. J. *Statistical Principles in Experimental Design*, 2d ed. New York: McGraw-Hill Book Co., 1971, 907 pp.

4. For the analysis of specific types of experimental designs, see Overall, John E., and Woodward, J. Arthur. "Unreliability of Difference Scores: A Paradox for Measurement of Change." *Psychological Bulletin*, 82, no. 1 (January 1975), pp. 85–86; Huck, Schuyler W., and McLean, Robert A. "Using a Repeated Measures ANOVA to Analyze the Data from a Pretest-Posttest Design: A Potentially Confusing Task." *Psychological Bulletin*, 82, no. 4 (July 1975), pp. 511–518; Poor, David D. S. "Analysis of Variance for Repeated Measures Designs: Two Approaches." *Psychological Bulletin*, 80, no. 3 (September 1973), pp. 204–209; Wagenaar, W. A. "Note on the Construction of Digram-Balanced Latin Squares." *Psychological Bulletin*, 72, no. 6 (December 1969), pp. 384–386; Lord, Frederic M. "Statistical Adjustments when Comparing Preexisting Groups." *Psychological Bulletin*, 72, no. 5 (November 1969), pp. 336–337; Elashoff, Janet D. "Analysis of Covariance: A Delicate Instrument." *American Educational Research Journal*, 6, no. 3 (May 1969), pp. 383–401. See also Glass, Gene V, Peckham, Percy D., and Sanders, James R. "Consequences of Failure to Meet Assumptions Underlying the Analysis of Variance and Covariance." *Review of Educational Research*, 42, no. 3 (Summer 1972), pp. 237–288; Greenwald, Anthony G. "Within-Subjects Designs: To Use or Not To Use." *Psychological Bulletin*, 83, no. 2 (March 1976), pp. 314–320.

5. See the following sources for various aspects of external validity: Bracht, Glenn H., and Glass, Gene V. "The External Validity of Experiments." *American Educational Research Association Journal*, 5, no. 4 (November 1968), pp. 437–474; Cronbach, Lee J. "Beyond the Two Disciplines of Scientific Psychology." *American Psychologist*, 30, no. 2 (February 1975), pp. 116–127; Bracht, Glenn H. "Experimental Factors Related to Aptitude–Treatment Interactions." *Review of Educational Research*, 40, no. 5 (December 1970), pp. 627–645; Snow, Richard E. "Representative and Quasi-Representative Designs for Research on Teaching." *Review of Educational Research*, 44, no. 3 (Summer 1974), pp. 265–291; Campbell, Donald T. "Reforms as Experiments." *American Psychologist*, 24, no. 4 (April 1969), pp. 409–429; Rosenthal, Robert. *Experimenter Effects in Behavioral Research.* New York: Appleton-Century-Crofts, 1966, 464 pp.; Oakes, William. "External Validity and the Use of Real People as Subjects." *American Psychologist*, 27, no. 10 (October 1972), pp. 959–962.

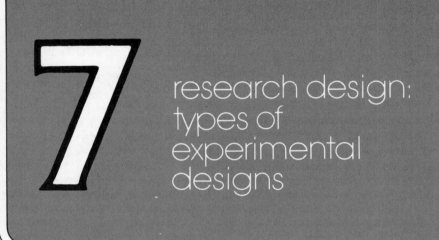

# 7

## research design: types of experimental designs

This chapter, which describes types of experimental designs, follows the graphic procedures used by Campbell and Stanley.[1] Thus, an $O$ will represent an observation or measurement, and an $X$ will represent the introduction of an experimental treatment. The progression of events is from left to right.

### Experiments Involving a Single Group

Single-group experiments do not involve a separate control or comparison group. These designs are classified by Campbell and Stanley as either "pre-experimental designs" or "quasi-experimental designs."

[1] Donald T. Campbell and Julian C. Stanley, "Experimental and Quasi-Experimental Designs for Research on Teaching," in N. L. Gage, ed., *Handbook of Research on Teaching* (Chicago: Rand McNally & Co., 1963), pp. 171–246.

*The One-Shot Case Study.* The one-shot case study may be diagrammed as follows:

$$X \quad O$$

A single group or person is exposed to some experimental treatment. Following this exposure, a measurement is obtained or an observation made on the dependent variable. No measurements are taken prior to the introduction of the experimental treatment.

The one-shot case study is so named because it is often used in case studies. It might also be appropriately called a "single-group after-only experiment" to point out that observations are made after the introduction of the experimental variable. The design is inefficient because it does not allow for either control of extraneous variables or of comparison of changes.

Suppose that $E$ is interested in studying the effects of coffee on $Ss$' ability to cross out $o$'s on a printed page. Suppose that the average number of $o$'s correctly crossed out was 18. What can $E$ conclude? Nothing, unless $E$ has some knowledge of how $Ss$ performed *before* they were given coffee.

To take another example, suppose that a group of teachers decides to evaluate a new method of teaching spelling. Each teacher tries the new method $(X)$; they then get together and compare notes. These comparisons are combined to form a single evaluation $(O)$. Still lacking, of course, is some measurement of the proficiency of $Ss$ before the introduction of $X$. In fact, there is no way of determining whether $Ss$ would have been better off with no spelling method than with the method under investigation.

*The One-Group Pretest–Posttest Design.* This is one form of repeated measurements design (see pages 135-136). This design can be diagrammed as follows:

$$O_1 \quad X \quad O_2$$

Consider an experiment on the effectiveness of aspirin to relieve headaches. $O_1$ could then be the initial observation that $S$ has a headache, $X$ could be the administration of some predetermined dosage of aspirin, and $O_2$ could be a report from $S$ on the progress of the headache.

Suppose that $S$ states that the headache is relieved after exposure to $X$. Can $E$ be sure that $X$ was responsible for differences between $O_1$ and $O_2$? If $O_2$ was obtained a number of hours after exposure to $X$, $E$ could not determine if $X$ relieved the headache or if it wore off by itself. Other events besides $X$, such as rest or relaxation, may have intervened to produce $O_2$. Thus, both history and maturation are left uncontrolled. Assume, however, that $O_1$, $X$, and $O_2$ all take place within a ten-minute period. If $Ss$ report a headache at $O_1$, they are not likely to change their minds by $O_2$. In other words, the very fact that *Ss* were questioned at $O_1$ could influence how they responded at $O_2$. Therefore, testing is also left uncontrolled.

Finally, there still remains the problem of instrumentation. Since there are two measurements for each *S*, there may be systematic differences in how *Ss* respond to $O_1$ and $O_2$ that reflect differences in what is considered to be a headache. Criteria may change independently of *X*, for example, so that even a very minor pain could be interpreted as excruciating at one time and be disregarded at another.

*The Time-Series Experiment.* The time-series experiment is a type of longitudinal research where *Ss* undergo repeated measurements both before and after the introduction of the experimental variable. It can be diagrammed in the following way:

$$O_1 \quad O_2 \quad O_3 \quad O_4 \quad X \quad O_5 \quad O_6 \quad O_7 \quad O_8$$

In other words, there are four observation periods (the actual number may vary considerably) preceding and following *X*. *E* hypothesizes that *X* is responsible for the difference between those observations that precede and those that follow *X*.

As an example of how the time-series experiment might be employed, suppose that *E* hypothesizes that the introduction of some curricular innovation will affect low achieving *Ss*. Test scores for one group of *Ss* are obtained 3 or 4 times prior to and again after the introduction of the innovation.

Although the time-series design is particularly simple to execute, the analysis and interpretation of the data are complex. Suppose that the test scores did increase following the presentation of *X*. Is *E* justified in concluding that these scores increased *because* of the innovation? The answer is affirmative *if E* is certain that the effects of history are absent; *E* must make sure no other events could account for increases in test scores. If other events intervened between $O_4$ and $O_5$ besides those produced by *X*, the effects of *X* alone cannot be evaluated.

Other than history, the only threat to the validity of the design is instrumentation. Bias is especially likely if the test scores fluctuate because of unreliability (i.e., lack of stability). In that case, it would be easy to mistake a gain or decrease in test scores for the effect of *X*. Evidence that the test scores are stable over time when *X* is not presented could help to eliminate this threat.

Campbell and Stanley have described some possible results of a time-series design (p. 154). Some of these outcomes have been reproduced in Figure 7-1. Conditions *A* and *B* show stable trend lines before and after the introduction of the experimental treatment except for the increase in performance between observation periods 4 and 5. That *X* has some effect is most

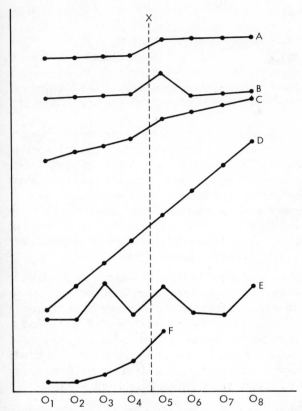

X

A

B
C

D

E

F

$O_1$  $O_2$  $O_3$  $O_4$  $O_5$  $O_6$  $O_7$  $O_8$

*Source:* Donald T. Campbell and Julian Stanley, "Experimental and Quasi-Experimental Designs for Research on Teaching," Chapter 5 in N. L. Gage, ed., *Handbook of Research on Teaching* (Chicago: Rand McNally & Co., 1963), p. 208, Fig. 3. Used with permission.

**Figure 7-1**
SOME POSSIBLE EFFECTS OF A TIME SERIES EXPERIMENT
(THE $O_4$ AND $O_5$ GAINS ARE EQUAL UNDER CONDITIONS *A* TO *F*).

plausible under conditions *A* and *B*. Condition *C* is less clear, however, since *Ss* were steadily improving from $O_1$ to $O_4$ and improved to the same extent from $O_5$ to $O_8$. Still, there is a greater gain from $O_4$ to $O_5$ in condition *C* than occurred before or after the introduction of *X*. In conditions *D*, *E*, and *F*, there is no basis for inferring a treatment effect.

*The Equivalent Time-Sampling Design.* One way to control history in some designs is to randomly vary the presentation of *X* so that at times it is present ($X_1$) and at times it is absent ($X_0$). The equivalent time-sampling design may be diagrammed as follows:

$$X_1O \quad X_0O \quad X_0O \quad X_1O \quad X_0O \quad X_1O \quad X_1O \quad X_0O$$

An alternative possibility is to compare $X_1$ and $X_2$. In this way, $E$ can compare the relative effects of two experimental treatments rather than of one treatment and a control. Additional treatments and control groups can also be introduced.

The equivalent time-sampling design eliminates the effects of history because $X$ is presented more than once, but it does introduce a few other problems. First, since $Ss$ are being constantly tested and retested, results may be generalized only to other groups examined in a similar manner. Second, if $X_1$ and $X_2$ are repeated over and over again, multiple-$X$ interference will also restrict generalizations to other conditions where $X_1$ may carry over to $X_2$. This means that $E$ has no way to generalize findings obtained in an equivalent time-sampling design to conditions where $X$ is constantly present or where there is a single presentation of $X$.

*The Equivalent Material Design.* In single-group repeated measurements designs, the introduction of $X$ may carry over from one occasion to another. In learning experiments, for example, the task may be to memorize passages of prose under different conditions of practice. If $S$ memorizes a given passage for $X_1$, the same passage cannot be used again for $X_2$ because of transfer effects. Under these conditions, $E$ has to prepare equivalent materials (passages) for each experimental treatment. Letting $M$ represent these materials, the equivalent material design can be depicted in the following way:

$$M_aX_1O \quad M_bX_0O \quad M_cX_0O \quad M_dX_1O \quad M_eX_0O \quad \text{etc.}$$

This design is exactly the same as the equivalent time-sampling design except that different materials are introduced throughout the course of the experiment. Assuming that these materials are equivalent, experimental controls would seem to be adequate. However, many of the problems concerning generalization of experimental findings in the equivalent time-sampling design also occur with the equivalent material design.

## Experiments Involving Separate Control Groups

As stated earlier, experiments require at least one comparison. The comparison may be between two or more experimental treatments or between groups exposed to $X$ and groups not exposed.

*The Static-Group Comparison.* Campbell and Stanley have classified the static-group comparison design as "pre-experimental" to differentiate it from "true experimental" designs. When applied to the static-group comparison (or to the one-shot case study and the one-group pretest–posttest design discussed in the preceding section), the term "pre-experimental" is unusually descriptive because this type of design leaves many factors uncontrolled.

Campbell and Stanley let dashes between rows mean that groups have not been equated. The static-group comparison may, thus, be diagrammed as follows:

$$X \quad O_1$$
$$\overline{\phantom{XO_1}}$$
$$O_2$$

The difficulty with the static-group comparison design is that $E$ has no way of knowing if the groups were equivalent before the introduction of $X$. Thus, selection is left uncontrolled, and differences between $O_1$ and $O_2$ could be due to initial differences between $Ss$ in experimental and control groups.

Much of so-called action research involves a static-group comparison design. For example, teachers may be concerned about their effectiveness in teaching moral values. They devise a series of lessons to give to their classes. To avoid some of the difficulties involved in designs of the $X\ O$ and $O\ X\ O$ types, they may ask other teachers in their school for permission to use their classes as controls. After the experimental group has been exposed to $X$, it is tested, as are the control groups. Suppose that the experimental group obtains a significantly higher score than the control groups. Nothing can be concluded because $E$ had no knowledge of how the groups differed *before* $X$ was introduced. It is possible that $O_1$ might have been higher than $O_2$ even if $X$ had not been present.

A second difficulty with the static-group comparison design is mortality. This could occur if the $O_1$ measurements were carried out on fewer (or different) $Ss$ than were in the original group that received $X$. $Ss$ in the experimental group may have transferred to other classes, and others may have replaced them after $X$ was introduced. Of course, there could be no experimental mortality if groups remained unchanged throughout the entire experiment.

*The Pretest–Posttest Control Group Design with Randomization.* This is the first of what Campbell and Stanley call a "true experimental" design because major controls are provided for internal validity and for at least some sources of external validity.

This design can be diagrammed in the following way:

$$R \quad O_1 \quad X \quad O_2$$
$$R \quad O_3 \qquad O_4$$

Selection is eliminated because $Ss$ have been assigned at random ($R$) to experimental and control groups. Instrumentation can also be controlled by having the same observers participate with both groups. To avoid any bias on their part, observers should not be told which group is the experimental and which is the control. Because there is a control group comprised of the same type of $Ss$ as are in the experimental group, regression can be ruled out as an explanation of $O_2 \ldots O_4$ differences. The effects of history can be disregarded because anything that affects the $O_1 \ldots O_2$ difference is also likely to affect differences between $O_3$ and $O_4$, assuming, of course, that experimental and control groups are tested together and at the same time. If they are tested at two different times or by two or more different persons, differences between $O_2$ and $O_4$ will not necessarily be due to $X$. The effects of experimental mortality can also be checked by examining the pretest scores of those who failed to show up for the posttest comparison.

There are, however, some difficulties in generalizing with this design. First, because both groups were pretested, $E$ has no way of knowing whether or not the same findings would hold for additional groups not initially tested. The concern is not with testing as a possible threat to internal validity since it is effectively controlled by having both groups pretested. The problem is that of generalization to other groups that have not been pretested.

As an example of how this design may be employed, consider the case of an investigator interested in studying the effects of drug $X$ on IQ. $Ss$ are randomly assigned to two groups. All $Ss$ are tested together by $E$ with an intelligence test. Without being informed whether they are in the experimental group or the control group, all $Ss$ are given injections that appear to be identical. They differ, however, because $Ss$ in the experimental group actually are given drug $X$ while those in the control group receive sterile water. All $Ss$ are then retested with an alternate form of the pretest.

The analysis of data for this design can be accomplished in a number of ways. The analysis of covariance can effectively take advantage of the pretest as a covariate. Another possibility is to compute a $t$-test or $F$ ratio between the two gain scores. Thus, $E$ could compute the mean $O_1 - O_2$ difference (symbolized as $M_{D1}$) and the $O_4 - O_3$ mean difference ($M_{D2}$). It is necessary then to determine if the $M_{D1}$ and $M_{D2}$ differ statistically. It is not sufficient merely to report that the $O_2 - O_1$ difference was significant but that the $O_4 - O_3$ difference was not since experimental and control groups were not directly compared with one another. It is also inefficient to compute only the posttests since the pretests would then be superfluous. One could run a $t$-test between $M_{D1}$ and $M_{D2}$.

*The Solomon Four-Group Design.* In an effort to eliminate some of the difficulties in generalizing with the pretest–posttest control group design with randomization, Solomon[2] proposed using four groups. His design can be diagrammed in the following way:

$$R \quad O_1 \quad X \quad O_2$$
$$R \quad O_3 \qquad \quad O_4$$
$$R \qquad \quad \; X \quad O_5$$
$$R \qquad \qquad \quad O_6$$

Note that the first two groups are formed in exactly the same way as in the pretest–posttest control group design. Because the last two groups receive no pretest and because all groups are initially equivalent through randomization, $E$ can determine the effects of pretest $O_1$ and $O_3$. A comparison of $O_2$ and $O_5$ provides evidence as to the effectiveness of $X$ with and without a pretest; a comparison of $O_4$ and $O_6$ provides evidence on the effect of the pretest without the presence of $X$.

Because most of the major variables are controlled with the Solomon four-group design, Campbell and Stanley consider it to be a true experimental design also.

*The Posttest-Only Control Group Design.* In this design, only the last two groups in the Solomon four-group design are employed, providing an experimental and a control group, but no pretesting. $E$ simply randomizes $Ss$ into two groups, introduces $X$ to one group and denies it to the other, and then tests both groups. The design can be summarized as follows:

$$R \quad X \quad O_1$$
$$R \qquad \quad O_2$$

This design is the third and last of the true experimental designs. All conditions in the preceding design are also controlled here. The difference is that $E$ has no measurement of the effects of the pretest in this design, although the effects of testing are controlled by eliminating the pretest from both groups. If $E$ does not need a pretest, this design may save much time and effort.

*The Nonequivalent Control Group Design.* This quasi-experimental design makes use of intact groups or classrooms which are formed on the basis of some natural grouping. Thus, experimental and control groups are not formed by randomly assigning $Ss$ although they could be matched. This

[2]Richard L. Solomon, "An Extension of Control Group Design," *Psychological Bulletin*, 46, no. 2 (1949).

design can be diagrammed in the following way:

$$\begin{array}{ccc} O_1 & X & O_2 \\ \hline O_3 & & O_4 \end{array}$$

There are two other designs which may be confused with this one: the one-group pretest–posttest design and the pretest–posttest control group design with randomization. The addition of a control group is the major advantage of the nonequivalent control group design over the one-group pretest–posttest design, but the failure to randomize $Ss$ is a distinct disadvantage. Nonetheless, there may be times when randomization is not possible, and $E$ may have to use existing groups. Even if $E$ decides to match experimental and control $Ss$, however, the pretest–posttest control group design with randomization is still to be preferred. Matching can only equate groups on a few variables, but randomization can assure $E$ that there are no systematic biases in groups containing randomly assigned $Ss$, and in cases where $Ss$ are already matched (twins, for example), it can determine which $S$ is to receive $X$ and which is not, thus eliminating systematic differences between groups.

Certainly, a minimum requirement for the nonequivalent control group design is that pretest scores for the experimental and control groups should be as similar as possible. It is especially important that the initial assignment to an intact class should not reflect systematic biases. It is one thing if students enter one of two classrooms without having any idea of the relative advantages or disadvantages that might occur by selecting one over the other; it is quite another matter if $Ss$ volunteer for one classroom because they either want to be exposed to $X$ or want to avoid exposure to $X$. Still, even if the initial mean scores do vary, the presence of a control group does aid interpretation.

*Separate-Sample Prestest–Posttest Design.* At times, $E$ may have to work with large but separate samples of groups of $Ss$ who can be considered equivalent, although subgroups may not be drawn randomly from any specified population. Samples may or may not be selected at the same time. Nonetheless, $E$ still maintains control over which $Ss$ will be measured and when $Ss$ will be observed. This design may be diagrammed as follows, where the top line is the control condition and the bottom line represents the experimental condition:

$$RO \quad (X)$$
$$R \quad X \quad O$$

As an example of the separate-sample pretest–posttest design, one can examine the design used to investigate the effects of a publicity campaign concerning the United Nations and UNESCO.[3] In this investigation, two equivalent samples of *Ss* were selected. The control group was interviewed before the publicity campaign was begun and the experimental group afterwards. The *X* is placed in parentheses because the control group was subjected to the effects of an irrelevant treatment. The difference between the two observations provides the basis for the experimental comparison.

There are a number of difficulties with this design. In the first place, history is uncontrolled because events other than the publicity campaign could account for differences between groups. Instrumentation may also have its effects, especially if interviewers are used to obtain data. If the same interviewers are employed twice, their skill in obtaining information will differ on the two occasions. If different interviewers are employed, there is no way of telling if differences between *O*'s reflect *X* or differences in the characteristics of the interviewers. One possible way to reduce the confounding effects of instrumentation is to randomly select half of the interviewers for the pre-experimental observation and use the remaining half for the posttest. If *Ss* are selected at the same time, mortality may be another problem.

The major advantages of this design lie in its ability to generalize research findings. We need not be concerned about pretest scores affecting posttest scores because two equivalent groups are used and only one is subjected to the pretest. The design also allows *E* to investigate groups in their natural surroundings, because there is only one observation required for each of the two groups.

In many of the designs we have considered so far, it is possible to add additional experimental or control groups to control for different types of effects. In the time-series experiment, for example, a control group can be added which is not subjected to *X*, the experimental variable. Similarly, it is possible to add a control group to the separate-sample pretest–posttest design. This could be diagrammed in the following way:

$$RO(X)$$

$$R \quad X \quad O$$
-----------
$$RO$$

$$R \qquad O$$

This allows *E* to make a comparison between groups receiving *X* and those not exposed to *X*. The reader should remember that only a few

[3]Shirley A. Star and Helen M. Hughes, "Report on an Educational Campaign: The Cincinnati Plan for the United Nations," *American Journal of Sociology*, 55, no. 4 (1950), pp. 389–400.

basic types of experimental designs have been presented here and that they can be modified as conditions change or as additional controls are needed.

## COUNTERBALANCING TECHNIQUES AND DESIGNS

In the counterbalanced design (variously called rotation experiments, crossover designs, or switchover designs),[4] each $S$ or group of $Ss$ is entered into all experimental treatments.

As an example of counterbalanced design, assume $Ss$ are required to memorize lists of words under two conditions, $A$ and $B$. Because there are repeated measurements involved in this study, $E$ realizes that learning $A$ and then $B$ might provide unfair practice effects for condition $B$. To counterbalance or control for any possible effects that the sequence $A$ to $B$ or $B$ to $A$ might have, $E$ might have $Ss$ learn one list under condition $A$, learn a second list under condition $B$, learn a third list under condition $B$, and then learn a fourth list under condition $A$. Because $A$ preceded $B$ on half of the occasions $(AB)$ and $B$ preceded $A$ on the other half $(BA)$, this method is called the $ABBA$ method of counterbalancing. The assumption is made that the effect of going from $A$ to $B$ represents the same amount of practice as that going from $B$ to $A$.

To see how the $ABBA$ method works, suppose that $Ss$ gain one unit of practice as they go either from $A$ to $B$ or from $B$ to $A$.[5]

The sequence $ABBA$ means that there would be no practice effect under the first presentation of $A$ because this would be the first exposure of $Ss$ to this condition. $E$ would then administer test or condition $B$, then $B$ again, and finally $A$. If each condition yields 1 unit of practice, the $ABBA$ sequence would yield 0, 1, 2, and 3 practice units, respectively. If the two $A$ conditions are combined, the cumulative practice effects for that condition would be $0 + 3 = 3$; the combined $B$ conditions would be $1 + 2 = 3$.

Thus, practice effects are effectively counterbalanced. Suppose, however, that practice effects are not equal, but that the initial sequence $(AB)$ yields 3 units gain while all subsequent conditions increase practice effects by only 1 unit. In this instance, counterbalancing would not be achieved by the $ABBA$ method since the $AB$ gain is greater than the $BB$ or $BA$ gains as shown below:

| Condition | A | B | B | A |
|---|---|---|---|---|
| Practice effect | 0 | 3 | 4 | 5 |

[4]Campbell and Stanley, p. 220.

[5]George H. Zimny, *Method in Experimental Psychology* (New York: Ronald Press Co., 1961), pp. 158–186.

The two $A$ conditions combine for 5 units of practice effect $(0 + 5)$, but the $B$ conditions combine for 7 units $(3 + 4)$. To effectively counter-balance these unequal practice effects, $E$ can combine the $ABBA$ method with the $BAAB$ method. Half of the $Ss$ receive the $ABBA$ sequence and the other half the $BAAB$ method as shown below:

|  | First Group | | | | Second Group | | | |
|---|---|---|---|---|---|---|---|---|
| Condition | $A$ | $B$ | $B$ | $A$ | $B$ | $A$ | $A$ | $B$ |
| Practice effects | 0 | 3 | 4 | 5 | 0 | 3 | 4 | 5 |

Again, it is assumed that the initial experience produces greater practice effects than subsequent ones. For group 1, the $AB$ sequence has 3 units of practice effect; for group 2, the initial gain is also 3 units but this gain occurs in the $BA$ sequence. Adding all values for condition $A$ in the two groups yields a total of 12 units of practice (i.e., $0 + 5 + 3 + 4 = 12$); for $B$, the total is also 12 (i.e., $3 + 4 + 0 + 5 = 12$). Thus, by giving half of the $Ss$ the $ABBA$ sequence and the other half the $BAAB$ sequence, $E$ can effectively counterbalance unequal practice effects. If in doubt, greater control of sequence effects is maintained by combining the $ABBA$ and $BAAB$ methods than by using either alone.

*The Latin Square.* The Latin square (named after an ancient puzzle, whose purpose was to determine the number of different ways Latin letters could be placed in a table so that each letter would appear only once in each row and column)[6] can be used for counterbalancing. In the Latin square below, four experimental treatments ($X_1$, $X_2$, $X_3$, and $X_4$) are assigned to four groups or persons ($A$, $B$, $C$, $D$) at four different times (1, 2, 3, 4).

|  |  | Time Periods | | | |
|---|---|---|---|---|---|
|  |  | 1 | 2 | 3 | 4 |
| Groups | $A$ | $X_1O$ | $X_2O$ | $X_3O$ | $X_4O$ |
|  | $B$ | $X_2O$ | $X_4O$ | $X_1O$ | $X_3O$ |
|  | $C$ | $X_3O$ | $X_1O$ | $X_4O$ | $X_2O$ |
|  | $D$ | $X_4O$ | $X_3O$ | $X_2O$ | $X_1O$ |

Note that three elements enter into the table: time periods, groups, and treatments. The Latin square contains the same number of groups as time periods; within each row and within each column, no treatment appears

[6]E. F. Lindquist, *Design and Analysis of Experiments in Psychology and Education* (Boston: Houghton Mifflin Co., 1953), p. 259.

more than once. It should also be clear that for any Latin square there are a number of ways that elements can be arranged and still maintain the general rule that rows and columns contain no element more than once. For reasons to be explained shortly, different Latin squares may be employed using different *Ss*, but whatever squares are used, they should be selected at random. If only a single Latin square is used, Campbell and Stanley consider the design to be quasi-experimental.[7]

There are some limitations to Latin square designs. In the first place, the number of degrees of freedom for the error mean square is $(t-1)(t-2)$, where $t$ is the number of treatments. Consider the extreme case where $t = 2$. With two treatments, there would be a two-by-two Latin square with zero degrees of freedom for the error mean square. Thus, to obtain an estimate of error requires $E$ to use a number of Latin squares, generally the more the better.

Another major difficulty with the Latin square design is that it is necessary to assume that interaction effects are zero. Take, for example, a Latin square where four *Ss* are given four tests on four occasions. The analysis of variance would then contain four sources of variation: treatments, subjects, occasions, and error, if one can assume that the relationship between treatments and orders is zero. In more complex analysis of variance designs (called *factorial* designs), these interaction effects can be separated and evaluated from the main treatment effects. In the Latin square, however, if there are treatments by order interactions, error estimates will be affected in the $F$ ratio,[8] making it difficult to reject the null hypothesis.

For counterbalancing, the Latin square can be quite useful indeed. History is eliminated because each treatment occurs at different times. Similarly, the effects of maturation, testing, instrumentation, etc. are also effectively controlled. If different Latin squares with different *Ss* randomly assigned to each square can be used, generalization can also be greatly facilitated.

*The Graeco-Latin Square.* At times it may be advantageous to have two Latin squares, each containing the same number of rows and columns. Each square contains a single, nonrepetitive entry in each row and column. If these Latin squares are superimposed, one set of squares can be represented by Latin letters and the other set by Greek letters. Such an arrangement is called a Graeco-Latin square. If additional Latin squares are superimposed, this is a *hyper-Graeco-Latin square.*

As an example of a Graeco-Latin square, consider the arrangement in Table 7-1. The purpose of the experiment might be to compare the effects

---

[7]The diagram comes from Campbell and Stanley, p. 222.

[8]Quinn McNemar, "On the Use of Latin Squares in Psychology," *Psychological Bulletin*, 48, no. 5 (1951), p. 400.

## TABLE 7-1

Four-by-Four Graeco-Latin Square

Testing Periods

| | | I | | II | | III | | IV | |
|---|---|---|---|---|---|---|---|---|---|
| | 1 | $D$ | $\alpha$ | $A$ | $\beta$ | $B$ | $\delta$ | $C$ | $\gamma$ |
| Groups | 2 | $A$ | $\delta$ | $D$ | $\gamma$ | $C$ | $\alpha$ | $B$ | $\beta$ |
| | 3 | $B$ | $\gamma$ | $C$ | $\alpha$ | $D$ | $\beta$ | $A$ | $\delta$ |
| | 4 | $C$ | $\beta$ | $B$ | $\delta$ | $A$ | $\gamma$ | $D$ | $\alpha$ |

of teaching spelling by methods $ABCD$ using four tests ($\alpha$, $\beta$, $\gamma$, $\delta$)[9] administered on four separate occasions (I, II, III, IV).

### Factorial Designs

Educational settings are complex and usually do not lend themselves to simple experiments where only one variable at a time can be manipulated and all other conditions can safely be assumed to have a negligible effect. Fortunately, experimental designs are available that allow for simultaneous comparisons of the effects of multiple independent variables. These are called *factorial designs*.

The simplest factorial design is the two-by-two design. In the experiment comparing spelling methods $A$ and $B$, methods $A$ and $B$ form one basis for classification; the other basis might be IQ levels (high versus low), sex (males versus females), or number of pupils per room (large versus small).

To take a simple example, suppose that $E$ wishes to test the hypothesis that there is a significant difference between $Ss$ exposed to some new method of teaching spelling and those serving as controls. However, suppose $E$ has a second hypothesis to test, namely, that there is a significant difference in spelling achievement between $Ss$ in large and small classes. $E$ could run a second experiment to test the effects of class size, but this would be an inefficient procedure. A better way is to construct a two-by-two table such as Table 7-2. Scores within each cell are means.

Assuming that differences are statistically significant, $E$ could say that experimental $Ss$ obtained higher scores than their counterparts in the control group and that those in small classes obtained higher scores than $Ss$ in large classes in both the experimental and control groups.

The analysis of variance for a two-by-two factorial design yields a sum of squares for columns and for rows. The $F$ ratio for columns usually

[9]$\alpha$, $\beta$, $\gamma$, $\delta$ are the Greek letters alpha, beta, gamma, and delta, respectively.

TABLE 7-2

Two-by-Two Factorial Design

|  | Experimental | Control |
|---|---|---|
| Large classes | 25 | 15 |
| Small classes | 30 | 25 |

compares various treatments; similarly, the $F$ ratio for rows would indicate that class size is related to spelling achievement. In addition, $E$ can also determine if there are any interaction effects between rows and columns. This is an extremely important advantage of the factorial design, because it permits $E$ to determine whether the experimental or the control method is more advantageous for large or small classes. A significant interaction could signify that: 1) additional factors were sufficiently important to have included them in the experiment; 2) a Type I error was committed, and the null hypothesis was incorrectly rejected; 3) principles of randomizing groups were violated; or 4) a combination of the variables used for classification was producing effects not attributable to either variable alone.

The testing of main effects and interactions requires the use of $F$ ratios. In factorial designs, the error term (denominator of the $F$ ratio) depends upon the type of *model* used. The *fixed constants model* applies where both bases for classification (class size and method) were predetermined and not selected at random.

The *random model* is appropriate where both bases for classification are obtained by sampling procedures. The particular variables under investigation are important only to the extent that they represent some predefined universe. As an example, consider the case where teachers form one basis of classification and students form the other. If both teachers and students are selected at random, the random method is applicable.

A third model is called a *mixed model* because one of the treatments is fixed and the other is selected at random. The mixed model is, therefore, a combination of fixed constants and random models. One basis for classification, for example, might be teachers randomly selected from a specified population of teachers. The second basis for classification could be nonrandomly selected teaching methods, schedules of reinforcement, testing periods, etc.

## More Complex Factorial Designs

The two-by-two factorial design represents the simplest factorial experiment. As additional treatments are added, the number of columns and rows changes. Instead of comparing two methods of teaching against class size, any number of teaching methods could have been studied. If four methods and sex were selected, there would be a two-by-four factorial design;[10] a comparison of four methods with three intelligence levels (bright, average, dull) would yield a three-by-four factorial design. There are still only two bases of classification in these examples.

In some experiments, however, $E$ has more than two variables to investigate. Suppose $E$ wants to compare the effects of five methods of teaching spelling to high and low intelligence males and females. In this case, there are three bases of comparison: methods, sex, and intelligence. Since there are two sexes, two levels of intelligence, and five methods compared, a two-by-two-by-five factorial design results. The layout is shown in Table 7-3.

**TABLE 7-3**

A Two-by-Two-by-Five Factorial Design

| | Methods | | | | |
|---|---|---|---|---|---|
| | I | II | III | IV | V |
| Males | | | | | |
| Bright | | | | | |
| Dull | | | | | |
| Females | | | | | |
| Bright | | | | | |
| Dull | | | | | |

In a two-way ANOVA, there is a sum of squares for rows, columns, interaction, error, and a total.[11] Higher-order designs permit an analysis of the total sum of squares into additional components: a sum of squares for each main effect, an estimate of error, and a number of higher-order interactions. For example, in a three-way classification such as the one in Table 7-4, there are three main effects: methods (designated $A$), sex ($B$), and intelligence ($C$). The analysis of variance could be arranged as in Table 7-4.

Thus, with a three-way classification, there are three main effects, three first-order interactions, and one second-order interaction.

The main effect for methods would involve comparing the five method means; sex differences would be analyzed by comparing the means for males and females; and the differences between intelligence levels would involve the mean of high and low IQ students.

[10]It is customary to report the numbers of rows first and then the number of columns.
[11]Interactions can be estimated only if the number of observations within each cell is larger than 1.

TABLE 7-4

Analysis of Variance Table Showing Sources of Variation
for a Three-Way Classification

| Source of Variation | Sum of Squares | Degrees of Freedom | Mean Square, or Variance Estimate |
|---|---|---|---|
| Between methods ($A$) | | 4 | |
| Between sexes ($B$) | | 1 | |
| Between intelligence ($C$) | | 1 | |
| Interaction: $A \times B$ | | 4 | |
| Interaction: $A \times C$ | | 4 | |
| Interaction: $B \times C$ | | 1 | |
| Interaction: $A \times B \times C$ | | 4 | |
| Within groups | | — | |
| Total | | $N - 1$ | |

Each of the first-order interactions ($A \times B$, $A \times C$, and $B \times C$) would also be tested for significance by an $F$ ratio. If the $A \times B$ (methods by sex) interaction is significant, the method means differ for males and females; an $A \times C$ (methods by IQ) interaction would signify that methods differ in effectiveness depending upon student IQ level; and the $B \times C$ (sex by IQ) interaction, if significant, would mean that one of the sexes obtained higher mean IQ scores while members of the other sex obtained lower IQ scores.

The meaning of the second-order interaction, $A \times B \times C$, is most easily explained by an example. For example, the interaction effect between methods and sex (i.e., the first-order interaction, $A \times B$) might differ depending on level of intelligence (see Figures 7-2a and b). If the $A \times B$ interactions

**Figure 7-2a**
INTERACTION OF METHODS-BY-SEX
FOR LOW INTELLIGENCE STUDENTS
(DATA ARE FICTICIOUS).

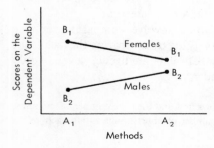

**Figure 7-2b**
ZERO INTERACTION OF METHOD-
BY-SEX FOR HIGH INTELLIGENCE
STUDENTS (DATA ARE FICTICIOUS).

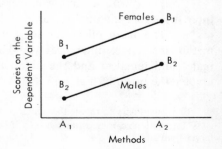

showed different patterns depending on condition $C$ (levels of intelligence), there would be a significant $A \times B \times C$ interaction. A significant $A \times B \times C$ interaction should also occur if the interactions between methods and intelligence (the $A \times C$ interaction) differed for males and females, or if the sex-by-intelligence interaction, $B \times C$, differed depending on the experimental methods employed. In short, a significant second-order interaction means that there are differences in the first-order interactions that are related to the third variable.

If the $A \times B \times C$ interaction is significant, that means that the $A \times B$, $A \times C$, and $B \times C$ interactions cannot be interpreted without reference to the third variable (for example, the $A \times B$ interaction has to be interpreted differently depending on $C$, student intelligence level). If the $A \times B \times C$ is not statistically significant, the first-order interactions can be interpreted without referring to the third variable.

## Some Advantages of Factorial and Higher-Order Factorial Designs

Purely from a statistical point of view, there is no reason for arbitrarily limiting the number of factors in an experiment. But increasing the number of factors also increases difficulty in interpretation.

There are several important advantages to factorial designs:

*1.* Factorial designs allow for a more complete interpretation of main effects. If interaction effects are not significant, each main effect can be considered independently and interpreted directly as being significant or not. But in studies where there are significant interaction effects, these interactions can affect the interpretation of the main effects. For example, it is possible for the combined effect of independent variables to be greater than either effect considered alone, just as two relatively innocuous chemicals could combine to produce a powerful effect. Or sometimes the main and interaction effects are both significant. The interpretation of the main effects then depends on the nature of the interaction.[12] For example, Figure 7-3 shows an example of an *ordinal interaction* in which the females obtained higher scores than the males regardless of method. With ordinal interactions, the lines on the graph do not cross even though the performance of the females is best under method $A_2$. Because the females outperform the males regardless of method, this is a significant main effect for sex. And because females do better under condition $A_2$ and males do better under condition $A_1$, there is an interaction effect between sex and method. If any significant interaction is ordinal, the main effects must also be significant.

[12]Geoffrey Keppel, *Design and Analysis: A Researcher's Handbook* (Englewood Cliffs, N.J.: Prentice-Hall, 1973), pp. 204–205.

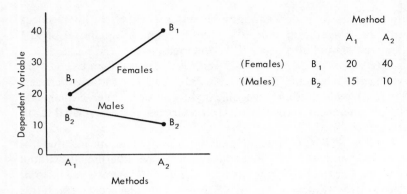

| | Method | |
| --- | --- | --- |
| | $A_1$ | $A_2$ |
| (Females) $B_1$ | 20 | 40 |
| (Males) $B_2$ | 15 | 10 |

**Figure 7-3**
AN EXAMPLE OF A SIGNIFICANT INTERACTION AND MAIN
EFFECT OF CONDITION $B_1$ OVER $B_2$.

Figure 7-4 depicts another type of significant interaction effect (called a *disordinal interaction*) where the interpretation of the main effects for methods lead to no general conclusion. Note that sex has been plotted along the horizontal axis instead of methods, but that the means have not changed. The disordinal interaction effect is clear since performance on methods $A_1$ and $A_2$ differ for males and females (i.e., females do better on $A_2$ and males on $A_1$). The main effect for method leads to no general conclusion since $A_1$ is superior to $A_2$ for males but not for females.

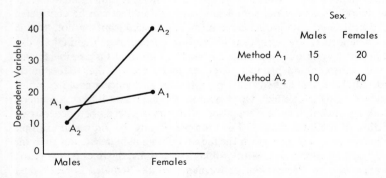

| | Sex | |
| --- | --- | --- |
| | Males | Females |
| Method $A_1$ | 15 | 20 |
| Method $A_2$ | 10 | 40 |

**Figure 7-4**
AN EXAMPLE OF A SIGNIFICANT INTERACTION EFFECT.

*2.* Another important advantage of the factorial experiment is that more than one variable can be manipulated at the same time. Extraneous variables can be deliberately entered into the design to evaluate their effects. In the earlier example of the spelling experiment, class size and sex could be included to study their possible interaction effects with methods.

*3.* Factorial designs are efficient and economical since any *S* is included in at least two comparisons (e.g., class size *and* method).

## Some Disadvantages of Factorial and Higher-Order Designs

As one might expect, there are some disadvantages to using highly complex designs that may outweigh their advantages. Among these are the following:

*1.* Interactions may become so complex that interpretations are impossible. Even with a three-way ANOVA there are 4 interactions to consider plus 3 main effects. With 5 factors, there would be 10 first-order interactions, 10 second-order interactions, 5 third-order interactions, and 1 fourth-order interaction, all of these in addition to the analysis of the 5 main effects!

*2.* The analysis of variance provides information concerning the relationships among a number of different means. If the *F* ratio is significant, this indicates that at least two of the means were drawn from different populations. What is not known is which means differ significantly. With a large number of means, many comparisons may have to be made following the analysis of variance.

Statistically, it is a mistake to run *t*-tests following an analysis of variance.[13] There are two reasons for this. In the first place, if there are 10 means to compare, there will be 45 different combinations to test. Not only does this entail much work, but it increases the probability that Type I errors will increase. Second, should *E* decide to select the 2 most extreme means to test, then the next 2, etc., an important assumption has been violated, namely, that all groups have been *randomly* sampled from the same population. See Keppel[14] for a summary of various methods that can be used to compare means following *F* tests.

## *EX POST FACTO* DESIGNS

The *ex post facto* design[15] is a cross between a descriptive and an experimental investigation. It is descriptive in the sense that *E* has no direct control of experimental conditions; it is experimental because an attempt is made to infer causal relationships between groups which differ in important ways.

Suppose, for example, that *E* is interested in studying the causes of

[13]The exception is when *E* specifies in advance of data collection which means are expected to differ.

[14]Keppel, pp. 133–163.

[15]In education, the *ex post facto* design has also been called the *causal comparative* design.

juvenile delinquency. In the *ex post facto* design, *E* selects two groups of *Ss* who *supposedly* differ only in that one group is composed of delinquents and the "control" group is composed of nondelinquents. Differences between the two groups are then considered to be *possible* causes of delinquency.

The word *possible* is italicized for an important reason. Certainly, samples of delinquents and nondeliquents are likely to differ in more than one way. *E* will then have multiple differences to evaluate. Some of these may indeed reflect causal conditions, but other differences may be unrelated to delinquency or may be due to sampling error.

In an effort to make groups more equivalent, *E* may be tempted to match *Ss* on such variables as IQ, socioeconomic level, or sex. However, the *ex post facto* design requires that matching be done *after* the groups have been formed. Thus, *E* can expect to lose a considerable number of *Ss* who cannot be matched. By the time matching is completed on one variable, sample size is reduced again. Each additional attempt to equate groups will result in a further loss of cases. In one investigation,[16] an orginal selection of 2127 *Ss* shrank to 46 after being matched on six variables. Commenting on this investigation, Campbell and Stanley said, "The tragedy is that his 46 cases are still not comparable, and furthermore . . . the shrinkage was unnecessary."[17]

The 46 *Ss* were still ineffectively matched because of regression effects and because differences between groups cannot be eliminated. Regression effects are present because *Ss* were selected on the basis of their being in extreme groups. As Campbell and Stanley have noted, these regression effects could have been eliminated by using an analysis of covariance design with the six matching variables as covariates. There would be no way to eliminate all the important extraneous variables, which are often unknown, but at least shrinkage could have been reduced.

## SUMMARY

**1.** A number of *single-group experimental designs* were described (see Table 7-5 for a summary of the advantages and disadvantages of various designs).

   **a.** The one-shot case study (*XO*) is an ineffective design since it fails to control extraneous variables and does not permit a measurement of change.

   **b.** One-group pretest–posttest design (*OXO*) controls for selection and mortality. It is a repeated measurements design.

[16]F. Stuart Chapin, *Experimental Designs in Sociological Research*, rev. ed. (New York: Harper & Brothers, 1955), pp. 99–124.
[17]Campbell and Stanley, p. 240.

# TABLE 7-5

## Major Advantages and Disadvantages of Different Experimental Designs

| | History | Maturation | Testing | Instrumentation | Regression | Selection | Mortality | Comments |
|---|---|---|---|---|---|---|---|---|
| **SINGLE-GROUP DESIGNS:** | | | | | | | | |
| 1. One-shot case study | − | − | | | | − | − | Does not allow for comparison of changes; no premeasures. |
| 2. One-group pretest–posttest design | − | − | − | − | ? | + | + | A type of repeated measurement design but with a single group. |
| 3. Time-series | − | + | + | ? | + | + | + | Leads to a complex statistical analysis. |
| 4. Equivalent time samples | + | + | + | + | + | + | + | Generalization is only to other groups which are repeatedly tested. |
| 5. Equivalent materials design | + | + | + | + | + | + | + | Generalization again restricted to groups tested repeatedly. |
| **SEPARATE CONTROL GROUP DESIGNS:** | | | | | | | | |
| 6. Static-group | + | ? | + | + | + | − | − | Along with designs 1 and 2, this is a pre-experimental design. |
| 7. Pretest–posttest control group design with randomization | + | + | + | + | + | + | + | A true experimental design; generalization restricted to other pre-tested groups. |
| 8. Solomon four-group design | + | + | + | + | + | + | + | Another true experimental design; requires use of multiple groups. |
| 9. Posttest-only control group design | + | + | + | + | + | + | + | A third true experimental design. |
| 10. Nonequivalent control group design | + | + | + | + | ? | + | + | Makes use of intact groups. |
| 11. Separate-sample pretest–posttest design | − | − | + | ? | + | + | − | Generalization facilitated. |

173

**c.** Time-series $(O_1 O_2 O_3 O_4 X O_5 O_6 O_7 O_8)$ is a repeated measurements design with multiple measures preceding and following the introduction of the experimental treatment. History and instrumention are not well controlled by this design.

**d.** Equivalent time-sample design $(X_1 O X_0 O,$ etc.) randomly presents experimental and control conditions to the same group of $Ss$. Although there are no threats to internal validity, generalizations may be limited to $Ss$ who have been tested repeatedly.

**e.** Equivalent materials design $(M_a X_1 O M_b X_0 O,$ etc.) is the same as the preceding design except that equivalent sets of experimental materials are presented to $Ss$ on each occasion.

2. Separate control group designs include the following.

**a.** Static-group comparison design $\left( \dfrac{X\ O_1}{\ \ \ \ O_2} \right)$ fails to control selection and mortality and possibly maturation. It is considered a weak design.

**b.** Pretest–posttest control group design with randomization

$$R\ O_1\ (X)\ O_2$$
$$R\ O_3\ \ X\ \ O_4$$

involves two groups randomly selected from a large population. One group is pretested and provided with an irrelevant treatment $(X)$; the other group receives the experimental treatment, $X$, and is posttested. History, maturation, instrumentation, and mortality are distinct threats. An additional control group may be added to this design for greater control.

3. *Counterbalancing* is used to control for sequence effects.

**a.** In the *ABBA* design, $Ss$ are presented with two conditions, $A$ and $B$, in the order $A \longrightarrow B \longrightarrow B \longrightarrow A$. Since $A$ precedes $B$ as often as $B$ precedes $A$, the order is counterbalanced. The assumption is made that the amount of improvement in going from $A$ to $B$ is equal to the improvement of $B$ to $A$.

**b.** Sometimes the *ABBA* sequence is combined with the *BAAB* sequence when *AB* may be supposed to yield greater improvement than any other sequence.

**c.** The Latin square is another counterbalancing technique where there are as many occasions as groups. Treatments are arranged so that they occur only once in each column and row. Any one study may include a number of different Latin squares. The Graeco-Latin square is simply a combination of Latin squares. It is possible to compare different methods, tests, and time periods by the Graeco-Latin squares as long as the number of methods, tests, and times are equal.

4. *Factorial designs* permit the simultaneous comparisons of two or more independent variables.

**a.** Different models of the analysis of variance determine what the denominator (error term) of the $F$ ratio will be. The *fixed constants* model assumes that all bases of classifying variables were predetermined; the *random* model assumes that the levels of all variables were selected randomly; the *mixed* model assumes combinations of the fixed constants and random models.

**b.** In complex factorial designs, a sum of squares may be computed for each main effect. In addition, there must be an estimate of error (as determined by the type of model employed), and interactions among the various independent variables. There is a main effect for each of the independent variables; a first-order interaction involves two variables; a second-order interaction involves three variables, etc.

**c.** Assuming three independent variables, $A$, $B$, and $C$, the first-order interactions involve the relationship between $A$ and $B$, $A$ and $C$, and $B$ and $C$. If the $A \times B$ interaction is significant, the different levels of variable $A$ are related to the different levels of variable $B$. The second-order interaction involves the relationships among the levels of variables $A$, $B$, and $C$. For example, the $A \times B$ interaction might differ depending on $C$, the $A \times C$ interaction might differ depending on $B$, or the $B \times C$ interaction could differ depending on $A$. Examples of these interactions were presented.

**d.** In factorial designs, there may be any number of independent variables. The higher-order interactions do become complex and difficult to interpret.

**e.** Factorial designs have a number of advantages over single-variable studies.

1) They permit for a greater degree of interpretation of the main effects. If interaction effects are significant, the main effects must be interpreted with this in mind.

2) They permit $E$ to vary a number of conditions at the same time.

3) They are efficient and economical.

**f.** Disadvantages of factorial designs, and especially of higher-order factorials, are:

1) Interactions may become difficult to interpret.

2) Special tests of significance are needed to determine which cell means differ.

**5.** The *ex post facto* design is an attempt to study causal conditions among already existing groups such as delinquents and nondelinquents, married and unmarried persons, etc. The use of the analysis of covariance was suggested as a reasonable way of statistically eliminating the effects of extraneous variables.

## PRACTICE EXERCISES

**1.** For each of the following examples, indicate the type of design employed:

**a.** A single group of *Ss* receives a pretest, experimental treatment, and posttest.

**b.** *Ss* are randomly assigned to experimental and control groups; the experimental treatment is given to one group and is withheld from the other. Both groups are posttested.

**c.** Except for the use of a pretest, this design is exactly the same as the one described in the preceding example.

**d.** *Ss* are observed on three occasions, then given an experimental treatment, and then observed again for three occasions.

**e.** An intact group is given an experimental treatment and then tested; another intact group receives the posttest only.

**f.** Except for the use of pretests administered to experimental and control *Ss*, this design is exactly the same as the one described in the preceding example.

**2.** Indicate the threats to internal and external validity that are uncontrolled in the preceding examples.

**3.** What are the advantages and disadvantages of using pretests if *Ss* have been assigned to groups randomly and if random assignment is not possible?

**4.** What factors are trying to be controlled in the following design in which *Ss* have been assigned randomly to treatment and pretest groups?

|  | Treatment | |
|---|---|---|
|  | YES | NO |
| Pretest yes |  |  |
| no |  |  |

**a.** Show how this design is related to the Solomon four-group design.

**b.** Interpret the findings graphed below.

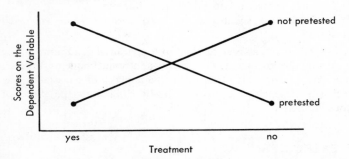

**5.** A study was conducted comparing the mean amount of food eaten by male and female dogs and cats of various ages (6 months, 2 years, and 4 years), and various weights (1 kg., 2 kg., 4 kg., 8 kg., and 16 kg.).

**a.** Construct an analysis of variance table for this study similar to the one shown in Table 7-3 (page 167).

**b.** What are the independent and dependent variables?

**c.** How many $F$ ratios for main effects will there be?

**d.** How many first-order interactions are there? second-order? third-order? fourth-order?

**e.** What model (fixed constants, random, or mixed) should be employed with this example?

**f.** If 5 animals were placed in each cell of the ANOVA table, what would the total $N$ be?

**g.** The researcher finds that age and animal weight interact. What does that mean?

**h.** Is it reasonable to suppose that there would be no significant interaction effect between animals and sex? between weight and age? sex and weight? Would these interactions be ordinal or disordinal?

**i.** Could the ANOVA show that heavy male dogs eat more than light female cats?

**j.** Give an example of a reasonable second-order interaction for this hypothetical study. In what way might the second-order interaction affect the interpretation of any of the first-order interactions?

**6.** An experimenter decides to rotate seating arrangements when $Ss$ observe films so that no one will have any advantage over any other person. Using as many occasions, seating locations, tests, and films as you like, develop some method of counterbalancing these conditions. Develop a layout such as is shown in Figure 7-1.

**7.** Develop an adequate experimental design to test each of the following hypotheses. Describe, in detail, how you will select $Ss$, what apparatus or instruments you will employ, what procedures you will follow, and what appropriate statistical analyses are relevant. Specify the independent and dependent variables and how extraneous variables will be controlled. Define operationally any terms which are unclear or ambiguous.

**a.** Elementary school $Ss$ exposed to creative dance classes will improve in social relationships to a greater extent than $Ss$ not exposed to creative dance classes.

**b.** The attitudes of high school freshmen toward minority groups will change as a function of direct contact with minority group members.

**c.** Delinquency among high school students results from broken homes.

**d.** The lecture method of learning is more beneficial for females than for males, whereas independent study will favor males rather than females.

**e.** Smoking reduces grades among high school $Ss$.

**f.** Playing fast music when students are tired (late in the afternoon or just after lunch) and slow music when they are overexcited will increase efficiency of learning among bright males but not among dull females.

**g.** Miss Jones can motivate bright students to a greater degree than can Miss Smith. Miss Smith, however, can motivate dull students to a greater degree than can Miss Jones.

## Selected Supplementary Readings

1. On the time-series experiments, see Glass, Gene V, et al., eds. *Design and Analysis of Time-Series Experiments.* Boulder, Colo.: Colorado Associated University Press, University of Colorado, 1975.

2. For further readings on the use of extended control group design, see Solomon, Richard L. "An Extension of Control Group Design." *Psychological Bulletin,* 46, no. 2 (1949), pp. 137–150; Carter, Ralph R., Jr. "The Use of Extended Control-Group Designs in Human Relations Studies." *Psychological Bulletin,* 48, no. 44 (1951), pp. 340–347.

3. On the nonequivalent control group design, see Kenny, David A. "A Quasi-Experimental Approach to Assessing Treatment Effects in the Nonequivalent Control Group Design." *Psychological Bulletin,* 82 no. 3 (May 1975), pp. 345–362.

4. Although the examples used in this text use analysis of variance procedures, there are advantages (and disadvantages) in using multiple regression approaches to serve the same purpose. For a general introduction to these topics, see Tatsuoka, Maurice M. *The General Linear Model: A "New" Trend in Analysis of Variance.* Champaign, Ill.: Institute for Personality and Ability Testing, 1975, 64 pp.; Woodward, J. Arthur, and Overall, John E. "Multiple Analysis of Variance by Multiple Regression Methods." *Psychological Bulletin,* 82, no. 1 (January 1975), pp. 21–32; Jones, Lyle V. "Analysis of Variance in Its Multivariate Development." Chapter 7 of Raymond B. Cattell, ed. *Handbook of Multivariate Experimental Psychology.* Chicago: Rand McNally & Co., 1966, pp. 244–266; and Kerlinger, Fred N., and Pedhazur, Elazar J. *Multiple Regression in Behavioral Research.* New York: Holt, Rinehart and Winston, 1973, 534 pp.

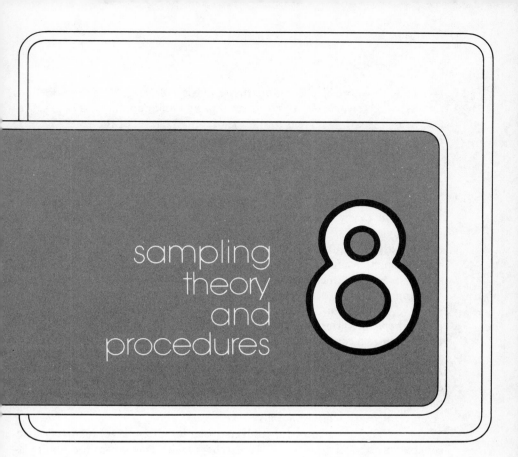

Empirical research in education often requires the use of children who differ considerably from one another in many attributes. Such variables as chronological age, sex, intelligence, socioeconomic background, and attitude are just a few of the characteristics in which human beings differ. This variability means that educators working with students may obtain results highly dependent on the nature of the particular students. The investigator has the responsibility for describing the relevant characteristics of persons selected for inclusion in a study.

The *Literary Digest* poll of 1936 has often been quoted as an example of faulty sampling procedures. After having predicted successfully the outcomes of the presidential campaigns of 1924, 1928, and 1932, the *Digest* sent out over 10 million ballots and confidently predicted the defeat of Franklin Roosevelt in a year in which he later carried 46 of the 48 states. What had gone wrong? An analysis of the procedures used by the editors of the *Digest* showed that they had obtained their list of potential voters largely from telephone directories, a procedure they had used successfully in their previous predictions. However, by 1936, political party affiliation and voting practices had become matters related to the socioeconomic level of the voter. The use of the telephone book to obtain lists of potential voters was likely to yield far more Republicans (who could afford telephones than Democrats. In previous elections, members of the two major political parties were not distinguishable by socioeconomic level, and the use of the telephone directory was a reasonable and impartial way of gathering lists of names.

Obviously, it would have been an impossibility to question each and every potential voter to determine voting preference. However, even if one could study all eligible voters (or any specified totality of persons, places, or events), such an undertaking would be prohibitively exhaustive, costly, and, as will be seen, unnecessary in most instances. Researchers usually prefer working with small but "representative" groups.

At this point, a number of terms need to be defined. To the general public, *population* signifies a totality of human beings residing in a given area, but in a more technical sense, *a population refers to the aggregate of all observations of interest to the researcher. Thus, it is possible to talk about a population of responses, test scores, characteristics, or traits.* The population (often called a *universe*) may be infinitely large (such as the scores of all children, past, present, and future) or finite (such as fourth-grade children attending a given elementary school on a given day).

Where populations or universes are infinitely large, relatively inaccessible, or expensive to obtain, researchers select *samples* from the population with which to work. *A sample is a limited number of elements selected from a population to be representative of that population.* Representativeness need not imply that the sample is a miniature population. To be representative in that sense would require that all relevant characteristics of the population be known, a circumstance that can only occur with finite populations which have been completely studied, as in census reprots. *Representative samples are ones which have been drawn in a random, unbiased manner* (terms which will be described in greater detail later in this chapter). It should be noted here, however, that *random sampling* refers to the process of selection and not necessarily to the extent to which samples approximate population characteristics, which are often unknown.

# DETERMINING THE CHARACTERISTICS
# OF THE SAMPLE

Determining which individuals, objects, or methods are to be included in the population (and therefore in the sample) depends upon the generalizations the researcher wishes to make. If, for example, generalizations are to encompass all students currently studying algebra throughout the United

States, the sample must necessarily include the attributes characteristic of that population. In essence, algebra students would have to be selected from various parts of the country, from all socioeconomic levels, and from all racial backgrounds if, through previous research studies, these variables are known or suspected to be related to achievement in algebra.

Usually, researchers must be content to generalize the results of their studies to a population delimited in both size and scope. By so doing, they allow themselves to select more limited samples; this in turn saves time, effort, and money. However, a sample drawn from a delimited population should not be generalized beyond that population unless evidence is available that the population being sampled is similar in relevant attributes to the population not being sampled.

The researcher should indicate the basis upon which generalizations are being made. If, for example, it is found that in one community a new method of teaching is superior to an older one, the investigator might be willing to hypothesize that similar results would be found in other communities and in other states having similar types of students and schools. Often, however, investigators are faced with a dilemma: whether to select populations difficult to obtain and study but which yield samples whose conclusions can be widely extended, or whether to limit themselves to restricted populations which yield easily accessible samples but may not be so widely generalized.

In practice, it is probably true that as many samples are selected because they are convenient as are selected by determining the extent to which one wishes to generalize research findings. Although intact groups may be quite convenient and accessible, they may not be representative of any desired population. Investigators who select individuals from an introductory education class, for example, have no way of knowing the extent to which that class is similar to other classes. Unless there is evidence that the characteristics of students remain constant from class to class, conclusions based upon the investigations of a single class can hold only for that one group. This places a definite limitation on the practical uses that can be made from research findings.

# METHODS OF SELECTING SAMPLES

Once the essential characteristics of the population have been decided upon, the researcher faces the problem of selecting the sample so that it will adequately reflect the characteristics of the population from which it has been drawn. Rarely is anyone concerned only with the data obtained from a sample, except insofar as these statistics (such as sample means or standard deviations) can be used to estimate the corresponding values (called *parameters*) in the population. Sampling involves: 1) defining the population, 2) selecting the sample, and 3) estimating the population's parameters from the knowledge obtained from the sample statistic.

Only a brief discussion of some of the problems involving the estimation of parameters from statistics is possible here, although specific methods of selecting samples will be described later in the chapter. Generalizing from known characteristics of a sample to unknown characteristics of a population or universe is known as *statistical inference*. Statistical inference provides an estimate of the parameter and the amount of error which can be expected. Many of these problems are considered in detail by Edwards[1] and Ferguson.[2]

Assume, for example, that investigators are interested in estimating the mean IQ of 900 fourth graders. They could, of course, test all 900 students and then compute the mean of all scores. The mean derived from all 900 cases in the population is a parameter.[3] Suppose, however, that they are unable to disrupt all fourth-grade classes to determine the mean IQ (which will be assumed to be 100), but that they can select a small number of students to test. Which students should be used? Each fourth-grade teacher could be asked for volunteers, but then the population is no longer scores of fourth-grade students in general but scores of fourth-grade volunteers. Students who volunteer (especially for testing) often differ systematically from those who refuse to be tested. Would it be reasonable to ask each teacher to select a few "average" students to be tested? Practical experience has led most researchers away from this procedure because of the difficulty of selecting "average" cases. Another way of selecting students (although a poor one) is to test all students in some conveniently accessible classes. Some of the difficulties involved in attempting to generalize from intact classes have already been mentioned.

Consider some of the problems involved in selecting samples in general. In the first place, samples are either *biased* or *unbiased*. Biased samples consistently overestimate or underestimate parameters. Thus, the use of volunteers is likely to yield mean IQ scores that are systematically too high; on the other hand, unbiased samples neither underestimate nor overestimate parameters. With unbiased samples, as the number of cases is increased, statistics tend to equal the corresponding value of the parameter. Increasing the size of a biased sample, however, cannot compensate for a faulty selection design. It is important, therefore, to select cases in some unbiased manner,

---

[1]Allen L. Edwards, *Statistical Analysis*, 4th ed. (New York: Holt, Rinehart and Winston, 1974).

[2]George A. Ferguson, *Statistical Analysis in Psychology and Education*, 4th ed. (New York: McGraw-Hill Book Co., 1976).

[3]It is not, however, the only parameter. Population values obtained on a given day may differ from values obtained on different occasions. In this sense, even a census or 100 percent sample is obtained only on a single occasion and is, therefore, technically a sample.

such as by *simple random sampling, stratified random sampling, systematic sampling*, or *area (cluster) sampling*.[4]

## Simple Random Sampling

A sample is selected randomly when every member of the population has an equal, nonzero chance of being included in the sample. This means that no population element has been either deliberately or inadvertently omitted or excluded from the sample except by chance.

The *Literary Digest* poll of 1936 described at the beginning of this chapter was an example of biased sampling. The population should have consisted of all persons able and willing to vote. The decision to use the telephone directory as the population of potential voters systematically excluded many persons who later voted for Roosevelt. Because the sample was biased, chance effects were not reduced, even though the sample was extremely large. The biased nature of the sample occurred because of the use of the telephone directory and because of the nature of the returns. Although 10 million questionnaires were sent out, only 2 million were returned. More Republicans, who voted for Landon, received and returned their questionnaires than did Democrats.

The selection of cases at random is most simply accomplished by using a table of random numbers, such as may be found in Snedecor and Cochran,[5] Kendall and Smith,[6] Peatman and Schafer,[7] or the Rand Corporation.[8] The researcher assigns a number to each member of the population, enters a table of random numbers at any point, and moving in any predetermined direction, reads the numbers of the individuals to be included in the sample. A portion of a table of random numbers may be found in Table 8-1. Note that the first 5 columns are labeled 00 to 04 and that rows are numbered 00 to 49.

---

[4]The present discussion is deliberately limited to probability sampling techniques and has omitted nonprobability sampling designs. The essential difference between the two is that in nonprobability sampling, subjects are selected by accessibility and convenience rather than at random. Doing so may make it possible to obtain more subjects and to substantially reduce costs over probability designs. However, the major defect of nonprobability designs is that statistical models are not applicable for their analysis. Nonprobability designs can be justified only on the grounds that costs may be reduced over random selection of samples. Amount of error cannot be estimated.

[5]George S. Snedecor and William G. Cochran, *Statistical Methods*, 6th ed. (Ames, Iowa: Iowa State University Press, 1967), pp. 543–546.

[6]M. G. Kendall and B. B. Smith, "Randomness and Random Sampling Numbers," *Journal of the Royal Statistical Society*, 101, Pt. I (1938), pp. 147–166.

[7]John Gray Peatman and Roy Schafer, "A Table of Random Numbers from Selective Service Numbers," *Journal of Psychology*, 14, (Oct. 1942), pp. 295–305.

[8]Rand Corporation, "A Million Random Digits with 100,000 Normal Deviates" (Glencoe, Ill.: Free Press, 1955).

## TABLE 8-1

### Twenty-Five Hundred Randomly Assorted Digits

|     | 00–04 | 05–09 | 10–14 | 15–19 | 20–24 | 25–29 | 30–34 | 35–39 | 40–44 | 45–49 |
|-----|-------|-------|-------|-------|-------|-------|-------|-------|-------|-------|
| 00  | 54463 | 22662 | 65905 | 70639 | 79365 | 67382 | 29085 | 69831 | 47058 | 08186 |
| 01  | 15389 | 85205 | 18850 | 39226 | 42249 | 90669 | 96325 | 23248 | 60933 | 26927 |
| 02  | 85941 | 40756 | 82414 | 02015 | 13858 | 78030 | 16269 | 65978 | 01385 | 15345 |
| 03  | 61149 | 69440 | 11286 | 88218 | 58925 | 03638 | 52862 | 62733 | 33451 | 77455 |
| 04  | 05219 | 81619 | 10651 | 67079 | 92511 | 59888 | 84502 | 72095 | 83463 | 75577 |
| 05  | 41417 | 98326 | 87719 | 92294 | 46614 | 50948 | 64886 | 20002 | 97365 | 30976 |
| 06  | 28357 | 94070 | 20652 | 35774 | 16249 | 75019 | 21145 | 05217 | 47286 | 76305 |
| 07  | 17783 | 00015 | 10806 | 83091 | 91530 | 36466 | 39981 | 62481 | 49177 | 75779 |
| 08  | 40950 | 84820 | 29881 | 85966 | 62800 | 70326 | 84740 | 62660 | 77379 | 90279 |
| 09  | 82995 | 64157 | 66164 | 41180 | 10089 | 4157  | 78258 | 96488 | 88629 | 37231 |
| 10  | 96754 | 17676 | 55659 | 44105 | 47361 | 34833 | 86679 | 23930 | 53249 | 27083 |
| 11  | 34357 | 88040 | 53364 | 71726 | 45690 | 66334 | 60332 | 22554 | 90600 | 71113 |
| 12  | 06318 | 37403 | 49927 | 57715 | 50423 | 67372 | 63116 | 48888 | 21505 | 80182 |
| 13  | 62111 | 52820 | 07243 | 79931 | 89292 | 84767 | 85693 | 73947 | 22278 | 11551 |
| 14  | 47534 | 09243 | 67879 | 00544 | 23410 | 12740 | 02540 | 54440 | 32949 | 13491 |
| 15  | 98614 | 75993 | 84460 | 62846 | 59844 | 14922 | 48730 | 73443 | 48167 | 34770 |
| 16  | 24856 | 03648 | 44898 | 09351 | 98795 | 18644 | 39765 | 71058 | 90368 | 44104 |
| 17  | 96887 | 12479 | 80621 | 66223 | 86085 | 78285 | 02432 | 53342 | 42846 | 94771 |
| 18  | 90801 | 21472 | 42815 | 77408 | 37390 | 76766 | 52615 | 32141 | 30268 | 18106 |
| 19  | 55165 | 77312 | 83666 | 36028 | 28420 | 70219 | 81369 | 41943 | 47366 | 41067 |
| 20  | 75884 | 12952 | 84318 | 95108 | 72305 | 64620 | 91318 | 89872 | 45375 | 85436 |
| 21  | 16777 | 37116 | 58550 | 42958 | 21460 | 43910 | 01175 | 87894 | 81378 | 10620 |
| 22  | 46230 | 43877 | 80207 | 88877 | 89380 | 32992 | 91380 | 03164 | 98656 | 59337 |
| 23  | 42902 | 66892 | 46134 | 01432 | 94710 | 23474 | 20423 | 60137 | 60609 | 13119 |
| 24  | 81007 | 00333 | 39693 | 28039 | 10154 | 95425 | 39220 | 19774 | 31782 | 49037 |
| 25  | 68089 | 01122 | 51111 | 72373 | 06902 | 74373 | 96199 | 97017 | 41273 | 21546 |
| 26  | 20411 | 67081 | 89950 | 16944 | 93054 | 87687 | 96693 | 87236 | 77054 | 33848 |
| 27  | 58212 | 13160 | 06468 | 15718 | 82627 | 76999 | 05999 | 58680 | 96739 | 63700 |
| 28  | 70577 | 42866 | 24969 | 61210 | 76046 | 67699 | 42054 | 12696 | 93758 | 03283 |
| 29  | 94522 | 74358 | 71659 | 62038 | 79643 | 79169 | 44741 | 05437 | 39038 | 13163 |
| 30  | 42626 | 86819 | 85651 | 88678 | 17401 | 03252 | 99547 | 32404 | 17918 | 62880 |
| 31  | 16051 | 33763 | 57194 | 16752 | 54450 | 19031 | 58580 | 47629 | 54132 | 60631 |
| 32  | 08244 | 27647 | 33851 | 44705 | 94211 | 46716 | 11738 | 55784 | 95374 | 72655 |
| 33  | 59497 | 04392 | 09419 | 89964 | 51211 | 04894 | 72882 | 17805 | 21896 | 83864 |
| 34  | 97155 | 13428 | 40293 | 09985 | 58434 | 01412 | 69124 | 82171 | 59058 | 82859 |
| 35  | 98409 | 66162 | 95763 | 47420 | 20792 | 61527 | 20441 | 39435 | 11859 | 41567 |
| 36  | 45476 | 84882 | 65109 | 96597 | 25930 | 66790 | 65706 | 61203 | 53634 | 22557 |
| 37  | 89300 | 69700 | 50741 | 30329 | 11658 | 23166 | 05400 | 66669 | 48708 | 03887 |
| 38  | 50051 | 95137 | 91631 | 66315 | 91428 | 12275 | 24816 | 68091 | 71710 | 33258 |
| 39  | 31753 | 85178 | 31310 | 89642 | 98364 | 02306 | 24617 | 09609 | 83942 | 22716 |
| 40  | 79152 | 53829 | 77250 | 20190 | 56535 | 18760 | 69942 | 77448 | 33278 | 48805 |
| 41  | 44560 | 38750 | 83635 | 56540 | 64900 | 42912 | 13953 | 79149 | 18710 | 68618 |
| 42  | 68328 | 83378 | 63369 | 71381 | 39564 | 05615 | 42451 | 64559 | 97501 | 65747 |
| 43  | 46939 | 38689 | 58625 | 08342 | 30459 | 85863 | 20781 | 09284 | 26333 | 91777 |
| 44  | 83544 | 86141 | 15707 | 96256 | 23068 | 13782 | 08467 | 89469 | 93842 | 55349 |
| 45  | 91621 | 00881 | 04900 | 54224 | 46177 | 55309 | 17852 | 27491 | 89415 | 23466 |
| 46  | 91896 | 67126 | 04151 | 03795 | 59077 | 11848 | 12630 | 98375 | 52068 | 60142 |
| 47  | 55751 | 62515 | 21108 | 80830 | 02263 | 29303 | 37204 | 96926 | 30506 | 09808 |
| 48  | 85156 | 87689 | 95493 | 88842 | 00664 | 55017 | 55539 | 17771 | 69448 | 87530 |
| 49  | 07521 | 56898 | 12236 | 60277 | 39102 | 62315 | 12239 | 07105 | 11844 | 01117 |

*Source:* Snedecor and Cochran, *Statistical Methods*, p. 10. Copyright The Iowa State University Press, reprinted by permission.

To return to the example of selecting a sample of fourth graders out of a population of 900 students, suppose that administrative problems prevents the testing of more than 35 students. Each of the 900 students in the population would be given a code number from 001 to 900. The researcher then enters a table of random numbers at any predetermined spot and simply reads all of the three-digit numbers. Suppose, for example, that the researcher picks column 10 to 12, row 15, of Table 8-1 to begin sampling, and suppose that the decision is to move down the page. The first number to be selected, 844, would be included in the sample. The next numbers, 448, 806, 428, etc., would also be included. Note, however, that when the researcher gets to row 35 the corresponding number is 957, which would have to be discarded since the highest number given to any student in the population is 900. The process is continued until the desired sample size is reached. Each student whose number was selected must then be tested and the mean IQ for the 35 students computed. Any number appearing more than once is disregarded after it has been included initially.

The important point to keep in mind is that the mean is likely to vary if another 35 cases are randomly selected. However, as long as each sample of 35 students is randomly selected, the population mean IQ of 100 will be (in the long run) neither systematically overestimated nor systematically underestimated. The mean computed from any random sample of 35 cases is considered to be an unbiased estimate of the population mean.

Ordinarily, of course, only one sample of 35 cases can be selected. The question that must be asked is how far the sample mean is likely to differ from the population mean. This can be estimated by computing the *standard error of a mean*, or

$$S_{\bar{x}} = \frac{s}{\sqrt{N}}$$

where $s$ is the standard deviation of the sample; and $N$ is the number of cases in the sample.[9]

Note that as $s$ increases, the standard error also increases and that the more cases added to the sample, the smaller the standard error will be. The least amount of error will occur when $N$ is large and $s$ is small.

## Stratified Random Sampling

Another sampling technique (which makes use of random sampling procedures as part of its design) is called *stratified random sampling*. Stratification is the process of dividing a population into a number of *strata*, or sub-

---

[9] $s = \sqrt{\dfrac{\Sigma (X - \bar{X})^2}{N - 1}}$

populations, so that the variability of elements selected within each stratum is more homogeneous than is the variability of elements between strata. Once the population has been subdivided into strata, samples are drawn independently and randomly from each stratum, and an estimate of the parameter is computed over all strata.

Stratified samples have a number of advantages over simple random samples. In the first place, stratification takes advantage of whatever information is known concerning the characteristics of the population. Having this information produces more efficient sampling than if it were unavailable. Second, it can be demonstrated that sampling errors arise only *within* strata, not *between* strata. If the variability within each stratum can be reduced, the estimate of the parameter will be more accurate than if there had been random sampling throughout an entire population without benefit of stratification. Third, stratified sampling allows selection of cases within each stratum in different ways and in different proportions.

An example will help to clarify the procedure of selecting a stratified random sample. Suppose that a school superintendent is interested in predicting whether or not local voters are likely to pass a proposed bond issue. Obviously, it would be impossible (or at least highly impractical) to assign a number to each potential voter to select a simple random sample. A more economical and reliable way to gather data is to divide the population of potential voters into such strata as sex, age, and socioeconomic level (it is assumed that this information is available from previous census reports). The intent is to stratify the population on the basis of those variables which have been demonstrated to correlate most highly with voting behavior and which do not correlate too highly with each other.

For the sake of simplicity, consider the age variable only. Suppose that on the basis of prior knowledge, derived from either earlier census reports or previous investigations, the superintendent knows that there are approximately 10,000 potential voters in the district who are younger than thirty years, 8,000 who are between the ages of thirty and fifty, and 6,000 who are older than age fifty There are, therefore, a total of 24,000 potential voters in this district.

As indicated earlier, it can be more advantageous to select potential voters randomly within each age stratum and then to estimate the percentage of the population in favor of the bond issue than it is to select randomly throughout the 24,000 potential voters. To determine the percentage of the population favoring the passage of the bond issue, the superintendent will first have to decide whether proportional or disproportional sampling within each stratum is preferred. That is, it is necessary to determine whether the percentage of units or elements selected within each stratum should be made proportional or disproportional to the percentage of units present in the population. Usually, the decision is to make the sampling proportional. Later it will be shown that this is not always desirable.

Suppose that the superintendent does decide in favor of proportional sampling and that a sample size of 500 will suffice. Table 8-2 is designed to demonstrate the procedures involved in drawing a stratified proportional random sample where the total number sampled is 500.

TABLE 8-2

Computational Table Demonstrating Method of Determining
Number of Cases to Be Selected within Each Stratum
for a Proportional Stratified Random Sample of 500 Voters

| Population and Sample Char- acterstics | Younger Than Thirty | Thirty–Fifty | Older Than Fifty | Totals |
|---|---|---|---|---|
| Population $N$ in each stratum | 10,000 | 8000 | 6000 | 24,000 |
| Proportion of no. of cases in each stratum to total no. of cases | $\frac{10,000}{24,000} = 0.42$ | $\frac{8000}{24,000} = 0.33$ | $\frac{6000}{24,000} = 0.25$ | 1.0 |
| No. in each stratum to be selected | $0.42(500) = 210$ | $0.33(500) = 165$ | $0.25(500) = 125$ | 500 |

(Age Groupings of Voters)

To determine the *number* of cases in each stratum to be selected, the proportion of cases within each stratum in the population must be known. For the three age groups in the present example, these proportions are 0.42, 0.33, and 0.25, respectively. Since there are a total of 500 cases in the sample, the number of cases to be included in each stratum can be determined by multiplying each of these proportions by 500. Thus, the superintendent would select 210 persons out of the first stratum, 165 from the second, and 125 from the third.

The next problem the superintendent faces is to estimate the percentage of the population favoring the passage of the proposed bond issue. As long as the sample size within each stratum is proportional to the number of cases within each stratum in the population (as it is in this example), the computation is relatively simple (this, by the way, is one advantage in using proportional stratified samples). In the sample of 500 cases, the superintendent has only to count the number of persons who indicated that they favor the bond issue and divide this number by 500 to obtain the proportion in the sample in favor of the issue. For example, if 160 persons out of the 210 who were less than thirty years of age favored the proposal (76 percent), while 85 out of 165 in the thirty–fifty age group were in favor (52 percent), and only 40 out of 125 older than fifty indicated that they were in favor of the bill (32 percent), a total of 285 out of 500, or approximately 57 percent, would have indicated a favorable attitude toward the proposed bond issue. This percentage derived from a sample is an estimate of the percentage of persons in the population who are in favor of the bond issue. Note that the older voters are less favorably inclined to vote for passage of the bill than are the younger voters. This knowledge helps the superintendent in allocating resources for persuasion where they will do the most good, namely, among the older voters.

How certain can the superintendent be that 57 percent of the voters will, in fact, vote for the measure? Is it possible, for example, that another randomly selected group of 500 voters might have yielded a different proportion? Here it is necessary to compute a standard error for the proportion, 0.57. The standard error for a stratified sample is not the same as for a simple random sample. Nor is the formula for the standard error of a proportional stratified random sample the same as for a disproportional stratified random sample. The references listed at the end of this chapter provide the appropriate formulas needed for determining these standard errors. It is sufficient at this point simply to state that, in general, estimates of parameters are more accurate (i.e., have smaller standard errors) when stratification is employed than when a simple random sampling design is chosen. Nonetheless, the amount of precision gained by stratification is usually not great.

At times it may be reasonable and desirable to "oversample" some element from one or more strata if that element occurs infrequently in the population. For example, in PROJECT TALENT,[10] it was necessary to overselect medium and large high schools and underselect smaller high schools to be included in the study. The question posed by the PROJECT TALENT staff was:

> How many schools would we need in order to draw a sample consisting of five per cent of high school students? Five per cent of the schools? Theoretically, yes—and, as it turned out, we did give the tests in approximately one out of every 20 schools. But it wasn't as simple as that.

[10]John C. Flanagan, John T. Dailey, Marion F. Shaycoft, William A. Gorham, David B. Orr, and Isadore Goldberg, *Design for a Study of American Youth*, Vol. I of *The Talents of American Youth* (Boston: Houghton Mifflin Co., 1962), p. 46.

The sizes of public high schools differ radically—from less than a hundred students to more than 5,000. The small high schools dotting the rural countryside are far more numerous than very large city high schools. To emphasize the contrast, the total enrollment of several dozen rural schools may fall far below the enrollment of one city school. To select one out of every 20 schools in the country without consideration of size differences would have resulted in so few large public high schools—and so very many small schools—that our later research on the effects of school size would have been inconclusive. The solution was to invite one out of every 20 medium-sized public high schools to participate in the study; one out of every 13 very large schools; and one out of 50 small schools.

The estimation of the value of a parameter when sampling is not proportional requires that the ratio of the number of cases in each stratum to the total number of cases be multiplied by the proportion of favorable responses in each stratum. A disproportional stratified random sample using the criteria established by the **PROJECT TALENT** staff and statistics provided by the U.S. Office of Education[11] is exemplified for American high schools by Table 8-3.

Note that if a 5 percent proportional sample were desired, approximately 472 small schools (0.39 × 1211), 727 medium-sized schools (0.60 × 1211), and about 12 large schools (0.01 × 1211) would be selected. However, a proportional sample would have included an excessive number of small schools and too few large ones.

Assume that an investigator is interested in estimating the number of high schools willing to participate in a new experimental program. Letters are sent to each school principal; assume that each of the 932 principals in the disproportional stratified sample answered the letter of inquiry. Of the 189 principals of small schools, only 40 are willing to participate (21 percent); of the 729 principals of medium-sized schools, 304 reply favorably (42 percent); and of the 14 principals of large high schools, 10 are in favor of the new experimental program (71 percent). If the sample were made proportional, the parameter estimate could be easily obtained by summing the favorable replies and dividing by the number of persons. However, with disproportional samples, it is necessary to weight the proportion of favorable replies by the ratio of the number of cases in each stratum to the total number of cases. Thus, the parameter estimate (the proportion of favorable replies) is

$$(0.39 \times 0.21) + (0.60 \times 0.42) + (0.01 \times 0.71) = 0.34$$

[11]U.S. Office of Education, *Statistics of Education in the United States*, 1958–1959 Series, No. 1 Public Secondary Schools, by Edmund A. Ford and Virgil R. Walker (Washington, D.C.: U.S. Government Printing Office, 1961), p. 7.

TABLE 8-3

Computational Table Demonstrating Method of
Determining Number of Cases to Be Selected within Each Stratum
for a Disproportional Stratified Random Sample

| Population and Sample Characteristics | Small | Medium | Large | Totals |
|---|---|---|---|---|
| Population $N$ in each stratum (no. of schools) | 9466 | 14,575 | 185 | 24,226 |
| Sample proportion desired | 1 out of 50 | 1 out of 20 | 1 out of 13 | 1 out of 5 |
| No. of high schools selected | 189* | 729* | 14* | 932 |
| Proportion of no. of schools in each stratum to total no. of schools | $\frac{9466}{24,226} = 0.39*$ | $\frac{14,575}{24,226} = 0.60*$ | $\frac{185}{24,226} = 0.01*$ | 1.0 |

*Rounded.

The important point is that parameter estimates derived from proportional stratified random samples differ from those derived from disproportional stratified samples. Proportional samples are already weighted and thus save some computational time. Otherwise, it would be necessary to apply the weighting procedure just described.

It may be of some interest to observe that if a proportional stratified sample is weighted, the results will be identical with those of the nonweighted procedure. In the earlier example of the superintendent's estimating the protion of voters favoring a proposed bond issue, 57 percent of the sample favored passage of the bill. Using the weighting procedure (which is unnecessary with proportional samples) would yield exactly the same results but with much more effort:

$$(0.42 \times 0.76) + (0.33 \times 0.52) + (0.25 \times 0.32) = 0.57$$

## Systematic Sampling

Sometimes a population is so structured that it is possible to select a sample by counting every fifth, tenth, or hundredth person until the desired sample size is obtained. This procedure is called *systematic sampling*. If a school district has students listed in alphabetical order, it may be possible to select every tenth or fifteenth name on the list for inclusion in a sample, instead of assigning numbers to each member of the population to select a simple random sample.

There are a number of important advantages in using a systematic rather than a simple random sample. In the first place, there is usually a considerable saving of work. Wherever population elements are listed (such as rosters, rolls, etc.), use of a table of random numbers is unnecessary, and the sample can be chosen by simply selecting every $n$th case. This procedure may also be of advantage in selecting cases within strata, as long as the elements are listed in some form. Systematic sampling also gives assurance that there is broad sampling throughout the population. It may, therefore, provide a more accurate sample.

To avoid bias, it is essential that the first element to be sampled be determined from a table of random numbers. For example, to select every tenth name in a telephone directory, enter a table of random numbers and select at random the first two-digit number between 01 and 10. If the number selected is 03, select the third name in the directory, followed by the thirteenth, twenty-third, thirty-third, etc., until desired sample size is reached.

Keep in mind that populations other than human beings can also be selected with systematic samples. House numbers, library call numbers, goods on grocery shelves, words in dictionaries, and names of cities in an atlas are just a few examples of situations where systematic sampling plans may be used.

Although systematic sampling usually leads to the same results as simple random sampling (and it often does so with much less effort), there are times when the method may yield a biased sample. This will occur whenever the elements to be selected are repeated in some form of repetitive cycle. Consider the following list of students and their IQ's in three classes:

|  | *Class I* |  |  | *Class II* |  |  | *Class III* |  |
|---|---|---|---|---|---|---|---|---|
| *1.* | Vern Jones | 143 | *11.* | Lois Brown | 149 | *21.* | Bob Moon | 146 |
| *2.* | Mary Smith | 139 | *12.* | Al Carp | 140 | *22.* | Rex Doll | 141 |
| *3.* | Ron Rogers | 130 | *13.* | Pete Ayer | 129 | *23.* | Charles Sal | 131 |
| *4.* | Alex Ruggs | 125 | *14.* | Vi Ellis | 124 | *24.* | Pat Rich | 123 |
| *5.* | Rory Paul | 115 | *15.* | Jay Pal | 117 | *25.* | Debbie Pop | 116 |
| *6.* | Karen Day | 110 | *16.* | Laurie Or | 109 | *26.* | Belle Lee | 111 |
| *7.* | Kathy Fay | 90 | *17.* | Jenny Fox | 93 | *27.* | Bernie Ep | 92 |
| *8.* | Mel Johns | 85 | *18.* | Carol Tom | 87 | *28.* | Ralph Law | 86 |
| *9.* | Paul Hyde | 80 | *19.* | Hugh Barr | 78 | *29.* | Will Ho | 79 |
| *10.* | Louis Kap | 70 | *20.* | Phil Dorr | 75 | *30.* | Thelma Lin | 73 |

Suppose now the researcher enters a table of random numbers and selects 03, and every tenth case is desired. The researcher would then select

Ron Rogers, Pete Ayer, and Charles Sal. Note that the mean IQ for these three students is 130, by no means typical of the 30 students in the three classes. Actually, the mean IQ for the entire group of 30 students is 109.5. However, because there is a cyclical fluctuation of listed IQ scores, systematic samples are inappropriate. Where cyclical fluctuations are not present, systematic samples can yield convenient as well as accurate estimates of parameters.

The mean derived from a systematic sample is computed in the same manner as are means derived from a simple random sample. The standard error of the mean for systematic samples presents, however, a "formidable problem,"[12] which can be resolved most easily by using or developing lists of the population elements that are organized in some completely random fashion. If this be the case, the formulas used in simple random sampling can be used with systematic sampling.

## Area or Cluster Sampling

Where lists of individuals are unavailable or the characteristics of the population are not well known, it is possible for the researcher to sample areas or clusters of elements first, and then to sample individuals or elements within the clusters. This procedure is called *area* or *cluster sampling*. Suppose, for example, an investigator is interested in sampling the attitudes of persons living in a large urban area. It would be both difficult and expensive to develop a list including *each* person. However, it may be possible to secure a map of the area which can be subdivided into city blocks or neighborhoods. Within each block or neighborhood some random method (usually systematic sampling) is used to select the actual units or elements to be polled. Similarly, although it may be possible to obtain a list of all students in a large school district, it may be easier and less expensive to select randomly a number of schools and then to select randomly students within these schools.

Both cost and the amount of tolerable sampling error determines whether cluster sampling or some other sampling procedure is to be preferred. Generally, cluster or area sampling costs less than does a simple random sample of the same size, but there is usually a corresponding decrease in the accuracy of predicting parameters. For example, a random selection of students throughout a large number of schools tends to be quite expensive when travel time is included in the costs. With cluster sampling, a few schools are randomly selected and a relatively larger number of students is selected within each school.

It is possible to arrange clusters and elements within clusters so that the sampling error is smaller than for simple random sampling or stratified

[12]Leslie Kish, *Survey Sampling* (New York: John Wiley & Sons, 1965), p. 117.

random sampling. To obtain this increase in accuracy, it is necessary to subdivide the population so that each cluster is as variable as possible with regard to the attribute under investigation and so that differences between clusters are kept as homogeneous as possible. If, for example, it would be possible to find one school that contained as heterogeneous a group of students as could be found in the population, and if other schools are similar to the first one, not only can costs be reduced by sampling solely within this school, but this would also be a very efficient sampling plan.

The characteristics which make for efficient sampling with stratification are exactly those factors that make cluster sampling inefficient. Stratified samples attempt to maximize differences between strata and minimize differences within each stratum; cluster samples should minimize differences between clusters and maximize differences within each cluster.

In practice, unfortunately, any given cluster is likely to be relatively homogeneous, and differences between clusters are likely to be quite large. Students within a given school are more likely to be similar than are students attending different schools. Under ordinary circumstances, then, cluster sampling is likely to be less expensive but will yield more error than simple random sampling or stratified random sampling.

The decision to use a cluster sampling design rather than a simple random sample can be determined from two different points of view. One can either begin by considering which of the two procedures will yield the smaller standard error for a given cost, or one can begin by specifying the amount of error which can be tolerated or allowed and then selecting the design that costs less. References at the end of this chapter will provide formulas needed to help determine the optimal sampling plan under different specified conditions.

# DETERMINING THE SIZE OF THE SAMPLE

The determination of sample size is a problem faced by every investigator. Too often, the inexperienced researcher considers large samples necessary if valid conclusions are to be drawn from research data. Cornell[13] has described an all too typical instance, which took place during World War II. A Congressional committee was interested in knowing the number of individuals trained in vocational schools who later went to work in war industries. Cornell states:

---

[13]Francis G. Cornell, "The Sampling Problem in Educational Research," in Raymond O. Collier, Jr., and Stanley M. Elam, eds., *Research Design and Analysis* (Bloomington, Ind.: Phi Delta Kappa, 1961), pp. 70–71.

In the final planning conference the statisticians were outnumbered ten to one. The proposed sample size was observed to be less than 5 percent of the population. The majority decision prevailed and the sample size was upped to 10 percent, since it was doubted that less than this magic minimum would yield reliable results. Rejection of the more efficient sample design as originally proposed resulted in additional costs of hundreds of thousands of dollars.

## Accuracy

Accuracy is not necessarily increased significantly by selecting large samples; this can be seen by examining data collected by Rowntree,[14] who complied information on the entire population of working-class households in York, England. One of the conditions Rowntree was interested in studying was the percentage of money spent on rent among members of five working classes, designated by the letters *A*, *B*, *C*, *D*, and *E*.

By interviewing every household, Rowntree found that 26.5 percent of the income from families in income class *A* was spent on rent, whereas only 11.3 percent of the income from group *E* was spent for rent. An examination of Table 8-4 shows that little or no accuracy was lost by systematically selecting only 1 household in 10 or even 1 household in 50 (a 2 percent sample).

TABLE 8-4

Percentage of Income Spent on Rent

| Income Class | No. of Families | Population Data | 1 in 10 | 1 in 20 | 1 in 30 | 1 in 50 |
|---|---|---|---|---|---|---|
| *A* | 1748 | 26.5 | 26.6 | 25.9 | 28.3 | 27.1 |
| *B* | 2477 | 22.7 | 22.9 | 23.5 | 22.3 | 22.6 |
| *C* | 2514 | 19.8 | 18.1 | 17.2 | 17.2 | 18.0 |
| *D* | 1676 | 15.8 | 16.0 | 14.4 | 17.1 | 16.9 |
| *E* | 3740 | 11.3 | 11.0 | 10.1 | 11.2 | 11.5 |

*Source:* Rowntree, p. 489.

Referring to the fifteen tables which he presented, Rowntree concluded:

They point to the fact that so long as one is dealing with fairly large figures . . . , results obtained by the sampling method are for the most

[14]B. Seebohm Rowntree, *Poverty and Progress: A Second Social Survey of York* (London: Longmans, Green and Co., 1941).

part (though not in every case) substantially accurate. . . . But when we come to analyze the causes of poverty we are dealing with less than a third of the total working class population, and dividing their number into seven groups. Consequently the classes are very much smaller and the degree of inaccuracy much greater.[15]

As discussed earlier in this chapter, the degree of accuracy (i.e., to what extent the sample mean obtained will differ from the population mean) that can be expected in any sample will depend on its standard deviation and the number of cases selected. These two statistics are used to compute the standard error of a mean, which has already been defined as $s/\sqrt{N}$. Extremely homogeneous populations will require a much smaller number of cases for any specified degree of error than will a heterogeneous population. If a proportion is of concern to an investigator, the standard deviation of the proportion, $\sqrt{p(1-p)}$, must also be computed. For example, if the proportion of respondents who favor some proposition is 0.60, the standard deviation will be

$$\sqrt{0.60(1-0.60)} \text{ or } \sqrt{0.60(0.40)} = \sqrt{0.24} = 0.49$$

The standard deviation must then be divided by $\sqrt{N}$, the square root of the number of cases in the sample, to compute the standard error of a proportion.

Suppose that with *simple random sampling* a superintendent found that 57 percent of a sample of 500 persons were in favor of a proposed bond issue and that a simple majority of yes votes would be sufficient to pass the issue. Because a percentage is 100 times the value of a proportion, the standard error of a percentage is

$$100\sqrt{\frac{p(1-p)}{N}} = 100\sqrt{\frac{0.57(0.43)}{500}} = 2.21$$

For the 0.95 confidence interval, the limits are $57 \pm 1.96(2.21)$ or 61.33 to 52.67; the 0.99 confidence interval is $57 \pm 2.58(2.21)$ or 62.04 to 51.96. Thus, the superintendent can be 99 percent confident that the percentage of favorable votes lies between 62.04 and 51.96.

Another way of looking at sample size as it relates to accuracy is to use the formula

$$N = \left(\frac{z}{e}\right)^2 (p)(1-p)$$

where $N$ is the sample size; $z$ is the standard score corresponding to a given confidence level; $e$ is the amount of tolerable sampling error in a given situa-

[15]Rowntree, pp. 479–480.

tion; and $p$ is the proportion of cases in the population that exhibit some particular attribute of interest. The formula assumes that the population consists of dichotomous attributes such as *present–absent, yes–no,* or *males–females.*[16]

As an example, suppose that a study can tolerate only 1 percent of error and that the researcher will establish a confidence level of 0.95. Assume that a particular dichotomous attribute, such as the percentage of favorable votes, is 15 percent. The $z$ corresponding to the 0.95 confidence level (for large samples) equals 1.96. Substituting in the above formula:

$$N = \left(\frac{1.96}{0.01}\right)^2 (0.15)(1 - 0.15)$$
$$N = 196^2(0.15)(0.85)$$
$$N = 38,416(0.1275)$$
$$N = 4898$$

That is, the researcher will need to select approximately 4900 cases from the population if the probability is to be 95 out of 100 that the sample proportion will differ no more than 1 percent from the population proportion. Rarely, however, does anyone need this degree of accuracy. For example, if the tolerable amount of error can be increased to 0.10, then:

$$N = \left(\frac{1.96}{0.10}\right)^2 (0.15)(0.85)$$
$$N = 19.6^2(0.1275)$$
$$N = 49 \text{ (rounded from 48.98)}$$

Also, if the confidence level can be reduced to 90 percent, the corresponding value of $z$ would be 1.65; $N$ could then be:

$$N = \left(\frac{1.65}{0.10}\right)^2 (0.1275)$$
$$N = 35$$

## Cost

The cost of securing additional samples should be considered before determining the final sample size. Cost, of course, includes expenditures of effort as well as of funds. Where individuals are to be interviewed, for

---

[16]For continuous measurements, the appropriate formula for estimating sample size would be

$$N = \left(\frac{z\sigma}{e}\right)^2$$

where $z$ is the standard score corresponding to a given confidence level; $\sigma$ is the estimated standard deviation in the population; and $e$ is the number of points of tolerable error.

example, much effort and time have to be expended, thus making the cost per sampled unit high. Under these conditions (especially if cluster sampling is not possible), it may not be possible to sample as many persons as one might prefer. On the other hand, where the unit cost of securing additional samples is relatively low (as in sending questionnaires through the mail), sampling error can be reduced by securing additional cases.

In large research organizations, it is important to estimate the approximate costs involved in any given study. However, graduate students are likely to have free access to many university facilities and resources and, therefore, will have relatively low costs in comparison with large research organizations working on commercial projects. Nonetheless, students would do well to try to estimate in advance of undertaking any study for what expenses they will be responsible and what size sample they can afford. A number of these factors have been identified in the literature. Table 8-5 is designed as an aid in estimating the approximate cost of undertaking a given sampling survey.

It should be clear that Table 8-5 is designed only to provide some general considerations to be kept in mind. Ideally, most of the time and money should go into designing, planning, collecting, and analyzing the data. If the student also has to pay for office space, equipment, or other services not directly related to obtaining reliable and valid data, and if these secondary costs are high enough to interfere with the collection of valid data, a less ambitious and more restricted design should be considered.

## Homogeneity of the Population

The homogeneity or heterogeneity of the population is a factor which must be considered before a sample size is considered adequate. From an intuitive point of view, it can be demonstrated that where the population is homogeneous in the attributes under investigation, a smaller sample is required than if the population is quite diversified. Consider a rather extreme example. Only a few drops of distilled water from a pitcher would be required to obtain a highly accurate picture of the rest of the water. In contrast, the selection of two students to "represent" an entire school body is not likely to be nearly so accurate.

In simple random sampling, the standard error of the mean is $s/\sqrt{N}$. By examination it can be seen that, for a given degree of accuracy, as the standard deviation increases, so will the size of the sample needed.

In stratified random sampling, an attempt is made to make each stratum as homogeneous as possible. This reduces the variability within each stratum and permits the researcher to select fewer cases for a given degree of reliability. The variability between strata does not enter into formulas for the standard error.

Cluster sampling increases the variability within each cluster but

## TABLE 8-5

### Factors Used in Estimating Cost to Conduct a Given Study

| Factor | Considerations |
|---|---|
| 1. Office space | a. Provided by school or home in most instances |
| 2. Calculators, typewriters, and other equipment | b. Usually provided by school; if not, add rental fee for period of time used |
| 3. Supplies (paper, stencils, misc.) | c. Number of reams of paper times cost per ream; add costs of stationery, duplicating, or printing |
| 4. Consultants | d. Paid consultants usually charge by the day plus transportation and accommodations |
| 5. Statistical work | e. For large amounts of data, compare computer time to hiring statistical clerks or doing own computations |
| 6. Secretarial help | f. Student help often satisfactory and relatively inexpensive |
| 7. Planning design of study, developing interview schedules or questionnaires, pretesting | g. Ordinarily done by student with help of faculty adviser; amount of personal time spent is a cost involved in the study. If the study is carried out in a number of different communities or schools, compare personal time involved with advantage of hiring data collectors |
| 8. Selecting the sample | h. Include cost of obtaining listings, rosters, or maps (for area sampling), and actual selection of participants |
| 9. Travel | i. Especially costly in interviews, but can be reduced in cluster sampling. Estimate car expenses; add travel time per hour to costs |
| 10. Selecting the data collectors | j. Compare cost of hiring trained interviewers with cost of training inexperienced interviewers; include training time, revising interview schedules to make items clear and unambiguous |
| 11. Interviewing | k. Preferable to pay by hour than by number of interviews completed |
| 12. Conference time | l. Include time spent with interviewers to obtain their reactions, time spent with respondents to check on validity of reports, time spent with consultants |
| 13. Writing the report | m. This is the investigator's responsibility; add to the time involved in completing the research |

attempts to reduce the variabilty between clusters. Thus, the standard deviation within a given cluster tends to be large; to increase accuracy in estimating the parameter, select a relatively large number of cases.

## SUMMARY

**1.** Because of the difficulty of studying populations, the educational researcher usually selects samples by methods that provide suitably close estimates of the relevant characteristics of the population.

**2.** Ideally, the population to which one plans to generalize research findings determines the selection of the sample. In actual practice, however, it is usually necessary to limit the scope of a population so that it may be sampled.

**3.** The process of sampling consists of three phases: 1) defining the population; 2) drawing a sample from the population; and 3) estimating the mean, standard deviation, proportion, or other parameter values from knowledge obtained from the sample statistic. The third step in the sampling procedure is known as *statistical inference.*

**4.** A sample was described as being *unbiased* when elements are drawn in some random manner. Unbiased samples approximate parameters as additional cases are drawn; *biased* samples yield statistics that consistently overestimate or underestimate parameters.

**5.** In *simple random sampling*, every element in the population has an equal probability of being selected. The use of a table of random numbers was described as an efficient and easy way of drawing a simple random sample.

**6.** With simple random sampling, the *standard error of a mean* is a ratio of the standard deviation to the square root of the number of cases. Thus, precision can be increased by reducing the variability of the sample and/or by increasing the number of cases.

**7.** *Stratified random sampling* involves: 1) dividing a population into strata; 2) sampling randomly within each stratum; and 3) estimating the value of the parameter. The major advantage to stratification is that sampling error arises only within each stratum and not between different strata. In addition, stratification permits the use of different methods of drawing samples within each stratum, which may help to reduce costs. Methods were described for estimating parameters for proportional and disproportional stratified sampling. Disproportional sampling requires a weighting procedure for estimating parameters; weighting is not necessary for proportional stratified sampling.

**8.** *Systematic sampling* was described as the selection of every $n$th case from a population listing or roster. The principal advantage of systematic sampling over simple random sampling is primarily one of convenience. The reason for drawing the first number randomly was described. The major disadvantage to systematic sampling is that it may be seriously in error if elements in the population are repeated at constant intervals. In addition, standard error formulas for systematic samples have not been satisfactorily developed.

**9.** In *area* or *cluster sampling* major areas or clusters are selected first and individuals second. The major purpose of cluster sampling is to reduce costs per element sampled, although this advantage is somewhat offset by the usual increase in error. To reduce error, clusters would have to be selected in such a way that differences *between* clusters are small in comparison to the variability *within* clusters.

**10.** The size of a sample is determined from a number of different factors:

**a.** *Accuracy*. That accuracy is not greatly lost in estimating parameters (as long as relatively large numbers of units in the population are considered) was demonstrated in a classic study by Rowntree. Methods for estimating confidence intervals for proportions and percentages were demonstrated.

**b.** *Cost*. A number of factors were noted that would increase the cost of undertaking any sampling survey. A worksheet to help the student estimate the cost of a sample survey was demonstrated.

**c.** *Homogeneity*. Some general considerations were noted for determining the number of cases needed when the homogeneity or heterogeneity of the population is considered. In simple random sampling, accuracy is increased as variability is reduced. In stratified random sampling, the investigator can afford to take fewer cases for a given degree of accuracy where each stratum is homogeneous and where differences between strata are heterogeneous. In cluster sampling, keep differences small between clusters and increase variability within each cluster. This increased variability within clusters means that, for a given degree of accuracy, more cases will be needed than if simple random sampling is used.

## PRACTICE EXERCISES

**1.** Explain why a physician may be satisfied with drawing only a few drops of a patient's blood before making generalizations about the patient's health, whereas the educational researcher is usually not satisfied with such small samples.

**2.** An educational psychologist studies the IQ's of penitentiary inmates and announces that the average person who has committed a crime has an IQ of 84. What logical error has this researcher committed? How could his error be corrected?

**3.** In a school district, principals spend one day per semester in the classroom of each of their ten teachers to assess teaching ability. Evaluate this sampling procedure. What suggestions could you make to improve sampling technique?

**4.** For each of the following sampling procedures, indicate the broadest population to which the researcher can legitimately extend research findings:

 **a.** Seventeen out of 174 students were chosen at random from an introductory philosophy class at college *Z*. The 17 students were each interviewed on his or her attitudes toward dictatorships.

 **b.** The subjects for this investigation included 350,000 army inductees selected at random during World War II. Each inductee was given form *X* of the Betterman Intelligence Test from which norms were to be developed for civilian groups.

 **c.** All of the parents in Johnson School District's Blake School were mailed questionnaires on their attitude toward education. Seventy-four percent of the parents responded.

**5.** A researcher advertises in the student newspaper for volunteers to participate in an experiment on learning. Each volunteer is to receive $3.00 per hour. Half of the volunteers are randomly assigned to one experimental treatment, while the other half act as a control or nonexperimental group. Suppose that the experimental group obtained higher scores than did the control group. What could the researcher conclude? What inferences could be made concerning the population? What sampling errors might have been committed?

**6.** The results of a math test for 20 students are as follows:

| Student | Score | Student | Score |
|---|---|---|---|
| *1.* Al Arneson | 9 | *11.* Kathy Kanner | 82 |
| *2.* Bill Bennett | 82 | *12.* Lionel Lummer | 85 |
| *3.* Carl Conner | 73 | *13.* Michael Monroe | 67 |
| *4.* Duane Dunn | 31 | *14.* Nancy Nannally | 57 |
| *5.* Elsie Emerson | 54 | *15.* Orvil Olson | 87 |
| *6.* Frank Fenner | 38 | *16.* Patricia Price | 16 |
| *7.* Gail Green | 18 | *17.* Quincy Queen | 5 |
| *8.* Henrietta Herman | 32 | *18.* Rodney Raney | 18 |
| *9.* Isabel Irving | 74 | *19.* Sally Samson | 47 |
| *10.* Jack Jones | 95 | *20.* Ted Thompson | 77 |

 **a.** Select 5 members of the class by using a table of random numbers. How close does the mean of your sample come to the mean of the class (52.35)? How could you determine whether your sample is biased or unbiased? Try again with $N = 10$ and $N = 15$. Does sample size make a difference? How?

 **b.** Using a systematic sample, select 5 individuals to be representative of the class. How does the mean of your systematic sample differ from the mean of the class? In this instance, is there likely to be any bias in the sample so selected?

 **c.** Select a stratified proportional random sample by dividing the class into males and females. The mean scores for the 12 boys and 8 girls are

55.58 and 47.50, respectively. How do these values compare to your selected sample of boys and girls?

7. Two investigators, A and B, select simple random samples from equally large populations that yield the following distributions:

| A | B |
|---|---|
| 14 | 72 |
| 13 | 19 |
| 15 | 43 |
| 14 | 12 |
| 14 | 99 |

Which investigator, A or B, will probably need to select the larger sample? Why?

8. In your own words, summarize the relationship between the number of cases in a sample, the standard deviation, and the amount of error.

9. Suppose that it is estimated that 20 percent of the students in a large high school hold part-time jobs. If a researcher selects a sample of 100 students at random, how accurately will such a sample statistic approximate population parameters?

10. You can allow an error of only 4 percent and want the level of confidence to be 0.99. You estimate that 80 percent of the population of students in a large school district do not have after-school jobs. What size sample would you recommend?

11. As a class project, predict the voting behavior of students throughout your school prior to some all-school election. Students should design a simple random sample, a systematic sample, a stratified random sample, and a cluster sample. Describe in detail how you would go about obtaining your sample. If time permits, one-fourth of the class can work on each sampling design. Actually carry out the interviewing of students and compare the results of each of the four sampling designs with the actual results of the election. Explain your findings.

## Selected Supplementary Readings

1. HANSEN, MORRIS H., and HURWITZ, WILLIAM N. "The Problem of Non-Response in Sample Surveys." *Journal of the American Statistical Association*, 41, no. 236 (1946), pp. 517–529. The authors suggest a plan for determining the characteristics of nonrespondents in mail surveys by mailing questionnaires in excess of the numbers actually required and by interviewing a sample of those who failed to return questionnaires by mail.

2. SUDMAN, SEYMOUR. *Applied Sampling.* New York: Academic Press, 1976, 249 pp. An excellent introductory text with numerous practical examples.

3. KISH, LESLIE. "The Design of Sampling Surveys," in Raymond O. Collier, Jr., and Stanley M. Elam, eds. *Research Design and Analysis*, Second Annual Phi Delta Kappa Symposium on Educational Research. Bloomington, Ind.: Phi Delta Kappa, 1961, pp. 45–63. The author presents an excellent taxonomy of sampling and workable criteria for sampling designs. See also Cornell, Francis G. "The Sampling Problem in Educational Research," pp. 65–80. The author discusses some of the misconceptions of sampling procedures that are inherent with the public and with researchers. He also indicates the advances that have been made in educational research by employing proper sampling techniques.

4. MARKS, ELI S. "Some Sampling Problems in Educational Research." *Journal of Educational Psychology*, 42, no. 2 (1951), pp. 85–96. A brief but excellent description of the need and the methods for defining population characteristics and drawing samples randomly. The article contains a bibliography which may be of value to students who need more advanced sampling procedures than can be described in this text.

5. KISH, LESLIE. *Survey Sampling*. New York: John Wiley & Sons, 1965, 643 pp. This text is difficult reading for the beginning student, but it contains a wealth of valuable information.

6. MCNEMAR, QUINN. "Sampling in Psychological Research." *Psychological Bulletin*, 37, no. 6 (1940), pp. 331–365. Professor McNemar is justifiably critical of the inappropriate uses of nonprobability samples. He examines the meaning of *homogeneous* populations and cites cases where adequate sampling procedures have allowed the researcher to draw reasonable conclusions about the population under consideration. In addition, the author shows clearly how selective and biased sampling has led to conclusions which are open to criticism.

7. POLITZ, ALFRED, and SIMMONS, WILLARD. "An Attempt to Get the 'Not at Homes' into the Sample without Callbacks." *Journal of the American Statistical Association*, 44, no. 245 (1949), pp. 9–31. The authors suggest a plan which can eliminate the need to return to homes to check on nonrespondents when using area survey techniques.

8. SLONIM, MORRIS JAMES. "Sampling in a Nutshell." *Journal of the American Statistical Association*, 52, no. 278 (1957), pp. 143–161. A nontechnical and highly readable introduction to sampling theory and procedures. Each of many methods is covered rather briefly.

9. WHITE, MARY ALICE, and DUKER, JAN. "Suggested Standards for Children's Samples." *American Psychologist*, 28, no. 8 (August 1973), pp. 700–703. The authors list essential characteristics of samples of children that should be reported in research articles.

9 obtaining
reliable
and valid
measures

Educational and psychological tests are used for a variety of research purposes. In experiments, tests are often used to equate groups on such attributes as intelligence, reading levels, or knowledge. Typically, one group (called an *experimental group*) is afforded some experimental treatment that is withheld from the members of the *control group*. Tests can then be employed to determine whether or not the experimental treatment produced any measurable effects.

In descriptive studies, tests are often used to gather information. The investigator may wish to know the mean IQ of students in a given district or the achievement levels of students in different curricula. Here again, tests can provide examinees with a common set of stimuli in the form of questions or items; this increases the likelihood that responses will be obtained under uniform conditions and will thus reflect differing levels of attainment on the same trait.

In still other types of studies, the tests themselves may be the primary focus of attention. The investigator may be concerned with such questions as "Do students who study for essay examinations retain more knowledge than those who study for multiple-choice examinations?" or "Is achievement facilitated more by taking 'hard' examinations or 'easy' ones?" These and related questions have been used to study the use of tests to motivate students, their influence on anxiety, test-taking strategies, etc.

Research findings requiring the use of tests can be no more accurate than the measures themselves. A poorly constructed examination may not yield accurate information about respondents. Because research findings are so dependent upon the instruments (i.e., tests, questionnaires, interview schedules, etc.) used to gather information, the researcher is responsible for selecting those instruments which best fit the requirements of the investigation.

## CONSIDERATIONS IN SELECTING A TEST

In selecting an examination, the researcher would do well to complete a copy of the *Test Analysis Form* (Appendix I) for each examination under serious consideration. Information concerning the examination that cannot be found in published research studies or in the test manual should be provided by the researcher. The investigator has the responsibility for providing evidence that the examination selected is the most appropriate for the purpose at hand.

One of the best sources for evaluating standardized tests is the *Mental Measurements Yearbooks*, edited by Oscar Buros.[1-9] These yearbooks

[1]Oscar Krisen Buros, "Educational, Psychological, and Personality Tests of 1933, 1934, and 1935," *Rutgers University Bulletin*, 13, no. 1 (New Brunswick, N.J.: School of Education, Rutgers University, 1936).

[2]Oscar Krisen Buros, "Educational, Psychological, and Personality Tests of 1936," *Rutgers University Bulletin*, 14, no. 2A, Studies in Education, No. 11 (New Brunswick, N.J.: School of Education, Rutgers University, 1937).

[3]Oscar Krisen Buros, *The 1938 Mental Measurements Yearbook* (New Brunswick, N.J.: Rutgers University Press, 1938).

[4]Oscar Krisen Buros, *The 1940 Mental Measurements Yearbook* (New Brunswick, N.J.: Rutgers University Press, 1941).

[5]Oscar Krisen Buros, *The Third Mental Measurements Yearbook* (New Brunswick, N.J.: Rutgers University Press, 1949).

[6]Oscar Krisen Buros, *The Fourth Mental Measurements Yearbook* (Highland Park, N.J.: Gryphon Press, 1953).

[7]Oscar Krisen Buros, *The Fifth Mental Measurements Yearbook* (Highland Park, N.J.: Gryphon Press, 1959).

[8]Oscar Krisen Buros, *The Sixth Mental Measurements Yearbook* (Highland Park, N.J.: Gryphon Press, 1965).

[9]Oscar Krisen Buros, *The Seventh Mental Measurements Yearbook* (Highland Park, N.J.: Gryphon Press, 1972).

contain critical evaluations of tests and provide information concerning costs, availability of alternate forms, administration time required, names of sub-tests, grade or age levels for which test were designed, and name of publisher. Each *Yearbook* usually covers only those examinations which have appeared since the publication of the preceding *Yearbook*. They are, therefore, some-what inconvenient to use unless one knows the approximate publication date of a test. However, references are available to help potential test purchasers locate test reviews, and to indicate which tests are still in print.[10,11]

In writing research reports that include the use of tests, inventories, questionnaires, or rating scales, the investigator should take the responsibility of evaluating all tests used in the investigation. Where a well-known stan-dardized test is used, relatively little space is needed in the research paper for its evaluation, unless it is being used in an unconventional manner. Ordinarily, a reference to the test manual or to research studies using the examination will be sufficient. However, where the researcher has found it necessary to construct a test or where new examinations are being employed, much care should be devoted to the objective evaluation of the instrument, and the findings of the evaluation should be in the research report. Usually, such information is included in theses or dissertations in the chapter titled "Proce-dure" or "Methods"; however, where the construction of an examination is the major purpose of writing the research report, or where the outcome of an investigation is determined primarily by the use of a particular examination, a separate chapter is ordinarily provided.

Even though evaluative criteria are available for educational and psychological tests, the researcher still faces the problem of deciding whether a given examination is suitable for his or her own purposes. Although such considerations as purchasing costs, simplicity of administration, ease of scoring, and appropriateness of norms should all be considered before deciding to use any examination, the problems of reliability and validity of the measurements themselves should be given the greatest consideration.

## THE MEANING OF RELIABILITY

*Reliability* may be defined as the extent to which measurements reflect true individual differences among examinees. Individual differences are considered to be "true" if they represent nonchance factors or conditions. A perfectly reliable set of measurements would be unaffected by random or chance events and would, therefore, be capable of measuring some educa-tional or psychological attribute perfectly (i.e., without error). Completely *unreliable* data would measure the effects of chance only. For example,

[10]Oscar Krisen Buros, *Tests in Print* (Highland Park, N.J.: Gryphon Press, 1961).
[11]*Tests in Print II* (Highland Park, N.J.: Gryphon Press, 1974).

assigning "scores" to student papers by selecting numbers at random would yield maximally unreliable values. Although it is unlikely that anyone would deliberately assign scores to students at random, some test items or scoring criteria may be so ambiguous that the effects are essentially the same.

Measurement theory often assumes that an individual's *obtained* score contains two components: a *true* score component and some degree of *error*. A true score is unaffected by chance conditions and would, therefore, increase individual differences along a continuum in which the role of chance or random error would be reduced to zero. However, in practice, all measurements (including those in the physical sciences) are subject to some effects of random error. The researcher's responsibility is to try to reduce random error as much as possible so that obtained and true scores will coincide as much as possible.[12]

The concept of a true score does not imply that the researcher has some magic formula for measuring true scores. A true score is usually thought of as the hypothetical mean of an infinite number of repeated testings with the same instrument when transfer effects from familiarity with the test are eliminated. The fact that an individual's true score remains unknown is not a particularly serious problem as long as it is possible to estimate the amount of random error present in a given set of measurements. As will be demonstrated, neither reliability nor estimates of error require knowledge of the true score. The only time a true score would be known is when reliability is perfect. In that case, obtained scores and true scores will be identical. As reliability decreases, there is a corresponding incongruence between obtained and true scores. In the extreme case where reliability is zero, the only relationship between true and obtained scores would be due to the effects of random error.

Most estimates of reliability require the use of correlation coefficients to measure how consistently true individual differences have been assessed. When correlations are 1.0, random errors must be 0.0; if correlations are 0.0, one explanation is that the measurement of at least one of the two variables being correlated was subject to the effects of complete random error.[13]

The *Standards for Educational and Psychological Tests*[14] describes four general types of reliability coefficients: *stability, equivalence, stability and equivalence,* and *internal consistency,* or *homogeneity.*

[12]Error can be *systematic* or *random*. Systematic error will increase *or* decrease all scores by a constant value. Systematic error does not affect reliability since it affects everyone in exactly the same way. Random error, however, will increase the scores of some persons and decrease the scores of others. Reliability is reduced if random error affects the measurement of individual differences.

[13]Correlations can be zero for at least two other reasons: (1) there may be no relationship between the variables being correlated, or (2) the relationship between the two variables is curvilinear.

[14]American Psychological Association, *Standards for Educational and Psychological Tests* (Washington, D.C.: American Psychological Association, 1974).

# TYPES OF RELIABILITY COEFFICIENTS

## Stability

If an investigation requires some estimate of the extent to which scores remain consistent over a period of time, the researcher may determine the consistency of these scores by readministering the same examination to the same group of individuals. The extent to which individuals retain their relative ranks on repeated administrations with the same instrument is an indication of their stability.

Suppose, for example, a researcher is trying to determine the consistency of the weight[15] of a group of individuals over a period of time. Perhaps the simplest procedure would be to weigh each person a number of times on the same scale. This could yield the following measurements:[16]

| Individual | Number of Pounds When First Weighed | Number of Pounds When Weighed Again |
| --- | --- | --- |
| A | 163 | 163 |
| B | 179 | 178 |
| C | 145 | 146 |
| D | 121 | 122 |

Note that each individual has maintained his or her relative rank in the group between the first and second weighing. The correlation between the two weighings is the coefficient of stability.

Similarly, test scores are stable if individuals retain their relative ranks when the same examination is administered twice. By correlating the scores that individuals obtain on the first test with their scores on the same test at a later time, a coefficient of stability is computed. Where the correlation is 1.0, the scores are perfectly reliable (i.e., stable); individuals have retained their ranks on both test administrations. Where the correlations are zero, the scores are completely unreliable; from a knowledge of scores on the first administration, one could not predict what the scores would be if the test were readministered.

The magnitude of stability coefficients can be greatly influenced by the amount of time that elapses between the two administrations of the examination. In the example concerning the reliability of a set of weighings,

[15]Stability coefficients assume that the measured trait itself does not change within the time interval of the repeated testings. Otherwise, a low stability coefficient might mean that the individual's weight changed and not necessarily that the scales were providing unreliable readings. Since few if any traits are perfectly stable, measurements of stability reflect changes in individuals as well as unreliability of the instruments.

[16]In practice, at least 20 or 25 individuals would be tested.

one factor which would affect the reliability of the measurements would be that some members of the group gained or lost weight over a period of time. This would affect the relative rankings of individuals and would thus lower the stability of the measurements. On the other hand, the chances of gaining or losing weight if one were to be weighed over a two-minute interval of time are fairly slight. In general, then, the longer the time that elapses, the lower the correlation between two sets of scores is likely to be. Similarly, individuals who are asked to retake an examination as soon as they have completed it will tend to respond the same way twice, yielding relatively high coefficients of stability. Researchers should report the amount of time elapsing between the two administrations of the examination.

## Equivalence

A second method of determining the reliability of a set of measurements is to administer equivalent or parallel forms of the same examination to the same group of individuals. In determining the reliability of the weight of a group of individuals, each person could be weighed on two different scales. A coefficient of equivalence could then be computed by correlating the weight obtained on one scale with that obtained on the second scale. Such data might be similar to those which follow:

| Individual | Weight on Scale One | Weight on Scale Two |
|:----------:|:-------------------:|:-------------------:|
| A | 161 | 161 |
| B | 137 | 138 |
| C | 126 | 125 |
| D | 119 | 119 |

Comparable or equivalent examinations are those designed to yield equal mean scores and equal standard deviations and which also correlate highly with each other. They are so constructed that an individual receiving a given score on one form would receive an equivalent score on the other. The essential difference between the two tests is in the specific items involved. Each form attempts to sample different items from the same universe. Form A of an examination, for example, might contain items measuring the ability to multiply two single-digit whole numbers; form B then would contain different specific items measuring the same trait.

Having equivalent forms of a test can be very useful in research. Sometimes, for example, it may be necessary to test under less than ideal conditions. To prevent students from looking at each others' answer sheets, two forms of a test can be distributed alternately. If the forms were perfectly equivalent, it would make no difference which form a student received.

The availability of parallel forms also permits the investigator to administer a second or third form of a test to students who might have been absent when their classmates were initially tested. Because items differ on each form, students would gain no advantage if their friends told them some of the specific items. Instead of having to eliminate absentees from a study, the researcher could use an equivalent form to retain these students in the study.

Having equivalent forms of a test also permits the investigator to administer both forms of the test at the same time to all students. It will be shown later in this chapter that reliability increases as the number of items on the test increases. By administering two forms of an examination, the length of the examination will double and reliability will increase.

If correlations are computed between scores obtained on alternate forms (equivalent-form reliability), they are likely to be lower than if a single form were administered twice over the same period of time (stability). Where measures of stability are concerned, the individuals taking the same examination twice will tend to respond consistently, especially if the time between testings is short. However, in equivalent-form reliability, the items differ in each form. Individuals are more likely to change their relative standings in a group when taking two different tests than when they have to respond to the same items twice. The change in relative rank will, of course, lower test reliability.

## Stability and Equivalence

A coefficient of stability and equivalence is obtained by administering two or more equivalent forms of a test over a period of time. This type of coefficient takes into effect any temporal changes that may occur in the examinees themselves, as would be true for stability coefficients. It also permits the investigator to use parallel forms at these different time periods. Using a coefficient of stability and equivalence to estimate the reliability of weight would yield data such as the following:[17]

| Individual | Weight on Scale One Now | Weight on Scale Two Later |
|---|---|---|
| A | 161 | 161 |
| B | 137 | 138 |
| C | 126 | 125 |
| D | 119 | 119 |

[17]Because individuals are being tested at two different times, coefficients of stability and equivalence are, at least to some extent, measuring changes within the individuals as well as the unreliability of the instruments.

The use of different forms (which may not measure the same attributes) over a period of time (which permits individuals themselves to change) are both potential sources of test unreliability. These two causes of change in rank (use of different items and variations in individual performance over periods of time) are likely to lead to low reliability coefficients. This calls for greater care and effort when constructing or selecting tests that must yield both stable and equivalent scores.

## Internal Consistency or Homogeneity

A minimum requirement for all tests should be that they yield a measurement of a single attribute. The researcher who uses or constructs a test designed to yield a single score but that contains numerous types of items (such as reading, math, spelling, and science) has compiled a hodgepodge of items resulting in a meaningless total score. Each item on a test should be a sample of the student's behavior derived from the same universe or population of items. If items are selected from different universes, a total score obtained by summing the number of correct items cannot represent a meaningful value any more than would adding the number of oranges to the number of apple crates.

Internal consistency means that each item in a test contributes to a meaningful total score. If it is necessary or desirable to construct a test that measures numerous objectives, each type of item (e.g., math, spelling, etc.) should allow students to be located along its own single continuum.[18] In other words, each test should be capable of standing on its own. Coefficients of internal consistency provide evidence that the test does, in fact, measure a single attribute. Measures of internal consistency or homogeneity may be determined in a number of ways. One procedure is to split an examination into two halves and correlate each person's score on the first half with the score on the second half. The correlation between the two sets of scores represents the degree of internal consistency or homogeneity of the scores. However, because many aptitude and achievement tests are arranged in ascending order of item difficulty, scores on the first half measure somewhat different traits than scores on the second half (fatigue and boredom are likely to occur on the latter parts of examinations). Thus, the correlation between halves is likely to be relatively low.

Where split-half techniques are used, most researchers prefer to correlate scores on odd-numbered items with scores on even-numbered

[18]Some intelligence tests may contain a wide variety of items, but each item should be capable of measuring a single attribute, i.e., intelligence. Other tests may *appear* to contain different kinds of items, but a coefficient of internal consistency could provide evidence that all items are measuring the same attribute.

items.[19] Thus, subjects $A$, $B$, $C$, and $D$ might obtain the following scores:

| Subject | Total Score | Score on Even-Numbered Items | Score on Odd-Numbered Items |
|---------|-------------|------------------------------|-----------------------------|
| A | 78 | 37 | 41 |
| B | 75 | 39 | 36 |
| C | 63 | 31 | 32 |
| D | 52 | 28 | 24 |

Each person's paper is scored twice. The first score is obtained by counting the number of even-numbered items (test items 2, 4, 6, 8, etc.) the subject marked correctly; the second score is obtained by counting the odd-numbered items marked correctly. The correlation between the scores on the even-numbered items and the scores on the odd-numbered items is a measure of their internal consistency[20]

Where items are arranged in *spiral-omnibus* form, odd–even splits are inappropriate. A spiral-omnibus form of item arrangement involves the use of two or more items measuring different content, the easiest items preceding the more difficult ones. The Henmon–Nelson Tests,[21] for example, contain vocabulary, arithmetic, and spatial relations items placed one after the other without separating each type of item into a different subtest. The use of odd–even techniques would place one type of item in one half of the test and other types in the other half. Reliabilities thus computed could be spuriously low, since the correlations would be between items measuring different content.

Other methods of determining the internal consistency of measurements were derived by Kuder and Richardson, the most important and useful being formula 20. In essence, this method provides the estimate of the average reliability for all possible combinations of splits (first half versus second half, odds versus evens, etc.). Like the split-half methods described earlier, Kuder–Richardson technique requires only a single administration of an examination to determine test reliability. A $KR_{20}$ reliability that approaches $+1.0$ means that the items are all measuring the same attribute, and the test, therefore, is internally consistent; coefficients that approximate 0.0 indicate that the test

[19]Odd–even splits often overestimate reliability since the two sets of items are spuriously parallel (equal levels of difficulty, fatigue, time spent working on solutions to problems, etc.).

[20]If split-half or odd–even methods are used, the Spearman–Brown formula will be needed to compensate for the smaller number of items used in correlating *half* of an examination with another *half*. This correction is discussed on pages 218-219.

[21]Martin J. Nelson, Tom A. Lamke, and Joseph L. French, *The Henmon–Nelson Tests of Mental Ability*, rev. ed. (Boston: Houghton Mifflin Co., 1973).

items are measuring a hodgepodge of attributes so that the total score is meaningless. Formula 20, the most widely used of the Kuder–Richardson formulas, is:

$$KR_{20} = \frac{n}{n-1}\left[\frac{s^2 - \Sigma\,p(1-p)}{s^2}\right]$$

where $n$ is the number of items on the examination; $s^2$ is the variance of the scores (standard deviation of the scores squared); $p$ is the proportion of individuals responding correctly to each item; and $(1-p)$ is the proportion of the subjects responding incorrectly to each item.

As an example, consider the following fictitious data obtained from five persons. Each $+$ refers to a correct response; each $-$ to an incorrect response.

| Individual | | Items | | | | Total Score |
|---|---|---|---|---|---|---|
| | 1 | 2 | 3 | 4 | 5 | |
| A | $+$ | $-$ | $+$ | $-$ | $+$ | 3 |
| B | $+$ | $+$ | $+$ | $+$ | $+$ | 5 |
| C | $+$ | $+$ | $+$ | $-$ | $-$ | 3 |
| D | $+$ | $-$ | $-$ | $-$ | $-$ | 1 |
| E | $-$ | $-$ | $-$ | $-$ | $-$ | 0 |
| | | | | | | $s^2 = 3.8$ |
| $p$ | 0.8 | 0.4 | 0.6 | 0.2 | 0.4 | |
| $(1-p)$ | 0.2 | 0.6 | 0.4 | 0.8 | 0.6 | |
| $p(1-p)$ | 0.16 | 0.24 | 0.24 | 0.16 | 0.24 | $\Sigma\,p(1-p) = 1.04$ |

For item 1, four out of five persons responded correctly; $p$, therefore, is 0.8 for that item; $1-p$ is $1-0.8$, or 0.2; and $p(1-p)$ is 0.8(0.2), or 0.16. The same procedure is followed for the remainder of the items. The $p(1-p)$ values are summed $(0.16 + 0.24 + 0.24 + 0.16 + 0.24)$ to 1.04. The variance of the scores 3, 5, 3, 1, and 0 is 3.8. With $n = 5$ (remember that $n$ is the *number of items* on the test), $KR_{20}$ can be found to be:

$$KR_{20} = \frac{n}{n-1}\left(\frac{s^2 - \Sigma\,p(1-p)}{s^2}\right) = \frac{5}{4}\left(\frac{3.8 - 1.04}{3.8}\right) = 0.907$$

## Assumptions

The use of the Kuder–Richardson and split-half formulas rests upon several assumptions. The first is that the test is a "power" rather than a "speed" test. That is, the test should attempt to measure the amount of knowledge rather than the speed with which an individual is able to respond. Speed tests, which tend to contain large numbers of very simple items, are too long to allow most people to finish within the established time limits. Thus, an examinee's score on a speed test ordinarily equals the number of items attempted. For example, on a 100-item test, suppose that all subjects are able to complete 42 items within the time limit and that all answers are correct. Furthermore, assume that this score of 42 is the lowest score in a class of 35 students. The proportion of the class responding correctly to each of the first 42 items would be 35/35 or 1.0, which is the value of $p$ in the K–R formula. With $p = 1.00$, $1 - p$ would equal zero and the product $p(1 - p)$ would be zero for each of these items. The K–R reliability would then be spuriously high. K–R formulas should *not* be used for speed tests.[22] It is, of course, reasonable to use separately timed measures of equivalence to determine the reliability of speed tests.

Second, remember that measures of internal consistency are not influenced by changes occurring in the examinees over periods of time as are measures of stability. Thus, any changes likely to affect performance over time will not be reflected by the use of measures of internal consistency.

Third, since all items enter into the formula for $KR_{20}$ (i.e., $s^2$ is based on the distribution of the *total* scores, and the value of $p(1 - p)$ is computed for *every* item and then summed), there is no need to use the Spearman–Brown formula after computing a $KR_{20}$ reliability. Unlike the split-half technique, which involves correlating the scores on *half* of a test (i.e., the odd- vs. even-numbered items), $KR_{20}$ provides an estimate of reliability for an *entire* test.

Fourth, $KR_{20}$ assumes that each correct item is accorded 1 point and each incorrect or omitted item, zero points. Note that the effect of violating this assumption is to *increase* spuriously the value of $KR_{20}$. If, for example, every correct response were given 5 points instead of 1, the standard deviation of scores would be 5 times larger, and the variance would be increased by a factor of 25. Thus, the $s^2$ values in the formula would be increased greatly. The $\Sigma\, p(1 - p)$, however, would be unaffected since $p(1 - p)$ is determined by the *proportion* of the group responding correctly and incorrectly to each item, and these proportions are unrelated to the number of points examinees receive for a correct response. A large $s^2$ value and a relatively small $\Sigma\, p(1 - p)$ will lead to extremely high coefficients. If it is necessary or desirable to give more than 1 point for each correct response, a modification in the formula can be made. Instead of computing $\Sigma\, p(1 - p)$ (which assumes each item has been scored 1 or 0), compute the differentially weighted

---

[22]The same assumption holds for split-half or odd–even methods. On a speed test, the student will ordinarily have equal numbers of correct responses on odd and even items (assuming no errors), making the correlation between them spuriously high.

variance for each item and sum those values.[23] Substitute the sum of the weighted item variances for $\Sigma\, p(1 - p)$ in the $KR_{20}$ formula.

# FACTORS AFFECTING RELIABILITY COEFFICIENTS

Conditions such as the variability of the group tested, the number of items on the examination, and the level of difficulty of the examination affect the reliability of measurements.

## Group Variability

The extent to which a group tends to be homogeneous or heterogeneous with regard to the trait being measured has a decided influence on the size of the reliability coefficient obtained. In general, the more heterogeneous the group, the higher the reliability coefficient is likely to be.

Suppose, for example, that a researcher wishes to determine the reliability of the weights of various persons. If one person weighs 275 pounds and another weighs just 90 pounds, their relative ranks are not likely to change even over extensive periods of time. However, suppose that two individuals initially differ in weight by only a fraction of an ounce and are put on strictly comparable diets. Under these conditions a fine measuring instrument would be needed to detect differences in weight. Thus, where the variability of the group being weighed is large, even an imperfect scale is likely to yield relatively stable rankings in weight, and conversely, a very fine instrument is required if small differences are to be measured consistently.

[23]Suppose that alternative $A$ is given a value of 5, $B = 4$, $C = 3$, $D = 2$, and $E = 1$. The variance for each item can be computed in the following manner:

| Response Alternative | Weight | Frequency | Weight-Item Mean | $X$ Frequency | $=$ | $x$ | $x^2$ |
|---|---|---|---|---|---|---|---|
| $A$ | 5 | 40 | $5 - 4 =$ 1 | $X$ 40 | $=$ | 40 | 160 |
| $B$ | 4 | 10 | $4 - 4 =$ 0 | $X$ 10 | $=$ | 0 | 0 |
| $C$ | 3 | 5 | $3 - 4 = -1$ | $X$ 5 | $=$ | $-5$ | 25 |
| $D$ | 2 | 10 | $2 - 4 = -2$ | $X$ 10 | $=$ | $-20$ | 400 |
| $E$ | 1 | 5 | $1 - 4 = -3$ | $X$ 5 | $=$ | $-15$ | 225 |
| | | $N = 70$ | | | | | $\Sigma x^2 = 810$ |

Item mean $= (5 \times 40) + (4 \times 10) + (3 \times 5) + (2 \times 10) + (1 \times 5) = \frac{280}{70} = 4.0$

Item variance $= \frac{\Sigma\,(X - M)^2}{N - 1} = \frac{\Sigma\,x^2}{N - 1} = \frac{810}{69} = 11.7$

An analogous problem is encountered in educational measurement. A test can be quite crudely constructed and yet be able to differentiate between very bright and very dull children. On the other hand, it may take a highly sensitive instrument to differentiate among individuals very similar with regard to some trait under investigation.

Similarly, reliability coefficients are likely to be much larger if they are computed using students in two or three different grade levels than if they are computed at one grade level only. Fifth *and* sixth graders, for example, vary more than *either* fifth *or* sixth graders considered separately. Reliability for combined groups tends to be higher than reliabilities computed over a single age or grade level.

In writing research reports, the investigator should indicate the variability (i.e., standard deviation or variance) of the scores for each set of measurements being correlated.[24] Thus, if equivalent-form reliability is being determined by correlating scores on one form with scores on another, the standard deviations should be reported for each form.

## Number of Items

In general, longer tests tend to be more reliable than shorter ones. Consider, for example, the extreme case of an examination consisting of only one item. An individual who changes an answer from one testing to the next would be maximally inconsistent. However, a very long examination may allow individuals to change their answers on some items without necessarily changing their overall position within the group.

The relationship between increasing the length of an examination and the resultant increase in test reliability may be demonstrated by the use of the Spearman–Brown formula. When the reliability of the initial test is known, this formula is useful in deriving an estimate of reliability for an examination whose length has been increased or decreased. The formula is:

$$SB = \frac{rk}{1 + [r(k - 1)]}$$

where $SB$ is the estimated reliability for an examination which has been increased or decreased in length $k$ number of times; and $r$ is the reliability of the initial measurements.

As an example, suppose that a 200-item examination requires four

---

[24]The standard error of measurement should also be reported since it takes into effect the variability of the group. The standard error of measurement $= s\sqrt{1 - \text{reliability}}$. The $SE_{\text{meas}}$ is the standard deviation of obtained scores around a hypothetical true score. For example, if $SE_{\text{meas}} = 5$, then 68 percent of the obtained scores will vary $\pm 5$ points around their hypothetical true score.

hours of administration time. Furthermore, assume that the investigator is allowed only one hour to administer the examination. If it is known that the original 200-item examination yielded a reliability coefficient of 0.90, then the researcher could estimate that the reliability of a comparable 50-item examination (having one-fourth the number of items as the original test) and requiring only one hour of administration time would be:

$$SB = \frac{(0.90)(0.25)}{1 + [0.90(0.25 - 1)]}$$

$$SB = \frac{0.2250}{1 + [0.90(-0.75)]}$$

$$SB = \frac{0.2250}{1 - 0.6750}$$

$$SB = \frac{0.2250}{0.3250}$$

$$SB = 0.69$$

Conversely, if the original examination yielded a reliability of 0.69, quadrupling the number of items would yield a reliability coefficient of:

$$SB = \frac{(0.69)(4)}{1 + [0.69(4 - 1)]}$$

$$SB = \frac{2.76}{1 + 0.69(3)}$$

$$SB = \frac{2.76}{1 + 2.07}$$

$$SB = \frac{2.76}{3.07}$$

$$SB = 0.90 \text{ (rounded from 0.8990)}$$

The problem of test length should be considered with regard to the discussion of split-half or odd–even reliability coefficients. In using these techniques, scores on part of an examination are correlated with scores on another part. A correlation so obtained would tend to underestimate the reliability of the whole examination because only half of the items are being correlated with another half. Correlations between halves should always be augmented by using the Spearman–Brown formula with $k = 2$ to provide an estimate of the reliability for an examination that is actually twice as long as the two halves. The "stepped-up" figure should be reported in the research paper, not the correlation between the halves.

One of the most effective ways for increasing reliability is to construct tests that are as long as practical. Long tests provide much better estimates of students' true knowledge, attitudes, or personality than do shorter tests.

## Level of Difficulty

A difficult test is one in which the mean tends to be low in relation to the number of items on the examination; conversely, an easy examination tends to yield a relatively high mean in comparison to the number of items.

Consider what would happen to test reliability on an examination in which everyone responded incorrectly to every item. Assuming that chance factors are inoperative, the mean and standard deviation of such a test would be zero. The simplest examination, on the other hand, would yield a perfect set of scores, with the mean equal to the number of items and the standard deviation equal to zero. In either instance, the lack of variability that exists when examinations are excessively simple or difficult will yield relatively low reliabilities.

The optimum level of difficulty for an examination depends on the purpose for which the examination is being given. If, for example, an examination is being used to select highly trained and competent individuals, it should be difficult enough so that only the most competent can be expected to do well. That is, the test should be able to discriminate among high-scoring persons. On the other hand, an examination should be rather simple if its purpose is to select individuals for remedial classes.

In general, for maximum discrimination along the entire scale, approximately half of the subjects should respond correctly to each item after the items have been corrected for guessing.[25]

On an examination consisting of 100 true-false items, the most likely score a person will attain by guessing is 50 (there is 1 chance out of 2 that the student will respond correctly by chance to each item; if there are 100 items, the most likely guessing score would be $\frac{1}{2} \times 100$, or 50). The optimal value of the mean may be found by adding to the guessing score half the difference between the maximum possible score and the guessing score. For the example presented above, the guessing score is 50, the maximum possible score is 100, and the optimal mean value would be $50 + (100 - 50)/2 = 75$. The optimal difficulty level for the test is determined by dividing 75

---

[25]The correction for guessing formula is $S = R - [W/op - 1]$, where $S$ is the correction for guessing score, $R$ is the number of items marked correctly, $W$ is the number of items actually marked incorrectly (not omitted), and $op - 1$ is the number of options per item minus 1. Omitted items are neither credited nor penalized. Essay and completion-type items are not subject to guessing.

by the number of items (i.e., 100), which would be 0.75. In other words, about 75 percent of the individuals would respond correctly to each item.

The optimal difficulties for other types of tests are provided below:

| Number of Alternatives | Optimal Level of Difficulty |
|---|---|
| 0 | 0.50 |
| 2 | 0.75 |
| 3 | 0.67 |
| 4 | 0.63 |
| 5 | 0.60 |

Looked at from a slightly different perspective, a 100-item completion (or essay) test should yield a mean of 50; a true-false test should have a mean close to 75; a 3-alternative multiple-choice test should have a mean of about 67.

## REQUIRED MAGNITUDES OF RELIABILITY COEFFICIENTS

Reliability coefficients may have magnitudes ranging from zero to unity; coefficients closer to unity indicate greater reliability than do lower ones. A question frequently posed by students is, "What is the minimum reliability coefficient that may be considered useful or acceptable?"

The answer to this question is related to 1) the availability of more reliable instruments; and 2) the purpose of the examination. In general, of course, the more reliable the measurements are, the better. However, the researcher may have no choice in some situations but to be satisfied with relatively low reliabilities if tests which yield higher coefficients are unattainable.

The intended use of an examination also influences the minimum size of reliability coefficient that may be acceptable. Important decisions which may have a permanent effect on the life of a given person should be determined by the most reliable instruments available. For example, an expensive or time-consuming program should be evaluated by highly reliable instruments. On the other hand, a lower degree of reliability is more tolerable in situations where an incorrect decision is of lesser consequence.

In addition to the considerations noted above, it is well recognized that reliabilities need to be higher when testing individuals than when testing groups. Group mean scores are less likely to fluctuate and are, thus, more dependable than are scores obtained by a single individual.

# VALIDITY OF MEASUREMENTS

Validity refers to the extent to which a test correlates with some criterion external to the test itself. In the physical sciences, there is little doubt that a scale is used to measure weight or that a ruler is intended to measure distance. However, in the behavioral sciences, tests are usually samples of behavior or of some trait, rather than direct measures. Thus, because a standardized test is titled *The Blank Test of Verbal Ability* is not sufficient evidence that the test actually does measure verbal ability. Evidence regarding validity should be provided to indicate the extent to which the test does in fact measure relevant criteria.

The essential difference between reliability and validity is that reliability coefficients always reflect the correlation of an examination *with itself* (or with a parallel form of itself), whereas validity coefficients require *some criterion external to the test itself.*

The validity of a set of measurements is not entirely independent of its reliability. Consider, for example, a clinical thermometer, which may yield true individual differences in temperatures and would, thus, be reliable but which would be quite invalid as a measure of the patient's intelligence, happiness, or attitude toward illness. High reliability, then, is not a guarantee of validity.

On the other hand, a perfectly valid examination must measure some trait without random error. If a clinical thermometer is valid for the measurement of body temperature, then it must reflect body temperature in a consistent and reliable manner. If two thermometers are placed in a patient's mouth and one yields a temperature of 98.6°F. and the other reads 104.2°F., they cannot both be measuring body temperature—one or both of the thermometers must then be invalid as a measure of body heat.

# TYPES OF VALIDITY

A number of techniques are available for determining the validity of psychological and educational tests for given purposes. The *Standards for Educational and Psychological Tests*[26] lists the following types of validity: *content validity, predictive validity, concurrent validity,* and *construct validity.*

## Content Validity

One method of determining the validity of a set of measurements is to study the items on an examination to see if they appear to be suitable measures of the objectives one has in mind. Ordinarily, to determine the content validity of a test the researcher will ask a group of individuals to examine

---

[26]American Psychological Association, 1974.

each item on the test to see if the items meet a predetermined set of criteria or objectives. To the extent that each item is judged to elicit responses relevant to established criteria, it may be said to have high content validity.

Assume, for example, that a researcher is interested in comparing the ability of two groups of students to do arithmetic problems. In the search for a suitable examination, the researcher would establish criteria to evaluate the relevance of a set of items for the type of behavior to be measured. For example, one could propose that each item measure one or more of the following objectives:

1. The student will add three whole numbers.
2. The student will identify arithmetic symbols (such as $=$, $-$, $\times$, $\div$).
3. The student will convert fractions into decimal equivalents.

In addition, the investigator could require that no item contain vocabulary above the difficulty level for fifth graders and that an equal number of items be presented for each objective. Items would then be selected for inclusion on the test by determining whether or not they met the objectives established by the investigator. To the extent that each item did in fact meet the criteria, the test would have high content validity.

It cannot be too strongly emphasized that an examination or subtest may not actually measure the content suggested in its title. Spelling, for example, can be measured by many different techniques:

1. Having students write words from a list dictated by the instructor
2. Asking the students to select the correctly spelled word from among a set of misspelled words
3. Counting the number of misspellings that occur spontaneously in student themes (either when dictionaries are made available or when they are not)
4. Having students check as many misspelled words as they can find in a paragraph (with or without benefit of a dictionary)
5. Requiring students to spell words orally
6. Asking students to write a dictated paragraph and counting the total number of misspelled words

Simply stating that a test measures spelling is accurate only if one believes that all measurement techniques are equivalent. If spelling ability is defined as the number of words students can write correctly from a dictated list, only a test that measures spelling in that way will do. All other approaches would be invalid.

Content validity is most frequently used in the evaluation of achievement tests because with this type of examination, test content is essential. On many other types of tests, such as intelligence, personality, and aptitude tests, the specific content of the questions is not so important as whether the items are useful in predicting the future performance of a group of individuals. Content validity might be used with personality inventories to judge whether a group of items appears to measure some trait. In this case, individuals would have to examine the content of the examinations and evaluate the extent to which the items measure specific predetermined criteria.

Because the use of judges to validate examinations and questionnaires is a widespread and relatively simple procedure, researchers may be tempted to use the technique inappropriately. Except on achievement tests, "expert opinion" probably should not be used where other, more suitable techniques are available. If the purpose of a personality inventory is to predict which respondents are going to require some form of psychotherapy in the future, judges cannot legitimately be used to examine the content of the questions except as an aid in reducing item ambiguity. To argue that four experts (in this instance psychotherapists) agree that the items on an examination will be predictive of some future behavior is irrelevant. What is required is evidence that the items are *in fact* predictive of future behavior.

## Predictive Validity

At times researchers are not so much concerned about the content of an examination as they are about trying to predict future behavior based upon present tested characteristics. Aptitude tests, for example, attempt to predict performance before an individual has been given the opportunity to study a body of knowledge or to engage in some type of work. Thus, if children are able to discriminate between various types of symbols, if their vocabulary scores are high, and if they are relatively bright, it might be concluded that they will be successful in a formal reading program. Usually, however, researchers are not too concerned about evaluating the specific content of the items on a test used to predict future performance so long as the scores correlate highly with a criterion.

In determining predictive validity, a correlation is computed between *predictor* scores and scores obtained on some criterion at a later time. For example, scores on an achievement test given in high school might be correlated with college grades, or present adjustment (indicated by scores on personality inventory) might be correlated with some other future behavior.

Predictive validity coefficients are influenced by the amount of time that elapses between the administration of the predictor test and the criterion measurements. In general, it is easier to predict events in the immediate future than it is to predict events further away. Thus, to evaluate predictive validity coefficients, one would need to know the amount of time elapsing between the administration of the predictor and the criterion. In this sense, *no test has just one validity coefficient.* Numerous validity coefficients may be obtained depending upon the nature of the criterion and the amount of time elapsing between the measurement of the predictor and the criterion.

## Concurrent Validity

Under some circumstances, it may be impossible or inconvenient to wait long periods of time to evaluate the predictive validity of a set of measurements. Some investigators have chosen to correlate the results of an examination with a criterion that is immediately available, rather than waiting as is required in predictive validity. Scores on a new intelligence test may be correlated with scores made by the same individuals on examinations whose characteristics are well-known, such as the Stanford–Binet[27] or the Wechsler Adult Intelligence Scale.[28] Often, teachers' ratings or evaluations made by psychologists or psychiatrists are used as concurrent criteria.

The major defense for using concurrent rather than predictive validity coefficients is usually one of convenience. However, if an examination has little concurrent validity, it is not likely to have any higher predictive validity so long as the same criteria measures are being used. That is, if an examination does not correlate highly with a criterion in the present, it is not likely to correlate with the same criterion where there is a lapse of time between the two measurements. Concurrent validity coefficients, then, may be used to establish upper limits for predictive validity coefficients. It is possible, for example, that a thermometer reading will be highly correlated with a physician's diagnosis and thus will have high concurrent validity. The same thermometer, however, may not be very predictive of the patient's future health.

Of course, criteria measures themselves may be no better than the scores with which they are correlated. A standardized achievement test may correlate insignificantly with school grades, but one could not assume that the achievement test is therefore of little value. It is possible that the grades themselves are so unreliable or invalid that no test could correlate highly with them. Under these conditions, the investigator should indicate just how reliable the criteria measures are.

## Construct Validity[29]

At times, researchers are less interested in the extent to which tests represent a body of knowledge (content validity) or the extent to which scores

[27]Lewis M. Terman and Maud A. Merrill, *Stanford–Binet Intelligence Scale: Manual for the Third Revision*, Form L-M (Boston: Houghton Mifflin Co., 1973).

[28]David Wechsler, *Wechsler Adult Intelligence Scale* (New York: The Psychological Corporation, 1955).

[29]The concept of *construct validity* has been attacked by some psychologists and just as vigorously defended by others. For detailed discussion of the problems involved, the student should consult the two following sources:

Harold P. Bechtoldt, "Construct Validity: A Critique," *American Psychologist*, 14, no. 10 (1959), pp. 619–629.

Donald T. Campbell, "Recommendations for A.P.A. Test Standards Regarding Construct, Trait, or Discriminant Validity," *American Psychologist*, 15, no. 8 (1960), pp. 546–553.

correlate with criteria scores (predictive and concurrent validity), and more interested in validating some theory which underlies or is assumed to underlie a given examination. Most personality inventories, for example, attempt to measure the theoretical position regarding the nature of personality held by the researcher. Thus, the *Blacky Pictures*[30] were designed by Blum to elicit Freudian psychosexual responses. To the extent that they are successful in eliciting these responses rather than some irrelevant response, the psychoanalytic theory involving psychosexual development will have gained supportive evidence. To be sure, if the pictures do not yield the type of responses Blum predicted, this fact could not be used as very strong evidence against traditional Freudian theory. All one could be justified in concluding is that the Blacky Pictures did not support the theory.

The validation of constructs or theories may require the use of many different techniques. One of the most useful of these techniques is *factor analysis*, a statistical technique used to analyze tests. Thus, a factor analysis of the present subscales of the *Minnesota Multiphasic Personality Inventory* indicated that some subscales could be further analyzed into separate and additional scales, whereas other subscales could be combined to form new and homogeneous sets of items.[31] Factor analysis is discussed in greater detail in Chapter 5.

# SOME DIFFICULTIES IN THE VALIDATION OF MEASUREMENTS

## The Criterion

One of the most difficult problems in determining the validity of any set of measurements lies in the selection of an adequate criterion. Criteria measures have ranged from grade point ratios to psychiatric evaluations. Too often criteria have been poorer than the instruments to be evaluated. As Ebel[32] has brought out:

> If the criterion is used as a standard for judging the accuracy of the scores from the test, it should always exemplify a measurement procedure clearly superior to [i.e., more relevant and precise than] that embodied in the test.

> In theory this could provide a useful distinction between test scores and criterion measures. In practice it seldom does. What usually happens is

[30]Gerald S. Blum, *The Blacky Pictures: A Technique for the Exploration of Personality Dynamics* (Ann Arbor, Mich.: Psychodynamic Instruments, 1950–1967).

[31]Andrew L. Comrey, "A Factor Analysis of Items on the M.M.P.I. Hypochondriasis Scale," *Educational and Psychological Measurement*, 17, 1957, no. 4 (1957), pp. 568–577.

[32]Robert L. Ebel, "Must All Tests Be Valid?" *American Psychologist*, 16, no. 10 (1961), p. 644.

that the test developer pours all the skill, all the energy, and all the time he has into the process of making an outstanding test. He has none left over to spend on obtaining measurements "clearly superior" to those his test will yield, and under the circumstances would have no stomach for the task anyway. Small wonder that many good tests go unvalidated or poorly validated by conventional psychometric methods.

On the other hand, tests are presumably given to measure important objectives, and it is not unreasonable to ask for evidence that the test in fact does measure these objectives. To be sure, the process of obtaining this evidence may be time-consuming and difficult, but without this information one could not feel justified in drawing valid conclusions from test data.

## CRITERION CONTAMINATION

In establishing adequate criteria, it is necessary that the researcher avoid the process known as *criterion contamination*. Criterion contamination refers to the unjustifiable practice of allowing raters whose judgments are to be used as criterion measures to examine predictor test scores, thus "contaminating" what should be independent judgments with prior knowledge of scores. Suppose that a group of psychologists is asked to classify a number of persons into clinical categories such as paranoids, schizophrenics, normals, etc. Assume also that before the psychologists' ratings are obtained, a test is devised and administered to categorize the subjects into these clinical types. It seems reasonable to ask that the psychologists make their decisions independently of their knowledge of scores made by the subjects on the examination. If the psychologists are allowed to examine the test scores obtained by the individuals whom they must ultimately classify, their judgments may be influenced by their knowledge of these scores, and the correlation between test scores and the criterion may be too high. In this instance, the criterion (i.e., the ratings of the psychologists) would be contaminated with knowledge of the scores on the predictor tests. The validity coefficients thus obtained would be spuriously high.

## CROSS VALIDATION

Another factor involved in validating a set of measurements is known as cross validation. Suppose that a researcher is constructing an examination which he or she hopes will be useful in predicting high school dropouts. The usual method of test construction in this instance would be to study the factors that lead to school dropouts and then to construct items that will discriminate between students who remain in school and those who drop out prior to graduation. The final form of the examination, then, is composed of items which empirically have been found to differentiate between students who remain in school and those who leave; all of the items shown to be of little value in discriminating between the two groups would have been eliminated. Unless the researcher cross-validates findings, he or she is likely to conclude that the examination is of great value in *predicting* potential high school dropouts. All that has been demonstrated so far, however, is that the items discriminate between two specific groups of students at a given period of time. Some, if not all, of the items may have discriminated between the two groups because of purely chance factors. No evidence has been presented that the same examination will actually predict other potential dropouts if the test is administered again to a new but similarly constituted group.

Cross validation is simply a procedure whereby a researcher reexamines the data by readministering a test to another group of persons. It is an attempt to substantiate or refute findings derived from an original item selection procedure by applying it to other groups of individuals. If cross-validating an instrument achieves results similar to those found in the administration of the original test, then the researcher has additional evidence that the relationship between predictor and criterion is genuine. If, on the other hand, cross-validation procedures do not substantiate earlier findings, the researcher is still faced with the problem of selecting tests or items that can adequately correlate with the criteria. If new tests are found that appear promising, then these too must be checked against new samples of subjects.

## SUMMARY

**1.** Reliability and validity are used to select tests for inclusion in a research project and to evaluate examinations prepared by the investigator. A *Test Analysis Form* is suggested as a guideline for selecting and evaluating tests (see Appendix I).
**2.** Reliability provides an estimate of how well measurements reflect true (nonrandom) individual differences.
   **a.** Obtained scores contain both true and error (random or chance) components. Reduction of random error increases reliability.
   **b.** A true score is defined as the mean of an infinite number of repeated tests when practice effects are presumed to be zero. If reliability is perfect (i.e., $+1.0$), true and obtained scores are equal, and there are no errors of measurement.
**3.** Four types of reliability coefficients were described.
   **a.** *Stability* is the extent to which individuals maintain their relative standings when the same examination is administered twice over a period of time. Long time intervals tend to lower stability coefficients since individuals are more likely to change over long than over short periods.

**b.** *Equivalence* is measured by correlating scores on two or more forms of an examination taken by the same persons. Different items on the various forms are designed to measure the same objectives and to yield equal means and standard deviations. Differences among the scores on the various forms are attributed to differences in item content.

**c.** *Stability and equivalence* involves correlating two forms of a test over time. Such coefficients are sensitive to changes in individuals that occur over time as well as to differences in item content on the various test forms.

**d.** *Internal consistency* or *homogeneity* refers to the extent that items are derived from the same universe or population of items. Internally consistent tests contain items that measure the same attribute.

    1) The *split-half* technique correlates each person's scores on the odd-numbered items with scores on the even-numbered items. The Spearman–Brown formula must be applied to the correlation between the halves to obtain an estimate of the total reliability. The split-half technique is not appropriate for tests arranged in spiral-omnibus format or for speed tests.

    2) The *Kuder–Richardson* technique also assumes that the test is a power and not a speed test. Unlike the split-half, $KR_{20}$ does not require correction by the Spearman–Brown formula, but it does assume that each correct answer will be given one point and incorrect answers, zero points.

**4.** A number of conditions affect reliability.

    **a.** Group variability has a decided effect on reliability. In general, the greater the degree of group variability, the easier it will be to measure individual differences reliably.

    **b.** Test length affects reliability since the number of items is related to the variability of scores. The Spearman–Brown formula was described as a way of estimating reliability when the number of items on a test is increased or decreased.

    **c.** Tests that are overly difficult or too simple tend to yield low reliability coefficients. Difficult and easy tests are unable to measure individual differences maximally. Although the optimal difficulty level of a test depends on the reason for testing, the highest reliability will be derived from tests where the mean score is equal to the chance score plus half the difference between a chance and a perfect score.

**5.** Researchers are obligated to select the most reliable instruments. The purpose of testing determines, in part, the minimum reliability coefficient that can be tolerated; another factor is the availability of more reliable instruments.

**6.** Validity refers to the extent to which measurements achieve the purpose for which they were designed. Reliable measures are not necessarily valid. Four types of validity were described.

    **a.** *Content validity* is used primarily to evaluate achievement tests or examinations in which the content is of primary importance. Usually, a group of persons is asked to evaluate the extent to which items measure predetermined criteria.

**b.** *Predictive validity* is used to indicate the extent to which previously obtained scores accurately predict criteria measures.

**c.** *Concurrent validity* is used when a researcher is concerned with the present behavior of a group of persons. Concurrent validity coefficients may be used as an upper-limit estimate of predictive validity coefficients.

**d.** *Construct validity* is used to gain supportive evidence for a theory or construct which a test is designed to measure. Although numerous techniques have been used to determine construct validity, factor analytic techniques have most often been employed.

**7.** The major difficulty in determining the validity of a set of measurements is in establishing adequate criteria. Criteria should themselves be highly reliable and relevant to the area under investigation.

**8.** Where ratings are used as a criterion, they should be obtained without the raters having knowledge of test scores which may later be used to predict these ratings. Failure to guard against this possibility leads to *criterion contamination*.

**9.** Researchers who construct empirically keyed examinations that initially correlate with some criterion should *cross-validate* their findings by recorrelating the scores on a different group. Cross validation is necessary because some or all items orginally selected for their ability to discriminate between criterion groups could do so as the result of chance.

## PRACTICE EXERCISES

**1.** Examine a standardized test manual using the evaluative criteria on the *Test Analysis Form* (see Appendix I). Find the reference to the test in Buros' *Mental Measurements Yearbook* to obtain additional information and opinions about the test.

**2.** For each of the following examples, indicate the type of reliability coefficient required (stability, equivalence, stability and equivalence, split-halves, Kuder–Richardson):

**a.** The Spearman–Brown formula must be used to obtain this type of reliability coefficient.

**b.** School counselors stated that they were not certain how often a particular intelligence test should be administered in the elementary schools of their district.

**c.** These reliability coefficients should *not* be used with simple and highly timed clerical aptitude tests, for example.

**d.** These reliability coefficients are *not* influenced by daily changes in the behavior of students.

**e.** Researchers wishing to determine the amount of student gain in knowledge over a period of time would probably use this type of coefficient.

**3.** Which method of validating tests is involved in each of the following examples (content, predictive, concurrent, or construct)?

**a.** The manual for a standardized test states that the test measures introversion and extroversion. The researcher administers the examination and obtains a normal distribution of scores.

**b.** A researcher constructs an examination and finds that it accurately discriminates between "normal" adults and those in mental hospitals.

**c.** At the end of the school year, an investigator correlates a newly developed aptitude test against teachers' grades.

**d.** Bill is told, from an examination of the results of a college aptitude test, that his chances for completing a four-year college program are excellent.

**e.** Members of the Board of Education unanimously agree that a particular test adequately covers the objectives of a given course of study.

**4.** Using the data below, indicate which of the two tests in each situation you would select for inclusion in a research project, other conditions being equal:

| Situation I | Standard Deviation | Kuder–Richardson Reliability |
| --- | --- | --- |
| Test *A* | 10 | 0.91 |
| Test *B* | 15 | 0.91 |

| Situation II | Stability | Amount of Time Elapsing between the Two Administrations |
| --- | --- | --- |
| Test *C* | 0.91 | 10 months |
| Test *D* | 0.91 | 20 months |

| Situation III | Type of Reliability Coefficient | Amount of Time Elapsing between the Two Administrations | Reliability |
| --- | --- | --- | --- |
| Test *E* | Stability | 10 months | 0.86 |
| Test *F* | Stability and equivalence | 10 months | 0.86 |

| Situation IV | Type of Validity Coefficient | Validity |
| --- | --- | --- |
| Test *G* | Predictive | 0.61 |
| Test *H* | Concurrent | 0.61 |

**5.** A test of 50 items yields a standard deviation of 5, and half of a group of 300 students gets each item correct (the other half obviously responds incorrectly). What is the Kuder–Richardson reliability for this examination?

**6.** What would the Kuder–Richardson reliability be if 150 items were administered instead of the 50 items? If 25 items were administered?

**7.** For each of the following situations, indicate the types of errors, if any, committed by the investigator and suggest ways of avoiding or correcting these errors:

**a.** An experimenter devises a rating sheet to evaluate standardized tests. A maximum of 20 points is given for validity, 15 for reliability, 10 for ease of administration, etc.

**b.** An examination which was given to seventh, eighth, and ninth graders yielded a stability coefficient of 0.92. A teacher decided to use this examination in an eighth-grade class and found the stability coefficient to be only 0.67. Although both tests were given over a two-month period, the teacher believes that the original figures must have been computed incorrectly.

**c.** A graduate student in education states that it is unnecessary to validate a newly constructed personality inventory because personality has been defined as the score an individual receives on that test.

**d.** A senior high school teacher discovers that in a test of 75 items, 5 seem to discriminate very highly between students who later go on to college and are successful and those who go on but are unsuccessful. From now on the teacher plans on giving only this 5-item exam.

**8.** Indicate the difficulties of using each of the following as criteria against which examinations could be validated:

**a.** Number of times students are sent to the guidance counselor is used as a measure of the effectiveness of a teacher's classroom control techniques.

**b.** Grade point ratios are used as a measure of student achievement.

**c.** Number of accidents are employed as a measure of the effectiveness of driver education classes.

**d.** Rate of teacher turnover is used as a measure of the effectiveness of administrative policies.

**e.** Conviction by a juvenile court is used as a measure of juvenile delinquency.

## Selected Supplementary Readings

1. For derivations of formulas described in this chapter, see Guilford, J. P. *Psychometric Methods.* New York: McGraw-Hill Book Co., 1954, 597 pp.; Gulliksen, Harold. *Theory of Mental Tests.* New York: John Wiley & Sons, 1950, 468 pp.; Horst, Paul. *Psychological Measurement and Prediction.* Belmont, Calif.: Wadsworth Publishing Co., 1966, 455 pp.; Magnusson,

David. *Test Theory*. Reading, Mass.: Addison-Wesley Publishing Co., 1966, 270 pp.; Nunnally, Jum C *Psychometric Theory* Second Edition. New York: McGraw-Hill Book Co., 1978, 701 pp.

2. Some excellent bulletins on testing have been published by the Psychological Corporation, Harcourt Brace Jovanovich, Educational Testing Service, and California Test Bureau. Most are available at no charge. Psychological Corporation (304 East 45th Street, New York, N.Y. 10017) has *Test Service Bulletins* related to reliability (e.g., No. 44, "Reliability and Confidence"; No. 50, "How Accurate Is a Test Score?"; and No. 53, "Comparability vs. Equivalance of Test Scores") and to validity (e.g., No. 37, "How Effective Are Your Tests?"; No. 38, "Expectancy Tables: A Way of Interpreting Test Validity"; No. 45, "Better Than Chance"; No. 47, "Cross-Validation"; and No. 56, "Double-Entry Expectancy Tables").

3. In addition to those sources that list and describe the content of various educational and psychological measures noted in the Selected Supplementary Readings for Chapter 12, see also Goldman, Bert A., and Saunders, John L. eds. *Directory of Unpublished Experimental Mental Measures, Volumes 1 and 2*. New York: Human Sciences Press, 1974, 1978, 233 pp. and 324 pp.

obtaining
information from
respondents:
interviews and
questionnaires

This chapter is designed to provide the reader with the techniques for collecting data by interviews and questionnaires. Chapters 11 and 12 will examine a number of other data gathering techniques.

## THE INTERVIEW

In a sense, any face-to-face conversation is a type of interview in which the roles of interviewer and respondent continually change. As a research method, however, the interview is more than an exchange of small talk. *It represents a direct attempt by the researcher to obtain reliable and valid measures in the form of verbal responses from one or more respondents.* The data obtained from interviews represent attempts to confirm or reject hypotheses. As such, they form one part of a research design and are not ends in themselves.

## Advantages of the Interview

The interview has a number of advantages. First, the interview is flexible and applicable to many different types of problems. It is flexible in the sense that the interviewer may change the mode of questioning if the occasion demands. If responses given by a subject are unclear, questions can be rephrased.

The interview is also useful in obtaining responses from young children or illiterates. Responses from such persons must be obtained orally rather than in written form.

The flexibility of the interview is also advantageous to respondents. Highly structured pencil-and-paper instruments do not allow respondents the freedom to enlarge upon, retract, or question items presented to them. In an interview (especially an *unstructured* one), the respondent has the opportunity to ask for further information.

The interview also allows the investigator to observe both what the respondent has to say and the way in which it is said. If the interview is *structured*, or standardized, it is similar to the administration of individual intelligence tests. How the subject responds may be as important as response content.

A third advantage of the interview is its usefulness in collecting personal information, attitudes, perceptions, or beliefs by probing for additional information. Inconsistent or vague replies can be questioned.

A fourth advantage of the interview concerns motivation. Almost all interviews attempt to develop rapport between the interviewer and the respondent. Once the respondent accepts the interview as a nonthreatening situation, respondents are more likely to be open and frank. This openness adds to the validity of the interview.

## Disadvantages of the Interview

The interview is subject to the same evaluative criteria as are other data collection methods. The flexibility of the interview generates its own special difficulties, especially if the interview is *unstructured*. In an unstructured situation, the questions asked by the interviewer are not completely circumscribed, and respondents are free to interpret questions as they see fit. Problems may arise when it is time to summarize, categorize, and evaluate responses to unstructured questions since each respondent may interpret the meaning of questions differently.

A second problem concerns the training of interviewers. Personal values, beliefs, and biases of interviewers can influence responses. To compensate for these subjective influences, interviewers need to be trained and evaluated. This training will add substantially to the costs of data collection.

A third difficulty is that the interview has often been used inappropriately. To save time, for example, a researcher may find it convenient to ask students to report their grade point averages or to estimate the number of books they have read from the school library. Here is where the difference between *facts* and *opinions* becomes an issue of paramount importance. If official records are available concerning students' grade point averages or the number of books they checked out of the school library, these records should be used or evidence provided that students are reporting valid information. The validity of student reports can be estimated by selecting a random sample (see Chapter 8) of reports and checking them against official documents. Parry and Crossley[1] found that respondents would report acccurately their age and telephone ownership but were more cautious when it came to indicating whether they possessed a library card or had contributed to the Community Chest. Evidently respondents will report information accurately as long as there is no threat to their self-esteem.

## Effects of the Interviewer on the Collection of Data

Interviewers take an active role in the data collection process. Their behavior, therefore, is subject to question. Not only must they observe and record, but they must also be able to obtain the cooperation of the respondents. If the interview is structured, the interviewer must be trained to ask questions and record responses accurately; if the interview is unstructured, much more time will be required to teach the interviewer how to probe for opinions or attitudes *without directing* what the respondent has to say.

The literature on interviewing contains many dos and don'ts that are either vague or unsubstantiated by research findings. However, Kahn and Cannell[2] have suggested some of the potential sources of error in any interview: errors in asking questions, errors in probing, errors in motivating, and errors in recording responses.

1. The *error in asking questions* occurs whenever the response to a question will not satisfy the objectives of the investigation. This could occur if words have different meanings to the interviewer and to the respondents.

The way in which a question is asked may determine the response. It is one thing to ask a child, "Do you like school?" and quite a different

[1]Hugh J. Parry and Helen M. Crossley, "Validity of Responses to Survey Questions," *Public Opinion Quarterly*, 14, no. 1 (1950), pp. 61–80.

[2]Robert L. Kahn and Charles F. Cannell, *The Dynamics of Interviewing* (New York: John Wiley & Sons, 1957), pp. 189–196.

matter to say, "Tell me about school." The first is a *limited-response* question[3] since it restricts the length and scope of questions and responses. Limited-response interviews are usually structured in advance.

The statement, "Tell me about school," is a *free-response* item. The respondent is free to define the boundaries of the topic as long as the subject discussed is not substantially changed. In free-response interviews, the interviewer must keep the respondent on the topic without influencing responses. Often, responses are lengthy, making it difficult to record and summarize them.

A third type of questioning is the *defensive-response* interview, or *stress interview,* used by Kinsey and others. Kinsey has described the advantages of the defensive-response interview:

> The interviewer should not make it easy for a subject to deny his participation in any form of . . . activity. It is too easy to say no if he is simply asked whether he has ever engaged in a particular activity. We always assume that everyone has engaged in every type of activity; consequently we always begin by asking *when* they first engaged in such activity. This places a heavier burden on the individual who is inclined to deny his experience. . . .[4]

The defensive-response interview requires that the interviewers be highly trained and sensitive to the problems faced by respondents. Because questions are of the "When was the last time you beat your wife?" variety, they may produce both anxiety and hostility. Unless the interviewer is predisposed by training and temperament to reduce these feelings in respondents at the conclusion of the interview, the defensive-response interview should not be used.

Errors in asking questions can often be reduced by keeping in mind the type of research which makes best use of each type of interview. Dohrenwend and Richardson[5] have suggested that the limited-response interview be restricted to circumstances where the interviewer and the respondent both "share a common vocabulary relevant to the issues and alternatives to be included in the interview." The limited-response interview has its greatest value in public opinion polling or in consumer evaluation studies where relatively simple choices are sufficient. In contrast, the free-response interview is most useful where interviewer and respondent face an ambiguously defined situation, and where the respondent will need help in interpreting questions

---

[3] Barbara Snell Dohrenwend and Stephen A. Richardson, "Directiveness and Non-directiveness in Research Interviewing: A Reformulation of the Problem," *Psychological Bulletin,* 60, no. 5 (1963), pp. 475–485.

[4] Alfred C. Kinsey, Wardell B. Pomeroy, and Clyde E. Martin, *Sexual Behavior in the Human Male* (Philadelphia: W. B. Saunders Co., 1949), p. 53.

[5] Dohrenwend and Richardson, pp. 483–484.

or in reporting feelings or opinions. Free-response interviews can also be used in the beginning stages of a study to get ideas on how later interviews can be structured.

2. *Errors in probing* occur when the interviewer does not allow the respondent sufficient time to respond or anticipates responses. Errors in probing also occur if the interviewer fails to clarify ambiguous responses.

The best way to reduce errors in probing is to train the interviewers not to anticipate replies and not to assume an informant is incapable of responding.

Errors in probing have been studied empirically. One study found that experienced interviewers were able to elicit significantly more responses and less typical responses than interviewers with limited experience.[6]

In another study, Guest[7] had 15 interviewers ask various types of predetermined questions of a respondent who, unknown to the interviewers, was trained to answer questions in a prearranged manner. Each interview was recorded (again unknown to the interviewers), and scored by counting the number of times an error occurred (an error was defined as any discrepancy between what interviewers were instructed to do and what they actually reported on the interview schedule or on the recording). By this method, Guest found that the 15 interviewers made a total of 279 errors, or an average of 18.6 errors for each interviewer (the range was from 12 to 36 errors). About 40 percent of the errors were due to inappropriate probing. Additional training sessions for interviewers were obviously needed.

3. *Errors in motivating* respondents can be another source of invalidity. Unless respondents are motivated by interviewers to answer questions candidly and accurately, responses may not be valid.

The problem of motivating respondents is important for another reason. Many research designs require that respondents be interviewed two or more times to determine reliability or to check on trends. If respondents find the initial interview boring or unpleasant, they are not likely to permit themselves to be interviewed again. Each respondent who refuses to be interviewed presents a potential source of sampling bias (see Chapter 8).

Cannell and Axelrod[8] have shown that more than 90 percent of those persons interviewed in four surveys found the experience interesting and about 75 percent were willing to be interviewed a second time. Generally, respondents enjoy being interviewed *if they perceive the interviewer as one who*

---

[6]J. J. Feldman, Herbert Hyman, and C. W. Hart, "A Field Study of Interviewer Effects on the Quality of Survey Data," *Public Opinion Quarterly*, 15, no. 4 (Winter 1951–1952), pp. 734–761.

[7]Lester Guest, "A Study of Interviewer Competence," *International Journal of Opinion and Attitude Research*, 1, no. 4 (1947), pp. 17–30.

[8]Charles F. Cannell and Morris Axelrod, "The Respondent Reports on the Interview," *The American Journal of Sociology*, 62, no. 2 (1956), pp. 177–181.

*is friendly and sincerely interested in them and their beliefs*. Of equal significance was the finding that the content of the interview (highly personal or factual knowledge) seemed to make little difference to the respondents. It should be added that all the interviewers had been trained in interviewing techniques.

4. *Errors in recording responses* occur when the interviewer inaccurately records respondent replies. Although recording errors are usually unintentional, some situation may encourage "cheating." In one study,[9] for example, a number of respondents were specially trained to act as either "punctilious liberals" or "hostile bigots." Fifteen interviewers were employed, and tape recordings were made of the "planted" interviews. Hyman reported the following conclusions:

> Every interviewer made at least one error of each of the three non-cheating varieties [probing errors, errors in asking questions, and recording errors]. . . . Although every interviewer cheated at least once in the "hostile bigot" interview, four of the nine interviewers who turned in completed schedules for this respondent did not really cheat to an appreciable extent. . . . Those interviewers who blatantly cheated in the "hostile bigot" situation also resorted to cheating slightly more frequently in the "punctilious liberal" situation than did the other interviewers.[10]

A number of factors seem to be responsible for the inaccurate recording of responses in the Hyman study. In the first place, a majority of the interviewers had no experience in interviewing and were more motivated by monetary rewards than by any interest to learn interviewing techniques. According to Hyman, these interviewers were not unlike other nonprofessional interviewers.

Hyman also indicated that interviewing "planted" respondents is more difficult than interviewing under more usual conditions. Nevertheless, he reported that, on a 50-item questionnaire, *each interviewer on the average made 13 errors in asking questions, 13 errors in probing, 8 recording errors, and 4 cheating errors on each report, where every error was accorded 1 point.* More than one type of error, of course, could be made on any given item. This points out the need for selecting interviewers with care and training them adequately.

The recording of responses during an interview may pose some special difficulties. At one extreme is the attempt to write the report from memory after the interview has terminated; at the other extreme is the

---

[9]American Jewish Committee, Department of Scientific Research (unpublished manuscript), as reported by Herbert H. Hyman et al., *Interviewing in Social Research* (Chicago: University of Chicago Press, 1954).

[10]Hyman et al., pp. 241–242.

attempt to record the entire interview. In favor of tape recording interviews is the now classic study by Payne,[11] which compared the number of errors in responses recorded from memory with those that were tape recorded. Payne reported that the use of tape recorders reduced errors of memory by 25 percent.

Unfortunately, tape recordings present other types of problems. Ethical considerations require that the respondent's permission be obtained before the interview is taped. Little evidence is available on the effect of a microphone on respondents, although Kahn and Cannell[12] have suggested that the microphone is more likely to make the interviewer nervous than the respondent.

Another problem with tape recordings is the necessity to transcribe reports so that they can be analyzed. Not only is this process time-consuming, but it is expensive as well. One possibility is to analyze the data directly from the tape recording without typing a script first.

If the interview is relatively unstructured, tape recordings can be useful; they are of less value as the interview becomes more structured. With limited-response questions, there is little need to use recording equipment.

Another way to reduce errors in recording is to take brief notes during the interview itself. Most respondents will not object to note taking. Rather than taking verbatim notes, interviewers should try to develop their own form of shorthand. These notes should be transcribed as early as possible into standard English to avoid forgetting the meanings attached to the symbols.

### Reliability, Objectivity, and Validity of the Interview

As a research method, the interview can be evaluated in much the same way as are psychometric measurements (see Chapter 9). However, instead of using tests as the primary data source, the interviewer records responses. The reliability and validity of the interview depend on the interviewer's skills and personal characteristics and on the respondent's ability and willingness to report the type of information requested.

The reliability of measurements produced by interviewing usually involves obtaining estimates of *stability*. The stability of interview data is obtained by having the same interviewer question each respondent twice. The correlation between the observations or measurements obtained during

[11]Stanley L. Payne, "Interviewer Memory Faults," *Public Opinion Quarterly*, 13 (1949), pp. 684–685.
[12]Kahn and Cannell, p. 255.

the original interview and those obtained after a time interval provides an estimate of the interview's stability.

*Objectivity* refers to the extent to which two or more interviewers or scorers agree on how a response is to be classified. Responses are classified *subjectively* if raters assign the same response to different categories. Unless responses are objectively categorized, they will be unreliable; the categorization will depend on who does the rating. Sometimes objectivity is referred to as *interobserver reliability*. It is similar to equivalent-form reliability except that there are two or more observers rather than two or more parallel sets of questions. Mosteller[13] has provided empirical evidence comparing the reliabilities of interviews under different conditions. Table 10-1 shows how the same interviewers reclassified respondents into five economic status groups after a period of three weeks. Mosteller indicated that 77 percent of the classifications were identical, which yielded a reliability coefficient of +0.79.

When different interviewers were assigned to the same respondents

**TABLE 10-1**

**Extent to Which the Same Interviewers Were Able to Reclassify Respondents over a Three-Week Period**

| Classification at First Interview | Classification at Second Interview | | | | | |
|---|---|---|---|---|---|---|
| | WEALTHY | AV. PLUS | AV. | POOR | ON RELIEF | TOTAL |
| Wealthy | 8 | 1 | | | | 9 |
| Average plus | 2 | 39 | 23 | | | 64 |
| Average | | 13 | 111 | 10 | | 134 |
| Poor | | | 10 | 56 | 1 | 67 |
| On relief | | 1 | 1 | 1 | 1 | 4 |
| Total | 10 | 54 | 145 | 67 | 2 | 278 |

*Source:* Mosteller, p. 99.

after two months, reliability dropped to +0.63, and the identical classifications dropped to 53 percent. This drop in reliability would be expected since the use of different interviewers over a longer period of time would increase error variance (see Table 10-2).

[13]Frederick Mosteller, "The Reliability of Interviewers' Ratings," in Hadley Cantril et al., *Gauging Public Opinion* (Princeton: Princeton University Press, 1944), pp. 98–106.

## TABLE 10-2

Extent to Which Different Interviewers Were Able
to Reclassify Respondents over a Two-Month Period

| Classification by First Interviewer | Classification by Second Interviewer | | | | | |
|---|---|---|---|---|---|---|
| | WEALTHY | AV. PLUS | AV. | POOR | ON RELIEF | TOTAL |
| Wealthy | 3 | 3 | 4 | | | 10 |
| Average plus | 4 | 20 | 21 | | | 45 |
| Average | 2 | 24 | 74 | 5 | | 105 |
| Poor | 1 | 2 | 57 | 59 | 6 | 125 |
| On relief | | | 8 | 9 | 9 | 26 |
| Total | 10 | 49 | 164 | 73 | 15 | 311 |

*Source:* Mosteller, p. 101.

It is often desirable to obtain some estimate of the composite reliability of $k$ number of interviewers or raters. It may also be important to obtain an estimate of the reliability of a single interviewer. The *intraclass correlation*, based on the analysis of variance, was described by Ebel[14] as a means for estimating the reliability of ratings or interviews.

The intraclass reliability for a single interviewer can be found by the following formula:[15]

$$r_{11} = \frac{V_p - V_e}{V_p + (k - 1)V_e}$$

where $r_{11}$ is the mean reliability of one interviewer; $V_p$ is the variance for persons or respondents being rated or interviewed; $V_e$ is the variance for error; and $k$ is the number of interviewers or raters. Note that if $V_e$ (error variance) is zero, the intraclass reliability ($r_{11}$) would equal 1.0. To the extent that error variance can be decreased, reliability increases.

Assume that seven students were each interviewed by four interviewers. Moreover, each interviewer rated the students on a 10-point scale. Table 10-3 summarizes the ratings made by the four fictitious interviewers.

The sum of squares for persons is found by assigning the mean rating of the four interviewers to each respondent. Albert, for example,

[14] Robert L. Ebel, "Estimation of the Reliability of Ratings," *Psychometrika*, 16, no. 4 (1951), pp. 407–424.

[15] J. P. Guilford, *Psychometric Methods* (New York: McGraw-Hill Book Company, 1954). Copyright © 1954, by McGraw-Hill, Inc. Used by permission of McGraw-Hill Book Company.

## TABLE 10-3

Ratings Given by Four Interviewers to Seven
Respondents (data fictitious)

| Respondents | Interviewers | | | |
|---|---|---|---|---|
| | MR. JONES | MR. SMITH | MS. HALEY | MR. HILL |
| Albert | 4 | 3 | 4 | 5 |
| Betty | 8 | 6 | 9 | 7 |
| Carl | 2 | 5 | 3 | 2 |
| Delbert | 4 | 7 | 9 | 4 |
| Evelyn | 1 | 1 | 2 | 1 |
| Frank | 7 | 3 | 9 | 1 |
| Gertrude | 9 | 3 | 6 | 1 |

would be assigned a value of 4.0 from *each interviewer*; Betty would be given 4 values of 7.5 (i.e., the sum of the 4 ratings is 30 divided by 4); and so on to Gertrude who would receive 4 ratings of 4.75 (19 ÷ 4 = 4.75). The mean of all 28 scores is 4.5. If 4.5 is subtracted from each of the 28 mean ratings and the differences squared, the sum of squares for persons or respondents can be found. This value is 98.5. The variance for persons is the sum of squares divided by $N - 1$, or 6. The value $V_p$ which appears in the numerator and denominator of the intraclass correlation is 98.5 ÷ 6, or 16.42.

The only other value needed is $V_e$, or error variance. This can be determined by computing the total sum of squares and the sum of squares for interviewers and persons. The error sum of squares can be found by the following formula: Error $SS$ = Total $SS$ − Persons $SS$ − Interviewers $SS$.

The total $SS$ is found by listing all 28 ratings, subtracting the mean (126 ÷ 28 = 4.3) from each, and squaring and summing the differences. The total sum of squares is 207.

The sum of squares for interviewers is found by disregarding differences in the ratings assigned to each person. The mean rating assigned to all persons by Mr. Jones is 35 ÷ 7 = 5.0; Mr. Smith's mean rating is 4.0; Ms. Haley's, 6.0; and Mr. Hill's, 3.0. Now replace all seven ratings by the interviewer's mean rating. There would be seven scores of 5.0, seven of 4.0, seven of 6.0, and seven of 3.0. Subtract the grand mean of 4.5 from each of the 28 ratings, square these differences, and sum them. This sum of squares for interviewers will be 35.00. The error $SS$ will then be 73.5, which is found by taking the total $SS$ (207) minus the persons or respondents $SS$ (98.5) minus the interviewer's $SS$ (35.00).

The number of degrees of freedom for error is found by multiplying the degrees of freedom for respondents ($N - 1 = 6$) by the degrees of freedom for interviewers $(4 - 1 = 3)$, or 18. The error variance is $SS$ for error (73.5) divided by 18, or 4.08. The intraclass correlation then becomes

$$r_{11} = \frac{16.42 - 4.08}{16.42 + (4 - 1)4.08} = \frac{12.34}{28.66} = 0.43$$

This index, 0.43, represents the mean reliability of a single interviewer. In this example, however, there were four interviewers, so the composite reliability would be expected to be larger than 0.43. The extent of this increase can be estimated by using the Spearman–Brown formula (see pp. 216–218), with $k$ equal to 4 and $r$ equal to 0.43.[16,17]

The validity of the interview is more difficult to obtain than are estimates of reliability. If criteria are available, predictive or concurrent validity may be used. For example, Parry and Crossley[18] were able to obtain accurate records of respondents' ages, amount (if any) contributed to the Community Chest, and ownership of a telephone. A simple percentage of agreement between information obtained from an interview and information from official files was used as a measure of validity.

A more difficult problem arises if the interview is designed to measure attitudes or opinions where no criterion other than the respondent's statement itself is readily available. At times, the validity of an opinion or attitude can be measured by considering how the information is to be used. If the purpose is to predict whether or not students will continue their education beyond high school, college attendance provides a useful criterion. But another possibility is simply to accept statements *as verbal responses*. These responses are, *ipso facto*, valid. If, for example, an investigator is interested in the attitude of parents toward their local school system, the statements of the parents can be accepted as *expressed* attitudes. They cannot be accepted, however, as evidence of predictive validity.

## Biasing Factors in the Interview

One of the most effective ways of increasing the reliability and validity of interviews lies in the training of interviewers. Interviewers not only have to record what the respondents say, but they also have to pose the

---

[16]If each interviewer has not been able to interview or rate each student, it will be necessary to modify the formula. For a more detailed discussion, the student should consult Ebel, pp. 412–413.

[17]If the data are ranked and there are only two interviewers, Spearman's rho, or rank order correlation, can be used. Where there are more than two interviewers who rank respondents, it is possible to use the coefficient of concordance. See, for example, George A. Ferguson, *Statistical Analysis in Psychology and Education*, 4th ed. (New York: McGraw-Hill Book Co., 1976), pp. 373–376.

[18]Parry and Crossley, "Validity of Responses to Survey Questions."

questions. They, therefore, must interact with the respondent, and that interaction can contribute to or detract from reliability and validity.

The personal characteristics of the interviewer can (and often do) determine the validity of the responses. It is important, then, to select and train interviewers who can obtain valid responses. The following variables have been shown to influence the responses obtained during interviews:

| *Variable* | *Effect on the Interview* |
|---|---|
| 1. Age of interviewer | a. Rapport is high if young interviewers work with middle-aged respondents. Respondent's age is unimportant for older interviewers.[19] |
| | b. The least amount of inhibition in responding occurs with young persons of same sex.[20] |
| | c. Most inhibition in responding occurs with persons of same age but different sex.[21] |
| | d. Interviewers between twenty-six and fifty years of age do a better job of interviewing than either younger or older interviewers.[22] |
| 2. College major | Interviewers trained in the behavioral sciences are rated as being more accurate than those in physical sciences; lowest rated are those who majored in fine arts, business, law, and the humanities.[23] |
| 3. Educational level | College graduates are rated higher than noncollege-trained interviewers, but differences are slight.[24] |
| 4. Experience in interviewing | Interviewers' accuracy increases as their experience in interviewing increases.[25] |
| 5. Racial background | Responses of blacks differ depending upon whether they are interviewed by Caucasians or other blacks.[26] |
| 6. Religious background | Negative responses concerning Jews tend to be withheld if the interviewers introduce |

[19]Hyman et al., *Interviewing in Social Research*, p. 155.

[20]Mark Benney, David Riesman, and Shirley A. Star, "Age and Sex in the Interview," *The American Journal of Sociology*, 62, no. 2 (1956), pp. 143–152.

[21]Benney, Riesman, and Star.

[22]Paul B. Sheatsley, "An Analysis of Interviewer Characteristics and Their Relationship to Performance—Part III," *International Journal of Opinion and Attitude Research*, 5, no. 2 (1951), pp. 191–220.

[23]Sheatsley.

[24]Sheatsley.

[25]Sheatsley.

[26]Cantril, pp. 114–116.

themselves by Jewish names or if they are "Jewish appearing."[27]

7. Sex of interviewer | Males obtain fewer interview responses than do females.[28]

8. Socioeconomic level | Middle-class interviewers report a greater degree of conservatism among working-class respondents than do working-class interviewers.[29]

# THE QUESTIONNAIRE

In many ways the interview and the questionnaire are similar. Both attempt to elicit the feelings, beliefs, experiences, or activities of respondents. They may also be as structured or unstructured as the situation demands. An interview may be so highly structured that it is necessary only to check a category corresponding to the response of the informant. If the interviewer is interested in knowing the respondents' salary, the *interview schedule* or list of questions to be asked should be highly structured; otherwise some interviewers might report the hourly income of respondents and others, yearly or monthly salaries, making data difficult to compare.

As indicated earlier, an advantage of the interview is its flexibility. Interviewers may ask questions in a variety of ways to make certain that the respondents understand the task; they may probe for additional information; they can note the manner of responding as well as the content of the response. In turn, respondents have the opportunity to question the interviewer should they desire or need to do so.

## Advantages of the Questionnaire

The most important advantage of the questionnaire over the interview is one of economy. Because many questionnaires are sent through the mail, the expense and time involved in training interviewers and sending them personally to interview each respondent are diminished. Also, the questionnaire can be sent almost anywhere, a condition that is usually impractical for interviews.

The use of the mails for questionnaires means that more persons can be reached than would be possible with interviews. To increase the size of a

[27]Duane Robinson and Sylvia Rohde, "Two Experiments with an Anti-Semitism Poll," *Journal of Abnormal and Social Psychology*, 41, no. 2 (1946), pp. 136–144.

[28]Benney, Riesman, and Star.

[29]Daniel Katz, "Do Interviewers Bias Polls?" *Public Opinion Quarterly*, 6, no. 2 (1942), pp. 248–268.

sample of interviews by one case may add many dollars to the cost of the investigation. The cost of mailing one additional questionnaire, however, is negligible.

Another advantage claimed for the questionnaire is that each respondent receives the same set of questions phrased in exactly the same way, as they are on standardized tests. Questionnaires are, thus, supposed to yield more comparable data than do interviews. The validity of this argument depends, in large part, on whether questions are structured or unstructured. If questions are structured, comparability in phrasing can help to standardize the response mode. Highly structured interviews, however, can easily become stilted.

Standardization requires more than a common set of questions or items; it also requires that responses be obtained under comparable conditions. With mailed questionnaires, there is little or no standardization in the response conditions. If item format and the conditions under which questions will be answered can be kept comparable, the questionnaire is favored over the interview.

## Disadvantages of the Questionnaire

The use of questionnaires poses some serious disadvantages. First, the motivation of the respondent is difficult to check, while an interview permits rapport to be established. Without knowing how motivated respondents are, the validity of their responses is difficult to judge.

A second disadvantage of the questionnaire, and especially those that are mailed, is the assumption that respondents are literate. Although this is probably not too serious a problem in many studies, it is a limitation in some populations.

Sampling is a third disadvantage of the questionnaire. Because each questionnaire that is not returned increases the likelihood of biased sampling, every effort should be made to obtain a 100 percent return. The percentage of returns depends on such factors as the length of the questionnaire, the reputation of the sponsoring agency, the complexity of the questions asked, the relative importance of the study as judged by the respondent, the extent to which the respondent believes that his or her responses are important, and the quality and design of the questionnaire itself.

In one study concerned with the percentage of returned questionnaires in published studies,[30] it was found that the average rate of return was about 75 percent. Many of these studies could have increased this percentage by sending two or three follow-up letters by registered mail, by calling

[30] J. R. Shannon, "Percentages of Returns of Questionnaires in Reputable Educational Research," *Journal of Educational Research*, 42, no. 2 (1948), pp. 138–141.

respondents by telephone or telegraph, or, if necessary, by including money to potential respondents as an inducement to return the questionnaire.[31]

In his highly readable book titled *How to Lie with Statistics*,[32] Darrell Huff stated that *Time* magazine reported the average income of Yale graduates (1924 class) to be $25,111 per year! This implied, of course, that Yale graduates were somehow superior to graduates from other universities. What Huff pointed out was the biased nature of the sample. First of all, not all members of the class of 1924 could be reached. Addresses of some of the class members were lost, and not all those who could be reached were willing to return the questionnaire. In this instance, it is most likely that the annual income for those persons whose addresses were known and who were willing to report their income was much higher than was the annual income of the nonrespondents. The failure to obtain a 100 percent return or a random sampling of returns from all members of the class clearly led to a spuriously high figure.

### Justifying the Use of the Questionnaire

A questionnaire, no matter how well designed, does not represent an end in itself. It is a means of gathering information *for specific purposes*. All too often a questionnaire is designed to gather information that is trivial at best and invalid at worst. The outcome is likely to be trivial whenever the investigator is unable to justify the need for the questionnaire. The decision to use a questionnaire (or any other instrument) presumes that the information requested is unobtainable in more reliable and valid ways. Too many studies have been done by persons determined to use a questionnaire without a single hypothesis established to justify its use.

The responsibility for selecting questions rests on the researcher. One recommendation is to prepare a work table (see Table 10-4) containing a list of questions related to the hypotheses under investigation. For each of these questions, the investigator can justify the need for collecting that type of information by questionnaire. In some instances, it might be more valid to check official documents and records for the required data.

Table 10-4 is not necessarily complete. A more thorough review of the literature might indicate that other variables should be included; as the invesitgation continues, further changes might have to be made in data collection plans. The work table is not designed to force the investigator into

---

[31]Marvin Bressler and William Kephart, "An Experience with the Use of the Mail Questionnaire," *Nursing Research*, 5, no. 1 (1956), pp. 35–39.

[32]Darrell Huff, *How to Lie with Statistics* (New York: W. W. Norton & Co., 1954), pp. 11–15.

# TABLE 10-4

Example of a Work Table Designed to Justify Various
Types of Data Collection Procedures

| Variable | Justification | Most Useful Method of Obtaining Information |
|---|---|---|
| I. INFORMATION WHICH CAN BE VALIDATED AGAINST OFFICIAL RECORDS | | |
| Name of teacher | Identification purposes | Code name on questionnaire |
| Grade level | Identification purposes | Include on questionnaire |
| Age | Prior investigations showing teachers' age related to discipline problems | Ask birthdate on questionnaire (validate sample of questionnaires against school records) |
| Sex | May correlate with student preferences | Questionnaire |
| Year of car | Omit—not sufficiently important to consider | |
| Address | Correlates with socioeconomic level | Questionnaire |
| II. OPINIONS OR ATTITUDES REGARDING EACH OF THE FOLLOWING VARIABLES | | |
| Control techniques used by teachers | Control techniques are related to students' attitudes | Questionnaire, but allow freedom to respond ("Do you think physical punishment is ever justifiable?") |
| Teachers' degree of respect for children | Measure of authoritarianism | Rosenzweig Picture Frustration Test |
| III. EXPLANATIONS OF REASONS BEHIND BEHAVIOR OR BELIEFS | | |
| Reason for teaching | Likely that teacher motivation related to pupil perceptions | Depth interview |
| Justification for type of disciplinary techniques used | Omit—Not needed in the present study | |

making hasty and irrevocable decisions, but rather to provide a means for consideration of alternative ways of dealing with data collection problems.

## Form of Items on Questionnaires

Now we will describe four types of measurement scales that can be used on questionnaires, tests, or inventories. Stevens[33] has called these four types of scales *nominal, ordinal, interval*, and *ratio* scales. Their consideration is important in order to point out the characteristics or properties of various types of scales.

The *nominal* scale involves the fewest assumptions. Names or labels for persons, objects, activities, or beliefs form this type of scale. Its purpose is simply to identify or categorize attributes. For example, names of schools, teachers, or objects of furniture are nominal forms of measurement. Even if the category is a numeral (such as those on the backs of football players), it is used only for identification, and any other numeral may be substituted as long as no two individuals have the same one. Categorizing persons into political parties, types of courses or subjects taught, or into different after-school activities in which students participate are all examples of nominal categories.

The *ordinal* scale has all of the characteristics of the nominal scale, but in addition attributes may be ranked (highest to lowest, most to least, or best to worst, for example). Grading systems that rank students within a class on some trait or combination of traits are examples of ordinal scales. These make no assumption that differences between successive categories such as bright, average, and dull represent equal differences.

The earliest type of attitude measurement was the social distance scale constructed by Bogardus.[34] Its intent was to measure the amount of social distance placed between oneself and members of various ethnic, religious, nationality, or racial groups. The directions for completing the Bogardus scale are as follows:

> *Directions:* According to my first feeling reactions I would willingly admit members of each race or nationality (as a class and not the best I have known, nor the worst members) to one or more of the classifications which I have circled.

---

[33]S. S. Stevens, "Mathematics, Measurement, and Psychophysics," in S. S. Stevens, ed., *Handbook of Experimental Psychology* (New York: John Wiley & Sons, 1951), pp. 23–30.

[34]E. S. Bogardus, "Measuring Social Distances," *Journal of Applied Sociology*, 9 (March–April 1925), pp. 299–308. The social distance scale presented in this chapter is a modification of Bogardus' early scale.

| | To Close Kinship by Marriage | To My Club as Personal Chums | To My Street as Neighbors | To Employment in My Occupation | To Citizenship in My Country | As Visitors Only to My Country | Would Exclude from My Country |
|---|---|---|---|---|---|---|---|
| English | 1 | 2 | 3 | 4 | 5 | 6 | 7 |
| Swedes | 1 | 2 | 3 | 4 | 5 | 6 | 7 |
| French | 1 | 2 | 3 | 4 | 5 | 6 | 7 |
| Russians | 1 | 2 | 3 | 4 | 5 | 6 | 7 |
| Blacks | 1 | 2 | 3 | 4 | 5 | 6 | 7 |
| etc. | | | | | | | |

The ordinal nature of the social distance scale can easily be seen by examining the categories making up the scale. The difference in social distance between category 1 and category 2 does not necessarily represent the same amount of social distance between any other two successive categories.

Another widely used type of ordinal measurement is the Likert (pronounced "Lick-ert") scale.[35] Although Likert used a 5-point scale ("strongly approve," "approve," "undecided," "disapprove," and "strongly disapprove"), it is possible to use fewer or more than 5 categories. In general, the more categories there are that can be reliably marked, the better.

The construction of a Likert-type scale involves assigning points to each of the categories being used. The most favorable response is usually given the most points. Thus, in a 5-point scale, "strongly approve" would indicate a value of 5 points, whereas "strongly disapprove" would receive only 1 point. It should be remembered that it is the favorableness of the attitude that is being scored and not the response category itself. If a question were worded, "The public schools should be abolished," the most favorable response would depend on the attitudes of those who constructed the questionnaire. If it were constructed by those who favored retaining the public schools, 5 points would be given for "strongly disagree" and 1 point would be given for "strongly agree." If, on the other hand, the questionnaire were constructed by those who favored abolishing the public schools, these scores would be reversed.

The score that an individual receives on a Likert-type scale is the sum of the scores received on each item. For example, if 25 items are on a questionnaire and if each item consists of a maximum of 5 points and a minimum of 1 point, the most favorable score would be 125 points ($5 \times 25$);

[35]Rensis Likert, "A Technique for the Measurement of Attitudes," *Archives of Psychology*, no. 140 (1932).

the lowest possible score would be 25 (assuming no items were omitted), which would represent the least favorable attitude.

In constructing Likert scales, the investigator attempts to develop items that correlate perfectly with total scores obtained by a group of respondents, that is, to develop an instrument which is as internally consistent as possible, so that all items will measure the same attitude. Perhaps the most defensible method of determining which items should be retained or eliminated is to correlate the item score with each individual's total score. For example, the following worksheet could be prepared:

| Item # _____ | | |
| --- | --- | --- |
| Individual | Item Score* | Total Score† |
| 1 | | |
| 2 | | |
| 3 | | |
| 4 | | |
| . | | |
| . | | |
| . | | |
| N | | |

*From 1 to 5 points (on a 5-point scale).
†From 25 to 125 points (on a 25-item questionnaire).

The final questionnaire would be composed only of those items that correlate highly with the total score. Items that correlate low with total scores or that correlate negatively would be eliminated. Some caution, however, must be observed here. Because total scores are sums of the individual item scores, the correlation between items and total scores will be spuriously high. This occurs because the items are not independent of the total score but rather are a part of it. Where there are a large number of items this is of minor significance, but for a questionnaire of just 25 items, each item plays a significant part in determining the total test scores. This still may not be serious if the correlation coefficients are considered only with regard to their relative magnitudes. Thus, while it is likely that all of the item–total score correlations will be spuriously high, the items can be ranked from those having the highest correlation to those having the lowest. The final form of the questionnaire would include those items having the highest item–total score correlations.[36]

[36]A much less laborious approach for selecting Likert-type items has been suggested

A technique which has been the subject of much controversy[37,38] is the *scalogram technique* proposed by Guttman.[39] Technically, it is more a method for determining whether a set of items is *unidimensional* than a method of constructing questionnaires.[40] A unidimensional scale is one that can predict, knowing a respondent's total score, how that person responded to each and every item on the questionnaire. A perfect Guttman scale would be one in which any two persons who obtained the same total score would also obtain identical item scores. An example of a set of items which conforms to Guttman's criterion might be the following:

*1.* I am over 10 years of age.
*2.* I am over 15 years of age.
*3.* I am over 20 years of age.
*4.* I am over 25 years of age.
*5.* I am over 30 years of age.

Note that a person who is over thirty years of age would respond positively to statements 1, 2, 3, 4, and 5. Any person obtaining a score of 5 would have had to agree with each and every statement on the list; a person with a score of 4 would have agreed with the first four items. With 1 point given for each statement to which the respondent can agree, a perfect Gutt-

---

by Gardner Murphy and Rensis Likert, *Public Opinion and the Individual* (New York: Harper & Row, 1938). The procedure involves the following steps: 1) scoring the papers and placing them in rank order; 2) selecting the highest- and lowest-scoring 25 percent of the questionnaires; and 3) summing the scores on each item and obtaining the difference in the scores for persons responding in the upper and lower groups. For example, if a questionnaire is completed by 100 persons, the upper and lower 25 percent would each contain 25 questionnaires. Suppose that on item 1, the sum of the scores for the upper group is 98, and the sum of the scores for the lower group is 47. The difference is 51, which can be taken as an index of item discrimination. Actually, Murphy and Likert divided each difference by the number of cases in the top or bottom group. However, because the divisor is constant, the additional step of dividing is unnecessary. This procedure is obviously much simpler to use than is the correlational method described earlier; according to Murphy and Likert, the correlation between the two methods of item selection was 0.91.

[37]Leon Festinger, "The Treatment of Qualitative Data by 'Scale Analysis,'" *Psychological Bulletin*, 44, no. 2 (1947), pp. 149–161.

[38]Jane Loevinger, "The Technic of Homogeneous Tests Compared with Some Aspects of 'Scale Analysis' and Factor Analysis," *Psychological Bulletin*, 45, no. 6 (1948), pp. 507–529.

[39]Louis Guttman, "A Basis for Scaling Quantitative Data," *American Sociological Review*, 9, no. 2 (1944), pp. 139–150.

[40]Allen L. Edwards, *Techniques of Attitude Scale Construction* (New York: Appleton-Century-Crofts, 1957), p. 172.

man scale would appear as follows:

| Respondent | Items | | | | | Total Score |
|:---:|:---:|:---:|:---:|:---:|:---:|:---:|
| | 1 | 2 | 3 | 4 | 5 | |
| A | 1 | 1 | 1 | 1 | 1 | 5 |
| B | 1 | 1 | 1 | 1 | 1 | 5 |
| C | 1 | 1 | 1 | 1 | | 4 |
| D | 1 | 1 | 1 | 1 | | 4 |
| E | 1 | 1 | 1 | 1 | | 4 |
| F | 1 | 1 | 1 | | | 3 |
| G | 1 | 1 | | | | 2 |
| H | 1 | 1 | | | | 2 |
| I | 1 | | | | | 1 |
| J | 1 | | | | | 1 |

Knowing a person's total score permits a perfect prediction of the responses to the individual items. The extent to which a scale conforms to this characteristic is called its *reproducibility index*[41] because scores on the individual items (given 1 or zero points) could be reproduced or predicted simply by knowing the total score.

The Guttman technique has been criticized on a number of grounds:

*1.* The technique cannot be used as a means of selecting items for a questionnaire. Only after items are selected can reproducibility be judged.

*2.* Guttman arbitrarily establishes a reproducibility index of 0.90 as the minimum value for a scalable test (other criteria are also required). Reproducibility indexes between 0.85 and 0.90 yield what Guttman has called "quasi-scales"; indexes below 0.85 are not considered to be scalable. One difficulty is that different groups of respondents yield different reproducibility indexes.

*3.* The value of the reproducibility index depends on the number of subtests, items, and categories to which these subjects respond. A high index of reproducibility can occur if the number of subjects, items, and categories is small.

Ordinal scales involve ranking but make no assumption concerning equality of difference between ranks. In contrast, the *interval* scale can be ranked, and the differences between successive ranks will be equal. A thermometer is an example of an interval measurement. Not only can temperatures be ranked (hottest to coldest), but the difference between 80 and 90 degrees is exactly the same as between 40 and 50 degrees.

---

[41]The *reproducibility index* is the proportion of *item* responses that can be reproduced from knowledge of the total score.

The most widely used method for developing interval-scale question-naires, proposed by Thurstone and Chave[42] in 1929, was based upon the psychophysical model called the *method of equal-appearing intervals*. The development of the scale involves the following procedures.

*Item Selection.* A large number of items (200 items are not con-sidered excessive) are selected and edited so that they are short, can be judged as favorable or unfavorable, and are not "double-barreled" in form. A double-barreled statement contains two propositions, such as "I am in favor of public education *and* am willing to have my taxes increased for support of the public schools." Although some persons could agree with the statement as a whole, some may favor public education without wanting their taxes raised.

*Sorting the Items.* Once the items have been selected, written, and edited, each item is typed on a separate card. Usually, 50 or more judges are asked to sort each statement on an 11-point scale (fewer categories have been used) ranging from "most unfavorable" to "most favorable." The only other category labeled by the investigator is the middle or "neutral" category. Each judge is asked to sort the statements into categories so that the differences in attitude expressed between successive categories appear to be equal. The *interval* nature of the scale rests on Thurstone's contention that the categories into which statements are sorted are independent of the values held by the judges, a contention that has been defended as well as attacked.[43]

*Determining Scale and Q Values.* The third step in constructing Thurstone scales is to determine the scale and $Q$ values for each item. Each category is numbered from 1 (indicating the most unfavorable category) to 11 (the most favorable category) after the judges have sorted the cards. The scale value is simply the category number corresponding to the median of the distribution of judgments; the $Q$ value is the interquartile range, or the difference between the category numbers corresponding to the 75th and 25th percentiles, which contains the middle 50 percent of the judgments.

[42]L. L. Thurstone and E. J. Chave, *The Measurement of Attitude: A Psychophysical Method and Some Experiments with a Scale for Measuring Attitudes toward the Church* (Chicago: University of Chicago Press, 1929).

[43]See E. D. Hinckley, "The Influence of Individual Opinion on Construction of an Attitude Scale," *Journal of Social Psychology*, 3, no. 3 (1932), pp. 283–296; Quinn McNemar, "Opinion–Attitude Methodology," *Psychological Bulletin*, 43, no. 4 (1946), pp. 289–374; and H. J. Eysenck and S. Crown, "An Experimental Study in Opinion–Attitude Metho-dology," *International Journal of Opinion and Attitude Research*, 3, no. 1 (1949), pp. 47–86. For exceptions and criticisms of Thurstone's point of view, see C. I. Hovland and M. Sherif, "Judgmental Phenomena and Scales of Attitude Measurement: Item Displacement in Thurstone Scales," *Journal of Abnormal and Social Psychology*, 47, no. 4 (1952), pp. 822–832; and Allen L. Edwards, pp. 106–116.

Assume that 80 raters are asked to sort 200 items concerning attitudes toward education. In addition, assume that the $n$th item is sorted in the following manner:

| Category | Number of Judges Placing $n$th Item into Each Category |
|---|---|
| 11   Most favorable | 3 |
| 10 | 6 |
| 9 | 6 |
| 8 | 8 |
| 7 | 12 |
| 6   Neutral | 20 |
| 5 | 14 |
| 4 | 6 |
| 3 | 2 |
| 2 | 2 |
| 1   Most unfavorable | 1 |
| | 80 |

The scale value is the median of this distribution, or 6.25; the $Q$ value is equal to the 75th percentile minus the 25th percentile, or 7.88 − 5.14 = 2.74. The same procedure is followed for determining the scale and $Q$ values for each of the remaining items.[44] $Q$ is simply a measure of the variability of judges' responses. Because $Q$ is unaffected by extremes in judgment, it was used in preference to the standard deviation which is affected by extreme responses.

*The Final Scale.* The final form of a Thurstone scale usually consists of 20 to 25 items selected so that scale values are as evenly distributed from 1 to 11 as possible. If there is a choice between two or more items having the same or essentially the same scale value, the investigator would select the one having the lowest $Q$ value. Low $Q$ values indicate that judgments are not too spread out; high $Q$ values are indicative of a relatively large dispersion of the judgments made by the sorters. Wherever possible, two equivalent forms of the questionnaire having equal scale and $Q$ values should be prepared. Items should be placed in random order on the final form.

*Sorting Procedure.* When the Thurstone type of scale is administered, respondents are asked to check the statements to which they can agree. Respondent scores can be determined by obtaining the median of the scale scores of those items. Because of the possibility that some respondents may

---

[44]The student is referred to any elementary textbook in statistics for help in computing medians and percentiles from grouped distributions.

be overly zealous (or overly cautious) in the number of categories they select, it may be a good idea to restrict the number of responses to 4 or 5.[45] Each person would then be responding to the same number of items. If, for example, a respondent could agree to statements having scale values of 8.9, 9.1, 9.6, 10.7, and 10.9, his or her score would be 9.6, the median of these 5 scale values, or the middle score after the values have been placed in ascending order. The spread of scale values for any one respondent may be taken as a measure of the extent to which that respondent has a clearly defined attitude. The more spread out the scale values are for a given person, the less certain it is that the respondent has an unambiguous and clearly defined attitude toward the topic under investigation.

## Arrangement of Items and Options

The arrangement of items on a questionnaire depends, in part, on the nature of the attitude scale. On social distance scales, the seven categories are fixed by order of favorableness. The ethnic, religious, or racial groups, however, could be presented in any order, although perhaps the least biased approach would be to place them randomly or to list them alphabetically.

On Likert scales, the placement of items should be randomized. Placing all of the favorably worded items first may produce a set or tendency for respondents to look favorably upon the items as a whole. The effect of item arrangement can be determined by administering the same questionnaire—but with the items arranged in different sequences—to comparable groups. If reliability and validity remain constant from group to group even though the items are presented in different sequences, then sequence can be disregarded.

On Thurstone scales, the cards to be used for sorting are presented to judges in random order *to determine scale and Q values*. The final form should also consist of items that have been randomly placed on the scale for presentation to subjects.

Item sequence can also be determined by considering how item format will affect the respondent. One technique is to present the most general items first, followed by questions which are more specific. Thus, it is advantageous to ask respondents about their attitude toward education in general, and then about some specific aspect of education such as the amount of homework that should be given to high school students.

Another approach has been described by Kinsey et al.,[46] although in reference to interviews. They suggest the wisdom of beginning with questions that are the least threatening, such as the respondent's birthplace,

[45]Guilford, p. 459.
[46]Kinsey, Pomeroy, and Martin, pp. 48–49.

interests, and health. Although Kinsey was especially interested in studying sexual behavior, he began by asking for less threatening information. The first sexual questions were those for which the subject could be held least responsible, such as his sources for obtaining information about sex. The questions next discussed the informant's overt sexual behavior as a child and then proceeded slowly to his adult behavior.

## Form of Item

Campbell[47] has distinguished four types of items: 1) *nondisguised–structured*, such as the Thurstone and Likert scales, in which respondents are given accurate information about the purpose of the questionnaire but are restricted in their responses by the investigator; 2) *nondisguised–nonstructured*, as found on the free-response type of questionnaire, where the subjects have unlimited possibilities to respond in any manner they see fit; 3) *disguised–nonstructured*, which restrict the responses of the respondents and at the same time conceal the purpose of the questionnaire. These will be considered in greater detail in Chapter 12.

Item format can be considered from another point of view. For example, on achievement tests, it is customary to refer to items as true–false, multiple-choice, completion, or essay. The advantages and disadvantages of each of these types can also be applied to questionnaires.

The true–false item is a statement which can be endorsed or not. On questionnaires, the statement could be: "I am willing to have my taxes increased to support the public schools." Two alternatives such as "Agree" and "Disagree" are provided, and respondents are asked to select the one option which best expresses their belief or opinion.

The Likert scale is presented in multiple-choice format. Respondents are instructed to select the one option that best describes their opinion or belief. On a three-option questionnaire, subjects may agree, disagree, or state that they are uncertain as to their beliefs.

On completion items, subjects are provided with an incomplete statement and are requested to write in a phrase or clause that will complete the sentence. On questionnaires, examples might be

*1.* Education is . . .

*2.* Teachers are . . .

*3.* I believe that smoking is . . .

On questionnaires, the statements reflecting different attitudes or beliefs may

[47]Donald T. Campbell, "The Indirect Assessment of Social Attitudes," *Psychological Bulletin*, 47, no. 1 (1950), pp. 15–38.

also be rank ordered on the basis of favorableness. Young children, for example, can rank the school subjects they like most and least.

The essay is the least structured (and probably the most unreliable) type of test. Within the boundaries established by the question, the subject is given the maximum amount of freedom in responding, which makes scoring a difficult chore. A relatively unstructured question on a questionnaire might be, "How good a job do you believe the public schools are doing in teaching reading?"

## Item Writing

The literature on item construction for questionnaires contains a large number of rules. While many of these suggestions may be useful,[48] they are not universally valuable. Take, for example, the admonition, "Statements should be clear to the respondent." While this might be a reasonable criterion in most instances, it is inappropriate for projective measures that are designed to be ambiguous.

Similarly, the double-barreled question may be inappropriate in developing statements for a Thurstone-type questionnaire. Nonetheless, students are usually warned against the use of double-barreled questions in *general*, even though they may want to compare only two alternatives. For example, a question may be worded: "Are you in favor of public education and willing to have your taxes doubled to help support the public schools?" If the intent is to select those persons who have a high enough interest in the public schools to be willing to increase their taxes, then a yes answer to this question would have helped accomplish this purpose. A no answer, however, would not mean necessarily that respondents are disinterested in the public schools. It could mean that they cannot afford to pay for additional support.

It is important to know the extent to which the wording of questionnaires is responsible for determining responses. Perhaps the best way to discover this effect is to prepare two forms of the same questionnaire which can then be given to random groups. If the two groups' responses differ significantly on any given item, the item would need to be rewritten in the final form. Another criterion for judging potential item bias is whether or not the attitude of the item writer can be discerned from the manner in which the item is written. A question such as, "Would you support the public schools if they continue to squander public funds?" forces respondents into assuming that public funds are being wasted. Replies to such questions are more a reflection of the item writer's biases than of the "true" opinions of respondents.

---

[48]See, for example, Stanley L. Payne, *The Art of Asking Questions* (Princeton: Princeton University Press, 1951).

## The Preliminary Run

Before the final form of the questionnaire is constructed, it is useful to conduct a pilot study to determine if the items are yielding the kind of information that is needed. Administer the questionnaire personally and individually to a small group of respondents (or to two or more comparable groups to test the effects of wording or item sequencing). Each respondent could be asked to answer questions, one at a time, and then discuss with the investigator the difficulties, if any, that he or she has in responding to each item. The respondent might state, for example, that a question such as, "How much money do you make per month?" caused some embarrassment, and that the type of response desired was unclear. Salaries might fluctuate from month to month depending upon tips and commissions; a second respondent might be paid $50.00 per hour to perform some specialized task but only find work for two or three hours per month; a third respondent might receive $1,000 per month, but this might be at a very low hourly rate. If salary is being used to estimate the respondent's socioeconomic level, the way the salary is paid (hourly, weekly, by commission) might be as important as the amount.

## The Cover Letter

If questionnaires are administered to an intact group (such as students in a class), the investigator has the opportunity to motivate respondents and to answer questions that may arise. However, with questionnaires sent through the mail, it may be difficult to motivate respondents to fill out questionnaires and to return them within a reasonable period of time. Unless respondents believe that the questionnaire is of value, that it is sponsored by a recognized and prestigious organization, that their personal attention to the questionnaire is important, and that not too much time will be required, the questionnaire is likely to be thrown into the nearest waste basket. To gain respondents' cooperation, a cover letter usually accompanies the questionnaire. The criteria for an effective cover letter may be summarized as follows:

*1.* The sponsor or sponsoring agency should be identified. As well as lending prestige to the questionnaire, this permits the respondent to verify the authenticity of the questionnaire. If the questionnaire has been developed by a student, the formal approval of a responsible university or college official should be solicited. The student's name as well as that of the sponsor should be included.

*2.* The purpose of the investigation should be stated clearly. The fact that the student expects to obtain a degree by means of the questionnaire should not be used as the purpose of the study. While this may be of importance to the student, it is unlikely to be considered important enough by potential respondents for them to take the time to fill out the questionnaire honestly and pain-stakingly. How the questionnaire will be used and its value to the investigation should be explained.

*3.* If the questionnaire is short, a double postal card may be used effectively and inexpensively; if it is relatively long, the cover letter should be enclosed in an envelope along with the questionnaire. Return postage should always be prepaid by the investigator.

*4.* The directions for responding should be stated clearly. They should indicate whether or not respondents are to identify themselves on the questionnaire, how the questions are to be answered, how the questionnaire is to be returned, some reasonable deadline for returning it, and any other necessary information.

Ethical considerations may require respecting the anonymity of respondents. Not only is this a matter of professional ethics, but it is also of importance in obtaining valid responses, especially if the data are personal. On the other hand, if respondents are not identified there will be no way of knowing which ones responded and which ones failed to do so. Follow-up letters encouraging nonrespondents to complete the questionnaire depend upon the identification of respondents. The dilemma is in having to decide whether replies will be anonymous (making it impossible to send selective follow-up letters) or identified (making it difficult to obtain valid responses). This dilemma cannot be resolved by using invisible ink or any other devious method.

Perhaps the best solution is to ask that respondents include their names on the questionnaire (or by typing it for them), assuring them that only the investigator will be permitted to see responses and that no one will ever be identified personally. Respondents should be told why it is necessary that they be identified. Names can be coded on the questionnaire so that no one will be able to associate responses with any individual. Any master list of names and codes must be kept in a secure place.

If items are so personal that respondents are likely to feel threatened, legitimate grounds exist for questioning whether the questionnaire is the most appropriate data collection method. More useful, perhaps, would be the interview. Trained interviewers may be able to elicit more valid responses by putting informants at ease and probing for needed information.

## The Reliability of Measurements Obtained from Questionnaires

The reliability of a set of measurements obtained from questionnaires may be determined by using coefficients of stability, equivalence, or internal consistency (homogeneity) as discussed in Chapter 9. Stability is determined by administering the same questionnaire twice over time to the same respondents. The correlation between their scores on the two administrations would be the coefficiency of stability. This coefficient is dependent upon the amount of time elapsing between the two administrations as well as on the extent to which the beliefs, attitudes, or opinions of the respondents actually change. In general, the longer the time lapse, the lower the coefficient of stability is likely to be. Also, if questions are poorly constructed, respondents may change their answers on repeated testings because they are uncertain what they are expected to do.

Equivalence, as a form of reliability, requires the construction of two or more forms of the questionnaire which, when given to the same group of respondents, yield equivalent responses. The construction of equivalent forms of a Thurstone-type scale has already been described (see page 254). Likert scales involve constructing parallel items having equal means, equal variances, and a high correlation between the two forms. If two forms of a questionnaire are equivalent, they are both measuring the same set of attitudes, opinions, or beliefs. If the two forms are administered over time, a coefficient of stability and equivalence can be obtained.

A third method for determining the reliability of measurements is internal consistency. The rationale is to construct a single form of a questionnaire so that each item correlates with the total score; those that do not correlate highly are eliminated. The result is a questionnaire measuring a single factor.

Guttman's scalogram technique is essentially a procedure for determining whether or not any given set of items is homogeneous or scalable. His index of reproducibility attempts to judge from knowledge of the total scores whether or not a particular set of items is reproducible. Any set of items which is so constructed would be internally consistent. Some of the difficulties in the use of Guttman's reproducibility coefficient have already been discussed.

## The Validity of the Questionnaire

Four types of validity coefficients were discussed in Chapter 9. They include content validity, predictive validity, concurrent validity, and construct validity. While these types were derived especially for psychological and educational tests, the same type of classification system can be used, with some modifications, for classifying the validity of questionnaires.

In measuring attitudes, it is useful to categorize them as *expressed, manifest,* or *inventoried.*[49] A respondent may *express* beliefs concerning a proposed school bond issue; the behavior *manifested* at the polls, however, may or may not be contradictory to these stated beliefs; and scores on an

---

[49]Donald E. Super and John O. Crites, *Appraising Vocational Fitness*, rev. ed. (New York: Harper & Brothers, 1962), pp. 378–380. Super and Crites were attempting to differentiate among different types of *interests*, but attitudes can be classified in the same way.

attitude scale designed to measure beliefs do not necessarily have to agree with expressed or manifest beliefs or attitudes.

As long as the concern is only with expressed or inventoried responses, content validity is appropriate. However, if predicting behavior is important, the use of judges to evaluate questionnaire items is inappropriate. The judges can, of course, state what the items *appear* to be measuring. Further empirical checks are needed to determine whether the items do in fact predict respondents' behavior (predictive validity). If the concern is not so much with prediction but with the present correlates of expressed or inventoried attitudes or beliefs, then concurrent validity of the scale can be determined.

## SUMMARY

**1.** The interview was defined as a direct or face-to-face attempt to obtain reliable and valid measures in the form of verbal responses from one or more respondents. A number of advantages in the use of the interview were noted:

   **a.** It allows the interviewer to clarify questions.

   **b.** It can be used with young children and illiterates.

   **c.** It allows freedom for informants to respond in any manner they see fit.

   **d.** It allows interviewers to observe nonverbal as well as verbal behavior.

   **e.** It is useful as a means of obtaining personal information, attitudes, perceptions, and beliefs.

   **f.** It reduces anxiety so that potentially threatening topics can be studied.

**2.** A number of disadvantages in using interviews were also discussed:

   **a.** Unstructured interviews often yield data that are difficult to summarize and evaluate.

   **b.** Training interviewers, sending them to meet and interview their informants, and evaluating their effectiveness all add to the cost of the study.

   **c.** Interviews have often been used to collect data inappropriately where other methods, which may be less convenient, would yield more valid results.

**3.** Four types of interviewing errors were analyzed:

   **a.** The error in asking questions occurs whenever questions are asked in a way which will not yield data needed to satisfy the purposes of the investigation. Limited-response, free-response, and defensive-response questions were discussed.

   **b.** Errors in probing occur whenever interviewers fail to probe or whenever they probe excessively. Training of interviewers can reduce this type of error.

**c.** Errors in motivating respondents to answer questions candidly also occur. Training procedures can reduce this type of error.

**d.** Errors in recording responses occur if interviewers fail to transcribe information accurately. Although tape recorders can reduce errors in recording, they introduce new errors when the taped report is transcribed. Typing transcriptions also wastes time if the interview is structured and if notes can be taken during the interview itself.

**4.** The reliability of the interview may be determined by having the same interviewer question informants twice over a period of time or by reclassifying statements obtained from informants over some time interval. Another possibility is to compute the interobserver reliability. The reliability of a single interviewer can be computed by using the formula for the intraclass reliability. The Spearman–Brown formula can then be used to estimate the composite reliability for any number of interviewers.

**5.** Where criteria are available, concurrent or predictive validity can be estimated by checking information obtained in an interview with official documents or with the actual behavior of informants. Where no apparent criterion is available (as in attitude or opinion measurement), the verbal responses are valid *as* verbal responses but cannot be used as evidence of predictive or concurrent validity.

**6.** Because interviewers have to interact with informants, they may influence the direction and intensity of the informants' statements. Such variables as the interviewer's age, college major, educational level, experience in interviewing, racial and religious background, sex, and socioeconomic level have been shown to influence interview responses.

**7.** The questionnaire, like the interview, is a means of eliciting feelings, beliefs, experiences, attitudes; both can be either structured or relatively unstructured.

**8.** A number of advantages were noted in using questionnaires:

**a.** For the same cost, many more responses to questionnaires can be obtained than can responses to interviews.

**b.** The argument that the questionnaire is a "standardized" data collection method was analyzed. Although items on a questionnaire are presented in the same way for each respondent, the meaning of each item may differ, especially if the items are vague or unstructured. In addition, standardization requires that respondents answer questions under similar circumstances, an unlikely possibility for mailed questionnaires.

**9.** There are a number of serious disadvantages in using questionnaires:

**a.** Respondent motivation is difficult to assess.

**b.** Questionnaires cannot be used with illiterates or persons who speak languages not spoken by the interviewer.

**c.** The failure to obtain a random sampling of returns leads to biased samples.

**10.** A work table was described which can be of value in selecting items for a questionnaire. The inclusion of an item depends upon the nature of the hypotheses under investigation and whether or not there are more objective means of obtaining the information.

**11.** Four scales of measurement were discussed: nominal, ordinal, interval, and ratio. Nominal scales simply categorize observations or responses; ordinal scales rank observations; interval scales have equal intervals between successive ranks; and ratio scales have equal intervals and an absolute zero.

**12.** Three types of ordinal scales were described: the social distance scale, the Likert technique, and Guttman's scale analysis or scalogram technique.

    **a.** The social distance scale measures the degree of social distance that respondents place between themselves and members of various ethnic, religious, racial, or nationality groups.

    **b.** Questionnaires making use of the Likert technique contain statements to which respondents indicate some degree of favorableness. The option representing the most favorable opinion is given the most points. The sum of the scores obtained on each item is the total score for the scale. Methods for determining the internal consistency of the items was described.

    **c.** Guttman's scalogram technique also makes use of ordinal measurements. This technique is not so much a method of constructing scales as it is one of determining whether existing scales are unidimensional (scalable), quasi-scalable, or nonscalable. The extent to which the items are scalable (or more properly, the extent to which the "universe of attributes" is scalable, quasi-scalable, or nonscalable) is a function of the reproducibility of the item scores from the respondent's total score.

**13.** The most commonly used method of scaling which forms equal intervals is the Thurstone and Chave method of equal-appearing intervals. A large number of items are typed separately on cards and given to 50 or more judges who sort them into 11 categories. The first, sixth, and last piles are marked "unfavorable," "undecided," and "favorable," respectively. For each item, scale and $Q$ values are determined. The scale value is the category number corresponding to the median judgment; the $Q$ value is the interquartile range. For inclusion on the final form of the scale, about 20 to 25 items are selected so that the scale values are as evenly distributed from 1 to 11 as possible. $Q$ values are kept as small as possible. The respondent's score on the revised scale is the median scale value of the number of items to which he or she can agree.

**14.** The arrangement of items on a questionnaire depends, in part, on the type of scale which is constructed. On social distance scales, various ethnic or religious groups can be arranged alphabetically or in random order.

Categories indicative of degree of social acceptability are, however, placed in rank order. Item arrangement should be random on Likert scales. Items should also be presented randomly on the final form of Thurstone scales.

**15.** Questionnaire items can be classified by form: nondisguised–structured, nondisguised–nonstructured, disguised–nonstructured, and disguised–structured forms. Each of these types was defined and examples given. Another approach is to classify items into true–false, multiple-choice, completion, or essay format.

**16.** No specific suggestions were made concerning the way items should be worded on questionnaires. The position was taken that wording is dependent upon the purposes of the investigation and the form of the item used. It was suggested that two or more questionnaires be constructed with different forms of item wording and given to comparable groups. If differences between groups are insignificant, item wording is not producing any measurable differences; if, however, differences are found between groups on any item, the item would have to be rewritten on the final form.

**17.** A preliminary tryout of the questionnaire should precede its actual administration. Preferably, the tryout should be administered individually to a number of persons to check on ambiguity of meaning, difficulties in responding, etc.

**18.** The form of the cover letter and its use in questionnaire construction was discussed. The cover letter should inform respondents of the purpose of the study, its potential values, the name of the sponsoring agency, and the name of the person responsible for the study. In addition, the directions and the methods for returning the questionnaire should be clearly stated.

**19.** If follow-up letters will be sent to encourage nonrespondents to complete and return their questionnaires, some means of identifying the returned questionnaires will be necessary. This means that respondents will have to be identified. Resorting to the use of invisible ink or to other unethical ways of coding questionnaires so that they can be identified without the knowledge of the respondents makes it impossible to send out follow-up letters without admitting to the respondents that the questionnaires were not anonymous. It was suggested that respondents be asked to identify themselves but that they be assured that responses will be kept in confidence.

**20.** The reliability of measurements obtained from questionnaires was discussed. The stability of measurements can be determined by administering the same questionnaire twice to respondents and correlating the responses or scores. Equivalence can be assessed by giving two forms to the same group of respondents. Items that correlate highly with one another are internally consistent.

**21.** The validity of questionnaires was discussed primarily in relation to expressed, manifest, and inventoried measurements. As long as the concern is with expressed or inventoried behavior, content validity may be used; if the purpose of the study is to predict behavior on the basis of either expressed or inventoried statements and responses, a measure of predictive validity can be obtained.

## PRACTICE EXERCISES

**1.** For each of the following problems indicate whether the questionnaire or the interview is more appropriate. Defend your choice. If neither the interview nor the questionnaire is appropriate, indicate what method you would recommend to obtain the needed information.

    **a.** The attitudes of five-year-olds toward school

    **b.** Expressed interests of teenagers in a given classroom

    **c.** The names of administrative officers in a distant school district

    **d.** Attitudes toward childrearing among blacks

    **e.** Attitudes toward segregation and integration throughout the United States

    **f.** Extent to which teachers differ in the number of high and low grades which they give to students for final course grades

**2.** For each of the above problems, indicate whether you would recommend using a structured or unstructured interview or questionnaire. Would the defensive-response type of interview be appropriate for any of these problems? Which ones? Why?

**3.** Classify each of the following statements as a limited-response, free-response, or defensive-response type:

    **a.** When was the last time you cheated on an examination?

    **b.** Have you ever cheated on an examination?

    **c.** If you have ever cheated on an examination, why did you do it?

    **d.** Do you think that President $X$ has done an excellent job while in office, or that he could have improved conditions?

**4.** Criticize each of the above statements. Ask each of these questions to a small sample of your friends. Were you able to determine whether the questions were limited-response, free-response, or defensive-response types before you asked the questions? If you changed your opinion after asking the question, what factors led you to do so?

**5.** Rewrite each of the above four questions as limited-response, free-response, and defensive-response questions. Readminister these questions to a new sample of persons. From the responses obtained, determine what type of question you have asked. Why is it difficult to classify limited-response, free-response, or defensive-response questions before they are administered to any given sample?

**6.** Individually administered intelligence tests contain many limited-response questions. Examine the manual for the Stanford–Binet Test, Wechsler Intelligence Scale for Children, or Wechsler Adult Intelligence Scale and determine how the authors have tried to control the error in asking questions, errors in probing, errors in motivating, and errors in recording responses. Under each of these types of errors, list the ways of controlling them that the authors of these tests suggest.

**7.** Examine the formula for finding the intraclass reliability for a single interviewer (page 240). Suppose that there is only one interviewer. Simplify the formula, with $k = 1$.

**8.** Using the data in Table 10-3, the reliability for a single interviewer was found to be 0.43. What is the composite reliability for the four interviewers?

**9.** Using only the ratings of Mr. Jones and Mr. Smith (page 241), find the reliability of their composite ratings.

**10.** The Parry and Crossley study referred to on page 242 used the percentage of agreement between responses and official records as a measure of the validity of the interview. What difficulties are there in using percentages rather than validity coefficients in the form of correlations?

**11.** A number of variables were shown to have an effect on the validity of data obtained by interviewers (pages 243–244). Suppose that you were able to afford only one interviewer and that you were working on those problems listed in Practice Exercise 1. What qualifications in interviewers would you want for each of these six problems? How could you determine whether or not interviewer bias was occurring? How could you reduce the effects of this bias?

**12.** Suppose that an investigator receives a 75 percent return from a mail questionnaire. How can you determine whether or not this sample is biased?

**13.** What suggestions can you think of to increase the percentage of replies in a mail questionnaire?

**14.** Compute the scale values and $Q$ values for each of the following five items:

| Category No. | 1 | 2 | 3 | 4 | 5 |
|---|---|---|---|---|---|
| 11 | 9 | 0 | 10 | 0 | 1 |
| 10 | 12 | 0 | 10 | 2 | 5 |
| 9 | 30 | 5 | 10 | 8 | 10 |
| 8 | 19 | 15 | 10 | 10 | 14 |
| 7 | 18 | 25 | 10 | 30 | 30 |
| 6 | 12 | 30 | 10 | 10 | 15 |
| 5 | 0 | 12 | 10 | 10 | 10 |
| 4 | 0 | 6 | 10 | 10 | 8 |
| 3 | 0 | 4 | 10 | 10 | 5 |
| 2 | 0 | 3 | 10 | 10 | 1 |
| 1 | 0 | 0 | 0 | 0 | 1 |
| | 100 | 100 | 100 | 100 | 100 |

Interpret your findings.

**15.** Find two of the five items above that have identical scale values but different $Q$ values. Of these two, which would you select for the final form of the questionnaire, other conditions being equal? Why?

**16.** Suppose that a final form of a Thurstone-type scale consists of 20 items administered to three students who are requested to check five which best represent their beliefs or attitudes. The scale values for each of these three students are given below:

| Albert | Betty | Carl |
|--------|-------|------|
| 10.6 | 6.1 | 10.6 |
| 8.4 | 5.2 | 8.4 |
| 7.2 | 4.1 | 7.2 |
| 6.1 | 2.9 | 4.1 |
| 5.2 | 2.1 | 2.9 |

**a.** What score would Albert, Betty, and Carl receive?

**b.** Whose attitude is most favorable? Whose is least favorable?

**c.** Who has the least clearly defined attitude? Who has the most clearly defined attitude?

**17.** Construct a Likert-type scale on "Attitudes toward the Public Schools." For practice in item selection, administer your scale to about 25 persons. Score the questionnaire and run an item analysis on it. Interpret your findings.

**18.** Write a cover letter for a questionnaire that incorporates the criteria discussed in this chapter.

## Selected Supplementary Readings

1. Techniques for categorizing and analyzing interview and other unstructured sources are discussed in Chapter 12 under "Content Analysis." For a linguistic approach to the analysis of conversations, see Harris, Z. S. "Discourse Analysis." *Language*, 28 (1952), pp. 29–32.

2. For a rather detailed description of the steps used to conduct an interview, see Cannell, Charles F., and Kahn, Robert L. "Interviewing." Chapter 15 of Gardner Lindzey and Elliot Aronson, eds. *The Handbook of Social Psychology*, 2d ed. Reading, Mass.: Addison-Wesley Publishing Co., 1968, pp. 526–595. Another excellent and detailed source of interviewing procedures can be found in the *Interviewer's Manual: Survey Research Center*, rev. ed. Ann Arbor: Institute for Social Research, University of Michigan, 1976, 142 pp.

3. PARTEN, MILDRED B. *Surveys, Polls, and Samples*. New York: Harper & Row, 1950, 624 pp. is still basic reading for anyone interested in conducting a survey. This book has been reprinted by Cooper Square Publishers. Two other classic sources of information can be found in Payne, Stanley L.

*The Art of Asking Questions.* Princeton: Princeton University Press, 1951 (see particularly pp. 228–237 for a checklist of 100 considerations in wording questions); and Cantril, Hadley, et al. *Gauging Public Opinion.* Princeton: Princeton University Press, 1944, now reprinted by Kennikat Press.

4. On the interviewer effect, see Rosenthal, Robert. *Experimenter Effects in Behavioral Research.* New York: Appleton-Century-Crofts, 1966, 464 pp.

obtaining
information
from respondents:
unobtrusive
measures
and observational
techniques

11

Interviews, questionnaires, tests, and inventories not only *measure* attributes, but they may *affect* them as well. Individuals who know they are participating in a study may respond as much to role expectations as to the content of an interview or test. The cooperation demanded of research participants may affect the way they respond to the research task itself. Instead of measuring an intended attribute, responses may be contaminated by irrelevant research demands that intrude upon respondents as research participants.

The intrusive nature of interviews and tests cannot be eliminated by disguising them—the participant still realizes that he or she is a participant, even though ignorant of the nature of the study. What is needed is a method (or methods) in which no one is required to do anything that will appear to be contrived or artificial. Unobtrusive measures[1] are those obtained without

[1]Eugene J. Webb, Donald T. Campbell, Richard O. Schwartz, and Lee Sechrest, *Unobtrusive Measures: Nonreactive Research in the Social Sciences* (Chicago: Rand McNally & Co., 1966), p. 225.

the direct cooperation of respondents. No one is asked or required to take tests, answer questions, or to do anything that in the normal course of events they would not have done otherwise.

Unobtrusive measures are considered to be *nonreactive* since research participants do not react with the knowledge that they are participants. When subjects realize that they are a part of a research study, some undesirable effects can occur to reduce the validity of the study. Unobtrusive or nonreactive measures are designed to reduce the following effects on the respondent:[2]

1. *The guinea pig effect* (acting in a way that affects research outcomes). If research subjects are made to feel that they are being experimented on, some subjects may try to anticipate the responses desired from the researcher; others may be antagonized by research procedures (no matter how innocuous they may appear to the investigator) and respond with animosity or spite. Such reactions, of course, invalidate the study.

2. *Role selection* (forcing the respondent to assume the role of a person being tested). When participating in a study, the respondent may not be defensive or even try to please the experimenter. Rather, the social demands imposed on respondents by being a part of a research study require that they react in *some* way, and whatever atypical role they select affects validity.

3. *Measurement as change agent* (the effect of pretests on subsequently obtained test scores). Sometimes the initial measurement of an attribute can produce change in the respondents. In observing a film designed to change attitudes of viewers to racial minorities, for example, pre–post differences might be attributed to the film's content when, in fact, the pretest itself could have brought about these changes. The reactive nature of the pretest can affect subsequent performance of respondents.

4. *Response biases* (the tendency to respond to item format or other irrelevant characteristics rather than to item content). A response bias is an unrecognized tendency on the part of a respondent that yields an undeserved and invalid score. For example, many respondents tend on personality inventories to make themselves appear more socially desirable than they really are. In other instances, some respondents facing a stringent time limit on a test respond accurately (but to a few items), whereas others in the same situation respond rapidly and may attempt many more items. If there is no correction for guessing, those who have a tendency to work quickly and guess are likely to obtain higher scores than will the more accurate but slower respondents.

Reactive measures can also suffer from errors that stem from the researcher. *Interviewer bias* (discussed in Chapter 10) is a case in point—responses are dependent, in part, on the interviewer's race, sex, age, and religion. These biasing factors may actually increase reliability (since bias is a stable trait) but reduce validity (since an irrelevant trait is being measured).

Webb and his associates have suggested five types of unobtrusive measures: *physical traces*, the *running record*, the *episodic* and *private record*, *simple observation*, and *contrived observation*.

### Physical Traces

Physical evidence may be categorized as traces of *erosion* or of *accretion*. Erosion measures refer to the amount of wear suffered by some object because of use. For example, it is not unreasonable to believe that worn spots in classroom carpeting have experienced more than the usual amount of use. Similarly, it is likely that those books in constant use will wear out more rapidly than less popular ones. The question is whether or not erosion is a measure of popularity and interest or whether it is an artifact produced by some other condition. A book, for example, may be ragged and frayed because it enjoyed extensive use or because of reader carelessness; a rug near a study work station may be worn because students enjoy the activity of the station or because the activity requires a great amount of physical movement. The more reasonable hypothesis can be determined by combining measures of erosion with other data-gathering procedures such as interviews, questionnaires, or unobtrusive observations.

Physical traces can also consist of *accretions* of evidence. The amount of dust on a book is a physical accretion as is the amount and type of graffiti found on school walls. An examination of garbage can measure not only degree of waste but also habits of thrift, knowledge of nutrition, approximate family income, and the ages of household members. Changes in food purchasing habits as measured by a grocer's order records can provide information on the effectiveness of a unit on nutrition at the local school. In all of these examples, the accretions could be used along with more reactive measures to provide for greater confirmatory evidence.

Erosion and accretion measures may be "controlled" by the researcher in nonreactive ways. The physical location of classroom stations can be manipulated by the researcher to make sure students are responding to the materials and content of the station and not to its location.

Physical traces suffer from "selective survival" and "selective deposit."[3] Not all "garbage" is thrown away (selective deposit) and what is thrown away decays at different rates (selective survival). One can assume that the most sensitive and potentially offensive graffiti will be the first to be eliminated. Nonetheless, physical traces can be used to good advantage to reduce the reactive effect of the more traditional data-gathering techniques such as the interview and questionnaire.

[3]Webb et al., p. 50.

## Archive Analysis: The Running Record

The running record consists of actuarial, political and judicial, and other archival records—in short, those continuous records left by a culture or society for its own purposes but which may be used by current researchers to test specific hypotheses in nonreactive ways.

Literacy, for example, can be measured in different ways and with different degrees of reactivity, but an analysis of the number of persons signing official documents such as marriage certificates with an "X" is unobtrusive.[4] Similarly, it would be possible to compare the amount of local taxes voted for education relative to income level as a nonreactive measure of willingness to support public education. The records of school board meetings, records of public appropriations of funds, salary schedules, and the like are all part of the analysis of public archives.

Political and judicial records may help answer such questions as whether or not blacks who commit the same crimes as whites receive the same punishment. The effectiveness of the public defender can also be evaluated by examining judicial reports, although the type of case referred to the public defender could differ in systematic ways from those accepted by private attorneys. Judicial records could also be used as criteria for evaluating driver education classes.

Selective deposit and survival are serious matters to consider in evaluating an archive. Not all records are maintained and those that are may not represent unbiased reporting. As noted previously (see Chapter 3), the *Congressional Record* permits contributors to modify their speeches before they are published.

## Archive Analysis: The Episodic and Private Record

Episodic records consist of private documents, letters, and reports that are written without the intent of creating an enduring record. Episodic records include sales records, institutional records, and personal documents not written for the public.[5]

Many episodic records are difficult to obtain. Sales records, for example, disclose information that might be useful to competitors. But the researcher might use them to rank various objects that have been sold to determine their desirability. Webb[6] listed the 1964 market value of original autographs of famous historical persons as a measure of their popularity, although figures had to be adjusted for the availability of these autographs.

Sales records could be used in education to measure consumer

[4]Webb et al., p. 60.
[5]Webb et al., p. 89.
[6]Webb et al., p. 93.

gullibility or knowledge. Institutional records would probably be of greater value. Vandalism records could be used to measure school morale; soap purchases could measure student concern with cleanliness; and the number of paper towels used could measure concern with saving environmental resources. Again, each nonreactive procedure could be compared with interview or questionnaire data as a validation technique.

Personal documents are the most difficult to obtain, but they can provide a rich resource of information and hypotheses. The correspondence of school boards, superintendents, principals, and teachers could provide an interesting perspective on their perceptions of different problems. An examination of tests constructed by teachers could be used as a measure of teacher competence not only in the technicalities of item construction but in their knowledge of subject matter as well.

## Simple Observation

Simple observation is the term used by Webb to refer to observations in which the researcher "does not intervene in the production of the material."[7] The role of the observer is to describe empirical phenomena as objectively and as unobtrusively as possible.

*Observational set* or readiness to respond to stimuli according to one's beliefs and values can interfere with the observer's ability to gather objective data. In one experiment,[8] for example, six words (equated for length and familiarity) for each of six value categories based on Spranger's *Types of Men* (i.e., theoretical, economic, aesthetic, social, political, and religious) were tachistoscopically presented, one at a time, to 25 Harvard and Radcliffe students who were also administered a test of values. The experimenters found, as hypothesized, that students who had high theoretical values could recognize significantly more tachistoscopically presented words relating to theory than could students with low theoretical values. Perception evidently depends on the student's observational set.

The investigator's decision to observe some behaviors and to disregard others is determined in part by the hypothesis being tested. If observers are unprepared, they are likely to observe and record irrelevant and incorrect data. Every lawyer is aware of the unreliability of observations. Witnesses, for example, are usually unprepared to make observations when an accident or crime occurs, and the passage of time can erode the effects of memory.

---

[7]Webb et al., p. 115.

[8]Leo Postman, Jerome S. Bruner, and Elliot McGinnies, "Personal Values As Selective Factors in Perception," *Journal of Abnormal and Social Psychology*, 43, no. 2 (1948), pp. 142–154.

The training of observers is the single most important task in obtaining reliable and valid observations. Usually the first step is to explain the purpose of the study so they understand its importance and the role they are expected to play. Adequate training requires that observers become competent in knowing what to observe and how the observations are to be reported. Training should be continued until all observers are able to objectively report the phenomena under investigation. Periodic reliability checks should be continued throughout the study.

The percentage of agreement between two observations is not a satisfactory way to estimate interobserver agreement. The percentage of agreement is likely to increase if the number of categories used for reporting is small. Also, the percentage of agreement fails to consider the role of chance. A better approach to the estimation of interobserver reliability has been proposed by Cohen.[9] The use of coefficient $k$ (kappa) can be demonstrated by an example provided by Cohen.[10] In this example, it is assumed that there are two observers, $A$ and $B$, who are required to observe 200 persons and to categorize them into one of three groups, such as autocratic, democratic, and laissez-faire.

TABLE 11-1

An Example of Categorical Judgments Made by Two Observers

| | | Observer $A$ | | | |
|---|---|---|---|---|---|
| | | AUTOCRATIC | DEMOCRATIC | LAISSEZ-FAIRE | TOTAL (OBSERVER $B$) |
| Observer $B$ | Autocratic | 88 | 14 | 18 | 120 |
| | Democratic | 10 | 40 | 10 | 60 |
| | Laissez-faire | 2 | 6 | 12 | 20 |
| | Total (Observer $A$) | 100 | 60 | 40 | $N = 200$ |

*Source:* Modified from Jacob Cohen, "A Coefficient of Agreement for Nominal Scales," *Educational and Psychological Measurement,* 20, no. 1 (Spring 1960), p. 45.

The two observers agreed in 140 judgments (88 + 40 + 12) out of the total of 200. The percentage of agreement would be $\frac{140}{200}$ or 0.70, but this value disregards the effect of chance agreement. What $k$ provides is an estimate of agreement after the effects of chance have been eliminated. Chance agreement can be determined using the same rationale for determining

[9]Jacob Cohen, "A Coefficient of Agreement for Nominal Scales," *Educational and Psychological Measurement,* 20, no. 1 (Spring 1960), pp. 37–46.

[10]Cohen, p. 45.

expected frequencies in a two-way chi square (see pages 399–402). For the autocratic category, the chance or expected value is $(100 \times 120)/200 = 60$; the democratic expected value is $(60 \times 60)/200 = 18$; and the laissez-faire expected or chance value is $(40 \times 20)/200 = 4$. The total expected or chance value is $60 + 18 + 4 = 82$. Kappa is defined as

$$k = \frac{fo - fe}{N - fe}$$

where $fo$ is the observed frequencies of agreement or $88 + 40 + 12 = 140$, and where $fe$ is the expected or chance agreement $(60 + 18 + 4 = 82)$, and where $N$ is the total number of persons observed. Substituting,

$$k = \frac{140 - 82}{200 - 82} = 0.49$$

In other words, after chance has been eliminated about half of the observations are in agreement.

Interobserver reliability or agreement increases as $k$ approaches $+1.0$; $k = 0$ when the observed agreement equals chance. If the value of $k$ is less than expected by chance, $k$ will be negative.

Theoretically, as the number of observers is increased, observational errors will cancel each other. This means it is advantageous to employ as many observers as possible. Assuming equally competent observers, interobserver reliability increases according to the Spearman–Brown formula (see pages 216–218). Thus, if the reliability of two observers is 0.50, the Spearman–Brown formula would predict a reliability of $+0.67$ if the number of observers were doubled.

Simple observation involves observers who work unobserved or who act as *participant observers* (i.e., they become a member of the group they propose to observe). If simple observation is to remain unobtrusive, the observer may have to depend upon eavesdropping or pretense, conditions which raise serious ethical and legal problems. The observation of *public* behavior is most defensible ethically. For example, observing how black and white children seat themselves on the first day of class could be used as an index of familiarity and prejudice. Also, the distance from teacher to pupils could be used to measure compatibility assuming, of course, that children are allowed to seat themselves where they wish.

## Contrived Observation

Contrived observation includes the deliberate modification of subject behavior by the researcher. The observer often arranges conditions that appear to be uncontrived but which have been carefully prepared to elicit the type of response desired.

Observations can be contrived in different ways. First, it is possible to use recording apparatus (i.e., tape and video, electronic counters, etc.) without the subjects' being aware of their presence. At the termination of the investigation the researcher may have accumulated many hours of permanent recordings and many thousands of feet of videotape. Such exhaustive accumulations of data permit the researcher to replay these materials as often as necessary but with two serious limitations: (1) not all recorded information is of equal importance and of equal validity, and (2) the obtaining of information without the consent or knowledge of the participants raises ethical questions.

Not all contrived observations force the researcher to resort to deception or lying. A contrived observation can simply set the stage so that specific responses can be noted. The type of toys children will select when given the opportunity to do so could be measured by placing a variety of toys in a room and counting the amount of time each toy is handled. The observations are contrived but not deceptive or demoralizing.

Other contrived studies may, however, be ethically questionable. At Yale University, for example, one researcher[11] selected a group of "teachers" who were instructed to deliver shocks to "learners" who failed to learn word pairs. Each failure to learn was to be punished by a greater shock (from a minimum of 14 volts to a potentially lethal 450 volts). Each teacher was administered a 45-volt shock so that he or she could experience the pain produced by the apparatus. Although the learners and teachers knew each other and ostensibly drew straws to determine which role each would play, the learner was actually one of Milgram's confederates and the drawings were fixed. The learners were moved out of sight (but not out of hearing range), and the teacher was told to punish each learner's error by increasing the amount of voltage. As shock was administered, a realistic tape recording of groans and screams was played, making the teachers believe they were causing excruciating pain. Over half of the teachers continued to increase voltage even to the point where they believed that the learners were receiving potentially lethal doses! Evidently, some of the "teachers" became highly traumatized by this experience which required them to blindly follow instructions that violated their own consciences.[12] Milgram did screen the "teachers" before the experiment and follow-up psychiatric services were provided.

Any study that involves deception (and particularly if participants are subjected to physical or psychological risks) requires a formal review procedure by the sponsoring institution. If the study is judged to be of poten-

[11]Stanley Milgram, "Behavioral Study of Obedience," *Journal of Abnormal and Social Psychology*, 67, no. 4 (October 1963), pp. 371–78.

[12]Herbert C. Kelman, "Human Use of Human Subjects: The Problem of Deception in Social Psychological Experiments," *Psychological Bulletin*, 67, no. 1 (1967), pp. 1–11.

tial social value and if the risks to the individual are minimal, some deception might be tolerated, but the investigator is ultimately responsible (both ethically and legally) for creating psychological or physical trauma.

One form of contrived observation is known as a *situational test*. A classic example of a situational test was conducted in a series of studies by Hartshorne and May,[13] who were interested in whether or not children would cheat or lie if given the opportunity to do so. Cheating, for example, was measured by having the children score their own examination papers after they had already been carefully scored by the investigators. Differences between the two sets of scores was used as a measure of cheating.

The U.S. Office of Strategic Services[14] used a series of situational tests in World War II to select potential candidates for military intelligence. Each candidate was given a construction job and two assistants. Unknown to the candidate, the assistants were actually psychologists who tried to frustrate the candidate by refusing to work, countermanding orders, ridiculing their superior's behavior, and the like. The candidate tolerance of stress was rated by the psychologists.

Most situational tests are expensive to set up, and behaviors tend to be *task specific* (i.e., the behaviors observed are not generalizable beyond the confines of the test itself). The expense and time required to set up complex situations limit contrived studies to those that cannot obtain data by less elaborate means. The task-specific nature of these studies can be demonstrated by referring to findings by Hartshorne and May in which they found that cheating on a test correlated practically zero with cheating in athletics. Evidently, whether students cheat or not depends on the specific situation and not on a generalizable character disorder.

The use of mechanical or electronic recording apparatus also serves to differentiate simple from contrived observation. In neither case, of course, would participants be aware of their role as "guinea pigs," but the use of hidden apparatus defines a contrived study.

*Film.* Movie film can be an accurate but expensive way to record behavior. A good deal of film is wasted if the camera must be kept in continual operation in the hope of filming a fairly rare occurrence.

If special lighting conditions are required, the unobtrusive nature of the study may become invalidated. Infrared film does permit photographing subjects in the dark but costs are high. In some studies costs can be reduced by using still cameras that automatically expose one picture at predetermined time intervals.

---

[13] Hugh Hartshorne and Mark W. May, *Studies in Deceit* (New York: Macmillan Co., 1928).

[14] U.S. Office of Strategic Services, *Assessment of Man* (New York: Rinehart, 1948).

*Audio Tape.* Tape cassettes and recorders can be used alone or in conjunction with movie or still cameras. They can be activated manually or automatically by a level of sound higher than some minimum threshhold. Cassette recorders are portable, relatively inexpensive, and permit reuse of the tape as often as necessary.

The problem with audio recorders is their lack of selectivity and their oversensitivity to sources nearest to them. In a group, individual responses might be difficult to discern, and the responses of persons some distance from the recorder could be eliminated by closer (or louder) persons. More than one recorder can be used simultaneously.

*Timing Instruments.* Timing instruments can be used to measure the duration of some activity. Hand-activated stopwatches are commonly used for this purpose. Although they are inexpensive and simple to use, they require manual operation and may yield rather subjective readings.

For more precise timing, a stop clock may be used. These clocks make one complete revolution per second, in contrast to stopwatches that usually make one revolution per minute. Clocks, then, tend to be more accurate than stopwatches, but both must be "read" by the investigator.

Control timers can provide both auditory and visual readings. Many are digital and can time electronically to the nearest hundredth of a second. In poorly lighted rooms and in studies where the experimenter must be reminded of time intervals, control timers can be used to good advantage. Many control timers can be coordinated with other equipment to present stimuli at constant speeds or to turn experimental apparatus on and off.

## SUMMARY

1. Unobtrusive measures are obtained in ways designed not to influence or affect subjects. The purpose of obtaining unobtrusive measures is to reduce:

   a. *The guinea pig effect.* Some subjects act differently if they know they are participating in research.

   b. *Role selection.* Some subjects believe they should act out a particular role as a participant in research.

   c. *Measurement as change agent.* Some subjects, when pretested, change their attitudes in a way that affects posttest scores.

   d. *Response biases.* Some subjects respond to irrelevant characteristics of a testing situation rather than to content.

2. Five types of unobtrusive measures have been identified:

   a. *Physical traces of erosion or accretion.* Objects and articles can be examined to determine such characteristics as amount of use or carelessness. A worn book is an example of an erosion physical trace; the amount of dust in a home could be used as a measure of neatness.

**b.** *The running record.* The "running record" consists of archival documents left by a group or culture for its own purposes. These records include but are not limited to actuarial records, political records, records of hospitalizations, etc.

**c.** *Episodic and private records.* Episodic and private records are written without the intent of creating an enduring or public document (e.g., sales records, personal letters, etc.).

**d.** *Simple observations.* Simple observation is the procedure used by researchers to gather firsthand data without intervening in or affecting the lives of subjects. Simple observation requires the training of observers so that reliable and valid data can be gathered. The extent to which two or more independent observers agree can be computed by *coefficient kappa*. As additional observers are utilized, idiosyncratic observations play a lesser role and interobserver reliability can be expected to increase as a function of the *Spearman–Brown formula*.

**e.** *Contrived observation.* In contrived observation, the conditions for observing are arranged by the researcher even though the subjects believe the situation is "natural."

**3.** Observations can be more accurately obtained by using various types of apparatus.

**a.** Film tends to be an accurate but expensive way to record behavior. Special lighting may affect subjects.

**b.** Audio-tape (cassettes and recorders) can be used to record sound.

**c.** Timing instruments can also be of value. Many different types are produced with various degrees of accuracy.

## PRACTICE EXERCISES

**1.** What unobtrusive measures can you think of that will satisfy the following needs?

**a.** Trying to measure the nightly amount of sleep first graders receive at home

**b.** Trying to measure the diet of children exposed to a unit on "Healthful Foods"

**c.** Trying to predict which of two potential candidates is most preferred by an audience

**d.** Trying to measure the effect of a stringent state marijuana law

**e.** Trying to evaluate parent attitudes toward a new grading system

**f.** Determining the popularity of five probationary teachers

**2.** For each of the above examples, what intrusive measures might be employed?

**3.** Is there any way that an intrusive test used for one purpose could become an unobtrusive measure for another? Give an example.

**4.** Indicate the purposes that could be served by each of the following unobtrusive measures:

   **a.** Keeping records of the number of students receiving grades of A, B, C, D, and F for a period of 10 years

   **b.** Keeping records of gas meter readings of a group of students

   **c.** Observing what times teachers arrive at and leave school

   **d.** Measuring the amount of distance students place their chairs from those of teachers

**5.** Give at least one original example of

   **a.** A physical trace of erosion

   **b.** A physical trace of accretion

   **c.** A running record

   **d.** An episodic and private record

   **e.** Simple observation

   **f.** Contrived observation

**6.** To what extent must unobtrusive measures involve deception?

## Selected Supplementary Readings

1. The best single source of information on unobtrusive measures is Webb, Eugene J., et al. *Unobtrusive Measures: Nonreactive Research in the Social Sciences.* Chicago: Rand McNally & Co., 1966, 225 pp.

2. Of somewhat broader scope is Angell, Robert C., and Freedman, Ronald. "The Use of Documents, Records, Census Materials, and Indices." Chapter 7 in Leon Festinger and Daniel Katz, eds. *Research Methods in the Behavioral Sciences.* New York: Holt, Rinehart and Winston, 1953, pp. 300–326.

3. On the use of various types of observational systems, see Medley, Donald M., and Mitzel, Harold M. "Measuring Classroom Behavior by Systematic Observation." Chapter 6 in N. L. Gage, ed. *Handbook of Research on Teaching.* Chicago: Rand McNally & Co., 1963, pp. 247–328.

4. For a compilation of different kinds of observational systems, see Simon, Anita, and Boyer, E. Gil, eds. *Mirrors for Behavior: An Anthology of Classroom Observation Instruments*, Vols. I–XII. Philadelphia: Research for Better Schools, 1967–1970.

5. A discussion of various types of observations including the observation of nonverbal behavior and methods of coding responses can be found in Lindzey, Gardner, and Aronson, Ellot, eds. "Systematic Observational Methods."

Chapter 13 in *The Handbook of Social Psychology*, 2d ed. Reading, Mass.: Addison-Wesley Publishing Co., 1968, pp. 357–451.

6. An interesting use of unobtrusive measures is provided by Ladd, Everett Carll, Jr., and Lipset, Seymour Martin. "98 to 2, That Professor in a Saab Is a Liberal." *The Chronicle of Higher Education*, 17, no. 6 (April 5, 1976), p. 18. The authors provide evidence that car ownership is related to political conservatism and liberalism.

7. On the effect of observers in the classroom, see Masling, Joseph, and Stern, George. "Effect of Observer in the Classroom." *Journal of Educational Psychology*, 60, no. 5 (October 1969), pp. 351–354.

# 12

## obtaining information from respondents: other techniques

Although most research projects in education have used interviews, questionnaires, and what Campbell[1] has called *nondisguised–structured* techniques (such as achievement or intelligence tests), it is necessary to consider the use of *disguised–nonstructured* methods (the "projective" techniques) and *disguised–structured* methods. This chapter will also devote some attention to sociometry, the $Q$ sort, the semantic differential, and content analysis as means of obtaining and analyzing information from respondents.

---

[1] Donald T. Campbell, "The Indirect Assessment of Social Attitudes," *Psychological Bulletin*, 47, no. 1 (1950), pp. 15–38.

# DISGUISED–NONSTRUCTURED METHODS

Suppose that a researcher is interested in studying the attitudes of children toward teachers. Although interviews or questionnaires could be used to elicit such information, responses are easily "faked" to conform to socially desirable or expected answers. Sophisticated respondents have learned to respond negatively to such direct questions as "Do you hate your teacher?" or "Don't you think it is better to drop out of school than to remain until you graduate?" Many respondents may try to disguise their real feelings, attitudes, or beliefs—perhaps out of fear of giving the "wrong" answer or out of the desire not to hurt the feeling of the investigator.[2,3]

Attempts have been made to devise disguised techniques to conceal the purposes of testing so that subjects will respond as frankly as possible. Ideally, these disguised scales should prevent respondents from fabricating their "true" feelings or attitudes and should allow investigators to obtain responses with higher validities.

Besides being disguised or nondisguised, questionnaires or scales can be *structured* or *unstructured*, depending upon the amount of freedom the respondent is given. If questions are unstructured, subjects can respond in any manner within the limits imposed by the investigator; if questions or items are structured, the limits imposed by the investigator are more restricted. Obviously, the difference between structured and unstructured scales is a matter of degree.

*Projective* techniques are disguised and unstructured. They allow respondents to project their feelings, attitudes, or beliefs onto a relatively ambiguous set of stimuli. Although many of the projective techniques (such as the Rorschach or the Thematic Apperception Test) have been widely used in clinical situations, they are not often used in research.

In part, the reluctance of many experimentalists to use projective techniques in research is understandable when one considers the evidence (or lack of it) presented by some authors of projective methods to substantiate their sometimes exuberant claims. Thus, in describing the Machover Draw-a-Person Test, Harriman[4] has stated:

> Here and there a bold generalization is supported by case notes, and then the case notes are cited as justification of the generalization. Just as an

[2] Allen L. Edwards, Carol J. Diers, and Jerald N. Walker, "Response Sets and Factor Loadings on Sixty-one Personality Scales," *Journal of Applied Psychology*, 17, no. 2 (1962), pp. 220–225.

[3] Allen L. Edwards and James A. Walsh, "Response Sets in Standard and Experimental Personality Scales," *American Educational Research Journal*, 1, no. 1 (1964), pp. 52–61.

[4] Philip L. Harriman in Oscar Krisen Buros, ed., *The Fourth Mental Measurements Year-book* (Highland Park, N.J.: Gryphon Press, 1953), pp. 187–188.

eloquent orator can obfuscate his auditors, so does Machover succeed in keeping the reader from asking such question as: What is the evidence? Are there any objective proofs? Why, for instance, is the Adam's apple sometimes indicative of sexual weakness . . . ? The style often becomes fervent and exhortatory, as if to induce a sort of religious conversion to the Machover technique.

The assumption involved in all projective techniques is that subjects are more likely to exhibit their "real" selves when the questions are disguised than when their intent is apparent. Considering the fact that most projective techniques have to be administered individually and usually require a great deal of time and training for their effective use and interpretation, they are less convenient to use than other types of measurement (i.e., disguised–structured tests or nondisguised tests) and probably should be avoided if less complex techniques are available. In one experiment,[5] it was found that responses obtained from projective techniques were *less* valid for subjects who were suspicious than were simple self-report techniques. Other studies,[6] however, have demonstrated correlations between projective and direct tests to run somewhere between 0.50 and 0.70, indicating that the direct tests and the projective methods are tapping roughly the same factors.

Should the student decide to use a projective technique in research, a number of cautions should be kept in mind. These may be summarized as follows:

*1.* No projective technique should ever be used without thoroughly understanding the assumptions, directions, scoring procedures, and limitations of the technique being used. Both the Rorschach and TAT, for example, require extensive training before they can be used. Expressive techniques are also rather complex.

*2.* The lack of norms on most projective devices is not too serious if these techniques are used only to compare two or more groups on some measured trait. However, norms can be useful in helping the investigator determine whether subjects in the experiment differ significantly from those in the standardization group.

*3.* The problem of validity remains the single most important factor in evaluating disguised–nonstructured methods. Of the various techniques used to determine validity, certainly content validity is inappropriate for projective methods. However, concurrent and predictive validity are relevant. Here, again, there is the problem of adequate criteria.

[5] Anthony Davids and Henry Pildner, Jr., "Comparison of Direct and Projective Methods of Personality Assessment under Different Conditions of Motivation," *Psychological Monographs*, 72, no. 464 (1958).

[6] Campbell, p. 33.

*4*. Determining the reliability of the projective technique used is another responsibility of the investigator. The appropriate type of reliability coefficient to employ is, in part, dependent upon the variable being measured. Certainly a minimum requirement is that independent testers agree in their scoring (interobserver reliability). Unless the variable under investigation is one that can be expected to change rapidly (such as mood), a measure of stability can be obtained. Equivalent forms can also be developed or internal consistency methods used.

*5*. The ethics of withholding from respondents information regarding the true intent of the research study is another serious matter to consider. If the nature of the study has to be disguised, it is particularly important to obtain an evaluation of the proposed methods by a review board that is in a position to suggest safeguards and to recommend whether or not the study is of sufficient importance to warrant deception.

# DISGUISED–STRUCTURED METHODS

Relatively unstructured projective techniques suffer from difficulties in administration, scoring, and interpretation. One way of reducing these difficulties is to provide subjects with questions they will interpret as having right or wrong answers, such as those found on achievement and aptitude tests. However, all alternatives will have to be so difficult that the choice selected by subjects will represent their own attitudes or beliefs, or the investigator will have to prepare options known to be unfamiliar to subjects. In either case, the response represents (hopefully) the attitude of the subjects rather than their knowledge. Campbell[7] has provided a "formula" for developing disguised–structured tests:

> Find a task which all your respondents will take as objective, and in which all will strive to do well. Make the task sufficiently difficult or use a content area in which the respondents have had little experience or opportunity for reality testing. Load the test with content relative to the attitude you study. Look among the responses for systematic error, or for any persistent selectivity of performance. If such can be found, it seems an adequate basis for the inference of an attitude.

This section will examine a number of different types of disguised–structured tests as described by Campbell.

## Information Tests

An information test contains items that are either so difficult or so far removed from the experience of the respondents that guessing is encour-

---

[7]Campbell, p. 19.

aged. The assumption is that guesses are not random but related to the respondents' attitudes or beliefs. In one study, for example, Hammond[8] administered three series of items to two groups of businessmen and to one group of employees in a labor organization. The first series of items contained answers that were equally wrong but in opposite directions, such as "Average weekly wage of the war worker in 1945 was (1) $37, (2) $57." In this first series of items, the actual wages were known. In the second series of items, the answers were nonfactual, such as "Molotov is known in diplomatic circles for his (1) excellent, (2) poor manners." A third series of items, although answerable, was not actually scored but was placed throughout the test to help disguise its actual purpose. The split-half reliability for the labor questionnaire was 0.78; for the Russia questionnaire, it was 0.87.

Cattell et al.[9] devised a *false belief* test using five alternatives. One of the ten items used by Cattell to measure religious beliefs was: "During the war church attendance increased greatly and since V-J day it has (declined slightly; tended to increase still more; stayed at its high peak; returned to its pre-war level; fallen to its lowest point since 1920)." The ten items yielded a split-half reliability of 0.53 when administered to 40 male subjects.

## Syllogistic Reasoning Tests

The assumption behind syllogistic reasoning tests is that drawing conclusions from premises may be distorted by the subject's own beliefs and attitudes. The prototype of syllogistic reasoning tests was proposed by G. B. Watson[10] in 1925 and expanded by Morgan and Morton[11] in 1943. The latter investigators were interested in studying public opinion concerning, among other things, the rationing of gasoline during World War II. One hundred students in a psychology class checked the one response which they considered to be the correct conclusion to each of two syllogisms:

If the reduction of tire mileage may be one way of saving rubber, and if the rationing of gasoline will reduce tire mileage, then

*1.* The rationing of gasoline will save rubber.

*2.* The rationing of gasoline may save rubber.

[8]Kenneth R. Hammond, "Measuring Attitude by Error-Choice: An Indirect Method," *Journal of Abnormal and Social Psychology*, 43, no. 1 (1948), pp. 38–48.

[9]R. B. Cattell, A. B. Heist, P. A. Heist, and R. G. Stewart, "The Objective Measurement of Dynamic Traits," *Educational and Psychological Measurement*, 10, no. 2 (1950), pp. 224–248.

[10]Goodwin B. Watson, "The Measurement of Fair-Mindedness," *Columbia University Contributions to Education* No. 176 (New York: Teachers College, Columbia University, 1925).

[11]John J. B. Morgan and James T. Morton, "Distorted Reasoning as an Index of Public Opinion," *School and Society*, 57, no. 1473 (1943), pp. 333–335.

3. The rationing of gasoline will not save rubber.

4. The rationing of gasoline may not save rubber.

5. None of the conclusions follows logically from the statements given.

If some girls are beautiful, and if Jane is a girl, then

1. Jane is beautiful.

2. Jane may be beautiful.

3. Jane is not beautiful.

4. Jane may not be beautiful.

5. None of the conclusions follows logically from the statements given.

The second syllogism was used as a control, and is presented in the same form as the first one except that it is less emotionally laden. Note also that responses 2 and 4 are essentially the same. Morgan and Morton found that most students responded to the second option (63 students in the rationing syllogism against 76 in the beauty syllogism) and none responded to the fourth option. This was explained as an example of the "atmosphere-effect" or the "tendency to accept for a conclusion a proposition which is of the same order as the premises." Thus, because the premises are stated in the affirmative, the tendency would be for subjects to select an affirmatively stated conclusion. Thirty-one students responded to the first conclusion on the rationing syllogism in contrast to only four students who responded similarly to the beauty syllogism. From this the authors concluded that the students tested believed that rationing of gasoline would save rubber.

Unfortunately, information is not available concerning the reliability or the validity of syllogistic reasoning tests. Reliability could be estimated by any of the approaches described previously (see Chapter 9). As far as validity is concerned, perhaps the simplest technique would be to administer the syllogisms to groups having known and differing characteristics, such as those favoring rationing and those known to disagree. If the responses differed in the expected directions, this would be some evidence in favor of the validity of the syllogisms.

## Tests of Perception and Memory

If it can be assumed that errors in perceiving or remembering reflect important aspects of personality and are not simply chance occurrences, there is a basis for constructing a disguised–structured test. Horowitz and Horowitz[12] studied the development of social attitudes of children in grades

---

[12]Eugene L. Horowitz and Ruth E. Horowitz, "Development of Social Attitudes in Children," *Sociometry*, 1, nos. 3, 4 (1938), pp. 301–338.

1 through 10 attending a consolidated school in a North–South border state. They developed a number of different tests; one of these, the *Aussage test*, was composed of ten pictures mounted individually in a scrapbook and presented one at a time to each subject for two to three seconds, depending on the age of the child. Considering the complexity of the pictures shown, distortions in perception and memory were likely to occur. Some of the pictures were included to help disguise the purpose of the testing and were neither scored nor analyzed. Following each presentation, questions were asked which would take advantage of any perceptual distortion. For example, one picture depicted four white boys reading in a library, but the children were asked, "What is the colored man in the corner doing?" The investigators found that 60 percent of the first graders reported seeing the nonexistent black engaged in some independent activity; some tenth graders failed to see the black engaged in independent activity, but about 50 percent did see him performing some menial task.

Horowitz and Horowitz also administered a *visual perception span test*, composed of ten pictures mounted on a single page, with each of the six pages exposed for ten seconds. After each page was exposed, the investigators asked the children to report all they could remember concerning the pictures. Although all six pages were administered, only the first page was judged to be of value because of the tendency of the children to give fewer and fewer replies on succeeding pages. The younger children were found to use the words "Negro" and "colored," or any synonym for these terms, less frequently than would be expected by chance; in contrast, the older children used these terms more often than would be expected by chance.

Cattell et al.[13] used a number of tests of perception and memory in their study of the measurement of attitudes. Their *immediate memory test*, for example, required subjects to recall tachistoscopically presented material. Twelve statements were exposed at six-second intervals and the subject was asked to recall "the phrases, statements or ideas presented in this last period." This procedure yielded a split-half reliability of 0.50.

Cattell's *distraction test* required subjects to study tachistoscopically presented statements related to attitudes. Around each statement there were 12 to 13 nonsense syllables, and subjects were asked to recall both the attitude statements and the nonsense syllables. A split-half reliability of 0.64 was found on attitudes concerning personal appearance and dress.

Another technique studied by Cattell and his coworkers was the *misperception test*, which was composed of ten attitude statements related to eating and drinking. Each sentence was tachistoscopically presented for one

[13]R. B. Cattell, E. F. Maxwell, B. H. Light, and M. P. Unger, "The Objective Measurement of Attitudes," *British Journal of Psychology*, 40, Part 2 (1949), pp. 81–90.

second, and the subject was asked to repeat it and to note all misspellings. Ten statements unrelated to eating or drinking were also presented. A split-half reliability of 0.43 was found.

## Judgment Tests

Different judgment tests have been devised to measure attitudes, opinions, and personality characteristics. In one study,[14] for example, children were asked to see how good they were at describing personalities from photographs of blacks and Caucasians. Measures of stability over a six-month period of time on a prejudice score were 0.50 and 0.36 for white and black children, respectively.

In a study of rationalization, Hsü[15] had three female graduate students divide 120 photographs of men into two groups: a "handsome" group and a "homely" group. When all the photographs were returned to them, the three women were asked to indicate which of the men were Communists and which were not. It was found that the two women who admitted to being somewhat anti-Communist tended to judge Communists as being ugly, whereas the one admitted pro-Communist represented Communists as handsome.

The *categories test* used by Horowitz and Horowitz[16] required children to indicate which one of five pictures "does not belong." They used five pictures mounted on a single page; thus, they could determine the basis upon which a given picture was being rejected from the remaining four pictures (i.e., race, sex, age, or socioeconomic condition). They found that race was the most important basis for determining differences.

Moral judgment tests were devised by Watson[17] and Seeman.[18] Watson provided his subjects with a variety of situations which were identical except for the persons or groups described. In one situation, an unwarranted search is being made on the headquarters of a suspected "radical"; in the parallel situation, an unwarranted search is being carried out on a business corporation suspected of being dishonest. The difference between the responses on the two parallel sets provided the basis for scoring. Seeman used essentially the same procedure, but with two equated groups; one group was

[14]Stuart Cook, *The Face Game* (Commission on Community Interrelations of the American Jewish Congress, unpublished manuscript, 1947–1948).

[15]E. H. Hsü, "An Experimental Study of Rationalization," *Journal of Abnormal and Social Psychology*, 44, no. 2 (1949), pp. 277–278.

[16]Horowitz and Horowitz. pp. 308–310.

[17]Watson, "The Measurement of Fair-Mindedness."

[18]Melvin Seeman, "Moral Judgments: A Study of Racial Frames of Reference," *American Sociological Review*, 12 (1947), pp. 404–411.

shown pictures and descriptions of black couples. Seeman found less disap-
proval for the behavior of the black couples than for the white couples on a
test of moral behavior concerning marriage and sex.

Humor has also been used as a basis for making judgments about
minority groups. Wolff, Smith, and Murray,[19] for example, selected 16 jokes;
half were made at the expense of Jews and were distributed randomly with 8
other jokes which contained no reference to minorities. They found, as
expected, that Gentiles and Jews differed in how they perceived the jokes, the
Gentiles tending to think the disparaging jokes funnier than did the Jewish
group.

## Evaluation of Disguised–Structured Methods as Research Tools

Certainly more information concerning the reliability and validity
of disguised–structured techniques is available than for disguised-non-
structured techniques. Much of this information has been provided by Cattell
et al.,[20] who found reliabilities to be comparable to those usually found for
many direct techniques. Campbell[21] has stated, however, that

> this consistency is in part conscious, voluntary, and possibly superficial—
> in contrast to the involuntary "bias" in performance achieved by many
> indirect tests. . . . And it is such consistencies, rather than consistency in
> voluntary self-description, which give vitality to current usage of the
> concept of attitude. In this, indirect attitude tests lie closer to contemporary
> attitude theory than do direct tests.

Conspicuously lacking is evidence that either disguised–nonstructured or disguised–structured techniques yield sufficiently high validity
coefficients to make them useful as research tools. While it is most difficult
to develop adequate criteria for determining the validity of projective techniques, this is also a limitation faced by constructors of all types of tests,
including disguised–structured tests. At least disguised–structured tests
simplify scoring rules. As an administrative convenience, then, disguised–
structured tests have much to recommend them.

Much of the work on attitude measurement has employed questionnaires of the Likert and Thurstone varieties. Relatively little research has
used disguised–structured methods. Nonetheless, these techniques may prove

[19]H. A. Wolff, C. E. Smith, and H. A. Murray, "The Psychology of Humor: 1. A
Study of Responses to Race-Disparagement Jokes," *Journal of Abnormal and Social
Psychology*, 28, no. 4 (1934), pp. 341–365.

[20]Cattell et al., "The Objective Measurement of Dynamic Traits"; Cattell et al., "The
Objective Measurement of Attitudes."

[21]Campbell, "The Indirect Assessment of Social Attitudes," p. 33.

to be of great value in educational research, because, for example, they are rather simple to construct, score, and evaluate. It is their disguised nature that raises ethical questions.

## SOCIOMETRY

Sociometry was developed by Moreno[22] as a technique for studying the interaction patterns among peer groups. The study of group behavior is especially important in education, where the class is a social group composed of students who interact with one another—often in complex ways not easily understood by the teacher. Sociometry requires the investigator to ask subjects to nominate their peers for a specific activity. Usually this activity is one in which the subject has some interest, such as nominating one or more persons he or she would like to sit next to, work with, or play with. Teachers often rearrange the group on the basis of choices made by the students, but this is not always necessary.

Although sociometry is often used by teachers to facilitate the organization of groups, to improve group cohesion, or to find those students who are popular or unpopular, it can also be used to operationally define such terms as "prejudice," "democracy," or "leadership." For example, a prejudice score could be obtained by asking the members of a newly formed group to indicate which persons they would prefer *not* to sit by, work with, or play with. If the group is composed of equal numbers of males, females, blacks, and whites (or if it is provided with pictures of such persons, or out-group members are identified only by names related to ethnic or nationality groups), then the consistent rejection of all persons of a given race or nationality group might be indicative of prejudice. Similarly, democracy could be defined as the absence of cleavages or cliques based on race, nationality, or religion.

The number of choices allowed members of the group depends upon their ages and the purpose of the investigation. If an attempt is being made to measure cordiality or the extent of social contacts, an unlimited choice is necessary. Furthermore, young children are not likely to nominate more than one or two persons,[23] although there is some evidence that reliability increases if five choices are allowed for upper elementary and older children.[24]

[22]J. L. Moreno, *Who Shall Survive? Foundations of Sociometry, Group Psychotherapy, and Sociodrama*, rev. ed. (New York: Beacon House, 1953).

[23]Robert F. Biehler, "Companion Choice Behavior in the Kindergarten," *Child Development*, 25, no. 1 (1954), pp. 45–50.

[24]Norman E. Gronlund and Fred P. Barnes, "The Reliability of Social-Acceptability Scores Using Various Sociometric-Choice Limits," *The Elementary School Journal*, 57, no. 3 (1956), pp. 153–157.

Perhaps the simplest procedure for analyzing sociometric choices is to list the "choosers" along one side of a table and those selected at the top. The numeral 1 could be placed in the cell representing the first person chosen by each subject; 2 would represent the second choice, etc. An *R* placed within a cell could represent subjects who are actively rejected, if this information is desired. Summing each column yields an index of the relative strength of the nominations received.

By examining the pattern of choices, different types of relationships can be described. The term "star" is used to describe the person who has been chosen most often; a "mutual pair" represents the pattern where individual *A* selects *B* and *B* selects *A*; a "chain" occurs when *A* selects *B*, *B* selects *C*, *C* picks *D*, etc.; an "isolate" is a person who has not been selected by anyone; and a "triangle" occurs when *A* picks *B*, *B* picks *C*, and *C* picks *A*. Any pattern which is developed because members of a group select each other but reject outside members or do not select them is called a "clique." A "rejectee" is anyone who has been actively rejected.

To show these relationships more easily, Moreno proposed using a *sociogram*, which pictorially describes the choice patterns of the group. Arrows are used to show the direction of choice; circles are often used for females and squares or triangles for males. Thus, if Alice selects Bill, this might be represented by:

In research, it is often advantageous to use an index number to represent various types of sociometric choices. *Emotional expansiveness*, for example, could be measured by counting the number of persons an individual will select if given an unlimited number of choices. However, many of these indexes are complex and of questionable value. Many indexes are too atomistic to yield an adequate picture of the social structure of the group, and this is the main purpose of sociometry. Many of these points are considered by Proctor and Loomis[25] and by Lindzey and Byrne.[26]

The reliability of sociometric choices has been investigated by using measures of stability and internal consistency. Stability can be estimated by

[25]Charles H. Proctor and Charles P. Loomis, "Analysis of Sociometric Data," Chapter 17 in Marie Jahoda, Morton Deutsch, and Stuart W. Cook, eds., *Research Methods in Social Relations*, Part 2, *Selected Techniques* (New York: The Dryden Press, 1951), pp. 561–585.

[26]Gardner Lindzey and Donn Byrne, "Measurement of Social Choice and Interpersonal Attractiveness," Chapter 14 in Gardner Lindzey and Elliot Aronson, eds., *The Handbook of Social Psychology*, 2d ed., Vol. 2, *Research Methods* (Reading, Mass.: Addison-Wesley Publishing Co., 1968), pp. 452–525.

correlating the number of choices received by subjects on one occasion with the number of choices received at some other time. Internal consistency is found by arbitrarily dividing the group into two halves and then correlating the number of choices an individual receives from one half of the group with the number received from the second half (the split-half technique). Gronlund[27] has summarized the results of studies involving the reliability of sociometric measures as follows:

*1.* The stability of sociometric results tends to decline as the time span between tests is increased.

*2.* There is a tendency for the stability of sociometric results to increase as the age of the group members increases.

*3.* Sociometric status scores based on general criteria [such as work or play] tend to be more stable and more consistent over various situations than those based on specific criteria [such as working on arithmetic or playing baseball].

*4.* Composite sociometric status scores based on several sociometric criteria tend to be more stable than sociometric status scores based on a single sociometric criterion.

*5.* The use of an unlimited number of sociometric choices, five positive choices, and three positive and three negative choices tends to provide similar sociometric results. The use of fewer choices provides less reliable sociometric results.

*6.* The social structure of a group tends to be less stable than the sociometric status of the individual group members.

*7.* The sociometric positions of leadership and isolation tend to be more stable and more consistent over various situations than those in the average sociometric categories.

The validity of sociometric measures is difficult to obtain. If the interest is in the choices made by subjects, sociometry operationally defines those choices and no further evidence of validity is required. On the other hand, it is important to relate sociometric choices to educational and psychological traits in order to know what these choices mean. Content validity will not suffice because the meaning of a choice or pattern of choices cannot be understood from the content of the questions asked. Predictive validity is appropriate if one is willing to assume that a leader in a given group now is going to be a leader among a different peer group later. Concurrent validity studies can be useful if they suggest those variables that are associated with sociometric choices.

[27]Norman E. Gronlund, *Sociometry in the Classroom* (New York: Harper Brothers, 1959), pp. 152–153.

Lindzey and Borgatta[28] have summarized the relationships between sociometric choices and characteristics such as leadership, prejudice, social adjustment, social sensitivity, morale, and group structure. Jennings[29] found that 18 out of 20 girls who were elected to a house council in a school for delinquents were overchosen (were one or more standard deviations above the mean number of choices received) on a sociometric test administered three months after the election. Evidence was presented that sociometric choice is related to other variables as well as to leadership, although not all results have been as striking as those presented by Jennings.

Although sociometry is a useful technique, it has a number of limitations:

*1.* Patterns of choices do not, in and of themselves, explain the reasons behind the choices. That is, it is difficult to assume that because *A* selects *B*, the reasons behind this choice are understood.

*2.* The understanding of group behavior depends on factors that must be obtained independently of sociometric choice. Case studies of the individuals comprising the group, for example, can be helpful in understanding group interaction.

*3.* Neither isolates nor stars are necessarily either well adjusted or poorly adjusted. The isolate may simply be unknown to members of the group, and many unhappy persons may be popular in certain situations.

*4.* The status of a subject within a given group does not necessarily imply equal status in another group. The star on the football field is not necessarily the star in mathematics, although many of these traits do seem to correlate positively.

*5.* The questions asked members of a group frequently determine the choices made. This points out the importance of asking questions relevant to the topic under investigation.

## THE Q-SORT TECHNIQUE

The *Q* technique was devised by Stephenson[30] for the study of *intrapersonal* relations. *Q* technique has its greatest appeal when the researcher must work intensively with few persons. It makes use of the correlation between persons rather than the correlation between tests.

[28]Gardner Lindzey and Edgar F. Borgatta, "Sociometric Measurement," Chapter 11 in Gardner Lindzey, ed., *Handbook of Social Psychology*, Vol. I, *Theory and Method* (Cambridge, Mass.: Addison-Wesley Publishing Co., 1954), pp. 405–408.

[29]Helen Hall Jennings, *Leadership and Isolation*, 2d. ed. (New York: Longmans, Green and Co., 1950).

[30]William Stephenson, *The Study of Behavior: Q-Technique and Its Methodology* (Chicago: University of Chicago Press, 1953).

$Q$ methodology begins with the development of items, usually 60 to 150, which originate out of some theoretical formulation. Each statement is printed on a separate card and presented to the respondents, who are asked to sort them into piles, much in the same way that judges are asked to sort items on a Thurstone-type scale. Generally, there are 11 piles, ranging from "most applicable to oneself" to "least like oneself" or "most liked" to "least liked." The $Q$ technique requires each respondent to sort the cards into a symmetrical distribution, with the number of cards to be sorted into each pile fixed by the investigator. Table 12-1 demonstrates the score values (from 0 to 10) and the number of cards to be sorted into each pile.

TABLE 12-1

Example of a $Q$ Sort

| | Most Applicable | | | | | | Least Applicable | | | | | |
|---|---|---|---|---|---|---|---|---|---|---|---|---|
| Score | 10 | 9 | 8 | 7 | 6 | 5 | 4 | 3 | 2 | 1 | 0 | |
| No. of cards to be placed in each pile | 2 | 3 | 5 | 7 | 9 | 13 | 9 | 7 | 5 | 3 | 2 | $(n = 65)$ |

Once the sorting has been accomplished, each statement or card is accorded the score corresponding to the pile into which it was placed. For example, if statement 24 is placed in pile 8, it is accorded a score of 8. One method of analysis is to have each person sort the deck twice under different conditions, such as, "How the teacher perceives me" and "How I perceive the teacher." The correlation between the ratings on the two sorts can then be used to measure compatibility between teacher and student.

$Q$ methodology has been applied to many kinds of problems in education. Sheldon and Sorenson[31] have described the use of the $Q$ technique to evaluate the extent to which a senior problems course affected adjustment, to determine the agreement between teachers and administrators regarding student-centered and subject-centered curricula, to determine changes in philosophical positions before and after taking a course, and to evaluate counseling interviews by correlating an ideal interview with a role-playing interview. Similarly, Revie[32] correlated the teacher's and school psy-

[31]M. Stephen Sheldon and A. Garth Sorenson, "On the Use of Q-Technique in Educational Evaluation and Research," *Journal of Experimental Education*, 29, no. 2 (1960), pp. 143–151.

[32]V. A. Revie, "The Effect of Psychological Case Work on the Teacher's Concept of the Pupil," *Journal of Counseling Psychology*, 3, no. 2 (1956), pp. 125–129.

chologist's attitudes toward pupils. Kerlinger and Kaya[33] demonstrated that progressivism and traditionalism in education tend to be relatively independent of one another.

However useful the $Q$ technique may be, it has been criticized by a number of persons.[34-36] For example, it has not been clearly established that a symmetrical distribution is the best form for studying individuals. In addition, the construction of items is time-consuming, as is the necessity of sorting many items one or more times. Nor is there any advantage in using cards when items can be printed in a booklet to facilitate scoring and administration.

## THE SEMANTIC DIFFERENTIAL

The *semantic differential* was developed by Osgood et al.[37-39] as a way of measuring the connotative meaning of concepts. Concepts such as home, father, or democracy have both *denotative* meanings (i.e., actual or lexical definitions) and *connotative* meanings, which reflect the attitude of the individual toward the concept. Denotatively, a home may be "any fixed shelter," but the connotations of home may be differentiated along continua which include such polar traits as comfortable–uncomfortable, warm–cold, or bright–dark. Actually, any concept or stimulus may be rated along a number of polar traits, and the rating will operationally define the connotative meaning of the concept for the individual doing the rating. Thus, the respondents may be asked to rate the concept "school" on the type of form shown in Figure 12-1.

Marking instructions follow closely those used on rating scales. In general, respondents are given some idea as to the purpose of the scale, how

[33] Fred N. Kerlinger and Esin Kaya, "The Construction and Factor Analytic Validation of Scales to Measure Attitudes toward Education," *Educational and Psychological Measurement*, 19, no. 1 (1959), pp. 13–29.

[34] O. Hobart Mowrer, "*Q* Technique: Description, History, and Critique," in O. H. Mowrer, ed., *Psychotherapy: Therapy and Research* (New York: Ronald Press Co., 1953), pp. 316–375.

[35] L. J. Cronbach and Goldine C. Gleser, "Review of W. Stephenson, *The Study of Behavior: Q–Technique and Its Methodology*," *Psychometrika*, 19 (1954), pp. 327–330.

[36] J. R. Wittenborn, "Contributions and Current Status of *Q* Methodology," *Psychological Bulletin*, 58, no. 2 (1961), pp. 132–142.

[37] Charles E. Osgood, "The Nature and Measurement of Meaning," *Psychological Bulletin*, 49, no. 3 (1952), pp. 197–237.

[38] Charles E. Osgood, George J. Suci, and Percy H. Tannenbaum, *The Measurement of Meaning* (Urbana: University of Illinois Press, 1957).

[39] James G. Snider and Charles E. Osgood, eds., *Semantic Differential Technique: A Sourcebook* (Chicago: Aldine Publishing Co., 1969), 681 pp.

**SCHOOL**

| good | ___: | ___: | ___: | ___: | ___: | ___: | ___: | bad |
| fair | ___: | ___: | ___: | ___: | ___: | ___: | ___: | unfair |
| clean | ___: | ___: | ___: | ___: | ___: | ___: | ___: | dirty |
| active | ___: | ___: | ___: | ___: | ___: | ___: | ___: | passive |
| varied | ___: | ___: | ___: | ___: | ___: | ___: | ___: | repetitive |
| fast | ___: | ___: | ___: | ___: | ___: | ___: | ___: | slow |
| hard | ___: | ___: | ___: | ___: | ___: | ___: | ___: | soft |
| sharp | ___: | ___: | ___: | ___: | ___: | ___: | ___: | dull |
| strong | ___: | ___: | ___: | ___: | ___: | ___: | ___: | weak |

**Figure 12-1**
AN EXAMPLE OF A SEMANTIC DIFFERENTIAL.

to mark it, and what criteria to use in making judgments. For heuristic purposes, a mark in the extreme left position is scored $+3$, the second column is scored $+2$, the third column in scored $+1$, and the middle column is scored zero; scores of $-1$, $-2$, and $-3$ are given for the corrresponding positions on the right side of the scale. A score of $-3$ on the *sharp–dull* dimension reflects the extreme connotation that school is maximally dull.

A number of factor analyses[40] described by Osgood et al. have confirmed the presence of at least three factors on the semantic differential: an *evaluative* factor (good–bad, fair–unfair, clean–dirty, etc.), an *activity* factor (active–passive, varied–repetitive, fast–slow, etc.), and a *potency* factor (hard–soft, sharp–dull, strong–weak, etc.); Husek and Wittrock[41] have found additional factors, which they labeled restraint, tenacity, predictability, and stability.

Of considerable interest is Osgood's concept of a "semantic space,"

a region of some unknown dimensionality and Euclidean in character. Each semantic scale, defined by a pair of polar ... adjectives, is assumed to represent a straight line function that passes through the origin of this space, and a sample of such scales then represents a multidimensional space. The larger or more representative the sample, the better defined is the space as a whole. ... To define the semantic space with maximum efficiency, we would need to determine that minimum number of *orthogonal*

[40]Factor analysis has been discussed in Chapter 5.

[41]T. R. Husek and M. C. Wittrock, "The Dimensions of Attitudes toward Teachers as Measured by the Semantic Differential," *Journal of Educational Psychology*, 53, no. 5 (1962), pp. 209–213.

dimensions [independent factors] . . . which exhausts the dimensionality of the space. . . .[42]

The semantic space may be described as being composed of $k$ number of mutually independent factors, each varying from $+3$ to $-3$, the zero position being the point of origin where the $k$ factors intersect. For example, if the concept "school" can be factor analyzed to yield three factors (evaluation, activity, and potency), it could be described by a three-dimensional model representing the semantic space. For any given group of subjects, then, the group's attitude can be placed in space at a point where the average scores on the three factors intersect.

As an example of how the semantic differential may be used, consider a study reported by Osgood concerning the attitudes of Taft Republicans, Eisenhower Republicans, and Stevenson voters during the 1952 presidential elections.[43] Each respondent was instructed to rate ten persons and ten issues, using the following bipolar traits: wise–foolish, dirty–clean, fair–unfair, safe–dangerous, strong–weak, deep–shallow, active–passive, cool–warm, relaxed–tense, and idealistic–realistic. The persons and issues were: 1) Robert Taft, 2) universal military training, 3) Adlai Stevenson, 4) U.S. policy in China, 5) Winston Churchill, 6) federal spending, 7) General MacArthur, 8) socialism, 9) Estes Kefauver, 10) government employees, 11) Josef Stalin, 12) government price controls, 13) Harry S Truman, 14) European aid, 15) General Eisenhower, 16) labor unionism, 17) Franklin D. Roosevelt, 18) use of the atomic bomb, 19) Senator Joseph McCarthy, and 20) United Nations. The semantic space model for Taft Republicans can be seen in Figure 12-2. The *fair–unfair* dimension represents the *evaluation* factor; *weak–strong* represents potency; and *active–passive* defines the *activity* factor. The broken lines reflect a *passive* rating whereas solid lines are *active* ratings. The length of each line measures the relative degree of the *active–passive* dimension.

As expected, Taft Republicans perceived Taft as fair, active, and strong, closely related to Eisenhower and MacArthur, and concerned with federal spending. Socialism is judged to be mildly active, weak, and unfair, and the policy in China is considered to be weak, passive, and unfair. Of greater theoretical interest is the finding that all three groups of voters could be rated on the same three dimensions (i.e., evaluation, activity, and potency).

Another contribution of the semantic differential technique is that it allows the investigator to examine the profiles made by two persons to see whether or not a given concept has the same meaning for both; the semantic differential may also be used to see how similarly a given subject perceives a number of concepts. One possibility is to use the correlation between two

[42]Osgood et al., p. 25.

[43]Osgood et al., pp. 104–124.

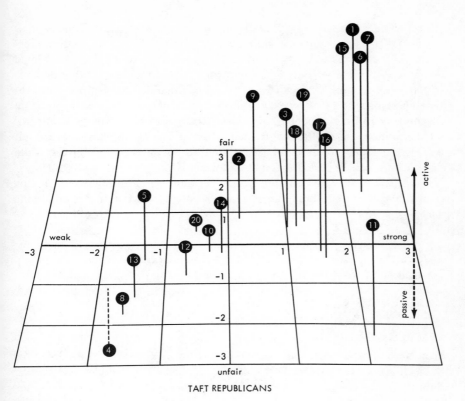

fair

active

weak

strong

passive

unfair

TAFT REPUBLICANS

**Figure 12-2**
THE SEMANTIC SPACE FOR TAFT REPUBLICANS.

profiles of scores, but Osgood and Suci[44] have argued that a measure of the differences between profiles is needed rather than the correlation between the scores. The measure or index of distance $D$ is the "square root of the sum of the squared differences between coordinates on the same dimension $(\sqrt{\Sigma d^2})$." While this may sound complex, it is really quite simple to compute. Assume, for example, that two subjects rate the concept "school" in the following way:

|  | Evaluation | Activity | Potency |
|---|---|---|---|
| Subject One | −3 | +3 | −3 |
| Subject Two | +1 | −2 | +2 |

[44]Charles E. Osgood and George J. Suci, "A Measure of Relation Determined by Both Mean Difference and Profile Information," *Psychological Bulletin*, 49, no. 3 (1952), pp. 251–262.

The difference between the scores on the evaluation dimension is $-4[-3-(+1)]=-4$; the difference for activity is $+5$; and the difference for potency is $-5$. Each of these differences is squared and summed $[-4^2+5^2+(-5)^2=66]$. The square root of $66=8.12$. Note that in place of Subject One and Subject Two it would be possible to substitute Concept One and Concept Two (such as "school" and "home" as rated by a single person or a group of persons). The use of $D$ assumes an approximate interval scale and independent factors. Evidence for the first assumption is presented by Osgood et al.[45] The second assumption, for any given set of bipolar traits or concepts, can be tested through factor analysis.

The distance index $D$ may also be found rather easily from the raw scores. Assume that three subjects rate a single concept in the following way:

|               | Subject One | Subject Two | Subject Three |
| ------------- | ----------- | ----------- | ------------- |
| hot–cold      | 5           | 2           | 6             |
| good–bad      | 3           | 6           | 4             |
| angular–round | 4           | 3           | 5             |

For illustrative purposes, only three scales with 7 points each have been used. For Subject One versus Subject Two, $D=\sqrt{19}$, or 4.36[46]; for Subject One versus Subject Three, $D=\sqrt{3}$, or 1.73; for Subject Two versus Subject Three, $D=\sqrt{24}$, or 4.90. Thus, the least amount of distance occurs between Subjects One and Three, and the greatest amount of distance occurs between Subjects Two and Three. Used in this way, a factor analysis need not be run prior to using the $D$ index.

In evaluating the semantic differential, a number of points can be made:

*a.* The semantic differential is not an entirely new procedure, but a combination of a graphic rating scale with factor analysis.

*b.* The technique is extremely flexible and is simple to construct, administer, and score.

*c.* The semantic differential is subject to all of the limitations which seem to be present in rating scales, namely, the possibilities of faking responses, the tendency to place marks in the middle position, and of having to mark a concept on some rather meaningless scales (e.g., is honesty fast or slow?).

[45] Osgood et al., *The Measurement of Meaning*, pp. 146–153.
[46] The value $\sqrt{19}$ was found in the following way:

$$
\begin{array}{rlrl}
5-2= & 3; & 3^2= & 9 \\
3-6= & -3; & -3^2= & 9 \\
4-3= & 1; & 1^2= & \underline{1} \\
& & & 19
\end{array}
$$

*d.* A number of studies have demonstrated validity for the semantic differential.[47] In one investigation, it was found that certain concepts (such as white rosebuds, gentleness, sleep—hero, virility, success—and quicksand, fate, death) clustered together in meaning as expected, thus providing some evidence of validity. Additional information concerning the usefulness of the semantic differential was obtained during the 1952 presidential election. Three and a half months prior to election day, 18 subjects indicated that they were uncertain whether they would vote for Eisenhower or for Stevenson. When the *D* indexes of those who stated that they were certain to vote either for Eisenhower or for Stevenson were compared with the semantic profiles of those who stated that they were uncertain, the fair–unfair scale predicted the actual voting behavior of 14 of the 18 subjects; the addition of the potency scale improved predictions to the point where 17 of the 18 subjects voted according to expectation. In this study, the activity scale was of no help in predicting voting behavior.

*e.* The semantic differential has found its widest application in the study of personality development, in the evaluation of psychotherapy, and in cross-cultural studies. Its use in education has not been widespread, although it appears to be a rather promising tool, especially in attitude measurement.

# CONTENT ANALYSIS

Content analysis has been defined by Berelson[48] as "*a research technique for the objective, systematic, and quantitative description of the manifest content of communication.*" Within the context of this definition, the meaning of communication is not restricted to spoken language, but is used to encompass both verbal and nonverbal behavior. Thus, one might be interested in studying the content of speeches, letters, essays, journals, documents, slogans, propaganda, films, music, textbooks, tests, interviews, or questionnaires. The purpose of content analysis is to classify and quantify relatively unstructured material to make it more meaningful and more easily understood.

The analysis of qualitative material involves the following procedures:

*a. Specification of objectives.* The categories selected for content analysis depend upon the purpose of the investigation. The purpose suggests relevant categories and ways to establish classification systems. Thus, for example, it is likely that two investigators would develop different classification systems to study popular trends in music if their purposes for doing so differed. To

---

[47]Osgood et al., *The Measurement of Meaning*, pp. 140–166.

[48]Bernard Berelson, *Content Analysis in Communication Research* (New York: Free Press of Glencoe, 1952), p. 18.

a historian of music, the tempo, instrumentation, melody, and harmony might be of extreme importance in characterizing a given period of music; to an educator concerned with determining the relationship between musical preferences and delinquency, lyrics (aggressive, suggestive, strong, etc.) may be of greater importance.

*b. Developing hypotheses.* Purposes are generally stated in broad terms, such as "having an interest in studying the changing conception of the teacher as this conception is reflected in the popular novel," or "I want to evaluate popular songs to better understand adolescent moral attitudes." It is at this point that specific hypotheses should be generated and terms defined according to the criteria developed in Chapter 4.

*c. Sampling.* Once hypotheses are developed and terms defined, the problem arises of selecting specific samples of content. Berelson[49] has stated that there are three universes from which samples may be drawn: *titles* (a specific newspaper, journal, radio station, etc.), *issues or dates* of titles, and *content* found within issues or titles. Specific titles are determined by examining the demands required by the hypotheses. If, for example, the interest is in studying changes in the teacher stereotypes as portrayed in popular literature, the researcher will have to limit the universe to specific titles of books or magazines likely to reflect these stereotypes. If magazines are selected, the specific issues or dates have to be determined in some unbiased way. Mintz[50] has pointed out the problems involved in selecting issues from a given title. In the first place, the amount of space devoted to a news story may fluctuate over a period of time. If the story builds up slowly, selecting an early issue will underestimate the amount of space devoted to it, while a late issue may overestimate its importance. Mintz has called this fluctuation a *primary trend. Cyclical trends* occur when every *n*th issue contains an element not found in other issues. A systematic sample of every Sunday paper, for example, would not yield a representative sample of newspapers in general. A third type of trend or problem occurs when there are *compensatory relations* between successive issues. For example, if a radio news report tends to devote a great deal of time to a given topic when first mentioned but less time on repeat broadcasts, a systematic sample of every other news broadcast would yield a biased sample.

After titles and issues have been selected, it is still necessary to determine what parts of the issue are to be analyzed. Berelson has suggested that newspapers be analyzed by the amount of space devoted to articles, location, headline size, and colors; radio by the length of the programs, order, intonation, sound, and music; and films by length, order, color, intonation, sound, and music. Similar types of analyses can be made for other media.

*d. Determining the categories.* Berelson has examined some of the major

[49]Berelson, pp. 176–182.

[50]Alexander Mintz, "The Feasibility of the Use of Samples in Content Analysis," in Harold D. Lasswell, Nathan Leites, and associates, eds., *Language of Politics: Studies in Quantitative Semantics* (Cambridge, Mass.: M.I.T. Press, 1965), pp. 127–152.

types of categories which have been used in content analysis and has organized them in the following way:

I. "What is said" Categories
   A. Subject matter: What is the communication about?
   B. Direction: Is the communication for or against the particular subject, or neutral toward it?
   C. Standard: On what grounds (strength, morality, etc.) is the classification by direction made?
   D. Values: What are the goals or desires which are sought?
   E. Methods: What are the means employed to attain values?
   F. Traits: What are the personality characteristics used to describe persons?
   G. Actor: Who or what is the initiator of acts?
   H. Authority: What person, group, or object is credited as the source of a statement or communication?
   I. Origin: In what locality did the communication originate?
   J. Target: Who is the intended recipient of the communication?

II. "How it is said" Categories
   A. Form or type of communication: Is the communication fiction, popular music, news, television, etc.?
   B. Form of statement: What is the grammatical or syntactical form of the communication? Is it fact, opinion, etc?
   C. Intensity: How emotional or exciting is the communication?
   D. Device: What devices are used to persuade or propagandize the reader?

*e. Category analysis.* Whatever type of category is selected to best fulfill the requirements of the investigation, it still has to be analyzed into components. For example, in the hypothetical study of the stereotypes of teachers as depicted in the "popular literature" from 1900 to 1976, one might want to use the categories of *direction, standard,* and *traits.* Direction can be described rather easily by evaluating an author's stereotype of a teacher in a story as favorable, unfavorable, or neutral. The analysis of standard and traits is somewhat more difficult. The simplest approach may be to use subcategories, such as strength and weakness or moral and immoral. These subcategories can be further subdivided if necessary. Similarly, traits may be divided into age, sex, religion, nationality, etc.; into more psychologically oriented traits such as introverted, extroverted, or ambiverted; or, perhaps, into a dimension such as awkward versus adroit.

*f. Quantification.* Much of the quantification used in content analysis involves determining the frequency with which various "units" occur. Berelson[51] has noted five major units which have been used in content analysis.

---

[51]Berelson, pp. 136–146.

*1. The word:* The word is the smallest unit in content analysis. Technically, this unit may include phrases as well as a single word. For example, a frequency count of the number of times words relating to aggression are used by a speaker might be used as an index of hostility. The difficulty is that word counts provide no idea of the context in which the word appears. It is possible that a very aggressive person will use words related to aggression as often as does a peaceful person, even though the contexts are quite different.

Another use of word counting may be found in readability formulas which attempt to analyze those factors making for reading ease. Readability can be measured by counting syllables, sentence lengths, personal pronouns, and the like.[52]

Russell and Fea[53] caution readers about some limitations of readability formulas:

Readability formulas do not: 1) give any measure of conceptual difficulty in textual material; 2) take into consideration the way the material is organized or arranged; 3) allow for variations in the meanings of multiple-meaning words; 4) accept the fact that a fresh or unusual word may make a sentence or idea clearer than a commonplace word; 5) vary their ratings in terms of different interests which persons may have at different developmental levels or in individual activities; 6) take account of physical factors such as format and illustration.

*2. The theme:* After the word, the theme is the next largest unit for analysis. A theme is simply a summary sentence describing the content of some communication. One could, for example, take the speeches of a political candidate and summarize his or her position on public education. This type of analysis may, however, be rather complex, especially if a simple sentence cannot adequately summarize the import of the communication.

*3. The characters:* Sometimes the most convenient unit for analysis is the personality or characteristics of the major and minor persons described in a communication. While this type of analysis is even broader than the theme, it is often used for analyzing plays, biographies, and similar types of communications. It will ordinarily be necessary to go through the entire communication before establishing categories for character analysis.

*4. The item:* Any whole, self-contained communication is considered to be an item. Examples include a book, an article, a story, or an entire radio program. A review of a book or play may be made on the basis of the work as a whole, categorizing it rather broadly as fiction or nonfiction, historical or contemporary, or perhaps realism or fantasy. Analysis by item is useful only if variations within the item are unimportant or secondary to the major classification.

[52]George R. Klare, "Assessing Readability," *Reading Research Quarterly*, 10, no. 1 (1974–1975), pp. 62–102.

[53]David H. Russell and Henry R. Fea, "Validity of Six Readability Formulas as Measures of Juvenile Fiction," *The Elementary School Journal*, 52, no. 2 (1951), p. 136.

5. *Space and time measures:* In analyzing the content of newspapers, the column inch devoted to a given topic has been used as a measure of importance or intensity. Similarly, the amount of time devoted to public information bulletins may be used as a measure of the radio or television companies' concern for the public interest, although there are obvious limitations to this criterion.

g. *Standardizing the coding procedure:* The coding procedure must be tried out with the persons who will actually do the categorizing. Many of the suggestions for the training of interviewers (see Chapter 10) are also applicable in content analysis. First, it is most important that the coders understand as completely as possible the purpose of the analysis. Second, it is necessary to conduct a "dry run" where all coders categorize the same material. Marked discrepancies in coding from rater to rater may, thus, be detected and eliminated. Third, it may be necessary to replace coders who are insensitive to the requirements of the task, even if the original selection of coders was rather complete and carefully planned. Raters may soon tire of the task unless they are motivated to be accurate.

h. *Reliability:* The reliability of qualitative data depends upon the accuracy of coding. In some instances, the extent to which a number of coders can consistently analyze the same data can be taken as a measure of interobserver reliability; in other cases, reliability may be considered from the point of view of one or more observers who are asked to code the same data over a period of time.

One rather serious limitation concerning the reliability of qualitative material should be mentioned. Often, reliability for coded material is presented in percentage form. For example, two coders might agree on 90 percent of their judgments. While this may sound high, the statement may be misleading, especially if the coding is rather simple and the number of categories small. See pages 274–275 for a possible resolution of this difficulty.

# SUMMARY

**1.** Disguised techniques can conceal the true purpose of an investigation if the study is controversial or potentially ego-threatening. Disguised techniques may be either structured or unstructured.

**a.** Disguised–structured techniques appear to be objective measures of achievement having a right or wrong answer, but they actually measure either attitude or personality.

**b.** Disguised–nonstructured tests allow the respondent more latitude in responding than do disguised–structured tests. They are essentially projective techniques.

**2.** Some cautions concerning the use of projective techniques were noted. Many of these techniques should be used only under the direct supervision of persons who have had the experience and training to use them competently. This is especially true for some of the more clinical instruments. The reliability and validity of these methods are open to question and the beginning student would do well to find some less demanding and less deceptive method if possible.

**3.** Four types of disguised–structured methods were described:

**a.** Information tests contain items that appear to measure achievement but which are so difficult to answer that guessing is necessary. It is assumed that the direction of guessing is an indication of the subject's underlying attitude or personality.

**b.** Syllogistic reasoning tests assume that the conclusions drawn from complex premises reflect the beliefs and hopes of the subject. Generally, two syllogisms are presented, one tapping the emotionally laden area under investigation and the other serving as a neutral or control syllogism. Differences in response between the two syllogisms are considered indicative of the attitude, biases, or hopes of the respondents.

**c.** Tests of perception and memory require the subject to examine some complex stimulus, such as a picture or sentence, and then to recall as many characteristics of the stimulus as possible. This chapter described the Aussage test, the visual perception span test, the immediate memory test, the distraction test, and the misperception test.

**d.** Judgment tests require the subject to judge a wide variety of different attitudes, opinions, or personality characteristics. These techniques often involve having subjects judge pictures or photographs, situations, or humor.

**4.** While there is not much evidence available concerning the evaluation of disguised–structured techniques, they do have some obvious advantages. In the first place they are easy to construct, administer, and score. Second, it is generally easier to evaluate disguised–structured techniques than it is to evaluate disguised–nonstructured techniques. Little evidence is available comparing disguised techniques with nondisguised methods (Likert or Thurstone methods, for example).

**5.** Sociometry was designed by Moreno as a method of studying peer group interactions. Although it has been used most often by teachers as a technique for discovering popular and unpopular students and for reorganizing classes on the basis of student preference, it can be used to study student interaction and preferences.

**a.** Sociometric choices have been analyzed by both tables and graphs. In tabular form an $N$-by-$N$ matrix can be prepared; graphically, a sociogram can be developed with arrows connecting choosers with those being chosen. Sociometric choices can be described by such terms as stars, mutual pairs, chains, isolates, triangles, cliques, and rejectees.

**b.** Although there are advantages in developing index numbers representing various types of group interactions, most are of dubious value. Index analysis has been criticized most often for its emphasis on isolated aspects of group relationships.

**c.** The reliability of sociometric choices has been determined by using measures of stability and internal consistency. Both of these methods were described and advantages and disadvantages noted.

**d.** The validity of sociometric choices was also considered. Generally, the most useful type of validity has been derived from studies employing concurrent validity coefficients.

**e.** A number of limitations concerning sociometry were noted: sociometry does not provide information concerning the reasons behind a choice; neither isolates nor stars are necessarily either well or poorly adjusted; the status of the individual varies from group to group; and the kind of question asked often determines how the choices will be made.

**6.** The $Q$ technique is another method of obtaining information about respondents. $Q$ methodology begins with the development of items to be sorted into piles approximating a symmetrical distribution. Each pile is given a number ranging from zero to 10 (if 11 piles are being used), and the subject is instructed to place each card into a forced-choice distribution with more of the cards placed in the center of the distribution than at the ends. Usually, each person sorts the cards twice under different sets of instructions or conditions. Correlations are then run between the two sorts. This procedure makes it possible to study a few individuals at a time.

Although a number of studies have established the value of $Q$ methodology, it has limitations. Forcing choices into a symmetrical distribution has been criticized, as has the sorting mechanics.

**7.** The semantic differential was designed to measure the connotative meaning of concepts. Typically, developing a semantic differential involves establishing a number of bipolar adjectives which can be rated on a continuum. These scores are usually factor analyzed and a "semantic space" defined.

**a.** The semantic differential allows the investigator not only to examine the connotative meaning of concepts, but also to compare the profiles made by two or more persons. It is also possible to compare the profiles of the same person on two or more concepts.

**b.** Although there are decided advantages in using the semantic differential, its limitations should be kept in mind. Being essentially a bipolar rating scale, it has all of the disadvantages this type of scale is known to possess (such as ease of faking and of the tendency to avoid extreme positions), as well as its advantages (simplicity in administration and scoring).

**c.** Evidence for the validity of semantic differential responses is highly promising.

**8.** Content analysis is the general term used to describe the process of quantifying and objectifying "qualitative" data, such as speeches, books, and letters.

A number of steps were described in running a content analysis:

**a.** *Specification of objectives.* Unless the objectives of the investigation are important, clear, and unequivocal, content analyses are likely to confuse rather than clarify.

**b.** *Developing hypotheses.* Hypotheses should be generated as early in the investigation as possible. By so doing, the investigator helps to specify relevant kinds of data.

**c.** *Sampling.* Samples may be drawn from any of three universes: titles, issues or dates, and content. A number of cautions were pointed out, especially in the selection of issues or dates.

**d.** *Determining the categories.* A number of categories were described that could be used to analyze content. In general, one may either consider what is said or how the message is said. Subcategories were described for each of these major classifications.

**e.** *Category analysis.* The categories used for analysis depend on the purpose of the investigator.

**f.** *Quantification.* Five major units used in content analysis were examined: the word, the theme, the characters, the item, and space and time measures. Readability formulas were described as essentially word counting procedures. A theme is a summary sentence describing the content of some communication. An analysis of content may also be made by studying the character or personality of one or more persons. Quantification by item refers to the analysis of the entire work as a whole. The amount of space or time devoted to a topic can also be used as an index of importance or intensity.

**g.** *Standardizing the coding procedure.* Coding may be standardized by training raters so that high agreement can be expected from different raters of the same material. This can be done by carefully selecting coders who are interested and capable of doing this type of work and by training them so that they will be fully aware of the procedures to be followed.

**h.** *Reliability.* The reliability of a content analysis may refer either to the extent to which two or more raters agree on their coding procedure or to the extent that a single rater codes the material the same way twice. However, unless tasks are equated, the percentage of agreement between ratings on different tasks may mislead rather than clarify.

## PRACTICE EXERCISES

**1.** To what extent do the projective techniques themselves help determine subject responses to them?

**2.** Suppose that a new projective technique might be of some value in an investigation you are planning. What criteria would you demand of this technique before you decide to use it?

**3.** Suppose it is hypothesized that the introduction of a unit on "Getting Along with Friends" will increase group cohesion among juvenile delinquents. Examine the two sociometric matrices which follow (assume that students can select none or all of their classmates). The first matrix was obtained after the first week of school; the second was obtained near the end of the semester. The persons on the left are selecting those at the top of the matrix.

### Before Matrix

|         | ALBERT | BEN | CARL | DELBERT | EGBERT |
|---------|--------|-----|------|---------|--------|
| Albert  | 0      | 0   | 0    | 1       | 0      |
| Ben     | 0      | 0   | 0    | 0       | 0      |
| Carl    | 0      | 0   | 0    | 0       | 1      |
| Delbert | 1      | 0   | 0    | 0       | 0      |
| Egbert  | 0      | 1   | 0    | 0       | 0      |

### After Matrix

|         | ALBERT | BEN | CARL | DELBERT | EGBERT |
|---------|--------|-----|------|---------|--------|
| Albert  | 0      | 0   | 0    | 0       | 0      |
| Ben     | 1      | 0   | 1    | 1       | 0      |
| Carl    | 1      | 1   | 0    | 0       | 0      |
| Delbert | 1      | 1   | 1    | 0       | 0      |
| Egbert  | 0      | 0   | 0    | 0       | 0      |

**a.** At the beginning of the semester, were there any cliques apparent? At the end? If there are cliques, what implications are there as far as the hypothesis is concerned?

**b.** What person(s) lost one or more "friends" by the end of the semester?

**c.** On the "after" matrix, who (if anyone) is the star? Who are the mutual choices? The chains? The isolates?

**d.** Which children have made the most improvement? The least?

**e.** If Delbert should run into any trouble, who might the teacher ask to help him?

**f.** Suppose the investigator concludes that the introduction of the unit was responsible for the changes in group structure. Is this conclusion justified? Why or why not?

**4.** In a study of personality change after placement in a special "problem" class, an investigator developed a $Q$ sort of 10 items (the small number is for illustration only) to be placed into 5 piles (again, the small number is for illustration only) in the following manner:

| Most Applicable | | | | Least Applicable |
|---|---|---|---|---|
| Score | 4 | 3 | 2 | 1 | 0 |
| No. to be placed in each pile | 1 | 2 | 4 | 2 | 1 |

Suppose that Frank, a student in the special class, sorts the 10 items as instructed, once before he enters the class and once at the end of the year. The items and the scores are given below:

| Item | Before | After |
|---|---|---|
| 1. I like my mother. | 1 | 2 |
| 2. I like my father. | 0 | 1 |
| 3. I like myself. | 4 | 2 |
| 4. I like my teacher. | 2 | 2 |
| 5. I like my brother. | 3 | 3 |
| 6. I like my friends. | 1 | 4 |
| 7. I like my uncle. | 3 | 3 |
| 8. I like my pet. | 2 | 1 |
| 9. I like my neighbor. | 2 | 2 |
| 10. I like the school principal. | 2 | 0 |

**a.** The correlation between the "before" and "after" scores is $+0.17$. What does this mean?

**b.** Using the 10 items above, complete the $Q$ sort by sorting on the basis of how you actually feel and then on the basis of how you would like to feel. Interpret the findings.

**5.** Complete the semanti differential for the concept "school" on page 297. What do your scores mean? What frame of reference were you using when you completed the form?

**6.** Compute $D$ indexes between your scores on the semantic differential and those of four other classmates or friends. Interpret your findings.

**7.** Take a picture from a popular magazine that shows a family doing something together. Have two or three children describe the kind of family that the picture shows. Develop some method of scoring (coding and quantifying) the responses. How reliable are the responses to this one picture? What other kinds of pictures would you recommend using, if any? Why?

**8.** Describe how you would analyze the words to three of the best-selling popular songs to determine current sttitudes toward "life." Conduct this analysis and compare your findings with those presented by other students.

Go through the six steps (specification of objectives to standardizing the coding procedure) described in this chapter. Suggest alternative ways of studying student attitudes other than the use of song lyrics. Which approach is the most defensible? Why? Might it be better simply to ask students what their attitudes are?

## Selected Supplementary Readings

1. The most comprehensive reviews of projective techniques are described in Buros, Oscar Krisen, ed. *The Mental Measurement Yearbooks*. Highland Park, N.J.: Gryphon Press.

2. CAMPBELL, DONALD T. "The Indirect Assessment of Social Attitudes." *Psychological Bulletin*, 47, no. 1 (1950), pp. 15–38. Campbell emphasizes disguised–structured tests of social attitudes and provides an excellent survey of research findings that use these techniques. Also, see Lindzey, Gardner. "On the Classification of Projective Techniques." *Psychological Bulletin*, 56, no. 2 (1959), pp. 158–168. Lindzey describes a number of classification systems for projective techniques.

3. Perhaps the most comprehensive study of content analysis has been done by Lasswell, Harold D.; Leites, Nathan; and associates. *Language of Politics: Studies in Quantitative Semantics*. Cambridge, Mass.: M.I.T. Press, 1965. See also Berelson, Bernard. *Content Analysis in Communication Research* (New York: Free Press of Glencoe, 1952). A shorter version of Berelson's text appears as Chapter 13 of Lindzey, Gardner, ed. *Handbook of Social Psychology*, Vol. I. Cambridge, Mass.: Addison-Wesley Publishing Co., 1954, pp. 488–522. See also Holsti, Ole R. "Content Analysis." Chapter 16 in Gardner Lindzey and Eliot Aranson, eds., *The Handbook of Social Psychology*, 2d ed., Vol. 2, *Research Methods*. Reading, Mass.: Addison-Wesley Publishing Co., 1968, pp. 596–692.

4. CHUN, KI-TAEK; COBB, SIDNEY; and FRENCH, JOHN R. P., JR. *Measures for Psychological Assessment: A Guide to 3000 Original Sources and Their Applications*. Ann Arbor, Mich.: Institute for Social Research, University of Michigan, 1975, 664 pp. This volume contains a comprehensive list of personality and mental health tests that have been cited in psychology and sociology journals from 1960 to 1970. It contains an author index, descriptor index, approximately 3000 references to journal articles, and an extensive list of instances in which the tests have been used.

   Another excellent source of tests has been published by Robinson, John P., and Shaver, Phillip R. *Measures of Social Psychological Attitudes*, Rev. ed. Ann Arbor, Mich.: Institute for Social Research, University of Michigan, 1973, 751 pp. This source contains approximately 125 tests including sample items and their descriptions, normative data, evidence of reliability and validity, publication dates, modes of administration, results and comments, and references. It includes chapters on measures of self-esteem, locus of control, observation, authoritarianism, sociopolitical attitudes, values, attitudes toward people, religious attitudes, and methodological scales. Each chapter contains a review of measurement and research problems. See also Miller, Delbert C. *Handbook of Research Design and Social Measurement*, Part 2. New York: David McKay Co., 1964, pp. 97–327. Miller provides a very readable description of published scales designed to measure social status, group structure and dynamics, morale, social participation, leadership, attitudes, family and marriage, and personality. See also Shaw, Marvin E., and Wright, Jack M. *Scales for the Measurement of Attitudes*. New York: McGraw-Hill Book Co., 1967.

5. For a general work on sociometry see Moreno, J. L. *Who Shall Survive? Foundations of Sociometry, Group Psychotherapy, and Sociodrama*. New York: Beacon House, 1953. A reasonably comprehensive description of index analysis and statistical analysis of sociometric data can be found in Proctor, Charles H., and Loomis, Charles P. "Analysis of Sociometric Data." Chapter 17 in Marie Jahoda, Morton Deutsch, and Stuart W. Cook, eds., *Research Methods in Social Relations*, Part 2, *Selected Techniques*. New York: Dryden Press, 1951, pp. 561–585.

6. The semantic differential has been described in greatest detail in Osgood, Charles E.; Suci, George J.; and Tannenbaum, Percy H. *The Measurement of Meaning*. Urbana: University of Illinois Press, 1957, 342 pp. The distance (*D*) index has been described in this book as well as in an article by Osgood, Charles E., and Suci, George J. "A Measure of Relation Determined by Both Mean Difference and Profile Information." *Psychological Bulletin*, 49, no. 3 (1952), pp. 197–237. See also Osgood, Charles E.; May, William H.; and Miron, Murray S. *Cross-Cultural Universals of Affective Meaning*. Champaign: University of Illinois Press, 1975, 486 pp.

7. Descriptions of *Q* methodology can be found in Stephenson, William. *The Study of Behavior: Q Technique and Its Methodology*. Chicago: University of Chicago Press, 1953, 376 pp. A more current evaluation of *Q* methodology has been presented by Wittenborn, J. R. "Contributions and Current Status of *Q* Methodology." *Psychological Bulletin*, 58, no. 2 (1961), pp. 132–142. An article by Guilford discusses some of the difficulties involved in finding an index of correlation for use in *Q* factor analysis when scores are dichotomized. See Guilford, J. P. "Preparation of Item Scores for the Correlations between Persons in a *Q* Factor Analysis." *Educational and Psychological Measurement*, 23, no. 1 (1963), pp. 13–22.

data
processing

Data processing includes those procedures used to convert raw information into a form capable of being interpreted. Sometimes this conversion involves taking test scores, questionnaire responses, etc., and transforming them into measures of central tendency, variability, or computing statistical tests of significance such as $F$ ratios or chi squares.

Whether the purpose of data analysis is to describe samples or to test hypotheses, it is essential that the researcher be familiar with modern data processing methods. This chapter is concerned with the principles and methods used in processing data.

## Planning for Data Processing

Because of the time and effort expended in collecting and analyzing data, some thought should be given to planning for data analysis during the initial stages of an investigation. Too often these considerations are delayed

313

until the researcher has already collected data. Judicious and early planning can prevent costly mistakes later.

The importance of planning for data analysis can be demonstrated by an example of a poorly designed study. The hypothesis was, "Subjects who are randomly assigned to an experimental and control group will differ significantly ($p < 0.05$) on a standardized reading test as a result of the experimental treatment." The investigator listed all students alphabetically along with their ages (in years and months such as 11-6, 10-9, etc.), sex, IQ, and grade levels (5, 6, or 7). A $t$-test for nonmatched groups was planned to compare experimental and control $Ss$ at the completion of the study.

The difficulty was that $E$ had copied pages of information of little or no relevance to the study. Any datum that cannot be used should not be collected, and conversely, data that are collected should have a reasonable chance of being useful. For example, if a $t$-test will be used to compare the means of two groups, what purpose will be served by knowing sex, age, IQ, and grade level?

If $E$ were interested in the interactions between methods and sex, age, IQ, and grade levels, a $t$-test would be inappropriate, and an ANOVA or ANCOVA should have been considered. However, with two methods, two sexes, three age levels, three IQ levels, and three grades, $E$ would have a $2 \times 2 \times 3 \times 3 \times 3$ design involving 108 *cells*. Obviously, 70 cases simply won't do. Either $E$ will have to consider obtaining a larger $N$ or some of the variables will have to be eliminated. Because chronological age and grade levels would be expected to correlate highly with one another, one of those variables could easily be dropped.

Data analysis is not independent of design considerations. The way data are gathered depends on the type of information one wants, and in turn, $E$'s desire for knowledge may have to be tempered by practical constraints. Unfortunately, if considerations of experimental design are delayed until after data are collected, $E$ may be forced to disregard the most effective and appropriate design because the required data were not obtained.

# DATA PROCESSING FORMS AND RECORDS

This section will describe criteria for evaluating record forms used for data collection.

*1. Accuracy.* One of the most important requirements for a record form is that there be sufficient room for recording information and preventing overcrowded confusion. On tables, all columns and rows should be clearly labeled.

2. *Completeness.* The form should provide room for all necessary and relevant information. This means that the investigator has to decide on the relevancy of data before they are collected. If uncertain, the investigator would probably be better off gathering more information than failing to gather data that may prove essential later on.

3. *Simplicity.* Other conditions being equal, simpler record forms are preferable to more complex ones. Little is gained by planning to use an electronic computer to calculate a simple mean or to use a desk calculator to determine multiple intercorrelations of tests.

4. *Speed.* Forms vary considerably in the speed with which data can be collected and processed. When it is possible, using the same form for data collection as for data analysis can reduce errors and avoid transcription of data obtained from one format to another for data processing.

5. *Cost.* The cost of record forms for data collection and analysis represents a substantial proportion of the funds expended for many research projects. By judicious planning, it is possible to conserve funds for other purposes. This means that costs should be estimated for various kinds of records and analysis procedures. In some cases, it may be worthwhile to incur high data processing costs if gains can be made in accuracy and speed.

6. *Availability.* Some equipment and materials for data analysis are readily available, and others may be located only at specialized centers. Since data processing costs and services vary considerably, estimates should be obtained from various sources.

Many different types of forms and records are available commercially. This text will describe only those having the greatest applicability and usefulness.

*Use of Machine-Scoring Answer Sheets.* Having $S$s mark their answers directly on test booklets is generally not recommended if it is possible to use separate answer sheets. Test booklets are expensive, especially if item analyses are needed. With separate answer sheets, test booklets can be reused, and research costs reduced considerably. Flipping through innumerable pages and counting errors takes time and encourages clerical mistakes. If all answers are located on a single sheet, scoring can be rapid and accurate. Children below the fourth grade, however, do experience difficulties in using separate answer sheets.

Most answer sheets contain space for 150 five-option items or 300 true–false questions[1] (see Figure 13-1). $S$s are usually instructed to mark their answers by blackening the space on the answer sheet that represents their desired response.

---

[1] Some machine-scoring answer sheets include those with room for answers on the reverse side. Others are available that provide room for 15 options for each of 50 items on each side of the page.

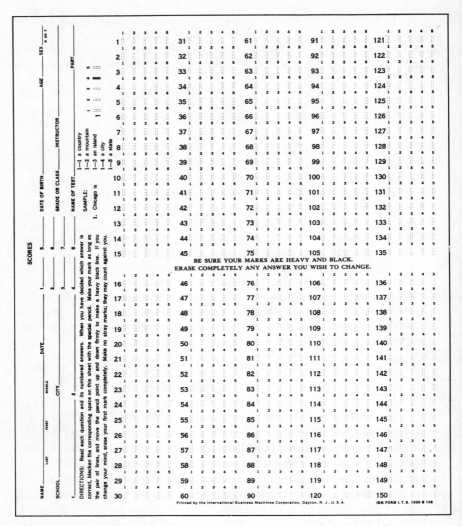

**Figure 13-1**
AN IBM ANSWER SHEET.

Answer sheets can be scored by machine or by hand. Hand-scoring is feasible if: 1) the number of papers to be scored is small; 2) there are not too many items; 3) item weighting is not contemplated; 4) a correction formula will not be applied; and 5) an item analysis is not needed. Perhaps the simplest way to way to hand-score answer sheets is to prepare a master stencil (a light cardboard stencil can be purchased from IBM) by punching holes corresponding to the positions of the correct choices. If the stencil is placed

316

over the answer sheet, the correct answers will appear through the stencil as black marks.

Test-scoring machines are of two types. The older type requires the use of answer sheets marked with an electrographic pencil; it operates by having electrodes come in contact with the graphite marks made by the pencil. Answer sheets are hand-fed into the machine one at a time, and scores are indicated on a dial. These machines are slow and errors in reading the dial are rather common.

Another type of machine-scoring system was developed by E. F. Lindquist at the Measurement Research Center, State University of Iowa. The services of the center are made available to the public, and profits are devoted exclusively to educational research at the State University of Iowa. According to Lindquist,[2] the system is capable of the following activities:

The machine accepts a stack of about 2,000 answer sheets at a time, and then automatically:

*1.* Passes the the sheets under its photoelectric "eyes" at the rate of 100 answer sheets per minute

*2.* Senses the marks on both sides of the sheet by means of light transmitted through the sheet

*3.* Compares the marks made by the examinee with the right answer key which has been stored in its "memory" (if desired, the same marks may be scored by different keys simultaneously)

*4.* Counts (at the rate of 10,000 per second) the number of right answers to each of as many as fourteen different tests on each answer sheet, or adds the weights for the right answers if weighted scoring is desired

*5.* Exercises its "judgment" while counting to ignore bad erasures and disallow multiple marks, thus eliminating the need for a preliminary visual scanning of the answer sheets

*6.* Converts each of the raw scores to one or more scaled scores according to conversion tables which it has previously memorized

*7.* Computes as many as four *weighted* composites of various combinations of scores on each answer sheet

*8.* If necessary, in turn converts these composite scores to scaled scores comparable to the subtest scaled scores

*9.* Reads the examinee's name from each answer sheet

*10.* Writes (types) the examinee's name, scaled scores, and composites on a multiple-carbon continuous report form

*11.* Notes, and records opposite each examinee's name, whether or not he has attempted all of the tests in the battery

[2]E. F. Lindquist, "The Iowa Electronic Test Processing Equipment," *Testing Today* (Boston: Houghton Mifflin Co., First Issue), pp. 2–3.

*12.* Notes, and records after each examinee's name, whether or not the answer sheet was in perfect registration and all sensing circuits were performing properly, during the scoring of that particular sheet

*13.* Punches all of this information about each examinee in an electronic accounting machine card which may be fed to other "brains" for subsequent processing if desired.

Clearly, large projects should find great savings in time and efficiency by making use of "optical scanning" machine-scoring systems. For smaller, less ambitious projects, the investigator can hand-score regular answer sheets or develop homemade answer sheets which can be mimeographed for hand-scoring. The slant key on the typewriter can be used for making answer spaces (see Figure 13-2).

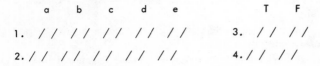

**Figure 13-2**
A HOMEMADE ANSWER SHEET.

*Use of Edge-Marked Cards.* If the amount of data to be recorded is relatively small, the student might consider the use of edge-marked cards. These cards are available commercially[3] or can easily be prepared by using mimeograph equipment. Cards of any size can be used, although three-by-five-inch cards are most common. An example of a homemade card is shown in Figure 13-3.

An advantage of the edge-marked card is that it facilitates sorting and collating. Each numbered space on the edge of the card is allotted only one type of information, such as sex, grade level, or IQ. For example, a 0 or 1 on the first line could be used to indicate respondent's sex. To sort cards into two groups by sex requires very little time. According to one investigator,[4] an unskilled clerical worker can sort 1000 cards into six piles in less than five minutes.

Edge-marked cards are of greatest value for sorting a relatively small number of variables; they are inefficient for recording larger amounts of data. If numbers or scores have to be combined to compute means or other

[3]The Psychological Corporation, 757 Third Ave., New York, N.Y. 10017, carries the Thurstone Edge-Marking Cards. They are five-by-eight inches and have 65 blank spaces on each side plus additional spaces in the center of the card for written comments.

[4]Mildred Parten, *Surveys, Polls, and Samples* (New York: Harper & Row, 1950), p. 463.

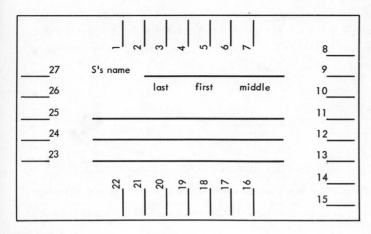

**Figure 13-3**
AN EDGE-MARKED CARD.

statistics, the edge-marked card is *not* recommended. It takes too long to sum numbers that appear on different cards.

*Use of Edge-Punched Cards.* The edge-punched card represents an elaborate modification of the edge-marked card. Instead of *marking* each numbered space, data are recorded by notching holes located around the perimeter of the card. For example, hole number 5 could be notched if S is in the experimental group or unnotched if S is in the control group. To separate experimental from control Ss, pass a needle through hole number 5 and lift the cards. All notched cards will drop, leaving the control group's cards on the needle. An example of an edge-punched card is shown in Figure 13-4 on page 320.

Some cards have single rows of holes; others have two or more rows, depending upon the amount and complexity of information to be recorded. Alphabetic information can be typed in the center of the card if desired.

Numbers can also be recorded with edge-punched cards. For example, some holes are numbered 1, 2, 4, and 7. By punching the 1 and 2 holes, a 3 can be recorded; $1 + 4 = 5$; $4 + 2 = 6$; $1 + 7 = 8$; etc. By reserving some of the 1, 2, 4, and 7 holes for *tens, hundreds,* or *thousands,* numbers of any size can be recorded, although there are always practical limitations.

Sorting with edge-punched cards is extremely rapid, although it does take time to punch the holes. However, for a large amount of sorting and for determining frequencies, the edge-punched card can be highly recommended.

*Use of Mark-Sense Cards.* The mark-sense card is designed to be used with electronic data processing equipment. However, instead of holes

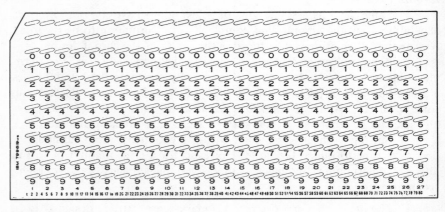

SAN FRANCISCO UNIFIED SCHOOL DISTRICT
JOHN A. O'CONNELL VOCATIONAL HIGH SCHOOL & TECHNICAL INSTITUTE

PERIOD | SEMESTER | CLASS | PREFIX | HUND | TENS | UNITS | ALPHABETIC CODE
SEMESTER
SPR/FALL/SUM 19

CHECK INDICATES IMPROVEMENT IS NEEDED  1 2 3 F  NAME, ADDRESS, TELEPHONE  ALPHA CODE
1 CAPABLE OF DOING BETTER WORK
2 REQUIRED WORK LATE OR INCOMPLETE
3 TOO MANY ABSENCES
4 CREATES A DISTURBANCE IN CLASS
5 WORK POORLY PREPARED
6 TESTS WERE UNSATISFACTORY
7 FAILURE TO FOLLOW DIRECTIONS

SUBJECT REPORT CARD
REPORT PERIOD  1  2  3  F
SUBJECT GRADE
CITIZENSHIP GRADE
NO. TIMES ABSENT
NO. TIMES TARDY

SHOP HOURS  1  2  3  F

SUBJECT
TEACHER
REMARKS
MAJOR CODE
ROOM
PERIOD
DOB

PARENTS ARE INVITED TO DISCUSS THE STUDENT'S PROGRESS IN THIS SCHOOL

INSTRUCTOR | ROOM | FLOOR | HONORS

*Source:* Permission by Indecks, Arlington, Vermont 05250, to reproduce the card shown in Figure 13-4 is gratefully acknowledged.

**Figure 13-4**
AN EDGE-PUNCHED CARD.

being punched on an electronic data processing card (EDP), information is entered on mark-sense cards by means of an electrographic pencil. Later, these marks can be "read" and automatically punched onto regular EDP cards without the intervention of a human operator. An example of a mark-sense card is shown in Figure 13-5.

The principal advantage of the mark-sense card is that it allows data to be obtained directly from $Ss$, much in the same way that one can gather data from an EDP answer sheet. The cards are then taken to a reproducing punch, a machine designed to reproduce punched cards from a variety of different sources including electrographic pencil marks. Once the data are on

**Figure 13-5**
MARK-SENSE CARD.

320

punched cards, they can be fed directly into an electronic computer for analysis.

The disadvantages of mark-sense cards are: 1) some cards may have to be specially printed, increasing costs substantially; 2) they are inappropriate for young children; and 3) they may be an inefficient means of recording data if, for example, information has to be transcribed from one source to a mark-sense card (it might be more efficient and ultimately less costly to record information by hand and punch it on cards later for electronic data processing).

*Use of Punched Cards for Electronic Data Processing.* The most rapid way of analyzing a large volume of data is to use electronic data processing equipment. The recording of information is accomplished by using a variety of *input–ouput* devices, including punched cards, punched paper tape, magnetic tape, magnetic ink characters, and optically readable characters (see Figure 13-6). For research purposes, the punched card is most often used to record data. Once information is recorded, it can be transferred to magnetic tape for high-speed processing, or the cards themselves may be fed directly into the computer for data analysis.

The standard EDP card (see Figure 13-7) is divided into 80 columns and 12 rows. Ten of the rows are numbered (0, 1, 2, 3, . . . , 9), and two are unnumbered. The unnumbered rows (rows 11 and 12) are called *zone punches* and are located above the row marked zero; they are used for recording minus and plus signs, respectively. These two rows are also used for recording alphabetic information.

Data are entered on cards by using a card punch, a machine resembling a typewriter. As each key is depressed, a rectangular hole is punched in an appropriate spot on the card. An experienced key punch operator can punch about 150 cards per hour.

Reading the punches on an EDP card is not difficult. Numerals are entered in each column by punching a hole in one of the numbered rows (0, 1, 2, . . . , 9). Only one number can be represented in any column. Alphabetic characters require two punches in each column. One of these punches has to be in the zero row, the minus row (one row above the zero), or the plus row (two rows above the zero); the other punch is represented by a digit. All letters from *A* through *I* are represented by a plus punch, *J* through *R* by a minus punch, and *S* through *Z* by a punch in the zero row. The letter *A* is punched automatically by depressing the *A* key of a card punch; when this is done, holes appear in the plus and 1 rows in a single column. *B* appears as a punch in the plus and 2 rows; an *I* is formed with a punch in the plus and 9 rows. In the same manner, other letters can be formed. The letter *J* is represented by holes in the minus and 1 rows, *S* by holes in the zero and 2 rows.

To facilitate card reading, a card punch can automatically print

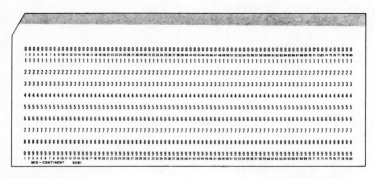

**IBM Card**

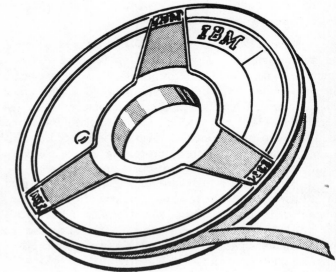

**Magnetic Tape**

**Paper Tape**

| Enter partial payment below | MUNICIPAL WATER WORKS | | | |
|---|---|---|---|---|
| | Account Number | Gross Amount | Net Amount | Last Day To Pay Net |
| | RL 45332 | 56 01 | 45 98 | 4 31 62 |
| | DISCOUNT TERMS 10 DAYS | | | |
| | Present Reading | Previous Reading | Consumption Gals | E D JONES |
| | 3255886 | 2369014 | 897 | 745 CHESTNUT ST ANYTOWN USA |
| | PLEASE RETURN THIS WITH YOUR PAYMENT | | | |

**Optically Readable Characters**

**Figure 13-6**
TYPES OF DATA RECORDING MEDIA.

322

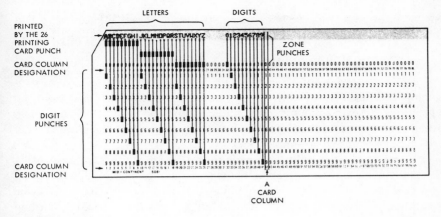

**Figure 13-7**
STANDARD EDP CARD AND CODE.

each character punched onto the card as has been done in Figure 13-7. Each printed character appears above its punched counterpart. If desired, colored cards can be used to identify or classify special groups. Cards are notched in one corner so that any card that must be kept separate can be located quickly simply by placing it backwards in a deck. It cannot, of course, be left that way for data processing.

The punched card is a highly efficient device for recording and analyzing data. Although card punching is relatively slow, data analysis is so rapid and accuracy so high that, at least for a large volume of data, card punching is usually only a minor problem. Other considerations, such as finding appropriate *programs* (i.e., machine instructions) and developing efficient coding procedures, take more time than running the data through the computer. Electronic computers will be examined in greater detail later in this chapter.

## COMPUTATIONAL AIDS

Prior to the development of the electronic computer, a number of devices had been designed to perform arithmetic operations rapidly and economically. Some of these devices have been used successfully for centuries. The abacus, for example, antedates Christ and is still currently used in many parts of the world. As an example of how effectively an abacus can be used, a contest was held in Japan in 1946 between an American Army private using a desk calculator and a Japanese clerk using an abacus. Although this was

323

hardly an example of a well-designed experiment, it was interesting to find the abacus superior to the calculator.[5]

## "Mental" Computations

Fortunately, not all computations are so complex or so time-consuming that mechanical aids become necessary. Much data processing in educational research requires only simple arithmetic easily performed with pencil and paper. Little is gained by using excessively complicated data processing systems when simpler ones will do.

Certainly, the ability to handle simple arithmetic skills differs widely. Few individuals can hope to emulate the performance of Mr. William Klein, who reportedly memorized the multiplication tables up to $100 \times 100$, the logarithms of all numbers up to 100, and all squares up to 1000. According to the same source, Mr. Klein was able to multiply $1,388,978,361 \times 5,645,418,496$ completely in his head in 64 seconds![6]

Many simple statistical computations can be performed economically by using pencil and paper. Means, standard deviations, and correlations can be computed using raw scores, but it is often much simpler to use shortcut methods that make use of arbitrary origins. If the amount of data is not large and if only a few statistics must be computed, pencil-and-paper methods work quite well. All computations should, of course, be double-checked.

## Tables and Nomographs

Should it become necessary to perform a large number of computations by hand, tables and nomographs can be used. The most commonly used tables are those involving squares, square roots, reciprocals, and logarithms. These tables can be found in most elementary statistics textbooks and can save the investigator much time and effort. In most cases, it is probably faster and more economical to perform a single numerical operation for a series of problems than to work through each problem separately. For example, if one has a number of $F$ ratios to compute, the squares could be computed at the same time.

The nomograph is another useful computational aid.[7] Instead of presenting data in tabular form, the nomograph makes use of curves or lines showing the relationship between two or more variables. If there is a single independent variable, the nomograph takes the form of a line with the independent variable on one side and the dependent variable on the other. Figure 13-8 is a nomograph for estimating the split-half reliability by

[5]Edmund Callis Berkeley, *Giant Brains or Machines That Think* (New York: John Wiley & Sons, 1949), p. 19.

[6]B. V. Bowden, "Thought and Machine Processes," in B. V. Bowden, ed., *Faster Than Thought* (London: Sir Isaac Pitman & Sons, 1953), pp. 312–313.

[7]The nomograph is sometimes called an *abac*, or an *alignment chart*.

*Source:* Edward E. Cureton and Jack W. Dunlap, "A Nomograph for Estimating a Reliability Coefficient by the Spearman–Brown Formula and for Computing Its Probable Error," *Journal of Educational Psychology,* 21, no. 1 (1930), pp. 68–69.

**Figure 13-8**
NOMOGRAPH FOR ESTIMATING A RELIABILITY COEFFICIENT BY THE SPEARMAN–BROWN FORMULA.

means of the Spearman–Brown formula (see Chapter 9). If, for example, the correlation between the halves is 0.40, the reliability of the examination as a whole would be approximately 0.57.

Even though intermediate values may have to be determined by interpolation, the nomograph is a convenient computational device unless extreme accuracy is required. In that case, tabular entries will be more exact.

## Electronic Desk Calculators

Electronic calculators have made the older mechanical models obsolete. Although there are many different kinds of electronic desk calculators, most have the following features:

*1.* They are small and portable; many can operate on rechargeable batteries or house current.

*2.* They can perform all basic arithmetic operations; some specialized models can compute means, standard deviations, correlations, regression equations, *t*-tests; determine areas under any part of the normal curve; store partial answers in "memory banks" for later computations; and can be programmed to repeat hundreds of sequential arithmetic operations.

*3.* Answers are displayed electronically on registers or on printed tapes.

*4.* They are less expensive than comparable electromechanical models and can process data much more rapidly.

Electronic calculators vary widely in the functions they can perform. The decimal point is usually automatic and in some models can be set for any number of places to a maximum of 9. Some can provide $N$, $\sum X$, and $\sum X^2$ automatically, and partial answers can be stored in memory for future recall.

Calculators especially designed for statistics can compute means and standard deviations, correlations, *t*-tests, etc. Most are able to extract any root and to raise a number to any reasonable power; some calculators even permit use of brackets and parentheses. Perhaps the most important feature, however, involves programming ability. By working out one problem, some calculators "remember" each step and simply substitute new values when entered by the operator. This permits the automatic calculation of most statistical problems.

The price of electronic calculators is much lower than the older electromechanical models that had few of their features or conveniences. Some calculators are available that are automatically programmed by using prepunched cards to control machine operations. Essentially, all the operator has to do is enter data.

Electronic desk calculators do have limitations. The number of storage locations, for example, is limited and may not be sufficient for the researcher who needs to store a good deal of information for later retrieval. Also, errors made by the operator in entering data may not be detected unless there is a printout of all entered data available. Printing calculators can resolve that problem but they tend to be rather slow. Most calculators also require the operator to repunch entry data if the instrument is turned off. With a large amount of data that will be entered at different times, this can be a very time-consuming process.

## THE USE OF ELECTRONIC COMPUTERS

Considering that the first electronic computer was developed in 1946, it is difficult to realize the impact it has had on research within such a short period of time. Many school districts, colleges, and universities now have their own computers or share computer time with each other to reduce costs.

### Advantages of Electronic Computers

The three advantages of electronic computers are speed, accuracy, and economy. As long as computational speeds are determined by the rotation of gears or the need to press keys for each entry, computation is bound to be slow.

Two factors account for the speed of electronic computers—the use of transistors and binary arithmetic. Instead of working with ten digits, modern computers use only the numbers 1 and 0. Thus, vacuum tubes or transistors are either on or off. With the use of only two numerals, computational time can be reduced.

Accuracy is a second advantage of using electronic computers. Not only is the computer a tireless worker, but it also can provide checks on its own procedures which can be built into machine programs. For example, the sum of squares, $\sum (X - \bar{X})^2$, must always be a positive number. If the answer is not positive, the machine can be programmed to indicate the error. Even unorthodox instructions to the machine can be read by the computer as errors and the human operator so informed.

Machines that can work rapidly and accurately are bound to save expenses in the long run. What formerly required as much as a week's time for pencil-and-paper calculation can now be accomplished in less than a second on an electronic computer.[8]

[8]W. J. Eckert and Rebecca Jones, *Faster, Faster* (New York: McGraw-Hill Book Co., 1955), p. 2.

## Noncomputational Uses of Computers

The advent of the modern high-speed electronic computer has opened vast opportunities in educational research. In many schools and colleges, computers are now handling problems previously performed by faculty, attendance officers, registrars, librarians, and clerks; they have been used in building school plants, in working out student assignments, in counseling and guidance programs, and in educational testing.

One of the most exciting areas of research involves *computer simulation*. Instead of actually performing an experiment, for example, the investigator programs the computer to *simulate* an experiment and predict results. Much in the same way that a model airplane represents a real one or a globe represents some aspects of the real world, so is it possible to develop models to represent more complex events, structures, or objects. The model can then be used to simulate whatever behavior is of concern to the investigator.

The computer program is a type of model that consists of a series of instructions "understood" by the machine. These instructions are written to correspond to whatever hypotheses $E$ wishes to investigate. For example, the computer can be programmed to act as a chess player, a business corporation, a student, a classroom, or a school district, in accordance with rules stipulated by the programmer. These rules tell the computer what it can and cannot do. In simulating a chess game, the machine can be instructed to perform no operation that may endanger the king; in simulating a learning situation, the computer can be taught to respond in much the same way as a human subject. The programmer can then compare the behavior of the machine with the actual performance of the subject, and the program can be modified and remodified until there is a closer correspondence between the two. Once this is accomplished, the computer can be used to predict human behavior.

Another use of computers is for data retrieval. For example, the CIJE (*Current Index to Journals in Education*) contains monthly listings of annotated journal articles along with a retrieval number. By using a key word thesaurus, a list of relevant terms can be compiled that will enable the computer to search through its storage to locate those articles having some bearing on the topic of interest. Although the investigator could examine each issue of CIJE for relevant listings, the computer can do so much more rapidly and efficiently. The ERIC system (Educational Resources Information Centers, see Chapter 3) can be searched by computer to locate information of interest to the user. University Microfilms at Ann Arbor, Michigan can locate titles of many doctoral dissertations written after 1938. The system is known as DATRIX (Direct Access to Reference Information).

# TYPES OF ELECTRONIC COMPUTERS[9]

Electronic computers are either analog or digital. An analog computer represents numbers by using physical analogies. For example, a yardstick may be used to perform simple calculations by converting various numbers into lengths. Lengths can, thus, be used as analogs of numbers. To perform the operation 12 + 5, place a ruler with its left edge on the yardstick's numeral 12 and move +5 units (inches) to the right. Other types of simple analog instruments include slide rules, clocks that measure time by the movement of their hands, and thermometers that represent temperatures by the height of a column of mercury.

In contrast to analog computers, digital computers work directly with binary numbers. They are much more accurate and flexible than analog computers and, thus, are used more often for computations.

## Forerunners of the Modern Digital Computer

One of the most fascinating stories concerns the attempt to produce machines that could process symbols, arithmetic or otherwise. It is difficult to say where the story began. Probably, the first digital "computers" were human fingers, which could be used for simple counting. Efficiency was most likely low because there were no means for "storing" or retaining partial solutions except in one's own memory. The use of pencil and paper represented tremendous advantages as far as storing information was concerned.

The first mechanical calculator was developed by Blaise Pascal in 1642. It consisted of a series of gears that could be turned with a hand crank. As each gear was moved one-tenth of a turn, a number from zero to nine was displayed above the gear. When the units crank was turned one complete revolution, a one would appear in the tens column and a zero in the units column.

The nineteenth century produced machines that more closely approximated modern computers. In 1801, Joseph Marie Jacquard was able to produce various patterns and colors of yarn in a weaving machine controlled by punched cards. Similar types of punched cards were later used to program electronic computers.

Another nineteenth-century contribution was the work of Herman Hollerith, who was hired by the United States government to collect and analyze data for the 1890 census. Knowing that it had taken over seven years

---

[9]Although *calculators* are limited to processing arithmetic symbols, *computers* are able to process many different kinds of symbols, including arithmetic calculations. See Allan B. Ellis, *The Use and Misuse of Computers in Education* (New York: McGraw-Hill Book Co., 1974), pp. 8–11.

to analyze the data from the 1880 census, Hollerith realized the need for more efficient ways of processing data. He resolved his problem by using three-by-five-inch punched cards divided into 240 squares. Each square contained only one bit of information that could be "read" and stored by an electro-mechanical machine.

Jacquard's work was known to Charles Babbage, who became interested in computing machines in 1812. The first machine he built was called a Difference Engine; it was designed especially to compute polynomials, which it could do to an accuracy of six decimal places. Not satisfied with this achievement, Babbage tried to build a larger Difference Engine, which would be accurate to twenty places. Unfortunately, it was impossible to engineer the parts, and the project was dropped in 1842.

In 1833, Babbage conceived of the Analytic Engine, which, at least in theory, could perform any numerical operation. Babbage realized the advantages of using punched cards for programming his Engine. The Analytic Engine was designed to operate on its own once it was programmed to do so, and could, much like a modern computer, vary its course of action in accordance with instructions. Babbage died in 1871 without completing the Analytic Engine. It was not until the 1940s that his works were rediscovered and found to anticipate many of the problems faced by developers of the modern electronic digital computer.

## Mark I

The Mark I was made operational at Harvard University in 1944, largely as a result of the work of Howard H. Aiken, who, interestingly enough, first learned of Babbage's work when his own was almost completed.[10] Seven years earlier, in 1937, Aiken was working on his doctoral dissertation in physics, which required the solution of a large number of complex equations. With the help of IBM engineers, he developed the first automatic digital computer. However, it was electromechanical and not electronic. Punched paper tape was used to feed instructions into the machine in a way analogous to the use of paper rolls to control player pianos. Because there were many moving parts, the Mark I required a great amount of computing time compared with present-day computers.

## ENIAC

ENIAC (Electronic Numerical Integrator and Calculator) was largely the product of a physicist, John Mauchly, and an engineer, J. R. Eckert, both of the Moore School of Electrical Engineering at the University

---

[10]Ellis, pp. 16–17, has pointed out the common historical error of attributing Aiken's success to Babbage's earlier attempts to contruct the Analytic Engine.

of Pennsylvania. Work was begun on ENIAC in 1943, one year before Mark I was completed. It was designed to help compute artillery firing tables for the Army but was not put into operation until 1946, after World War II had ended.

ENIAC was the first electronic digital computer. Instead of using relatively slow relays as did Mark I, ENIAC made use of vacuum tubes having no movable parts. Although much faster than Mark I, ENIAC required a large amount of time to change electrical connections in preparation for feeding new problems into the computer.

## Whirlwind I

Whirlwind I was developed at the Massachusetts Institute of Technology and was made operational in 1951; it was the first large machine to use *magnetic cores* for storing data. The use of cores increased the speed with which information could be located in the computer and processed.

Whirlwind I was also the first computer to incorporate *marginal checking*, by which various operations of the computer could be checked for reliability to reduce costly machine errors.

## ILLIAC

The University of Illinois was the first university to provide a computer for general research purposes. ILLIAC (University of Illinois Automatic Computer) was made operational in 1952, at the Digital Computer Laboratory.

ILLIAC did much more than provide computer time for faculty members at the University of Illinois. In the early 1950s, ILLIAC was in use such a small proportion of the time that faculty members from other universities were able to use the facilities at Illinois. Their experiences generally were so favorable that considerable pressure was placed on their institutions to provide computer facilities. These facilities eventually spread into every major university.

# "MODERN" COMPUTERS

In a field changing as rapidly as electronics, it is always dangerous to describe what is "modern." In a period of only a few years, numerous computers have been replaced by faster, larger, and more efficient machines. Probably, the major changes that will occur in the next few years will include more efficient programming techniques and more efficient methods for getting data into and out of the computer. Vocal and written programming instructions are likely to develop to the point where they can be used routinely.

## Computer Components

Modern computers contain five elements or components: an *input* system, *storage* or *"memory,"* a *control* system, an *arithmetic* unit, and an *output* system. Although each of these components varies from one machine to another, they all are sufficiently similar to warrant describing them in general terms. The components of an electronic digital computer can be seen in Figure 13-9.

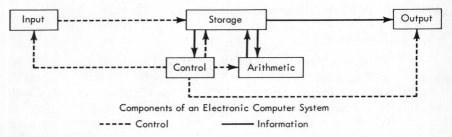

Components of an Electronic Computer System

----- Control ———— Information

**Figure 13-9**
COMPONENTS OF AN ELECTRONIC COMPUTER SYSTEM.

*Input.* The input system of an electronic computer is designed to take information from an external source so that it can be processed by the computer. The computer uses input data for two different purposes: 1) as a means of programming or controlling the operation of the equipment, and 2) as a means of feeding data into the computer for processing.

Various media have been used to enter data into the computer, but the most common are punched cards and magnetic tape. The computer responds to these media by reading either the holes in punched cards or magnetized spots on the tape. Magnetic tape is prepared from punched cards, or a special machine can be employed for converting data directly from a typewriter keyboard onto the tape.

Tapes and cards have both advantages and disadvantages. Although cards have visible punches that allow them to be read without special equipment, input speeds tend to be relatively slow. Cards also tend to be bulky in contrast to tape. The decision to use cards or tape will probably be determined by the staff of the computing center where the data will be run.

*Storage or "Memory."* One of the most important characteristics of a computer is its ability to store instructions and data according to some predetermined plan. The computer works like an income tax form, where information is "stored" on various lines and the machine is instructed, for example, to "add lines 5 and 6" or "subtract line 8 from line 7." The machine is even able to perform "if" statements, such as "If payments (line 17c) are less than tax (line 16), enter Balance Due," or "If payments (line 17c) are larger than tax (line 16), enter Overpayment." However, instead of using lines, the computer automatically stores information in different locations called *addresses*.

Data can be stored by *serial access* or by *direct access* (often called *random access*). In serial access, the computer goes through all intermediate locations until the desired one is found; in direct access, a specific address can be found directly. Serial access works like a tape recorder; direct access works more like a jukebox. Unfortunately, faster access times are usually accompanied by smaller storage facilities and greater increases in cost.

The two major types of internal storage are magnetic cores and magnetic disks. Magnetic cores are tiny rings of ferrous material strung along vertical and horizontal wires. When a current is sent through both wires, a magnetic core at a specific location is magnetized in only a few millionths of a second. A core magnetized in one direction represents a 1 in the binary system; magnetized in the other direction, it represents 0. Magnetic cores are found on large, rapid computers.

Magnetic disks offer relatively large storage capacities with fast access times. They resemble phonograph records and are mounted on a rotating vertical shaft. They thus resemble a jukebox and operate in much the same way. To find a specific address, an access arm locates first the correct disk and then the specific magnetized spot corresponding to the desired storage location.

*Control.* The purpose of the control unit is to interpret and decode instructions found in storage and to direct the operations of the computer. The control unit transfers data into and out of storage.

The *control console* is the means by which the human operator communicates with the machine. The operator can start and stop all operations and control the flow of data and information throughout the entire computer system. In return, the console provides flashing lights and buzzers so that the machine is in constant communication with the operator. The computer can indicate what steps are being performed at any given moment and what parts, if any, are malfunctioning.

*Arithmetic.* The control and arithmetic make up the computer's *central processing unit*, which contains the electronic circuits needed to control and regulate machine operations and arithmetic processes. The purpose of the arithmetic unit is to perform basic mathematical operations such as addition, subtraction, multiplication, and division, as well as to perform certain kinds of logical operations of the "if" variety described earlier.

*Output.* The function of the output system is to take information out of storage so that it can be read by the operator. Output may be in the form of graphs or plots. Cards and tapes are useful if output from one machine is going to be used as input for another. If answers are to be read directly, they can appear as printouts from electric typewriters or lineprinters. If graphs or plots are needed, they can be obtained directly from a special type of plotter.

# PREPARING DATA FOR ELECTRONIC PROCESSING

Much of the information concerning electronic data processing is too technical and specialized to be described in an introductory research text. Fortunately, a happy division of labor has developed in the electronic computing field. Most computing centers in universities employ a staff of technical advisers who are responsible for the actual operation of the machines and who can be counted upon to provide technical skills. Usually, these persons have had extensive training in mathematics and engineering, but they may have only superficial knowledge of the kinds of problems faced by investigators in the behavioral sciences. The responsibility for understanding the assumptions and limitations of the statistics being used falls upon the investigator and not computer specialist.

The following sections will cover only the minimum essentials needed by the beginning investigator who is contemplating the use of electronic data processing equipment. References at the end of the chapter should be consulted for more advanced instruction.

## Amenability of the Problem to Electronic Data Processing

Theoretically, there is no reason why any problem could not be run on an electronic computer if the same problem could be solved by pencil and paper. Whether it is worth the effort or not is a more basic question. Generally, the decision to use electronic data processing depends on such factors as: 1) the number of variables of interest to the investigator; 2) the number of cases for each variable; 3) the complexity of the analysis; and 4) the availability of a computer program to handle the specific job requirements.

*1. Number of variables.* The greater the number of variables entering into the research design, the greater is the justification for using electronic data processing equipment. However, computer programs are limited in the number of variables they are capable of processing. Program descriptions usually provide information of this type.

*2. Number of cases.* In general, the larger the $N$, the more advantageous electronic data processing will be. Again, computer programs will specify both the maximum and minimum number of cases which they can process.

*3. Complexity of the analysis.* Because complex computations are particularly susceptible to error, and because they tend to require much time and effort, the use of electronic processing is recommended.

*4. Availability of a computer program.* Unless a program is available to handle a specified problem, a great deal of time and trouble may have to be expended writing one. Generally, program writing requires experience with computer languages, and professional programmers are often so busy that they may not have time to modify existing programs or write new ones. All university computing centers have program libraries, but often they contain only the programs most widely requested. To overcome this deficiency, a number of cooperative agencies have been established to share programs with one another. IBM Corporation, for example, periodically abstracts new developments in programming. SHARE (Society to Help Avoid Repetitive Effort) and USE (Univac Scientific Exchange) were developed to facilitate the exchange of computer programs on a cooperative basis. The Western Data Processing Center at UCLA has worked out its own programs (called BIMD or BMD, and pronounced "By-Med"). Many students have found it particularly convenient and simple to use the *Statistical Package for the Social Sciences* (SPSS), which requires little background in computers or programming.[11] Computing center staff members are usually quite willing to help students locate appropriate programs. Some fundamentals of programming will be considered in the next section.

## An Introduction to FORTRAN

FORTRAN (Formula Translation) is a special "language" used to communicate with electronic computers, especially the larger ones. Before the development of FORTRAN and similar *problem-oriented languages*, the programmer had to be trained to communicate with the computer in a *machine language* that made use of numbers to represent instructions. Because each type of computer had its own "dialect," the programmer had to become familiar with a variety of languages and dialects. Obviously, this was both cumbersome and inefficient.

In machine language, the programmer had to be able to tell the computer what to do and in what locations (addresses) data were to be stored. These operations were performed by using code numbers and by specifying storage locations. For example, +99 meant to clear the accumulator (the register where arithmetic operations are performed); +21 was a storage instruction; +10 meant add; +15, subtract; +19, multiply; +14, divide; +72 was used for printing answers for output, etc. Thus, the instruction +10 0008 meant "add whatever number is in storage location 0008 to the

---

[11]See, for example, William R. Klecka, Norman H. Nie, and Hadlai Hull, *SPSS Primer* (New York: McGraw-Hill Book Co., 1975), 134 pp.

accumulator." The programmer had to remember the type of information to be found in each storage location. Mistakes were common and often difficult to find.

In problem-oriented languages such as FORTRAN, the programmer's work is simplified considerably by using a language similar to standard English. The computer uses a *compiler program* to translate FORTRAN statements into machine language. Although this requires an extra step for the computer, the machine can process information so rapidly that it is a minor concession and a great time-saver for the programmer.

Although FORTRAN statements are not particularly difficult to read, detailed instruction in programming is clearly beyond the scope of this text. Many universities offer special short-term classes in FORTRAN fundamentals, and a number of teaching aids have been prepared if students prefer to learn programming on their own. Some of these are listed in the supplementary readings at the end of the chapter. However, a relatively simple program, designed to compute a mean and standard deviation, can be instructive in learning some of the basic principles of FORTRAN programming (see Figure 13-10).

**Figure 13-10**
FORTRAN PROGRAM TO COMPUTE MEAN AND STANDARD DEVIATION.

```
1  2 3 4 5  6  7                                                              7

        1      READ (5, 101) N
     1  0 1    FORMAT (I3)
        2      DO 5 I = 1, N
        3      READ (5, 102) X
     1  0 2    FORMAT (F10.6)
        4      SUMX = SUMX + X
        5      SUMSQ = SUMSQ + X**2
        6      ZN = N
        7      XBAR = SUMX/ZN
        8      VAR = (SUMSQ - SUMX**2/ZN)/(ZN - 1.0)
        9      STDEV = SQRT(VAR)
     1  0      WRITE (6, 103) N, SUMX, SUMSQ, XBAR, VAR, STDEV
     1  0 3    FORMAT (14H SAMPLE SIZE =,I3, 18H SUM OF X VALUES =, F15.6/17H SUM
            1  OF SQUARES =, F15.6/14H SAMPLE MEAN =, F15.6/18H SAMPLE VARIANCE
            2  F12.7/28H SAMPLE STANDARD DEVIATION =, F12.7)
     1  1    STOP
            END
```

The purpose of the program is to provide a set of instructions to the computer so that data can be "read" into the computer, processed by it, and a readable output obtained. Each line of a program is punched onto a separate card. The program in Figure 13-10 contains 17 FORTRAN statements, each to be punched onto a separate card. The computer "memorizes" each statement and later processes data in accordance with these instructions. Note that two sets of punched cards or two tapes are used for electronic data processing: one for the program and one to contain raw data to be processed.

Column 1 on program cards either can be left blank or a "C" may be punched to indicate to the computer that the programmer wishes to comment on some aspect of the program. The comments are usually included to remind the user about some aspect of the program.

Columns 2 through 5 on program cards are usually reserved for statement numbers. These numbers may be assigned arbitrarily and in any order, since the sequence of operations is not affected by the specific numbers assigned. The statement numbers are used for identification purposes as well as to control computer operations. The use of these numbers will be described later in this section.

Column 6 is used to identify continuation cards. If any FORTRAN statement requires more than 72 columns, any character or symbol (except zero) may be punched in the next card. Up to 19 continuation cards can be processed by most computers. Although all EDP cards contain 80 columns, FORTRAN instructions are punched in columns 7 through 72. The remaining columns are not processed by the computer but can be used to identify cards if they have to be placed in serial order.

Statement number 1 in Figure 13-10 says, "READ (5, 101) N." This instruction tells the computer to enter the number of cases into central storage according to format statement 101. The computer then searches through the program until it finds statement 101, which reads "FORMAT (I3)." This format statement indicates that $N$, the number of cases in the sample, will consist of integers ($I$) containing 3 digits. The "5" indicates that input will consist of punched cards.

Statement 2, "DO 5 I = 1, N," is a shorthand method of telling the computer to do all of the statements down to and including statement number 5. The first time this is done, let $I$ equal 1, then 2, etc., until the $N$th case is reached.

Statement 3 is an instruction to the computer to enter data into central storage according to format number 102. The values entered into the computer are $X$'s (raw scores). Format statement 102 means that $X$'s will consist of "floating point" (decimal) values having a maximum of 10 digits with 6 to the right of the decimal.

Statement 4 tells the computer to add $X$ to the previous value of the sum of $X$ (which initially is set equal to zero) and to store the resulting figure in the storage location assigned to the sum of $X$ by the computer. Statement 5 is interpreted in the same manner, except that it refers to the sum of squares. Note that exponents are written in FORTRAN by using double asterisks.

Statement 6 is used to convert an integer variable $N$ into a floating point or decimal mode. All FORTRAN names beginning with letters from $I$ through $N$ in the alphabet are automatically read as integers by the computer. To convert an integer to a floating point mode requires that the variable name be preceded by some letter other than $I$, $J$, $K$, $L$, $M$, or $N$.

The seventh statement defines $XBAR$ to be equal to the sum of $X$ divided by $N$. Note that if the mean is to involve a decimal, one could not refer to this value as "MEAN = SUMX/ZN," since "MEAN" begins with a letter reserved for an integer and means are often wanted in decimal form.

Statement 8 defines the variance, and statement 9 states that the standard deviation is the square root of the variance.

Statement 10 contains the instructions to the computer for writing out the answers to the values of $N$, the sum of $X$, the sum of $X$ squared, the mean, the variance, and the standard deviations according to format number 103. In this example, the computer was told that there are exactly 14 "Hollerith" characters in the expression "SAMPLE SIZE =," including all letters, spaces, signs, and punctuation marks. The sample size will be an integer having a maximum of 3 digits. The "SUM OF X VALUES" will consist of decimals having a maximum of 15 digits with 6 to the right of the decimal point. The slash (/) tells the computer to skip a line in printing out the information that follows. The "STOP" statement terminates the execution of a program. The "END" is the last program statement.

## Selecting an Appropriate Program

Before deciding to use a particular program, it is wise to read in detail the program's description, which can be found in computer program manuals published by the organization or person responsible for that program. For example, program descriptions usually indicate the kind of computer which can process the program; types of data the program can produce (e.g., means, standard deviations, etc.); the maximum number of variables it can accommodate; the maximum sample size; and the kinds of decisions possible regarding zeros and blank spaces. A sample output is often provided.

Because there are many programs that can compute the same statistics, it is important to select the most applicable and efficient program. Some programs will contain much more information than is necessary and thus waste computer time and research funds. Again, the student should not hesitate to ask for help in selecting programs.

## Checking the Program

One responsibility of the programmer is to make certain that the program is free from error. The process of locating and eliminating errors in the program is called "debugging," and is a time-consuming but very important procedure. Ordinarily, "canned" programs have been debugged, but from time to time these programs may contain errors. As a partial check on this, students should compute some of the data on their own and compare their answers with the computer's. Any discrepancy should be thoroughly investigated and resolved.

## Preparing Data for Card Punching

Once a program has been selected, the investigator can begin planning how to record input data so that they can be punched on cards for processing. Unless planning is begun early, data collected on one form may have to be transferred to another. This not only is inefficient, but it also encourages errors as data are transferred from one source to another.

Before data can be punched on cards, each column on the card has to be reserved for a specific type of information. In some cases the program itself will dictate the kind of information that can be punched in each column; in others, it may be possible to modify the program to accommodata the user. The computing center staff will be able to decide which of these alternatives is most feasible.

Most computing centers are able to provide the 80-column coding sheets used to record data to be keypunched for machine processing (see Figure 13-11). Each row is used to record information on a single subject. For example, column 1 could be designated to signify a project number or letter; columns 2 and 3, the card number; columns 4 through 7, student code number; etc. If more than 80 columns are needed, a second or third sheet can be used.

A complete description of the type of information recorded in each column should be kept by the investigator. The descriptions should be specific and detailed. An example of a convenient description form is shown in Figure 13-12.

Every column used has to be accounted for and clearly labeled. The letter "B" punched in column 1, for example, must refer to Project *B* and to no other. A "3" in column 11 must include all persons preparing to become secondary school teachers. Columns 14-16 must contain three numerals, one in each column, referring to grade point average at the time of graduation. If all 80 columns are needed, there must be a description for every column.

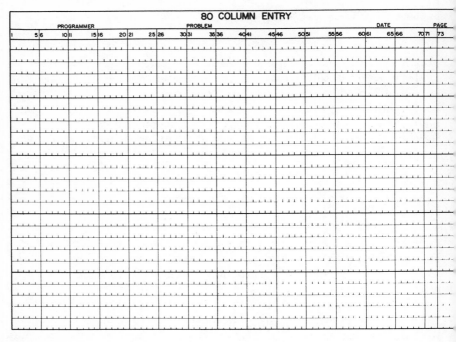

**Figure 13-11**
AN 80-COLUMN CODING SHEET.

## Card Punching

If raw data are placed on 80-column coding sheets, the key punch operator can punch data directly from the sheets to cards, saving time and reducing errors. Most computing centers employ key punch operators who are trained to work rapidly and accurately. If these services are available, they can usually be had at relatively low costs. If they are not available or if costs are too high, the investigator will find keypunching rather simple.

Card punch machines resemble typewriters. Alphabetic characters are located in the same positions on card punches as they are on standard typewriters. Numerals appear over the alphabetic characters operated by the right hand. Information to appear on all cards may be duplicated automatically by the key punch.

*Verifying.* All data punched on cards should be verified for accuracy. This may be accomplished by using a machine called a *verifier*. Machines are also avilable that will print out all data on cards for visual verification.

*Reproducing Punches.* Once data are punched on cards, they can be duplicated automatically by using a *reproducing punch*. To avoid having to

340

| CARD 01 | | |
|---|---|---|
| Cols. | Type | Variable |
| 1 | Alph | Project <u>A</u> or <u>B</u> : <u>B</u> = teacher characteristic and prediction study; <u>A</u> = curriculum study |
| 2-3 | Num | Card type = 01 |
| 4-7 | Num | Student code number |
| 8-9 | Num | Year student entered College of Education |
| 10 | Num | Standing granted at entrance to College of Education: 1 = 1st year Freshman (0-24 credits) 2 = 2nd year Sophmore (25-54 credits) 3 = 3rd year Junior (55-88 credits) 4 = 4th year Senior (89 credits and above) 5 = 5th year or Professional Certificate Candidate |
| 11 | Num | Education major code 1 = Preschool (kindergarten and grade 1) 2 = Elementary (grades 2-6) 3 = Secondary (grades 7-12) 4 = Undeclared |
| 12-13 | Num | National Teachers Exams: scale scores, Professional Information subtest |
| 14-16 | Num | Grade point average at time of graduation |

**Figure 13-12**
CARD DESCRIPTION RECORD.

repunch cards by hand if they become lost or torn, it is probably a good idea to duplicate all cards.

*Sorting and Collating.* Punched cards can be sorted automatically by using a *sorter.* This machine can arrange cards into 12 stacks, each stack corresponding to one of the 12 punching positions in a column. For example, the sorter could be set to segregate information punched into column 10 into as many as 12 categories.

For more complex stacking and sorting operations, a *collator* can be used. If, for example, two decks of data cards are used, they can be combined in any desired order or sequence.

## SUMMARY

**1.** Data processing involves those methods used to convert raw data into a form capable of being interpreted.

**2.** Data processing should be planned for in the early stages of the investigation. To collect data and then to consider their processing is both inefficient and risky.

**3.** Six criteria were presented for evaluating data collection forms:

**a.** *Accuracy.* All entries on record forms should be clearly labeled to avoid misinterpretation.

**b.** *Completeness.* The record form should be complete, with room for all necessary information.

**c.** *Simplicity.* Data processing methods and forms should be no more complex than necessary.

**d.** *Speed.* Data processing methods should be selected to allow completion of the project in as short a time as possible.

**e.** *Cost.* Data collection and analysis may be one of the most expensive items in an investigation. Cost has to be evaluated against other criteria such as speed and accuracy of processing.

**f.** *Availability.* Some methods of data analysis may be readily available, whereas others may be difficult to obtain. Researchers should obtain estimates of data analysis costs and services.

**4.** A variety of different record forms can be used to gather data:

**a.** Machine-scoring answer sheets can be used for both data collection and analysis. They can be hand- or machine-scored. Machine-scoring is recommended if there is a large amount of scoring to be done or if item analyses are needed. Light scanning and graphite sensitive machines were described.

**b.** If sorting and counting are the basic operations to be performed, edge-marked cards can be used rapidly and inexpensively. Specific types of information can be coded along the sides of a three-by-five-inch or larger card.

**c.** For more rapid sorting, edge-punched cards may be made or purchased. These consist of three-by-five-inch or larger cards containing one or more rows of holes along all four edges. A notched hole can be coded to have a specific meaning. Sorting is accomplished by passing a needle through a deck of cards and lifting. Notched cards will drop, and the cards with holes will remain on the needle.

**d.** Mark-sense cards record information by means of electrographic pencils. Cards can then be reproduced automatically for electronic data processing.

**e.** Punched cards are designed for use with electronic data processing equipment. They can be fed directly into a computer or their data placed on magnetic tape for even more rapid processing. The IBM card code was described.

**5.** A number of manual methods were described for performing relatively simple calculations:

   **a.** For a limited amount of data, computations may be done by pencil-and-paper methods. One or two simple means, standard deviations, or correlations require no special computing equipment.

   **b.** Tables and nomographs can be used to facilitate hand computations. Most of the commonly used tables are available commercially or can be produced rather easily by the investigator. Many rather complex computations may be done by nomographs or abacs if extreme accuracy is not required.

   **c.** Perhaps the greatest aid to hand calculations is the electronic desk calculator, which can perform all of the basic arithmetic processes, some of them simultaneously (such as counting $N$ and computing $\sum X$ and $\sum X^2$). They are simple to use and relatively inexpensive, but require the presence of a human operator to perform all operations. The amount of information to be processed is limited in comparison to electronic computers, and errors in entry data are common.

**6.** Electronic computers can be used most efficiently with large amounts of data requiring complex analyses. They are extremely rapid and accurate.

**7.** Electronic computers can be used to simulate experiments, persons, etc. This is accomplished by programming the machine to operate in some desired fashion according to rules established by the programmer. The performance of the computer can then be compared with the actual behavior under investigation and remodified to correspond in greater detail with this behavior. Computers can also be used for data retrieval.

**8.** Electronic computers may be analog or digital. Analog computers use variables such as length to represent numbers. Digital computers represent numbers with digits.

**9.** The development of modern computers began when humans first learned to use fingers for counting. In 1642, Pascal invented the first mechanical calculator. Punched cards were used as early as 1801 to weave patterns of cloth.

The conception of the modern computer is usually credited to Charles Babbage, who designed an Analytic Engine but was unable to make it operative. In theory, the Analytic Engine could vary its course of action in accordance with instructions.

**10.** The Mark I was the first electromechanical computer; it was completed in 1944. The first electronic computer, ENIAC, was completed two years later. Magnetic cores for data storage were introduced in 1951 by Whirlwind I. In 1952, the University of Illinois developed its own computer, called ILLIAC, and introduced electronic computers into a major university for general research purposes.

**11.** Modern electronic computers contain five components:

**a.** An input system is designed to control the operations of the computer and to enter raw data for processing. Punched cards and magnetic tape are most often used for these purposes.

**b.** A storage or memory system retains instructions and data for processing. Data may be stored serially or by direct access. Magnetic cores and magnetic disks may be used for storage.

**c.** A control system interprets and directs the operations of the computer.

**d.** An arithmetic unit performs various mathematical operations.

**e.** An output system takes data out of storage so they can be understood by a human operator.

**12.** Use of electronic data processing equipment is suggested if a) there are a large number of variables to be processed; b) $N$ is relatively large; c) the analysis is complex; and d) a program is available.

**13.** Computer languages are of two types. *Machine languages* can be understood directly by the computer but require a great deal of programming time and skill. In contrast, *problem-oriented languages* (such as FORTRAN) are easier for the programmer to use but must be converted by the computer into machine language by means of a compiler or translation program. An example of a program used to compute a mean and standard deviation was described.

**14.** The preparation of data for electronic processing requires the following steps:

**a.** Selecting an appropriate program

**b.** Checking it for accuracy

**c.** Preparing data for card punching

**15.** Once data are on cards, they should be verified for accuracy. Machines are available to print, verify, reproduce, sort, and collate information.

## PRACTICE EXERCISES

**1.** In a particular study, the following information was collected:
   IQ scores
   Mental ages
   Socioeconomic level
   Sex

Suggest various ways that this information could be entered on a) edge-marked cards; b) edge-punched cards; and c) electronic data processing cards. What factors would you take into consideration before deciding to use one of these methods?

**2.** Read the data punched on the following IBM card.

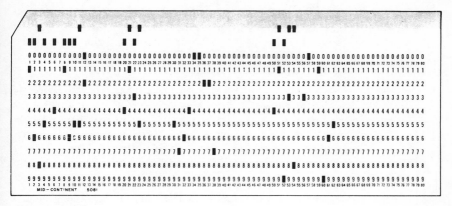

**Figure 13-13**

3. Using the nomograph in Figure 13-8, if the initial reliability of a set of measurements is 0.65, what would the reliability be if the number of items were doubled? If the number of items were halved?

4. In what ways does an electronic computer resemble a human brain? In what ways do they differ? Use the references at the end of this chapter to gather additional information.

5. Explain in your own words how a computer works, using Figure 13-9 as a reference.

6. What aspects of an electronic calculator correspond to the input, storage, control, arithmetic, and output of an electronic computer?

7. Suppose that a particular study requires the following data to be collected: a) Stanford–Binet IQ scores; b) mental ages; c) chronological ages; d) socioeconomic levels; e) grade levels; f) overall grade point ratios; and g) scores on a 200-item multiple-choice test in arithmetic.

Devise a card description form, similar to the one in Figure 13-12, that can accommodate this information. Describe each variable completely, indicating what each column is to contain.

8. If possible, punch your own IBM cards using fictitious data for the categories listed in exercise 7. Use an 80-column coding sheet for listing data.

9. Examine a comparable BMD or SPSS program. What are their relative advantages and disadvantages?

## Selected Supplementary Readings

1. On the use and limitations of mark-sense cards, see Appel, Valentine, and Cooper, George. "A Refinement in the Use of Mark-Sense Cards for Test Research." *Journal of the American Statistical Association*, 50, no. 270 (1955),

pp. 557–560. See also Bass, Bernard M., and Wurster, Cecil R. "Using 'Mark Sense' for Ratings and Personal Data Collection." *Journal of Applied Psychology*, 40, no. 4 (1956), pp. 269–271; and Deemer, Walter L., Jr. "The Use of Mark Sensing in a Large Scale Testing Program." *Journal of the American Statistical Association*, 43, no. 241 (1948), pp. 40–52.

2. The historical development of computing machinery is described in an article titled "Calculating Machines," in *Encyclopædia Britannica*, Vol. 4. Chicago: Encyclopædia Britannica, 1962, pp. 548–554. Bernstein has written a highly readable account of the development of modern computers and his experiences in learning to operate them. See Bernstein, Jeremy. *The Analytical Engine: Computers—Past, Present, and Future*. New York: Random House, 1964.

3. For the use of specific electronic desk calculators, consult the owner's manual with each calculator. Some general sources of information on the use of calculators include the following: Feldzamen, A. N., and Henie, Faye. *The Calculator Handbook*. New York: Berkley Medallion Books, 1973, 127 pp.; Gilbert, Jack. *Advanced Applications for Pocket Calculators*. Blue Ridge Summit, Penn.: Tab Books, 1975, 303 pp.; Mullish, Henry. *The Complete Pocket Calculator Handbook*. New York: Collier Books, 1978, 309 pp.; and Sippl, Charles J. *Calculator Users' Guide and Dictionary*. Champaign, Ill.: Matrix Publishers, 1976.

4. General references on programming include Sherman, Philip M. *Programming and Coding Digital Computers*. New York: John Wiley & Sons, 1963; and McCracken, Daniel D. *A Guide to FORTRAN IV Programming*, 2d ed. New York: John Wiley & Sons, 1972.

5. For additional information on the use of edge-marked cards, see the following source: Thurstone, L. L. "The Edge-Marking Method of Analyzing Data." *Journal of the American Statistical Association*, 43, no. 243 (1948), pp. 451–462. Thurstone suggests various uses of edge-marked cards, including using them in the preparation of bibliographies and tables, and as answer sheets. See also Lester, A. M. "The Edge Marking of Statistical Cards." *Journal of the American Statistical Association*, 44, (1949), pp. 293–294. He presents a novel coding system to facilitate card sorting.

6. A number of important tables have been published by the U.S. National Bureau of Standards, National Applied Mathematics Laboratories, Computer Laboratory. Many have little relevance to education, but there are others which may be quite useful, including logs of integers from 1 to 10,000, reciprocals of integers from 100,000 to 200,009, fractional powers, etc. See also the index of Vol. 35–50, "List of Selected Mathematical Tables and Charts." *Journal of the American Statistical Association*, 11 (1959). Another useful source of tables is Greenwood, J. Arthur, and Hartley, H. O. *Guide to Tables in Mathematical Statistics*. Princeton, N. J.: Princeton University Press, 1962. A now classic book of tables is Comrie, L. J., ed. *Barlow's Tables*

*of Squares, Cubes, Square Roots, Cube Roots, and Reciprocals of All Integers up to 12,500*, 4th ed. New York: Halsted Press, John Wiley & Sons, 1965. See also the publications of the National Research Council, *Mathematical Tables and Other Aids to Computation*. Washington, D.C.: National Research Council.

# glossary

**Action Research**   Sometimes called "cooperative research"; the application of principles of group dynamics to implement research innovations in the schools.

**Analog Computer**   A computer that represents numbers by using physical analogs.

**Analysis of Covariance**   A statistical procedure used to equate experimental and control groups by adjusting posttest scores for initial differences between groups; abbreviated ANCOVA.

**Analysis of Variance**   A statistical procedure used to compare the significance of the difference between two or more means; usually abbreviated ANOVA.

**Analytic Research**   Research that derives knowledge primarily through deduction (e.g., philosophical, mathematical research).

**Applied Research**   Research designed to create knowledge having relatively immediate applications.

348

**Aptitude–Treatment Interactions** The *interaction* or relationship between various levels of student characteristics and different levels of *treatments* or methods; used in *factorial* ANOVA designs and to increase *external validity* of experiments.

**Arithmetic Unit** That part of an electronic *data processing* system that performs basic arithmetic processes.

**Authority** An individual whose position on a topic is accepted. Authorities should be identified, recognized as such, living (or no new evidence made available following the authority's death), and be unbiased.

**Basic Research** Research designed to contribute to theory.

**Beta Weights** ($\beta$) The weights assigned to each variable in a multiple *regression equation* to maximize predictability.

**Carryover or Transfer Effects** The systematic increase (or decrease) of scores as a result of being exposed to multiple practice periods or materials.

**Case Study** The detailed description of a person, event, institution, or community designed to create *nomothetic* knowledge.

**Central-Limit Theorem** The principle that the *sampling distribution* of means will be *normally distributed* if the *population* is normal or if the *sample* is large.

**Chi Square** ($\chi^2$) A statistical technique used to determine the probability that observed and expected preferences differ.

$$\chi^2 = \frac{\Sigma (f_o - f_e)^2}{f_e}$$

where $f_o$ = an observed frequency, $f_e$ = an expected frequency.

**Common-Factor Variance** The proportion of *variance* held in common by two or more *factors;* common-factor variance is responsible for the *correlation* between variables.

**Communality** ($h^2$) In *factor analysis*, the proportion of *common-factor* variance contributed by all *factors; validity* is dependent on the communality.

**Confidence Interval of a Mean** The probability that a range of *sample* means encompasses a *parameter* mean ($\mu$).

**Content Analysis** Any of a number of methods used to quantify and analyze qualitative communications (e.g., letters, song lyrics, books).

**Contrived Observation** Techniques designed to elicit behavior but which appear natural to the subject.

**Control Group** In experimentation, a group administered a placebo treatment; alternatively, it may refer to a group receiving no treatment.

**Control System** The part of an electronic *data processing* system that transfers data into and out of *storage*.

**Correction for Guessing** A penalty applied to the scores of individuals who respond incorrectly to an item.

**Correlation** A measure of the extent to which variables are related to one another.
(a) Correlation ratio or *eta*: A measure of correlation used when *linearity of regression* cannot be assumed.
(b) Multiple correlation: The correlation between two or more predictors and a criterion; symbolized *R*.

**Counterbalancing** Techniques used to control for carryover or transfer effects produced because subjects are exposed to repeated measurements.

**Covariate or Adjusting Variable** In the *analysis of covariance*, the variable on which subjects are statistically equated.

**Criterion Contamination** The unjustifiable procedure of permitting raters whose judgments are to serve as criterion measures to examine the test scores of subjects *before* providing the ratings. The criterion ratings are thus contaminated with knowledge of the subjects' performance on the test when the two measures should be obtained independently.

**Cross-Sectional Method** A method used in *developmental studies* in which random samples of subjects at different developmental stages are selected at the same time to study changes in growth and development (cf. *longitudinal method.*)

**Cross Validation** The readministration of a test to a second sample of subjects to see if item characteristics have changed.

**Determination, Coefficient of** ($r^2$) The proportion of *variance* held in common between two correlated variables.

**Development** An aspect of research used to increase the efficiency of products, practices, or conditions.

**Digital Computer** A computer that is capable of performing arithmetic operations with numbers.

**E** Abbreviation for experimenter or researcher.

**Eigenvalue (Latent Root)** The sum of the *common-factor variances* for each *factor*.

**Episodic and Private Records** A type of archival, nonreactive measure that consists of private documents written without the intent of creating an enduring record.

**Error Score** The hypothetical difference between an *obtained* and a *true* score.

**Eta or the Correlation Ratio** A measure of correlation between two nonlinearly related variables.

**Evaluation** A decision-making process designed to study whether a given program or method should be continued, modified, or eliminated.

**Experimental Research** Research designed to study causal relationships.

**Ex Post Facto Study** A study that attempts to discover the preexisting causal conditions between groups already formed.

**External Validity** The extent to which experimental findings can be generalized to other persons, conditions, and settings.

**F Ratio** In the *analysis of variance*, a ratio formed by dividing the between-group variance by the error variance; more generally, any ratio of independent variances.

**Factor Analysis** A statistical procedure used to determine the minimum number of factors or traits that are measured by a series of tests or items.

**Factor Loading** In *factor analysis*, the correlation between a test (or item) and a *factor*.

**Factor Matrix** In *factor analysis*, a table showing the correlation between tests (or items) and *factors*.

**Factorial Designs** Experimental designs that measure the simultaneous effects of two or more *independent variables*.

**Fixed Model** In a *factorial design*, the assumption that all levels of the independent variables were deliberately predetermined and not selected at random.

**FORTRAN ("Formula Translation")** A symbolic language used in computer programming.

**Free-Response Question** An item asked during an interview or presented on a questionnaire that gives the respondent the freedom to answer questions within relatively undefined boundaries.

**Guttman Scale** Sometimes referred to as the *scalogram technique;* a method of determining whether or not a set of items measures a single universe.

**Hypothesis** (a) Research hypothesis: A statement expressing a tentatively held expectation or relationship between variables.
(b) Null hypothesis: A statistical statement that expresses a parameter value, usually that $\mu_1 - \mu_2 = 0$.
(c) Alternative hypothesis: A statement that the null hypothesis is wrong (e.g., $\mu_1 - \mu_2 \neq 0$).

**Idiographic** Any study designed to create nongeneralizable knowledge; (cf. *nomothetic*).

**Input System** That part of an electronic *data processing* system that receives information from an external source for processing.

**Interaction Effect** The relationship between two or more *independent variables* in a *factorial analysis of variance*. Variables interact if one level of a treatment (such as a method) depends on the specific values of a second variable (such as level of intelligence).

**Intercept** The point where the regression line crosses the vertical axis.

**Internal Validity** In experimental design, the extent to which relationships between *independent* and *dependent variables* are not confounded with the presence of *extraneous variables*.

**Intervening Variable** A hypothetical variable that represents the relationship between a stimulus and response variable.

**Interviewer Bias** Personal characteristics of interviewers that influence subject responses.

**Intraclass Correlation**   A statistical method based on the *analysis of variance* used to estimate the reliability of a single interviewer, rater, or observer.

**Kappa (*k*)**   A coefficient used to measure the degree of interobserver agreement on nominal scales.

**Latin Squares**   A type of experimental design used to control for multiple *carry-over effects*; a Latin square has an equal number of groups, time periods, experimental treatments, etc.

**Levels of a Variable**   As used in the *analysis of variance*, the qualitative or quantitative differences in categories that comprise each *independent variable*.

**Likert Scales**   A type of ordinal attitude scale on which respondents express degrees of agreement or disagreement to a series of statements related to the attitude being measured.

**Linearity of Regression**   The assumption that variables being correlated are best represented by a straight line.

**Longitudinal Method**   A method used in *developmental studies* in which the same subjects are measured at two or more time periods (cf. *cross-sectional method*).

**Main Effect**   In *factorial designs*, the difference produced by the *levels* of each *independent variable*.

**Mark-Sense Cards**   Data processing cards on which responses are marked with special pencils that can be "read" by computers.

**Matching**   The equating of members of experimental and *control groups* on extraneous variables that correlate with the dependent variable.

**Mean**   A measure of central tendency found by adding all scores and dividing by the number of scores.

**Median**   The middle value of a series of sequentially ordered scores.

**Method of Equal-Appearing Intervals**   A method designed to create differences between successive levels of an attitude that are equal.

**Mixed Model**   In a *factorial design*, the assumption that the *levels* of one factor are *fixed* while levels of the other are *random*.

**Model**   A physical or abstract (e.g., mathematical) representation of an object, person, concept, or set of relationships.

**Naturalistic Observation**   Any of a number of methods used to study educational or psychological phenomena by observing how subjects respond when uninfluenced by the observer.

**Nomograph**   A computational aid that makes use of lines or curves to show the relationship between variables; sometimes referred to as an abac.

**Nomothetic**   Any study that permits generalization beyond the specific person, event, institution, or community studied (cf. *idiographic*).

**Nonreactive Measure or Observation**   See *unobtrusive observation*.

**Nonstructured Items**  Broadly worded questions that allow subjects the freedom to clarify and expand upon responses.

**Normal Curve**  A mathematically defined bell-shaped curve that is often approximated when large numbers of cases are selected randomly.

**Observational Set**  The tendency on the part of observers to respond to stimuli in accordance with the observers' backgrounds, values, beliefs, and expectancies.

**Obtained Score**  An individual's score on a test that is composed of *true* and *error* scores.

**One-Tailed Test**  The test of the *null hypothesis* that specifies the direction of the expected values of the *alternative hypothesis*.

**Orthogonal**  In *factor analysis*, the lack of relationship between two factors; factors are orthogonal if they are uncorrelated.

**Output System**  That part of an electronic *data processing* system that takes information out of *storage* so that it can be read by the human operator.

**Parameter**  Any value (such as a *mean* or *standard deviation*) computed from a *population* of scores.

**Parsimony, Law of**  Sometimes referred to as the *Principle of Occam's Razor*; the principle that scientists tentatively "accept" the simpler of several equally good explanations or theories.

**Partial Correlation Coefficient**  The statistical procedure of eliminating the usually *spurious* effect of a third variable from the correlation between two variables.

**Participant Observation**  The process of obtaining information by having observers live or participate with those persons being observed.

**Physical Trace**  A type of *unobtrusive measure* characterized by physical evidence of *erosion* or *accretion*. *Erosion* refers to evidence produced by the amount of wear in an object. *Accretion* refers to the qualitative or quantitative accumulation of physical evidence.

**Population**  In statistical inference, the aggregate of *observations* (scores, ratings, etc.) to which one wishes to generalize. The term is also used to refer to the total supply of potentially available individuals for a study.

**Probability**  The ratio of a specified event to the total number of possible events; a likelihood; symbolized *p*.

**Program**  In electronic *data processing*, the instructions provided to operate the machine and arrive at the solution to a problem.

**Q Sort**  A technique for the study of intrapersonal relations in which subjects are asked to sort statements twice into one of eleven (usually) categories reflecting differences along a dimension of similarity to oneself. The two sets of ratings can be correlated by assigning the category number of each item on the first sort with the category number on the second sort. The number of cards to be sorted into each category is fixed by the researcher.

*Q* **Value**   On Thurstone *equal-appearing interval scales*, the *Q* value is the interquartile range or difference between the ratings corresponding to the 75th and 25th percentile; a measure of variability not strongly affected by extreme ratings.

**Random Error**   Differences between a set of *obtained* and *true* scores that, in the long run, sum to zero.

**Random Model**   In a *factorial design*, the assumption that the *levels* of both variables were selected randomly.

**Randomization**   In experimentation, the unbiased assignment of subjects to *treatments* to eliminate systematic differences.

**Randomized-Block Design**   An experimental design in which subjects are matched or equated on one or more *variables* that *correlate* with the *dependent variable*. Subjects within each matched block are then assigned random treatments.

**Rationalism**   The belief that reason and deduction provide ultimate knowledge.

**Readability Formulas**   Any of a number of equations used to estimate the difficulty level of materials to be read.

**Regression Equation**   A formula used to predict a criterion value from knowledge of one or more predictor scores.

**Regression Line**   A line fitted to a series of paired scores so as to minimize the sum of squared differences between each paired score and the line.

**Reliability**   The extent to which scores or observations measure true individual differences; also the ratio of true variance to total or obtained variance. Four types of reliability coefficients have been described:
(a) Equivalence: The extent to which scores on parallel forms on a test are related.
(b) Homogeneity or internal consistency: A measure of reliability estimated by correlating scores on one part of a test with scores on another part of the same test.
   (1) Split half: Reliability estimated by correlating scores on the even-numbered items of a test with scores on the odd-numbered items. This correlation must be augmented by the *Spearman–Brown* formula.
   (2) Kuder–Richardson 20: An estimate of reliability that measures the extent to which all items on a test measure the same trait.
(c) Stability: The extent to which measures are related on the same test for the same persons over time.
(d) Stability and equivalence: The extent to which scores on parallel forms of a test correlate over time.

**Repeated Measurements Design**   In *experimental* research, the exposure of the same subjects to two or more *treatments* to ensure comparability and increase the likelihood of rejecting the *null hypothesis*.

**Replication**   The procedure of repeating a study to check on the validity of findings; replication may also refer to the addition of a greater number of subjects to a study.

**Reproducibility Index**   The proportion of items in a *Guttman scale* that can be predicted or reproduced from knowledge of a person's total score.

**Research**   The assumptions, techniques, methods, and procedures used to create knowledge by empirical and rational means; the study of such procedures.

**Response Biases**   The tendency on the part of subjects to respond to irrelevant characteristics of items or test format.

**Running Record**   A type of archival analysis that consists of records used by a culture for its own purposes; a form of *nonreactive measurement*.

*S; s*   The abbreviation for a subject who participates in a research study; the lower-case *s* refers to a *sample standard deviation*.

**Sample**   A limited number of elements selected from a population.
(a) Representative samples: Samples drawn in an unbiased manner from a population.
(b) Random samples: Samples drawn from a population so that *parameter* values are neither under- nor overestimated in the long run.
(c) Biased samples: Samples drawn so that not all elements of the population have an equal chance of being drawn.

**Sample Survey**   A type of descriptive research in which data are obtained by sampling questionnaire responses or test scores.

**Sampling**   The process of drawing *samples* from *populations*.
(a) Area or cluster sampling: The sampling of areas (blocks, locations) followed by the sampling of elements within areas.
(b) Simple random sampling: The selection of cases from a population by enumerating all elements and drawing randomly from the population.
(c) Statified sampling: The selection of elements drawn from each of a number of subpopulations; elements can be drawn proportionally or disproportionally from the number of cases in each stratum.
(d) Systematic sampling: The selection of elements by drawing every *n*th case from a roster.

**Sampling Distribution**   An empirical or mathematically determined distribution of a *statistic* such as a *mean*.

**Sampling Unit**   The type of element that comprises a *sample* such as individuals, classrooms, or districts.

**Scales of Measurement**   Characteristics or properties of measurements that depend on the level and complexity of assumptions that can be met.
(a) Nominal scale: Measurements are assumed to exist in independent categories.
(b) Ordinal scale: Measurements can be rank-ordered only.
(c) Interval scale: Measurements are assumed to possess equality of differences between successive levels of the scale.
(d) Ratio scale: Measurements possess equal intervals and an absolute zero.

**Scale Values**   On Thurstone *equal-appearing interval scales*, the median rating assigned to an item by a large number of judges; scale values usually range from 1.0 to 11.0 where 1.0 is usually the most unfavorable category.

**Scalogram Technique** See *Guttman scale;* a method used to determine whether item responses can be predicted from knowledge of a subject's total score.

**Selective Deposit** A deficiency in analyzing documents resulting from the fact that not everyone privy to an event produces a document.

**Selective Survival** A deficiency in analyzing documents produced by the failure of all documents to be found.

**Semantic Differential** A method that measures the connotative meaning of concepts. Subjects rate each concept along a number of bipolar adjectives, and the concept's meaning is measured along (usually) three factors: evaluative (good–bad), activity (passive–active), and potency (strong–weak).

**Semantic Space** In the interpretation of a *semantic differential*, the graphic representation of a concept's meaning along a number of different and *orthogonal* dimensions defined by a *factor analysis.*

**Sensitivity** The extent to which experiments are capable of detecting true differences between experimental and control groups.

**Serendipity** The accidental discovery of an important finding when an investigator is actively studying a different problem.

**Shrinkage** The attenuation or lowering of multiple-correlation coefficients when they are *cross-validated.*

**Sigma** The capital Greek letter, $\Sigma$, used as a statistical symbol for "add" or "sum"; the lowercase sigma, $\sigma$, represents a *parameter standard deviation.*

**Significance Level** In statistics, an arbitrary but agreed upon probability level that is needed to reject the *null hypothesis* with a certain degree of risk (usually 5% or 1%).

**Significance Test** A *statistical* procedure used to reject or fail to reject the *null hypothesis*, such as the *F ratio, t-test,* or *chi square.*

**Simple Observation** Any observation in which the observer's role is entirely *nonreactive.*

**Situational Test** A form of contrived observation that involves *participant observation* in nonreactive settings.

**Slope** The degree of "steepness" of a line; more technically, the ratio of the vertical to the horizontal distance from a line.

**Social Distance Scale** An ordinal scale developed by Emory Bogardus in 1925 that measures the degree of acceptance or rejection between oneself and members of various ethnic, religious, or racial groups.

**Sociogram** In *sociometry*, a pictorial representation of the choice (and sometimes the rejection) patterns of peer group members.

**Sociometry** A technique developed by Jacob Moreno for studying peer group relationships.

**Spearman–Brown Formula**   A formula used to estimate reliability of a test increased or decreased in length $k$ number of times.

**Specific Variance ($v^2$)**   In *factor analysis*, the proportion of variance related only to a single test and its equivalent forms; $v^2$ contributes to *reliability* but not to *validity*.

**Spurious**   Not genuine, artificial, such as a "spurious finding" or a "spurious correlation."

**Standard Deviation**   A measure of variability of scores around the *mean* of a distribution; the square root of the sum of squares divided by the degrees of freedom;

$$s = \sqrt{\frac{\Sigma (X - \bar{X})^2}{N - 1}} \quad \text{or} \quad \sigma = \sqrt{\frac{\Sigma (X - \bar{X})^2}{N}}$$

Standard deviation of a proportion:

$$\sqrt{p(1 - p)}$$

where $p$ is the proportion of persons responding favorably.

**Standard Error**   The *standard deviation* of a *statistic*.

(a) Standard error of a mean: The *standard deviation* of a *sampling distribution* of means; $s_{\bar{X}} = s/\sqrt{N}$

(b) Standard error of a proportion:

$$\sqrt{\frac{p(1 - p)}{N}}$$

(c) Standard error of measurement: The *standard deviation* of *error scores:*

$$SE_{\text{meas}} = s\sqrt{1 - \text{reliability}}$$

(d) Standard error of estimate: The *standard deviation* of scores around the regression line:

$$SE_{\text{est}} = s_Y\sqrt{1 - r_{XY}^2} \quad \text{(where } Y \text{ is predicted from } X\text{)}$$
$$s_X\sqrt{1 - r_{XY}^2} \quad \text{(where } X \text{ is predicted from } Y\text{)}$$

**Standard Score**   Any of a number of statistics that describes a score by the number of *standard deviations* the score is from the *mean*; *z-scores* are *standard scores.*

**Standardization**   The process of writing, administering, timing, scoring, and norming tests to produce scores that are as comparable as possible.

**Standardization of Error**   The continued and uncritical belief in unsubstantiated research findings.

**Statistic** A computed value (such as a *mean* or *standard deviation*) derived from a *sample*.
(a) Biased statistic: A statistic that consistently over- or underestimates its corresponding parameter.
(b) Unbiased statistic: A statistic that, in the long run, neither over- nor underestimates its parameter.

**Statistical Inference** The process of generalizing from *statistics* to *parameters*.

**Storage Unit** That part of an electronic *data processing* system that retains data for future processing.

**Structured Items** Items that set predetermined and limited boundaries on the responses of subjects.

**Sum of Squares (SS)** The sum of the squared differences between a score and the *mean*; the numerator of the *variance* and *standard deviation*; $\Sigma (X - \bar{X})^2$.
(a) Between-groups $SS (SS_{BS})$: The sum of the squared differences between the *mean* of each group and the grand mean weighted by the number of observations in each group.
(b) Total $SS (SS_T)$: The sum of the squared differences between each score and the grand mean.
(c) Within-groups $SS (SS_{WG})$: The combined sum of squared differences between the scores within each group and that group's *mean*.

**Systematic Error** Nonrandom error; the difference between a set of *obtained* and *true scores* that does not sum to zero.

**Theory** A unified system of principles, definitions, postulates, and observations organized to explain some phenomenon.

**Time Sampling** A technique of studying behavior by recording all responses that occur during randomly selected time segments.

**Treatment** An experimental condition imposed on subjects.

**True Score** The hypothetical mean of an infinite number of repeated testings with the same instrument after eliminating practice effects.

*t*-**test for Means** A statistical test designed to measure the significance of the difference between two *means*; the ratio of the differences between *means* to the standard error of the difference between means.

**Two-Tailed Test** The test of the *null hypothesis* that does not specify the direction of differences.

**Type I Error** The incorrect rejection of the *null hypothesis*; reporting a statistically significant difference when the *parameter* differences are zero.

**Type II Error** Failing to reject the *null hypothesis* when there are differences in the *population*.

**Unbiased Statistic** A *statistic* that neither under- nor overestimates *parameter* values if repeated *samples* of a given size are drawn from the *population*.

**Unobtrusive Observation** Any observation obtained without affecting behavior or responses of subjects.

**Validity**   The extent to which a test satisfies the purpose for which it was constructed.

(a) Concurrent validity: The *correlation* between test scores and a criterion when both are measured at approximately the same time.

(b) Construct validity: The extent to which a construct or theory is supported by evidence that the construct can be measured.

(c) Content validity: The extent to which test items are judged to measure stated objectives.

(d) Predictive validity: The *correlation* between test scores and a criterion when there is a time interval between the two measurements.

**Variable**   Any condition or quantity that can assume different values.

(a) Dependent variable: A response variable.

(b) Extraneous variable: A variable that correlates with the dependent variable but is not a part of the independent variable.

(c) Independent variable: Any manipulated variable under the control of the experimenter.

(d) Organismic variable: Characteristics of subjects that are related to the dependent variable but which cannot be manipulated by the experimenter (e.g., sex, intelligence).

**Variance**   In statistics, the *sum of squares* divided by the number of degrees of freedom:

$$s^2 = \frac{\Sigma (X - \bar{X})^2}{N - 1}$$

sometimes referred to as a mean square.

(a) Variance between groups: The *sum of squares between groups* divided by the number of groups minus 1.

(b) Variance within groups: The *sum of squares within groups* divided by the total $N$ minus the number of groups.

**z-scores**   A *statistic* that describes the number of *standard deviations* that a score is above or below the mean:

$$z = \frac{X - \bar{X}}{s}$$

**z-test**   A statistical test of the difference between a *statistic* and a *parameter mean*; sometimes called a critical ratio.

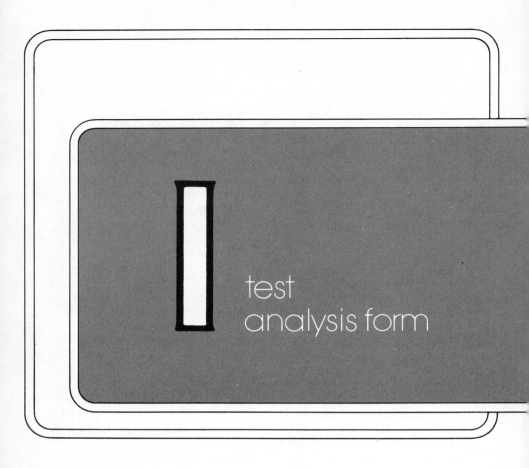

test
analysis form

Reference Data
Title
Author
Publisher
General Type (aptitude, intelligence, etc.)
Test Administration Time
Number of Alternate Forms
Appropriate Age or Grade Group

*Source:* Adapted from American Psychological Association, Joint Committee of the American Psychological Association, American Educational Research Association, National Council on Measurement in Education, Frederick B. Davis, Chairman. *Standards for Educational and Psychological Tests* (Washington, D.C.: American Psychological Association, 1974), 76 pp. The *Test Analysis Form* presents only those recommendations in the *Standards* that are relevant to the research use of tests. Letters and numbers in parentheses refer to related paragraphs in the *Standards*.

**1.** Manuals and promotional materials are available, recent, and accurate. (A1)
**2.** Complete description of the test's development and rationale is provided. (A3)
**3.** Information designed to facilitate correct interpretation of tests and sub-tests is available. (B1)
   a. Names of tests and subtests are not misleading.
   b. Effects on test performance (if known) of such variables as social class, race, ethnicity are specified in manual.
   c. Frequent errors of misinterpretation are explained.
**4.** Purposes for which test is recommended are explained. (B2)
**5.** Nature of the trait being measured is specified. (B3)
**6.** Qualifications needed to administer, score, and interpret test for each recommended use are stated. (B4)
**7.** Directions to the examiner and to examinees for test administration are clear. (C1)
**8.** a. Time limits allowed are specified.
   b. Instructions to examinees regarding guessing are clear.
   c. Methods examinees are to use in marking responses to items are specified.
   d. Amount of freedom that examiners are allowed in answering examinees' questions is included.
**9.** Scoring standards and methods are provided. (C3)
**10.** Up-to-date norms are in manual. (D1)
**11.** Populations on which norms have been developed are described. (D2)
   a. Extent to which norms are generalizable to different groups is specified.
   b. Methods used to sample norm groups are clearly stated.
   c. Extent to which sample is obtained by an unbiased procedure is specified.
   d. Manual includes number of individuals sampled and the number of sampling units (schools, classrooms, districts).
   e. Characteristics of the sample are described in sufficient detail to facilitate test interpretation and to help judge the relevance of norms for a specified sample.
   f. Norms are reported only if data are presented on their reliability and validity.
**12.** Means and standard deviations are reported for each norm. (D3)
**13.** If groups (schools, districts, classes) rather than individuals are to be measured, group norms are provided. (D7)
**14.** Evidence regarding validity of the test to perform each function for which it was designed is reported. (E1)
   a. The manual refers to validity for specific purposes and not to test validity in general.
   b. The manual cautions the examiner that judgments derived from a very few items are less valid than those derived from a larger sample.

    c. The extent to which each item measures whatever the test as a whole measures is not described as "item validity" (this coefficient can be described as an item-discrimination coefficient).

**15.** The use of a test requires that the user obtain the needed evidence (reliability, validity, relevant norms for selected samples, etc.) to justify that use. (E2)

**16.** If judges are used to provide criteria data, their judgments are not contaminated with knowledge of examinee performance on the tests being validated. (E4)

**17.** Reported validity studies employ samples of individuals sufficiently similar to those who will be given the test so that the user can evaluate the appropriateness of the test to particular situations and examinees. (E6)

    a. The characteristics of the validation sample are described in detail.

    b. Individuals used in the validation sample are in the same educational circumstances as are those who will be taking the test.

**18.** The amount of time that intervenes between the administration of a test and the obtaining of criteria data is reported. (E7)

    a. Validity studies report the date of test administration and the date that criteria data were accumulated.

    b. The manual warns against the difficulties of long-term prediction.

    c. The manual makes clear that evidence of long-term predictability cannot be assumed from concurrently obtained relationships between test scores and a criterion.

**19.** Evidence of criterion-related validity is presented using 1) means and standard deviations of test scores and the criterion, 2) correlations between scores and criteria, and 3) reliability data for scores and criteria. (E8)

    a. If validity coefficients are corrected for attenuation (i.e., errors of measurement are eliminated statistically), the reported correction should be for the criterion and not for the fallible scores.

    b. Both corrected and uncorrected coefficients should be reported.

    c. Evidence of the test to misclassify individuals (omitting students from a category to which they belong or falsely including students who do not belong) should be provided in the manual.

    d. The manual should provide evidence that any test added to a battery of tests will result in significantly increased validity.

**20.** The test user is responsible for investigating the extent of test bias by establishing validity for specific purposes with relatively large samples of minority members. (E9)

**21.** The manual reports validity data on a sample of persons other than those on whom the original items were selected (i.e., items are *cross-validated*). (E10)

**22.** If *content validity* is appropriate, the manual should state the characteristics of the universe and the manner in which items have been sampled from that universe. (E12)

**23.** In establishing *construct validity*, the theoretical construct (trait, characteristic, or attribute) being measured should be described fully and differentiated from similar terms; empirical evidence should be presented to substantiate the author's interpretation of that construct. (E13)

**24.** The manual presents estimates of reliability and of errors of measurement that allow a test user to judge if measurements are sufficiently reliable for each recommended purpose. (F1)

**25.** Samples on which reliability estimates are obtained permit the user to determine whether the test is reliable for an intended use. (F2)

   a. Standard deviations should accompany reliability data.

   b. If scores are *corrected for range*, corrected and uncorrected coefficients should be reported.

   c. Separate reliabilities should be reported for each independent subsample for whom the test is recommended (i.e., fifth, sixth, *and* seventh graders, boys and girls, etc.).

   d. The standard error of measurement should accompany the presentation of each reliability coefficient.

**26.** Reliability estimates should be expressed in commonly understood statistics, or relatively unfamiliar terminology and formulas explained with reference to their derivation. (F3)

**27.** Equivalent-forms reliability coefficients should present the means, standard deviations, and correlations among forms. (F4)

**28.** Estimates of internal consistency are not appropriate for speed tests. (F5)

**29.** Stability coefficients should express the amount of time elapsing between the successive administrations of the test. (F6)

**30.** Anyone selecting tests or interpreting test scores is expected to have the competency to do so and to be aware of limitations in training and background. (G1)

**31.** Discriminatory practices involved in test selection, administration, scoring, and interpretation are to be avoided. (G4)

**32.** The background of research and development afforded each test should be considered by potential users. (H3)

**33.** The use of electronic scoring systems requires that accuracy be checked periodically. (I3)

**34.** Both the test user and developer are responsible for test security. (I5)

**35.** A test score is a sample of behavior and should be so interpreted. (J1)

Reviewers' Comments:

# 11
# ethical considerations in conducting research

The selection of a research topic carries with it the obligation to behave ethically. A code of ethics prescribes the general conditions under which the investigator may and may not conduct research.

The most complete set of guidelines for researchers has been published by the American Psychological Association.[1] The following principles should be considered in planning and conducting research with human subjects.

## Acceptance of Personal Responsibility and Review

The researcher accepts the responsibility for following certain principles involved in conducting research with human subjects. It is especially important that the researcher obtain advice and guidance from institutional review committees (as

[1]Adopted from the Ad Hoc Committee on Ethical Standards in Psychological Research, "Ethical Principles in the Conduct of Research with Human Participants" (Washington, D.C.: American Psychological Association, 1973), 104 pp.

required by the Department of Health, Education and Welfare), advisers (if a student), or colleagues regarding behavior of participants that may be harmful, damaging, anxiety-producing, debasing, etc. Advice to proceed will ordinarily be given only if the benefits of the proposed research outweigh the potential harm to the participants. Each collaborator in a study accepts equal responsibility for following these principles.

## Informed Consent

The researcher has the responsibility to inform participants of those conditions that might affect their decision to participate in the study. This disclosure implies that questions by potential participants be answered completely by the researcher.

*Unobtrusive Public Observations.* Sometimes researchers engage in studies where they observe individuals who are unaware of their participation in a research study (e.g., observing the behavior of persons waiting in lines). If participants remain completely anonymous (not identified by name, or by personal descriptions, videotapes or audio-recordings), the problem of obtaining consent is somewhat lessened, but still limited by the advice of colleagues, advisers, and institutional review boards. But if individuals can be identified even though their behavior may be public, asking individuals to give their consent for the *use* of data is recommended.

*Unobtrusive Private Observations.* When individuals are persuaded by deceptive means to divulge personal information, there is an explicit invasion of their privacy and a violation of these principles.

*Intrusive, Disguised, and Public Observations.* Intrusive research involves manipulating the behavior of the respondent. Such manipulations are disguised if respondents are unaware that they are participating in a study. For example, an intrusive, disguised, and public observation would occur if a researcher hired students to pick fights on a playground for the purpose of observing the behavior of the other students. Such research should be conducted only with the advice of colleagues since informed consent would not be possible.

*Evaluation Studies and Other Research in Institutions.* Sometimes a decision must be made whether to introduce a particular treatment or method to individuals in an institution such as a school. For example, a textbook company may want to evaluate a text being used in a school district by testing the students. Or students in a control group may be tested even though they received no benefit from a study. Although informed consent would be desirable in these studies, the potential harm to subjects is minimal and is especially so when subjects normally expect to be tested and are treated in an acceptable manner. Again, the advice of colleagues is important in these cases. It is important to realize that informed consent implies that potential participants in a research study are competent to give their consent. When working with minors, the mentally retarded, or psychotics, consent should be obtained from guardians, those persons acting as parents or parents under the law (e.g., superintendents of correctional institutions), and if at all possible, from the potential participants as well.

## Freedom from Coercion

Individuals should not be forced to participate in research as a requirement for enrollment in a course unless it can be demonstrated that students are participating in a study of direct benefit to them educationally (e.g., requiring students in a course on test construction to develop experimental tests). If students are allowed reasonable alternatives to participating in research, if they are informed about the participation requirement before they enroll (assuming the course is not required), if the students can withdraw from a research project at any time, and if there is no penalty for withdrawing, these matters can be readily resolved. The desire to withdraw from a study may also include the participant's right to remove his or her research data from a study.

## Honoring Agreements with Participants

For research to be ethical, the participants and researcher must have a clear understanding of their respective roles, their agreement must be fair, and the researcher must fulfill all commitments. Any promises made must be honored, and individuals must not be deceived into participating in a study by promises of high rewards that may obscure any risks they may be taking.

## Protection against Risk

A participant is placed at risk if the study involves physical or emotional danger or potential danger. Any such potential danger must be explained to the participant in readily understood terms and consent obtained. The investigator has the obligation to reduce all forms of stress. Research on human subjects is unethical if it is likely to produce long-term and serious problems. Individuals must be carefully screened to make sure that unanticipated consequences of an experimental treatment are eliminated (e.g., screening out persons with liver problems in studies on the effects of alcohol). The use of drugs is regulated by state and federal laws. Stress should be monitored throughout the study and follow-up services planned.

## Clarification and Explanations of the Study

At the termination of a study, the investigator has the obligation to debrief all participants. If providing such information puts the participant in greater risk than would otherwise have been likely, potentially damaging information may be withheld. For example, children who were told they had performed well during an experiment need not be told afterward that their performance was actually poor.

## Diagnosing and Eliminating
## Undesirable Experimental Effects

Any possible stressful conditions, physical or mental, must be detected and eliminated as rapidly as possible. Participants—and especially children—must not be allowed to experience undesirable effects resulting from a research study. The investigator needs to consider the possibility of such effects and either prevent them from occurring or forego the study. Follow-up procedures should be planned to make sure participants have not been placed at risk and to plan for eliminating any undesirable effects incurred by participants. If, for example, students are given extremely difficult tasks, it may not be sufficient merely to tell them that they are not expected to perform these tasks perfectly. The follow-up should provide students with tasks on which they do extremely well to minimize previous negative treatment effects.

In considering whether or not to undertake a given study, the researcher is obligated to weigh the consequences of the participants' expectations when the study terminates. If, for example, children from low-income homes are found to benefit from special diets at school, the investigator needs to provide for the continuance of these diets when the experiment is ended. Failure to do so could seriously affect participants who may have developed strong expectations and dependent relationships.

## Anonymity and Confidentiality

The participant has the right to know which persons are privy to personal information obtained during the course of an investigation. If possible, data should be obtained anonymously to avoid the possibility that any individual could be identified. However, if research is being carried out with a small number of persons, anonymity cannot always be assured. Participants must be fully informed of such conditions. It is a clear violation of ethical principles to pretend that anonymity is being protected if, in fact, it would be possible to identify participants.

Some studies require a comparison of participant responses on two or more occasions. Under such conditions, participants must be informed that identification is necessary. Nonetheless, confidentiality can be assured (and, of course, must be honored). Participants can also be asked to identify themselves by a code name or number of their choice. They might also be told that it would be advantageous if the investigator could keep a separate and confidential list of code names with the names of the participant to prevent participants from forgetting their pseudonyms. On questionnaires, it would be necessary to keep this list separate from participant responses.

In conducting research with minors in a school setting, all persons providing consent (e.g., parents, school principal, teachers, and students) need to understand what information will and will not be provided to them. The investigator is responsible for developing an explicit "contract" regarding confidentiality and for making sure that those persons giving consent receive the information agreed upon.

Data collected in a research study can usually be subpoenaed by the courts whether or not confidentiality has been promised to participants. In studies where such information is likely to be required by the courts, this fact must be communicated to participants before any data are collected. Completely anonymous data, of course, pose no threat to participants.

Sometimes a researcher obtains information that threatens the life or well-being of a third party or of the research participant. Under these conditions, confidentiality cannot be maintained, and the appropriate authorities should be informed.

Nonetheless, the danger must be evident, and the participant must be warned that confidentiality may be violated under such circumstances.

## Acceptance of Research Funds

Researchers need to be aware of the potential effects that the acceptance of funds from certain agencies or organizations may have. Certainly, it would be unethical—and scientifically meaningless—to deliberately bias procedures to produce an effect "acceptable" to the sponsoring agency. But perhaps a more difficult judgment faces the researcher who is offered funds or who solicits funds from an organization whose policies or practices might be contradictory to those of one's colleagues or of the institution for which one works. The American Psychological Association only suggests that these matters be considered in planning research, but it leaves the final decision to solicit funds to the investigator and the policy-making board of the institution receiving the funds.

## Potential Misuse of Research Findings

The researcher needs to consider the potential effects and possible misuses and misinterpretations of research findings. To be sure, the results of any study can be misunderstood and used for socially undesirable goals, but some studies are particularly susceptible to this type of problem.

Other ethical considerations may persuade a researcher to forego a particular study. For example, a study may require the cooperation of atypical children (mentally retarded, neurologically handicapped, blind, etc.) and their parents. It may be tempting to ask the teacher of these children or the school principal for permission to contact the parents. The problem, however, is that the parents may not want it known that their children are attending a special class. One way to avoid this difficulty is to request the teacher or principal to ask parents if their children can participate in the study. This procedure may take more time and may require the cooperation of a third party, but it does protect the parents' rights of privacy.

### Selected Supplementary Readings

1. The single best source of ethical principles used in conducting research has been published by the American Psychological Association (see reference on page 364). See also Schultz, Duane P. "The Human Subject in Psychological Research." *Psychological Bulletin*, 72, no. 3 (September 1969), pp. 214–228. See also *American Psychologist*, 22, no. 5 (May 1967), which contains articles on privacy, the Surgeon General's Directives on Human Experimentation, the ethical use of drugs and personality measures, and ethical considerations on research with children.

2. On the effect of deception and ways to avoid it, see Stricker, Lawrence J.; Messick, Samuel; and Jackson, Douglas N. "Evaluating Deception in Psy-

chological Research." *Psychological Bulletin*, 71, no. 5 (May 1969), pp. 343–351.

3. On the various roles taken by subjects who participate in research, see Weber, Stephen J., and Cook, Thomas D. "Subject Effects in Laboratory Research: An Examination of Subject Roles, Demand Characteristics, and Valid Inference." *Psychological Bulletin*, 77, no. 4 (April 1972), pp. 273–295.

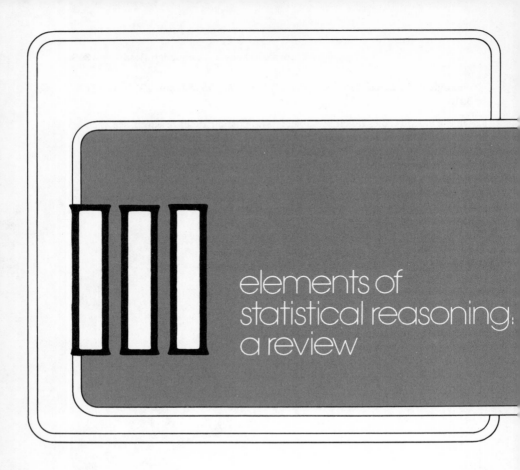

elements of
statistical reasoning:
a review

The purpose of this appendix is to review the elements of statistical reasoning needed to interpret research findings. The approach will be to explain how and why statistics are used in research but not to attempt to derive formulas mathematically. References at the end of this chapter can take the student beyond the elementary approach presented here.

Statistical methods may be categorized as being *descriptive* or *inferential*. Descriptive statistics describe and summarize relatively large amounts of data into manageable and more easily interpretable form. More specifically, descriptive statistics attempt to answer such questions as

*1.* How many individuals participated in the research?

*2.* How well did they perform "on the average"?

*3.* To what extent is there variability in some trait or characteristic within a group?

*4.* To what extent are traits related to one another?

In each of these examples, the intent is to describe one or more attributes (traits or characteristics) of a group. Sometimes, however, the intent is to estimate how closely an attribute derived from a sample approximates the same attribute in the population from which the sample was drawn. Statistical inference involves those procedures that are used to generalize from sample to population attributes. For example, researchers often can study characteristics of *samples* of students that are later used to make inferences about the populations from which the samples were drawn. Typically, the researcher also wants to know how well the sample data approximate the corresponding data in the populations. Such endeavors are known as *statistical inference*.

# POPULATIONS AND PARAMETERS

A population is the aggregate of all possible observations (scores) to which the researcher has an interest in generalizing. A population may be finite (limited to a specific number of cases) or infinite (unlimited and therefore of unknown size). Students enrolled in a given classroom, school, or district represent finite populations. Ten-year-olds in the nation or world, however, represent infinite populations, since it is not possible to identify or study all members of those groups.

Attributes of finite populations can be measured from each element (e.g., person) in that population; the characteristics of infinitely large populations cannot be measured directly, but they can be estimated by studying the characteristics of samples drawn from their corresponding populations. Any characteristic derived from a population (such as "average" IQ) is called a *parameter*, and any characteristic of a sample is called a *statistic*. The definitions of a population and parameter do not necessarily imply that the observations are derived from human beings. It is perfectly reasonable to talk about observations derived from television sets or from automobile accidents and to compute parameters from these populations.[1]

A sample is a limited number of cases selected to represent a population or universe. If populations are finite but very large, it would be possible and certainly economically advantageous to work with samples rather than with populations; if populations are infinite in size, sampling will be necessary.

Customarily, statistics are represented by roman letters ($A$, $B$, $C$, etc.) and parameters by Greek letters ($\alpha$, $\beta$, $\gamma$, $\Delta$, etc.). This practice is not universally accepted, and the student needs to be aware of possible inconsistencies.

# DESCRIPTIVE STATISTICS

## The Mean

The mean is the most commonly used descriptive statistic. It is exactly the same as the arithmetic average that is found by summing all values and dividing by

---

[1]The term *universe* is often used instead of population if the aggregate is inanimate or an event. One could, for example, refer to all test items that measure some given trait as a universe of items.

the number of cases. The mean of a sample (i.e., a *statistic*) is computed in the same way as is the population mean or parameter. The symbols differ, however. A sample mean is designated by either $M$ or $\bar{X}$ (pronounced "$X$-bar"); the population mean is represented by the Greek letter *mu*, symbolized by $\mu$. The formulas for $X$ and $\mu$ are

$$\bar{X} = \frac{\Sigma X}{N_{sample}} \quad \text{and} \quad \mu = \frac{\Sigma X}{N_{population}}$$

where $N$ = the number of cases, observations, or scores. As an example, the mean of the numbers 8, 2, 7, 3, and 5 is found by adding these values $(8 + 2 + 7 + 3 + 5 = 25)$ and dividing the sum by 5, the number of cases. Therefore, the mean is $\frac{25}{5} = 5.0$.

The mean is probably the most commonly used measure of central tendency or average. Its usefulness is derived from the fact that the sample mean more closely approximates its parameter than does any other statistic. In part, this is true because the mean is computed from every score value and, therefore, makes use of all available data. The mean is also highly "sensitive" to extremes in the score distribution. For example, the sum of the differences between the mean and each score value is always at a minimum (i.e., zero) as is seen in the example below. The mean acts as a balance point for all scores that enter into its computation. No value can represent its scores as well as does the mean.

| Scores | Minus | Mean | = | Difference |
|--------|-------|------|---|------------|
| 8 | — | 5 | = | +3 |
| 2 | — | 5 | = | −3 |
| 7 | — | 5 | = | +2 |
| 3 | — | 5 | = | −2 |
| 5 | — | 5 | = | 0 |
| | | $\Sigma (X - \bar{X}) =$ | | 0 |
| | | (Sum of the differences) | | |

## The Median

The median, like the mean, also indicates how the group as a whole performed, but it is insensitive to the effects of extreme scores. The median is the score associated with the center point of a series of values when these values are arranged sequentially.

If the scores 65, 8, 2, 7, 3, 5 are rearranged in order of magnitude, these values become 65, 8, 7, 5, 3, 2. The median is halfway between the 5 and 7, or 6.0. The median is the value that divides the sequentially arranged scores so that there is the same number of scores above (65, 8, 7) as below it (5, 3, 2). If there is an odd number of scores (65, 8, 7, 5, 3), the median is simply the middle score or 7.0 since two values are above and below that point.

In research, the median is not reported as often as the mean because it fails to take advantage of all available information. For example, the median is the same if the distribution of scores is 65, 8, 7, 5, 3 or if it is 650, 8, 7, 5, 3. The median is insensitive to extreme values. If data contain extreme values, the median may be used to minimize their effects. If in doubt, both the mean and median can be reported.[2]

## The Sum of Squares, Variance, and Standard Deviation

Variability is as important as central tendency. The two most commonly used measures of variability in research are the variance and the standard deviation.

Again, consider the values 8, 2, 7, 3, 5 and compute their mean (5.0). Remember that when the mean is subtracted from each score, the sum of those differences is always zero. Thus, there seems to be no way to calculate the *average difference* of each score from the mean, since the sum of the differences is always zero. Nonetheless, the differences can be squared to eliminate all negative values (the square of any negative number is always positive). In the example below, the sum of the squared differences is 26.0. This value, $\Sigma (X - \bar{X})^2$, is of great practical use in research, and is technically referred to as the *sum of squares*. The student should keep in mind that the sum of squares is actually the sum of the squared *differences* between each score and the mean.

| Score | Minus | Mean | = | Differences | Squared Differences |
|---|---|---|---|---|---|
| 8 | — | 5 | = | +3 | +9 |
| 2 | — | 5 | = | −3 | +9 |
| 7 | — | 5 | = | +2 | +4 |
| 3 | — | 5 | = | −2 | +4 |
| 5 | — | 5 | = | 0 | 0 |
| | | | | 0 | $\Sigma (X - \bar{X})^2 = 26$ |

To understand the sum of squares, the variance, and the standard deviation, plot the difference scores on a number line as shown below:

Difference scores

The individual with a score of 8 is 3 units above the mean of 5.0. A dot has been placed on the number line corresponding to a difference score of +3. The score of 2 is 3 units below the mean (−3) and has been indicated by a dot on the line by the −3. The same has been done for the 3 remaining difference scores. Think of each dot as representing a distance (or difference) between that score and the mean of the 5 scores.

[2]The mean and median are known collectively as measures of *central tendency*. Another measures of central tendency is the *mode* or score value that occurs with the greatest frequency (e.g., the scores 1, 2, 3, 3, 3 have a mode of 3.0). Because the mode is rarely used in research, it will not be described in greater detail.

Now square each of the differences to eliminate negatives. The person who obtained the score of 8 is 3 units above the mean and that squared value is 9.0. If $+3$ is thought of as a measure of horizontal distance on the number line from zero, then 9.0 represents an area circumscribed by a perimeter that extends 3 units horizontally and 3 units vertically, yielding an area of 9.0 square units. Similarly, individuals with a difference score of $+2$ or $-2$ on the number line would be accorded an area of 4 square units each. The number of square units can be summed for the 5 difference scores ($+3^2 = 9$; $-3^2 = 9$; $+2^2 = 4$; $-2^2 = 4$; $0^2 = 0$) to equal an area of 26 square units. Since there are 5 scores in this example, the mean number of square units accorded each person is $\frac{26}{5} = 5.2$. This value, 5.2, is the variance. For a population, the variance, $\sigma^2$,[3] is

$$\sigma^2 = \frac{\Sigma\,(\Sigma\,X - \mu)^2}{N}$$

for a sample, the variance, or $s^2$, is

$$\frac{\Sigma\,(X - \bar{X})^2}{N - 1}$$

The explanation for $N - 1$ is forthcoming.

The numerator for the variance, $\Sigma\,(X - \bar{X})^2$, or $\Sigma\,(X - \mu)^2$, is the "sum of squares" although it represents the sum of the squared *differences* of the mean from each score. The larger the sum of squares is in relation to $N$ (the number of cases), the larger will be the variance. If every individual received the same score, the sum of squares would be zero.

The $N - 1$ in the formula for $s^2$ is needed to increase the numerical value of the sample variance. When $N$ instead of $N - 1$ is used as the denominator for $s^2$, $s^2$ systematically underestimates the corresponding parameter, $\sigma^2$. This is because the variability of the sample is always smaller than the variability of scores in the population. The $N - 1$ increases $s^2$ to make it more equivalent to $\sigma^2$. The value of $N - 1$ is known as *degrees of freedom*.[4] A sample variance ($s^2$), then, involves the sum of squares divided by the appropriate number of degrees of freedom.

The standard deviation is the square root of the variance:

$$\sigma = \sqrt{\frac{\Sigma\,(X - \mu)^2}{N}} \qquad s = \sqrt{\frac{\Sigma\,(X - \bar{X})^2}{N - 1}}$$

---

[3] $\sigma^2$ is the lowercase Greek *sigma* squared (remember that Greek letters represent parameters). The corresponding statistic is symbolized by $s^2$. The student should note that the formulas for $\sigma^2$ and $s^2$ are not the same.

[4] *Degrees of freedom* is not always $N - 1$. In this example, there were five difference scores ($+3$, $-3$, $+2$, $-2$, 0). Since the sum of these scores must be zero, any combination of four scores ($N - 1$) can be selected and are "free to vary," while the fifth score is fixed. Pick the last four scores, for example, and the fifth must be $+3$ since the sum of differences is always 0. Other statistics also involve the freedom to vary, but this freedom does not necessarily involve the number of cases.

The variance involves a measure of area, while the standard deviation provides a measure of distance. This is because differences were squared when the variance was computed. The square root of the variance will then estimate length or distance. Using the previous example,[5]

$$\sigma = \sqrt{\tfrac{26}{5}} \text{ or } 2.28 \qquad s = \sqrt{\tfrac{26}{4}} \text{ or } 2.55$$

The standard deviation is a relative value that partly depends on the unit of measurement. Intelligence test scores, for example, ordinarily have standard deviations of 16 IQ *points*; grade equivalent norms are expressed in *years* and have standard deviations of from about 0.5 to 1.5 years. Obviously, it would be misleading to compare standard deviations computed using different units of measurement since one year and one point are not necessarily equal.

The interpretation of a standard deviation is most understandable in relation to the so-called normal curve (see Figure III-1). Although this curve is defined mathematically, it is approximated in many research studies. The theoretical

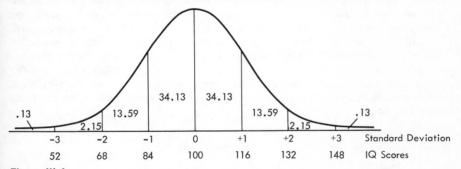

**Figure III-1**
THE NORMAL CURVE SHOWING PERCENTAGES OF CASES BETWEEN SELECTED STANDARD DEVIATIONS AND A HYPOTHETICAL DISTRIBUTION OF IQ SCORES HAVING A MEAN OF 100 AND A STANDARD DEVIATION OF 16.

curve is symmetrical and extends infinitely in both directions (below and above the mean). The total area under the normal curve is equal to 1.0 (expressed as a proportion or 100 percent). Between the mean and $1\sigma$ above the mean lie 34.13 percent of the cases; almost 14 percent fall between 1 and 2 standard deviations, and from 2 standard deviations to infinity lie some 2 percent. Thus, if the mean of a set of intelligence test scores is 100 and the standard deviation is 16 points, about 68 percent (34.13 + 34.13) of all individuals, or roughly two-thirds, will fall between the mean and $1\sigma$ above and below that value. Approximately 95 percent will fall between $\pm 2\sigma$; almost all cases fall between $\pm 3\sigma$. In other words, some 68 percent of the individuals vary in intelligence test scores between 84 and 116.

[5]The use of the $N - 1$ in the denominator for $s$ assumes that sampling was employed to estimate $\sigma$. If this were so, the sum of squares for $s$ would be smaller than the sum of squares for $\sigma$, and $N - 1$ would be a reasonable correction. Because the same data were used for both $\sigma$ and $s$, dividing the sum of squares by $N - 1$ will make $s$ larger than $\sigma$.

## Correlation

Correlations measure the extent to which paired sets of data are related to one another. For example, a researcher might be interested in knowing whether there is some relationship between number of absences and grades or whether there is a relationship between educational expenditure in different districts and crime rates in those districts.

Correlations are described as being positive ($+$) if the same individuals are above or below the means of the two sets of data, or variables, being correlated. If, however, those who are above the mean on one variable tend to be below the mean on the other, the correlation is negative ($-$). Height and weight, for example, correlate positively, as do intelligence and achievement test scores, or age and the number of birthdays. A negative correlation would occur between age and the amount of hair on the heads of male adults. It is negative because the *older* individuals have less hair (conversely, those adults having the *most* hair tend to be *younger*).

In addition to being positive or negative, correlations can vary in magnitude between 0.0 and 1.0. A correlation of $\pm 1.00$ means that the two variables are measuring the same attribute (e.g., height measured in inches and centimeters). A correlation of 0.00 means that the two variables are completely unrelated. A correlation can be most easily interpreted by converting it to a coefficient of determination, which is $100r^2$ where $r$ is a symbol for correlation. When $r$ is 0.50, $100r^2 = 25$. This means that 25 percent of the variance associated with one variable is also associated with the other variable. If $r = 0.80$, the coefficient of determination would be 64 percent.

## Characteristics and Assumptions Underlying Correlation

A number of assumptions and cautions in interpreting correlations need to be understood.

*1.* Correlations are not percentages and should not be interpreted as such. A correlation of 0.80 is referred to as "point eighty"; a coefficient of 0.04 is referred to as "point 0 four." Coefficients of determination are, however, percentages and may be so interpreted.

*2.* Correlations assume linearity. That is, the paired variables should form a straight line when plotted as in Figure III-2a. In that figure, each dot represents an individual's score on the $X$ and $Y$ variables. Figure III-2b indicates that increases in $X$ are not always associated with an increase in $Y$. Rather, $X$ and $Y$ tend to increase together at the lower end, remain unchanged in the center of the plot, and then decrease. If $X$ is time of day and $Y$ the amount of student productivity, a nonlinear relationship would be expected and special correlational techniques would be needed (see references at end of chapter for eta, the correlation ratio used for nonlinear relations). The effect of computing correlations when plots are nonlinear is to spuriously reduce the magnitude of the computed correlation value.

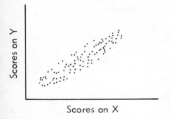

**Figure III-2a**
A LINEAR RELATIONSHIP BETWEEN
VARIABLES X AND Y.

**Figure III-2b**
A NONLINEAR RELATIONSHIP BETWEEN
VARIABLES X AND Y.

*3.* Correlations do not imply causal relationships, even if $r = \pm 1.00$. The one exception is that of a nonspurious correlation of 0.0 which indicates no relationship, causal or not. In all other instances, a correlation only indicates some association between the two variables but not necessarily a causal one (inches and centimeters are highly correlated, but one does not cause the other).

*4.* Differences between successive correlations are not necessarily equal. For example, the difference between correlations of 0.90 and 1.0 represents a difference of about 19 percent when both values are converted to coefficients of determination ($100 \times 0.90^2 = 81\%$; $100 \times 1.0^2 = 100$; $100 - 81 = 19\%$). But on the same basis, there is a difference of only 9 percent when the coefficients of determination corresponding to correlations of 0.40 and 0.50 are compared. Because differences are not equal, correlations should not be averaged [e.g., the mean of $+1.0$ and a $-1.0$ correlation is *not* zero. Instead, a median correlation may be reported or $r$ can be converted to Fisher's $z$ transformation and then averaged (see references at end of chapter)].

*5.* The value of $r$ is not affected if either or both variables are added, subtracted, multiplied, or divided by a constant. But doing so will modify the mean by the amount of the constant and may modify the standard deviation.[6]

*6.* The correlation coefficient is strongly influenced by the size of the standard deviation. Correlations tend to increase or decrease in magnitude as $s$ increases or decreases. This means that correlations must be interpreted in relation to $s$. Since $s$ increases when extreme scores are included, correlations computed from such a set of scores will be higher than if the extreme scores were eliminated. For this reason, whenever $r$ is computed, $s$ should be reported for both variables.

## STATISTICAL INFERENCE

The purpose of statistical inference is to draw conclusions about populations from the information obtained from samples. This process assumes that the sample has been drawn randomly so that every element of the population has an

---

[6]The standard deviation is not affected by adding or subtracting constants from either or both variables being correlated. Multiplying or dividing by a constant will increase or decrease the standard deviation by the value of the constant.

equal opportunity of being included in the sample (see Chapter 8 for a description of random sampling procedures). Decisions regarding the parameter are made from the statistics (such as $\bar{X}$ and $s$) computed from the sample data.

## Sampling Distributions

Every sample statistic drawn from a population is likely to differ not only from one another but from the parameter it is attempting to estimate. Most statistics do approximate their corresponding parameters reasonably well, but any given sample can be expected to underestimate or overestimate these parameters. If a distribution of a statistic is determined empirically or mathematically, that distribution is known as a *sampling distribution*. The sampling distribution provides an estimate of how frequently a given value of a statistic can be expected to appear, assuming random sampling from the parent population.

Suppose that a researcher wants to estimate the intelligence of students in a rather large school. Suppose also that 5 samples are selected from the population and that each sample contains 10 students. Sample 1 is selected and yields a mean IQ of 105; sample 2 has a mean of 106.8; sample 3, 99.2; sample 4, 101; and sample 5, 103. The mean of the sampling distribution of means is 103.0 and the standard deviation is 3.0. As more and more samples of 10 cases each are drawn, this empirically obtained sampling distribution of means would more closely approximate the mathematical or theoretical sampling distribution of means. In practice, researchers are much more likely to depend on theoretical sampling distributions since they are easier to obtain than empirical sampling distributions.

## Standard Errors

The mean of the sampling distribution referred to in the preceding paragraph was 103.0. This value is the best estimate of the population mean. The standard deviation of these 5 means is 3.00 and is referred to as the *standard error of the mean*. The standard error of any sampling distribution is the standard deviation of that distribution. The standard error of the mean, symbolized by $s_{\bar{x}}$, indicates the amount of variability among the sample means. The larger the value of $s_{\bar{x}}$ is, the greater will be the dispersion of sample means around the parameter. Only if $s_{\bar{x}}$ is zero will there be no error or variability of sample means around $\mu$, the population mean.

Statisticians have developed formulas that can be used to estimate $s_{\bar{x}}$ from a single sample since the process of drawing successive samples empirically is tedious, expensive, and unnecessary. If the parameter standard deviation, $\sigma$, is known, the standard error of the mean is $\sigma_{\bar{x}} = \sigma_x/\sqrt{N}$. IQ scores, for example, are converted so that they yield standard deviations of 16 points. If the researcher selected a sample of 100 students, $\sigma_{\bar{x}} = 16/\sqrt{100} = 1.6$ points.[7] In most instances,

---

[7]Because $\sigma_{\bar{x}}$ is the standard deviation of means, it may be interpreted as such. If a large sample were selected (e.g., > 30), the sampling distribution of means would approach the normal distribution and one could argue that approximately 68 percent of the sample means would vary one standard deviation on either side of the population mean.

however, $\sigma$ is unknown but can be estimated by computing $s$, the standard deviation of the sample. When $\sigma$ is unknown, $s_{\bar{x}} = s_x/\sqrt{N}$.

The formula for $s_{\bar{x}}$ shows that a large standard deviation among the scores or observations in the sample increases the value of $s_{\bar{x}}$ as does a small number of cases. Increasing the sample size reduces $s_{\bar{x}}$. Only if all observations from a given sample are identical will the researcher be certain that the sample and population characteristics coincide exactly. Since this almost never occurs, statistics are not likely to be identical with their parameters and a certain amount of *error* can be expected. The size of this error depends on how far the sample means vary from sample to sample, and, as noted, this can be estimated by computing the standard deviation of the observations from a single sample and relating that value to the square root of $N$.

Although only the standard error of the mean has been discussed in this section, all statistics have sampling distributions from which it is possible to estimate their standard errors. The standard error of a median, for example, is given by the formula $s_{\text{med}} = 1.253s/\sqrt{N}$. Comparing this with the formula for the $s_{\bar{x}}$ shows that medians involve more error and that therefore the variability or dispersion of sample medians is greater (by about 25 percent) than is the variability of means.

Statistical estimates of parameters will increase in accuracy and usefulness if they meet the following criteria:

*1. Unbiased* (i.e., neither underestimate nor overestimate parameters if repeated samples of the same size were drawn from the population). A *biased* statistic tends to under- or overestimate a parameter as repeated samples are selected. The mean, $\bar{X}$, for example, is an unbiased estimate of $\mu$ since $\bar{X}$ will approach the value of $\mu$ "in the long run." The use of $N$ rather than $N - 1$ in the denominator of the *sample* standard deviation ($s$) would yield a *biased* estimate of $\sigma$; the use of $N - 1$ would not.

*2. Consistent* (i.e., they increase in accuracy as $N$ increases). The value of $\bar{X}$, for example, can be expected to approach $\mu$ as larger samples are selected. Even biased estimates will closely approximate parameters if they are consistent and if enough cases are selected.

*3. Efficient* (i.e., they are precise or vary minimally from sample to sample). Efficient statistics lack variability in different samples and thus are able to estimate parameters accurately.

*4. Sufficient* (i.e., they contain all of the information regarding a parameter that the observations can provide).

## Steps in Statistical Inference

Statistical inference involves the following steps: 1) stating a research hypothesis; 2) identifying one or more populations to which one wishes to generalize; 3) drawing samples; 4) expressing the research hypothesis in *null* form and specifying the *significance level* required to reject the null hypothesis; 5) describing the *decision rules* that will specify the conditions under which the null hypothesis will be rejected; 6) computing the *significance test*; and 7) arriving at a decision regarding the parameter or parameters.

## Stating the Research Hypothesis

Suppose that a new drug is claimed to raise intelligence test scores. The research hypothesis that expresses a testable expectation is formulated (e.g., "a random sample of fifth-grade pupils administered 2 cc. of drug $X$ daily for 10 weeks will obtain a mean IQ that differs significantly from the mean IQ of fifth graders not treated with drug $X$"). Chapter 4 describes in greater detail how research hypotheses are expressed.

## Identifying the Populations

The research hypothesis implies two populations: one consisting of the scores of fifth graders administered drug $X$ and another consisting of the scores of a comparable group not treated with drug $X$. Since the mean IQ of any random untreated group is defined as 100 (with a standard deviation of 16 points), those values will be used as parameters for the untreated group.

## Drawing the Sample

The researcher may have the resources to test 50 pupils who will be treated with drug $X$ for 10 weeks. These 50 pupils have to be selected so that they are as comparable as possible to the untreated pupils. The methods used to draw random samples are described in Chapter 8.

## Stating the Null Hypothesis and Significance Level

The research hypothesis specifies two mutually exclusive statistical hypotheses. The first is known as the *null hypothesis* (symbolized by $H_0$) which specifies a particular value for the *parameters* (e.g., the IQ's of the drugged and non-drugged groups are equal; therefore drug $X$ was ineffective).[8] Note that if $H_0$ states that $\mu_1 - \mu_2 = 0$, it is the same as stating that the two parameters are equal. The second statistical hypothesis (called the *alternative hypothesis* and symbolized by $H_1$) states that $\mu_1 - \mu_2 \neq 0$ (e.g., the IQ's of the two groups are not the same; therefore drug $X$ had an effect, whether good or bad).

Obviously, $H_0$ and $H_1$ cannot both be true. The researcher usually wants the alternative hypothesis to be true since this would mean that drug $X$ had an effect unlikely to be attributable to the effects of chance. The problem is that $H_1$ can refer to numerous parameter values and still satisfy the condition that $\mu_1 - \mu_2 \neq 0$. $H_0$, in contrast, is a specific and unambiguous statement. For these and other reasons, the researcher first assumes that $H_0$ is true and then gathers data that will reject $H_0$ or fail to reject $H_0$.

---

[8]The null hypothesis could also be that $\mu_1 = 100$; if there is no difference between the parameters, $\mu_2$ would also have to be 100 and $\mu_1 - \mu_2 = 0$.

In the drug experiment, rejection of $H_0$ would mean that the drug has a nonchance effect on intelligence test scores, but not necessarily that the drug *increased* test scores. Rejection of $H_0$ does require the acceptance of $H_1$ (i.e., $\mu \neq$ 100 in the treated group), but $H_1$ could be true if $\mu > 100$ or if $\mu < 100$. Of course, if it turned out that $\mu < 100$, there would probably be a public outcry for the immediate destruction of drug $X$ since it *lowered* IQ scores. But even so, $H_0$ would have been rejected and $H_1$ accepted, suggesting that drug $X$ had *some* effect.[9]

Neither $H_0$ nor $H_1$ can be rejected or accepted with certainty. Rather, a certain amount of risk accompanies each rejection of the null hypothesis. Researchers are usually willing to reject the null hypothesis if the amount of risk in being incorrect is 5 percent or less. If one is unwilling to take a 5 percent risk of incorrectly rejecting the null hypothesis, a 1 percent or lower risk may be specified instead. These two values—5 percent or 1 percent—are known as *significance levels*. If the null hypothesis is rejected at the 0.05 significance level, then the risk is 5 in 100 that the researcher will incorrectly or erroneously reject the null hypothesis; if the 0.01 level of significance is specified, then the researcher is willing to take only 1 chance in 100 of incorrectly rejecting $H_0$.

Although the 0.05 and 0.01 levels of significance are most commonly used to reject $H_0$, there is nothing sacred about those two values. A 0.10 or even a 0.30 significance level might be acceptable if the social and economic consequences of rejecting $H_0$ are slight. Being wrong 30 times out of 100 is not particularly serious under those conditions. But if the consequences are serious (e.g., death, exorbitant costs), the error rate for rejecting $H_0$ might well be lowered to 0.005 (5 chances out of 1000) or 0.001 (one chance in 1000).

## Specifying the Decision Rules

The decision rules specify the conditions under which $H_0$ will be rejected or not rejected.[10] Sometimes a researcher may reject $H_0$ when in fact $H_0$ is true. Just how often this will be done depends on the significance level required to reject $H_0$. For example, a significance level of 0.05 means that the researcher will reject $H_0$ *incorrectly* 5 percent of the time. If the significance level is 0.01, $H_0$ will be rejected incorrectly only 1 percent of the time. An incorrect rejection of $H_0$ means the researcher will report that the treatment is effective when, in fact, it is not. Rejecting $H_0$ incorrectly is known as a *Type I error*, and the risk or probability in making a Type I error depends entirely on the significance level established by the researcher.

Why not, then, always set the significance level at 0.001 or smaller? Although this would reduce Type I errors, it would have the concomitant effect of failing to reject $H_0$ when, in fact, $H_0$ should have been rejected. This type of incorrect decision is known as a *Type II error*. A Type II error would occur if the

---

[9]If $H_0$ specifies that $\mu = 100$, $H_1$ could be that $\mu > 100$ *or* $\mu < 100$. In either case, the direction of $H_1$ is specified. The test of $H_0$ when the direction of $H_1$ is specified is called a *one-tailed test of significance*, for reasons to be described later; if the direction is not specified, then the test of $H_0$ is called a *two-tailed test of significance*. A two-tailed test need only specify that $\mu_1 \neq \mu_2$.

[10]The statistical procedure that permits the rejection or the failure to reject $H_0$ is known as a *significance* or *statistical test*.

researcher reported that drug $X$ made no difference when it really did. The risk of a Type II error increases in part as the level of significance is reduced, and that level is always determined by the researcher.

The other factor that affects Type II errors (i.e., incorrectly failing to reject $H_0$) is the extent to which differences between parameters can be detected. For example, $H_0$ may specify that $\mu = 100$, and one possible value of $H_1$ could be 80. Incorrectly failing to detect that large a difference (a Type II error) would be serious, but could occur if $N$ happened to be quite small, if unreliable measures were used, or if the *statistical test* used to reject $H_0$ was not powerful enough to detect differences even that large. Not finding something that is actually present means one is working with relatively insensitive "equipment," if by that term one can include low-powered statistical tests, along with other conditions noted above that increase Type II errors.

The researcher is always in the uncomfortable position of not knowing for sure whether the decision to reject $H_0$ was correct or whether a Type I or Type II error was committed. Neither error is desirable, nor is one necessarily better than the other. A common assumption in statistics, however, is that most if not all treatments should make some difference that will be detected by the use of sensitive tests of significance and large samples.

In the drug study, the researcher needs a significance test to determine the likelihood that $\bar{X}$, the mean IQ score of 50 fifth graders administered drug $X$, is a random sample from a much larger population of the IQ scores of students not administered drug $X$. This larger population is known to have $\mu = 100$ and $\sigma = 16$. The significance test used to test $H_0$ is called a $z$-test. Assume that to reject $H_0$, the 0.05 level of significance will be required.

The formula for the $z$-test is

$$z = \frac{\bar{X} - \mu}{\sigma_{\bar{X}}}$$

The numerator expresses the disparity between the sample mean and the population mean. The denominator, $\sigma_{\bar{X}}$, is the standard error of the mean $\left(\frac{\sigma}{\sqrt{N}}\right)$ computed from known values in the population. The formula relates the difference between the two means to the standard error of the mean. In other words, the $z$-test expresses the number of standard errors that separates $\bar{X}$ from $\mu$.

To better understand the $z$-test, remember that the researcher wants to know if the null hypothesis is true or false; that is, does $\mu_1 = \mu_2$ or does $\mu_1 \neq \mu_2$? The researcher has also specified that an error of 5 percent or less in incorrectly rejecting $H_0$ is tolerable. The null hypothesis is that the two population means are identical. The value of $\mu$ in the formula for the $z$-test is the mean of the population of IQ scores of the undrugged students or 100. The best estimate of the mean of the population of IQ's for students receiving drug $X$ is the mean ($\bar{X}$) IQ of the 50 students in the sample. Thus, $\bar{X}$ can be used as an estimate of $\mu$.

Since $\bar{X}$ is computed from empirical data, it is most unlikely that it would be exactly 100, the value of $\mu$ in the numerator of the $z$-test. Values very close to 100 would probably not persuade most people to reject the null hypothesis since even the injection of sterile water instead of drug $X$ would not yield a sample mean of exactly 100. The question, of course, is how far the sample mean, $\bar{X}$, needs to differ from $\mu$ in the numerator for the $z$-test to conclude that drug $X$ had some effect?

The central-limit theorem is a basic principle in statistical inference. This theorem states that a sampling distribution of means will be normally distributed if the sample is large, no matter what the shape of the population may be.

Compare Figure III-3 with Figure III-1. Figure III-1 on page 375 is a normal distribution of *scores* or *observations* plotted in standard deviation units around $\bar{X}$, the sample mean. Figure III-3, in contrast, plots the variability in means (i.e., the standard error of sample means) around $\mu$, the parameter mean. In Figure III-1, 68 percent of the scores vary around their mean; in the second example, 68

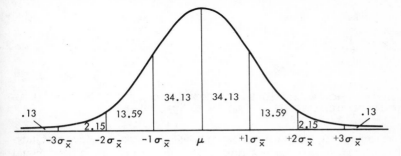

**Figure III-3**
AN EXAMPLE OF A SAMPLING DISTRIBUTION OF MEANS.

percent of the sample means vary around $\mu$. This is the same as saying that the probability is 68 percent that any single sample mean will be within $\pm 1$ standard error of the mean. With a table of areas under the normal curve (found in any statistics text), it can be shown that the probability is 95 percent that a sample mean will fall $\pm 1.96$ standard errors of the mean. This is depicted in Figure III-4a.

Figures III-4a and III-4b are important because they help to point out the type of reasoning used by statisticians. The hypothetical drug study required an estimate of the likelihood that $\bar{X}$ was drawn randomly from a specified population having a mean of $\mu$ and a standard error of $\sigma/\sqrt{N}$. If the probability is 0.68 that sample means will vary $\pm 1$ standard error around $\mu$, then statisticians would argue that any sample mean that does fall within those limits is not sufficiently different to reject the null hypothesis. Although any sample mean *could* have been drawn randomly from the population from which $\mu$ is the mean, some values of $\bar{X}$ are so far from $\mu$ that most persons would be willing to argue that $\bar{X}$ is not likely to be a random sample drawn from $\mu$. Then, the null hypothesis would be rejected since $\bar{X}$ differs so much from $\mu$.

Coin-tossing experiments are often used to demonstrate the point that any number of heads or tails can be expected by chance to occur some proportion of the time. In tossing 10 coins, for example, 10 heads can be expected to occur 1 out of every 1024 times, simply on the basis of chance. Admittedly, this is rare, but it will happen.

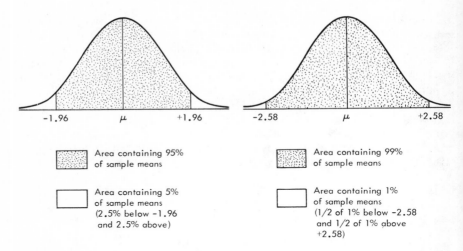

Area containing 95% of sample means

Area containing 5% of sample means (2.5% below -1.96 and 2.5% above)

Area containing 99% of sample means

Area containing 1% of sample means (1/2 of 1% below -2.58 and 1/2 of 1% above +2.58)

**Figure III-4a and Figure III-4b**
NORMAL DISTRIBUTION OF $\bar{X}$ VALUES PLOTTED AROUND $\mu$ FOR TWO-TAILED TESTS OF SIGNIFICANCE; 0.05 LEVEL (Fig. III-4a) and 0.01 (Fig. III-4b).

At some point, the researcher has to be willing to make an incorrect judgment and argue that some value of $\bar{X}$ is so unlikely that the null hypothesis should be rejected. The amount of error generally will not exceed 5 percent, or 0.05. To reject the null hypothesis with a 0.05 error is the same as saying that a significance level of 0.05 will be required to reject $H_0$.

Note that 68 percent of the sample means in Figure III-3 fall between $\pm 1$ standard error of the mean and that, therefore, 32 percent of the sample means fall outside that region. Some 4.56 percent of sample means can be expected to vary 2 or more standard errors from $\mu$ (2.15 + 0.13 + 2.15 + 0.13). Assuming random sampling, 95.44 percent (i.e., 100 − 4.56) of the sample means will be between $\pm 2$ standard errors. The probability is 0.9544 (it is common to express probabilities as proportions rather than as percentages) that $\bar{X}$, by chance, will fall $\pm 2$ standard errors around $\mu$; the probability is 0.0456 (almost 0.05, or 5 percent) that $\bar{X}$ will fall outside those limits by chance. If a researcher is willing to take a 0.0456 risk of being wrong, then any value of $\bar{X}$ that falls outside the limits of $\pm 2$ standard errors will be judged to be so unlikely that the null hypothesis will be rejected.

To reject $H_0$ at exactly the 0.05 level, a sample mean would have to be $\pm 1.96\sigma_{\bar{x}}$ from $\mu$. The comparable value needed to reject $H_0$ at the 0.01 level is $\pm 2.58$. Note that these values, $\pm 1.96$ and $\pm 2.58$, include 95 percent and 99 percent of the sample means. Any sample mean that *exceeds* these values will be judged to be sufficiently far from $\mu$ to reject $H_0$ at the 0.05 and 0.01 levels, respectively. Figures III-4a and III-4b represent two-tailed tests of significance since the researcher will reject $H_0$ if $\bar{X} > \mu$ or if $\bar{X} < \mu$.

Figures III-5a and III-5b and Figures III-6a and III-6b represent one-tailed tests of significance.

384

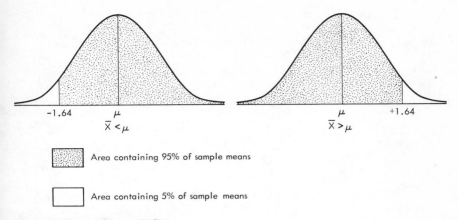

**Figure III-5a and Figure III-5b**
NORMAL DISTRIBUTION OF $\bar{X}$ VALUES PLOTTED AROUND $\mu$ FOR ONE-TAILED TEST OF SIGNIFICANCE, 0.05 LEVEL.

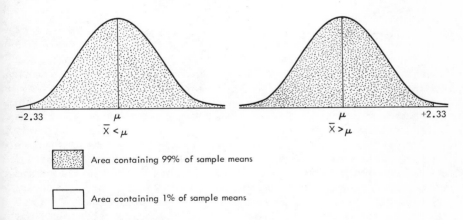

**Figure III-6a and Figure III-6b**
NORMAL DISTRIBUTIONS OF $\bar{X}$ VALUES PLOTTED AROUND $\mu$ FOR ONE-TAILED TEST OF SIGNIFICANCE, 0.01 LEVEL.

To reject $H_0$ at the 0.05 level for a one-tailed test requires only that $\bar{X}$ fall in the unshaded areas of Figures III-5a and III-5b since 5 percent of sample means will fall in that region. In Figure III-5a, the directional hypothesis is that $\bar{X}$ is at least $1.64\sigma_{\bar{X}}$ *smaller* than $\mu$; in III-5b, $\bar{X}$ must be at least $1.64\sigma_{\bar{X}}$ *larger* than $\mu$. The comparable values needed to reject $H_0$ at the 0.01 levels are shown in Figures III-6a and III-6b. $\bar{X}$ must equal or be smaller than $2.33\sigma_{\bar{X}}$ if $H_1$ is that $\bar{X} < \mu$; if $H_1$ is that $\bar{X} > \mu$, then $\bar{X}$ must equal or be larger than $2.33\sigma_{\bar{X}}$.

385

To estimate the number of standard errors that a sample mean is from some value of $\mu$, use the formula $Z = (\bar{X} - \mu)/\sigma_{\bar{x}}$. If $\sigma$ is unknown, it can be estimated by $s$.[11] The decision rules for the drug problem are:

1. Reject $H_0$ if $z \geq +1.96$ or if $z \leq -1.96$ ($\geq$ means "equals or surpasses"; $\leq$ means "equals or is smaller than").
2. Do not reject $H_0$ if $z$ is any value between $-1.96$ and $+1.96$.

Essentially, these rules state that the 0.05 level will be used to reject $H_0$ and that a two-tailed test is required (see Figure III-4a).

## Computing the Statistic

The parameter mean IQ is 100 and $\sigma$ is 16. The research question concerns the probability that a sample mean of $N = 50$ differs from a population mean. Since $\mu$ and $\sigma$ are known, the appropriate formula is $z = (\bar{X} - \mu)/(\sigma/\sqrt{N})$. Assume that the sample mean is 103. Then $z$ would be

$$\frac{103 - 100}{16/\sqrt{50}} = \frac{3}{16/7.07} = +1.32$$

## Arriving at Decisions Regarding the Parameter

The computed value of $z$ indicates that the sample mean is only $+1.32$ standard errors from the population mean of 100. The decision rule states that the null hypothesis cannot be rejected at the 0.05 level for a sample of 50 cases if $z$ is between $-1.96$ and $+1.96$. Since this is the case, the researcher is forced to conclude that there is no significant difference between those exposed to drug $X$ and other students in the population.

What would have happened if $N$ were increased to 1000? First, the standard error of the mean would have become $16/\sqrt{1000}$ or 0.5059 (compare this with $\sigma_{\bar{x}}$ of 2.263 where $N = 50$). Clearly, increasing the number of cases reduces $\sigma_{\bar{x}}$. Second, $\bar{X}$ will more closely approximate the value of $\mu$ from which it was drawn. If it were drawn from the population where $\mu = 100$, one would expect $\bar{X}$ to more closely approximate that value. If, on the other hand, the drug were highly effective, $\bar{X}$ would probably be larger than 103 and $H_0$ could be rejected.

## Statistical Significance vs. Practical Significance

Rejecting $H_0$ means that the researcher has found differences unlikely to be the result of chance. Because the denominator of both the $z$- and $t$-tests involves

---

[11] If $s$ is used to estimate $\sigma$, the appropriate statistical test requires the use of the $t$-distribution which approximates the normal distribution as the sample size approaches infinity. At the 0.05 level a sample of 50 cases and a two-tailed test, $t$ would have to surpass the value of $\pm 2.01$; at the 0.01 level, $t$ would have to surpass $+2.68$. Tables of $t$-values can be found in any elementary statistics book.

the standard deviation ($\sigma$ or $s$, respectively) divided by $\sqrt{N}$, statistically significant differences could occur by reducing $\sigma$ or $s$ (perhaps by taking care to treat all subjects alike and by using the most reliable measures available) or by increasing $N$. In the hypothetical drug study, for example, when $N = 50$, the $z$-ratio was only $+1.32$; with $N = 1000$, $z = +5.93$ (assuming $\bar{X} = 103$), large enough to reject $H_0$ at the 0.01 level. Still, the difference between $\bar{X}$ and $\mu$ was only 3 points. The question is whether or not a difference of that magnitude warrants much enthusiasm. In a practical sense, there is little difference between the behavior of students with IQ's of 100 and 103. A statistically significant difference may not make a practical difference. Even smaller differences between $\bar{X}$ and $\mu$ could be statistically significant with large enough $Ns$. For example, if $\bar{X}$ turned out to be 100.03, it is clear that drug $X$ failed to produce a difference of any practical importance. Yet, it would be possible to reject $H_0$ at the 0.01 level if the researcher had an extremely large sample ($N$ would, admittedly, have to be approximately 1.9 million). The moral is simple but important: *consider not only whether or not statistically significant results have been attained but also whether or not the results make any practical difference.*

# THE ANALYSIS OF VARIANCE: ONE-WAY RANDOMIZED GROUPS

The analysis of variance (often abbreviated ANOVA) is a statistical procedure that can be used to test the hypothesis that any number of parameter means differ. The $z$- and $t$-ratios are actually subtypes of the analysis of variance since both are restricted to comparing no more than two means. The ANOVA can compare two or more means and is the more general model.

## Stating the Research Hypothesis

Consider the following research hypothesis: "Final spelling test scores of eighth-grade students will differ significantly as a function of the amount of feedback they receive on spelling tests (zero, 50 percent, and 100 percent feedback)." Fifteen students will be assigned randomly to one of three groups, and all students will be given five spelling tests, one on each of five days. Those in the zero feedback group will be given no feedback on how well they have performed; the 50 percent feedback group will be given feedback on half of the spelling words each day; and the 100 percent group will learn how well they performed on all words after each test. Spelling test scores on a final examination will be the criterion measure. Because the groups are classified only by method (amount of feedback), the ANOVA is referred to as a one-way analysis of variance.

## Identifying the Population

The population will consist of spelling scores of eighth-grade students attending Q Junior High School as of a given date.

## Drawing the Sample

The names of every eighth grader attending Q Junior High School will be placed on a 1- by $1\frac{1}{2}$-inch card. These cards will be thoroughly shuffled and 5 names drawn at random. These students will be placed in the zero feedback group; the next two groups will be placed in the 50 percent and 100 percent feedback groups, respectively.

## Specifying the Null Hypothesis and Significance Level

The null hypothesis is that the final spelling test scores of the students will differ only by chance. Put another way, $H_0$ is that the three groups of students will have equal means in the populations after exposure to the experimental treatment. The 0.05 significance level will be used to reject $H_0$.

## Specifying the Decision Rules

The logic of the analysis of variance requires a comparison of the amount of variability *between* the various group means and the variability *within* groups. Variability may exist between groups[12] for one of two reasons: either the differences between means accurately portray population differences or the differences have arisen by chance. Variability also exists within each of the three groups. One could not reject $H_0$ if all means were identical or if there were more variability within groups than between groups. Variability within each group represents "error" or the amount of individual differences in that group.[13] The null hypothesis is that the 3 population means are equal.

The $F$ distribution is used for the test of significance for the analysis of variance. The numerator for $F$ is the variance between groups; the denominator is the variance within groups. If the between-group variance is greater than the variance within groups, it may be possible to reject $H_0$ at the 0.01 or 0.05 levels of significance; if there is greater variability within groups than between them, $H_0$ cannot be rejected. The assumptions for ANOVA are that the *population* from which each group is sampled is normally distributed, individuals are assigned randomly to each group, and the variances are approximately equal within each of the various groups being compared.

The decision rules for rejecting $H_0$ involve the use of the $F$ table (see Table III-1). If, for example, there are three groups of individuals (zero, 50 percent, and 100 percent feedback groups) with 5 cases within each group, one enters the $F$ table with the numerator having $k - 1$ degrees of freedom (where $k = $ the number of groups) and the denominator having $N - 1$ degrees of freedom. At the 0.05 level, the tabled value needed to reject $H_0$ is 3.74 (i.e., $k - 1 = 2$ and $N - 1 = 14$). If

---

[12]The term "between groups" is grammatically incorrect if more than two groups are being compared. Nonetheless, it is customary to use "between groups" rather than the more grammatically precise term "among groups."

[13]Error in a statistical sense does not refer to computational mistakes. It refers to sampling variability within groups.

## TABLE III-1

### F Values Required to Reject $H_0$ at the 0.05 Levels (Roman Type) and 0.01 Levels (Boldface Type) for Various Degrees of Freedom*

| Within-Groups Degrees of Freedom | Between-Groups Degrees of Freedom | | | | |
|---|---|---|---|---|---|
| $(N - 1)$ | 1 | 2 | 3 | 4 | 5 |
| 1 | 161 | 209 | 216 | 225 | 230 |
| | **4,052** | **4,999** | **5,403** | **5,625** | **5,764** |
| 2 | 18.51 | 19.00 | 19.16 | 19.25 | 19.30 |
| | **98.49** | **99.01** | **99.17** | **99.25** | **99.30** |
| 3 | 10.13 | 9.55 | 9.28 | 9.12 | 9.01 |
| | **34.12** | **30.81** | **29.46** | **28.71** | **28.24** |
| 4 | 7.71 | 6.94 | 6.59 | 6.39 | 6.26 |
| | **21.20** | **18.00** | **16.69** | **15.98** | **15.52** |
| 5 | 6.61 | 5.79 | 5.41 | 5.19 | 5.05 |
| | **16.26** | **13.27** | **12.06** | **11.39** | **10.97** |
| 14 | 4.60 | 3.74 | 3.34 | 3.11 | 2.96 |
| | **8.86** | **6.51** | **5.56** | **5.03** | **4.69** |

*F tables found in virtually all statistics texts provide degrees of freedom from one to infinity.

the $F$ ratio is equal to or greater than 3.74, reject $H_0$ at the 0.05 level; if $F$ is less than 3.74, do not reject $H_0$ at the 0.05 level.

## Computing the F Ratio

The $F$ ratio is the variance between groups divided by the variance within groups. Consider the hypothetical data displayed in Table III-2.

Recall that a variance is found by dividing the sum of squares, $\Sigma (X - \bar{X})^2$, by degrees of freedom, $N - 1$. The variance *within* each of the three groups is 6.5, 6.5, and 17.5, respectively. To combine these 3 variances in order to obtain an overall estimate of the within-group variance in the population, add the 3 sums of squares and divide by the sum of the degrees of freedom within each of the three groups. The 3 sums of squares when combined will equal $26 + 26 + 70 = 122$. Each of the three groups has $N - 1$ or 4 degrees of freedom for a total of 12 degrees of freedom within groups. The ratio of 122 to 12 is 10.16 (i.e., $\frac{122}{12} = 10.16$). This value, 10.16, represents the within-group variance and is the denominator of the $F$ ratio.

The between-groups variance is found by replacing all score values within each group by the group's mean score. The zero feedback group has a mean of 5.0, the 50 percent feedback group has a mean of 10.0, and the 100 percent group, a mean of 15.0. Note that setting the scores within each group to equal their respective means yields differences between groups of 5.0, 10.0, and 15.0, respectively, and

## TABLE III-2

Hypothetical Final Spelling Test Scores Obtained by Three Groups of Randomly Assigned Eighth-Grade Students Exposed to Different Feedback Schedules

|  | Zero Feedback | 50 Percent Feedback | 100 Percent Feedback |
|---|---|---|---|
|  | 8 | 13 | 16 |
|  | 2 | 7 | 9 |
|  | 7 | 12 | 17 |
|  | 3 | 8 | 13 |
|  | 5 | 10 | 20 |
| Sums = | 25.0 | 50.0 | 75.0 |
| Means = | 5.0 | 10.0 | 15.0 |
| Variances | $\frac{26}{4} = 6.5$ | $\frac{26}{4} = 6.5$ | $\frac{26}{4} = 17.5$ |

that the variance within groups is now 0.0. To compute the variance between groups, calculate the mean of the 15 substituted values. Their mean will equal the sums divided by $N$ or

$$\frac{25 + 50 + 75}{15} = \frac{150}{15} = 10.0$$

This value is the *grand mean* or the mean of all 15 means. Now subtract the grand mean, 10.0, from each of the 15 means (i.e., compute $\bar{X} - GM$ where $GM$ is grand mean), square each difference, and sum these squared differences [i.e., compute $\Sigma (\bar{X} - GM)^2$]. This is the sum of squares between groups. For the zero feedback group,

$$\Sigma (\bar{X} - GM)^2 = \Sigma [(5 - 10)^2 + (5 - 10)^2 + (5 - 10)^2 + (5 - 10)^2 + (5 - 10)^2)]$$
$$= 125$$

for the 50 percent group,

$$\Sigma (\bar{X} - GM)^2 = \Sigma [(10 - 10)^2 + (10 - 10)^2 + (10 - 10)^2 + (10 - 10)^2$$
$$+ (10 - 10)^2] = 00$$

and for the 100 percent group,

$$\Sigma (\bar{X} - GM)^2 = \Sigma [(15 - 10)^2 + (15 - 10)^2 + (15 - 10)^2 + (15 - 10)^2 + (15 - 10)^2]$$
$$= 125$$

The sum of squares between groups is $125 + 0 + 125 = 250.00$.

The between-group variance required for the numerator of the $F$ ratio is the between-groups sum of squares divided by the appropriate number of degrees of freedom. The degrees of freedom for any number of groups is $k - 1$, where $k =$ number of groups. For three groups, the degrees of freedom between groups is $3 - 1$, or 2. Since the sum of squares between groups is 250 with 2 degrees of freedom, the variance between groups is $\frac{250}{2} = 125.00$.[14]

The $F$ ratio is found by dividing the between-groups variance by the within-groups variance ($125/10.16 = 12.30$). Since this ratio is equal to or larger than the tabled value of 3.74 with 2 and 14 degrees of freedom, $H_0$ is rejected at the 0.05 significance level.

It is customary to prepare an ANOVA table that summarizes computations. Table III-3 presents an ANOVA table for the data presented in Table III-2.

## TABLE III-3
### A Summary Analysis of Variance Table

| Source of Variation | Sum of Squares | Degrees of Freedom | Variance Estimate or Mean Square | $F$ |
|---|---|---|---|---|
| Between groups | 250 | 2 | 125.00 | 12.30* |
| Within groups | 122 | 12 | 10.16 | |
| Total | 372 | 14 | | |

*$p < 0.05$ (i.e., the probability is less than 5 percent that the difference among the three means are attributable to sampling error or chance. The differences among the means are significant at the 0.05 level of significance as hypothesized). Indeed, the $F$-ratio is sufficiently large to reject $H_0$ at the .01 level.

The total sum of squares can be computed by taking all 15 scores and disregarding their original classification into three groups. The mean of all 15 scores is 10.0; the value of 10.0 is subtracted from each of the 15 scores, and these differences are squared. The sum of the squared differences is the sum of squares or 372. Note that the between- plus the within-groups degrees of freedom equals $N - 1$ or 14.[15] Note also that the total degrees of freedom between groups sum to 14. By computing all three sources of variance (between groups, within groups, and total) a check on the accuracy of the calculations can be made. The between- and within-groups sums of squares and their respective degrees of freedom must add up to the totals.

[14]Some researchers use the term *mean square* instead of *variance*. The symbols $MS_B$ and $MS_W$ refer to the mean square between and within groups, respectively. *Mean square* is the mean (at least in the sense that there is a division by degrees of freedom) of the sum of the squared deviations around the mean.

[15]The between-groups degrees of freedom is number of groups minus 1; the within-groups degrees of freedom is number of persons minus 1 for each group; the total is found by taking all subjects minus 1.

## Arriving at Decisions Regarding Parameters

The ANOVA has indicated that the populations means differ significantly, but what is not known is which means are significantly different. It may be tempting to select the two most discrepant means and to compute a $t$-test between them. But this violates an assumption underlying $t$-tests, namely, that the groups must be selected randomly. If the two most extreme means are selected, randomization has been violated, and the tabled values of $t$ no longer hold. Duncan,[16] Tukey,[17] Scheffé,[18] and Dunnett,[19] among others[20] have proposed methods of determining which means differ following a significant $F$ ratio. The researcher should avoid using $t$-tests following ANOVA unless two specific groups were hypothesized to differ from one another prior to the collection of data.

If two and only two groups are being compared, it is possible to use a $t$-test or an ANOVA. In this limited case where only two groups are involved, $t = \sqrt{F}$ and $t^2 = F$. Thus, the computed value of $t$ will equal the square root of $F$.


# THE ANALYSIS OF VARIANCE: FACTORIAL EXPERIMENTS

A one-way analysis has a single basis of classification such as methods, treatments, *or* amount of feedback. There may be any number of methods, but if all means are method means, there is only one basis of classification.

The rationale behind the analysis of variance can be extended to two or more bases of classification such as methods and levels of intelligence, methods and grade levels, or methods and types of teachers. Indeed, any number of different bases for classification may be employed. When two or more classifications are involved in an experiment, the researcher has employed a *factorial experiment*.

Suppose, for example, that a researcher hypothesizes not only that amount of feedback will have a significant effect on spelling achievement but also that males will differ from females. Although two experiments could be conducted (one to test the effect of the amount of feedback and a second one to determine whether males differ from females in spelling achievement), it is possible and advantageous to combine the two studies to form a factorial experiment. The factorial experiment

[16]David B. Duncan, "Multiple Range and Multiple $F$ Tests," *Biometrics*, 11 (1955), pp. 1–42.

[17]John W. Tukey, "Comparing Individual Means in the Analysis of Variance," *Biometrics*, 5 (1949), pp. 99–114.

[18]H. Scheffé, "A Method for Judging All Contrasts in the Analysis of Variance," *Biometrika*, 40 (1953), pp. 87–104.

[19]Charles W. Dunnett, "A Mutual Comparison Procedure for Comparing Several Treatments with a Control," *Journal of the American Statistical Association*, 50, no. 272 (1955), pp. 1096–1121.

[20]See Geoffrey Keppel, *Design and Analysis: A Researcher's Handbook* (Englewood Cliffs, N.J.: Prentice-Hall, 1973), pp. 133–163, for a discussion of these topics and numerical examples.

permits the researcher to determine the effects of feedback, sex, and the *interaction* between feedback and sex. The interaction effect is extremely important since it allows the investigator to determine whether there is some relationship between sex and amount of feedback. If a significant interaction is present, this might suggest that males respond with higher levels of achievement under one type of feedback but lower under a different type.

Examine the data in Table III-4. The design is restricted to 2 levels of feedback (50 percent and 100 percent) and 2 levels of sex (males and females). Because

## TABLE III-4

Hypothetical Data Showing Spelling Scores of Male and Female Students under 2 Conditions of Feedback

|         | 50% Feedback | 100% Feedback |
|---------|:------------:|:-------------:|
| Males   | 1            | 4             |
|         | 2            | 5             |
|         | 3            | 6             |
| Females | 7            | 10            |
|         | 8            | 11            |
|         | 9            | 12            |

there are 2 bases of classification (feedback and sex), this would be called a 2 × 2 (read "two by two") factorial design. A 2 × 3 factorial design would result if a third feedback group (zero feedback) were included in the study. The same assumptions hold for a factorial design that held for a one-way ANOVA. An additional assumption for a factorial design over the one-way ANOVA is that the number of cases in each group be equal.[21] That assumption has been met in Table III-4 since there are 3 scores or observations in each of the 4 groups.

In a factorial design, the researcher is interested in determining whether or not there are significant differences between columns (usually methods or treatments), between rows (usually aptitude, sex, grade level, or other subject or teacher characteristics) and the interaction between columns and rows.

## The Between-Methods Sum of Squares

The between-methods sum of squares is found by replacing the scores in each column with the column mean score.[22] The grand mean (6.5) is then sub-

---

[21]For modifications in computation should this assumption be violated, see Allen L. Edwards, *Experimental Design in Psychological Research*, 4th ed. (New York: Holt, Rinehart and Winston, 1972), pp. 217–220.

[22]The method demonstrated here is used to help the student understand the rationale behind the factorial analysis of variance. References at the end of the appendix should be consulted for more efficient computational procedures.

tracted from each of these replaced values, and the differences are squared and summed. Each squared difference is 2.25, and there are 12 of these values to yield a between-columns or -methods sum of squares of 27.0 (see Table III-5, page 396).

| | Original Column Scores (Methods) | | Replaced Column Scores | |
|---|---|---|---|---|
| | 50% | 100% | 50% | 100% |
| | 1 | 4 | $5 - 6.5 = -1.5^2 = 2.25$ | $8 - 6.5 = 1.5^2 = 2.25$ |
| | 2 | 5 | $5 - 6.5 = -1.5^2 = 2.25$ | $8 - 6.5 = 1.5^2 = 2.25$ |
| | 3 | 6 | $5 - 6.5 = -1.5^2 = 2.25$ | $8 - 6.5 = 1.5^2 = 2.25$ |
| | 7 | 10 | $5 - 6.5 = -1.5^2 = 2.25$ | $8 - 6.5 = 1.5^2 = 2.25$ |
| | 8 | 11 | $5 - 6.5 = -1.5^2 = 2.25$ | $8 - 6.5 = 1.5^2 = 2.25$ |
| | 9 | 12 | $5 - 6.5 = -1.5^2 = 2.25$ | $8 - 6.5 = 1.5^2 = 2.25$ |
| Sums | 30 | $+$ 48 $= 78$ | | |
| N | 6 | 6 | Grand mean $= \frac{78}{12} = 6.5$ | |
| Mean | 5.0 | 8.0 | | |

## The Between-Sexes Sum of Squares

The sum of squares between rows or characteristics (males and females) is computed in exactly the same way. The original scores attained by the males and females are listed without regard to the amount of feedback. These original scores are replaced by their respective means. The grand mean is subtracted from each replaced mean and these differences are squared and summed. The between-sexes sum of squares is 108.0 ($9 \times 12 = 108$). These data are also summarized in Table III-5 (see page 396).

| | Original Raw Mean (Sex) | | Replaced Column Scores | |
|---|---|---|---|---|
| | Males | Females | 50% | 100% |
| | 1 | 7 | $3.5 - 6.5 = -3^2 = 9$ | $9.5 - 6.5 = 3^2 = 9$ |
| | 2 | 8 | $3.5 - 6.5 = -3^2 = 9$ | $9.5 - 6.5 = 3^2 = 9$ |
| | 3 | 9 | $3.5 - 6.5 = -3^2 = 9$ | $9.5 - 6.5 = 3^2 = 9$ |
| | 4 | 10 | $3.5 - 6.5 = -3^2 = 9$ | $9.5 - 6.5 = 3^2 = 9$ |
| | 5 | 11 | $3.5 - 6.5 = -3^2 = 9$ | $9.5 - 6.5 = 3^2 = 9$ |
| | 6 | 12 | $3.5 - 6.5 = -3^2 = 9$ | $9.5 - 6.5 = 3^2 = 9$ |
| Sums | 21 | $+$ 57 $= 78$ | | |
| N | 6 | 6 | Grand mean $= \frac{78}{12} = 6.5$ | |
| Mean | 3.5 | 9.5 | | |

## The Interaction Sum of Squares

The interaction sum of squares can be determined in a $2 \times 2$ table by examining the sums of the original scores in each of the 4 cells.[23] Add the sums indicated by the arrows in the $2 \times 2$ table below (i.e., $6 + 33$ *and* $24 + 15$); subtract the 2 sums, and square the difference $(39 - 39)^2 = 0$. Since this value is 0.0, the interaction sum of squares is zero. A difference greater than 0.0 means there is *some* interaction. The amount of interaction is found by dividing the squared difference by $N$, the number of cases. If the interaction is not significant, the effect of each variable may be considered separately; if the interaction is significant, this means that the effect of the variables can only be considered in relation to one another. An example of a nonzero interaction will be shown shortly.

|         | 50%  | 100% |              |       |
|---------|------|------|--------------|-------|
| Males   | 6.0  | 15.0 | $6 + 33 =$   | 39    |
| Females | 24.0 | 33.0 | $24 + 15 =$  | $-39$ |
|         |      |      |              | 00    |

## The Within-Groups Sum of Squares

The within-groups sum of squares is found by adding the sum of squares within each of the 4 groups. The sum of squares in each group is the numerator of that group's variance. Because there are 4 groups, each having 2.0 as its sum of squares, the within-group sum of squares is 8.0 (see Table III-5 on page 396).

|                 | Males 50% Reinforcement | Males 100% Reinforcement | Females 50% Reinforcement | Females 100% Reinforcement |
|-----------------|-------------------------|--------------------------|---------------------------|----------------------------|
|                 | 1                       | 4                        | 7                         | 10                         |
|                 | 2                       | 5                        | 8                         | 11                         |
|                 | 3                       | 6                        | 9                         | 12                         |
| Sums            | 6                       | 15                       | 24                        | 33                         |
| Means           | 2                       | 5                        | 8                         | 11                         |
| Sums of squares | 2.0                     | 2.0                      | 2.0                       | 2.0                        |

## Degrees of Freedom

Note that there is 1 degree of freedom for methods and 1 degree of freedom for sex since there are 2 methods and 2 sexes. Within each group there are 2 degrees

---

[23]See Edwards, *Experimental Design in Psychological Research*, p. 160. By interaction is meant that the effect of one factor (e.g., amount of feedback) depends on or interacts with the conditions of the second factor (e.g., sex). For example, if the effectiveness of feedback depended on being a male (or female) there would be an interaction between the two variables.

of freedom and there are 4 groups. Therefore, there are 8 degrees of freedom within groups. The degrees of freedom for interaction are found by multiplying the degrees of freedom for methods by the degrees of freedom for sex. The total degrees of freedom is $N - 1$ or 11. All of these values have been included in Table III-5.

TABLE III-5

Summary Table for a Two-Way ANOVA*

| Source of Variation | Sum of Squares | Degrees of Freedom | Variance Estimate or Mean Square | $F$ |
|---|---|---|---|---|
| Methods | 27.0 | 1 | 27.0 | 27.0** |
| Sexes | 108.0 | 1 | 108.0 | 108.0** |
| Interaction (methods × sex) | 0.0 | 1 | 0.0 | 0.0 |
| Within groups | 8.0 | 8 | 1.0 | |
| Total | 143.0 | 11 | | |

*The student should note that the total sum of squares is the sum of the method, sex, interaction, and within-groups sum of squares. The interaction may be computed by summing the methods, sexes, and within groups and subtracting them from the total.

**There are significant differences between methods and between sexes. Evidently 100% feedback is more effective than 50%. Also, females outperformed the males in the spelling test.

## The Meaning of Interaction

Suppose that the interaction were significant. Examine another set of four different sums obtained from a total $N$ of 20 below:

| | Method 1 | Method 2 |
|---|---|---|
| Characteristic 1 (males) | 40 | 20 |
| Characteristic 2 (females) | 20 | 40 |

Clearly, males seem to perform better under method 1, whereas females perform better under method 2. The amount of interaction between methods and sex is

$$\frac{(80 - 40)^2}{20} = \frac{40^2}{20} = 80$$

This relationship can be seen in Figure III-7 where a dot has been placed across from the sum of 40 and above method 1 to depict the performance of males under method 1; a second dot for males has been placed where the sum of 20 intersects with method 2. The two dots are joined by a line. A second line is plotted for the females. The two main conditions (method and sex) *each* provide a separate *main effect*, and the relationship between them is known as the *interaction effect*. In this

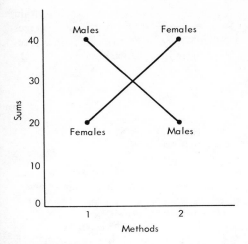

**Figure III-7**
SHOWING THE INTERACTION BETWEEN METHODS AND SEX AND NO SIGNIFICANT
MAIN EFFECTS (DATA ARE FICTITIOUS).

example, the two method means[24] are equal as are the two sex means. Thus, the
two main effects are not significant. Some interaction is present if the lines are not
parallel as is the case in Figure III-7. Figure III-8 depicts zero interaction.

In Figure III-8, females consistently outperform males; sex, therefore, yields
a possible significant main effect. Methods also differ since 100 percent feedback
is superior to 50 percent feedback. Since the lines are perfectly parallel, however,
there can be no significant interaction effect.

Figure III-9 shows four hypothetical means where there is a possible signi-

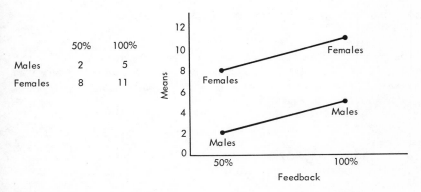

**Figure III-8**
SHOWING POSSIBLE SIGNIFICANT MAIN EFFECTS FOR FEEDBACK
AND SEX WITH NO INTERACTION EFFECTS.

[24]It is possible to plot either sums or means. Ordinarily, means are plotted.

397

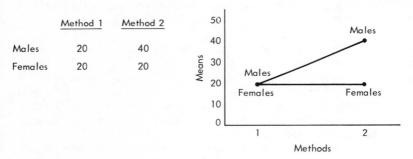

|         | Method 1 | Method 2 |
|---------|----------|----------|
| Males   | 60       | 60       |
| Females | 30       | 30       |

**Figure III-9**
MEANS AND PLOTS OF A 2 × 2 FACTORICAL DESIGN WITH
A POSSIBLE SIGNIFICANT MAIN EFFECT FOR SEX ONLY.

ficant main effect for sex, but no significant main effect for methods and no interaction. Since males performed at a higher level than females regardless of method, there is no interaction effect. Note that the two lines are parallel.

Figure III-10 shows yet another possibility in outcome. Because males perform at a higher level than females under method 2 (but not method 1), there is

|         | Method 1 | Method 2 |
|---------|----------|----------|
| Males   | 20       | 40       |
| Females | 20       | 20       |

**Figure III-10**
MEANS AND PLOTS OF A 2 × 2 FACTORIAL DESIGN SHOWING POSSIBLE
SIGNIFICANT MAIN EFFECT FOR SEX, METHODS, AND INTERACTION.

a main effect in favor of males. There are also differences favoring method 2 and an interaction effect since the lines are not parallel. Chapter 7 contains a section on the interpretation of interaction effects when the lines converge (as they do in Figure III-10) and when they cross (as in Figure III-7).

Differences between method means are shown in Figure III-11. Method 1 has a grand mean of 10, whereas the grand mean for method 2 is 5. Thus, there is some difference between the means. Males and females, however, both yield grand means of 7.5. Since males and females perform equally well, there can be no significant main effect for sex, and since the two lines are identical, no significant interaction exists between methods and sex.

The analysis of variance is not limited to 2 × 2 designs. Chapter 7 discusses more complex functional designs and shows how results obtained from such designs can be interpreted. The advantages and disadvantages of *repeated*

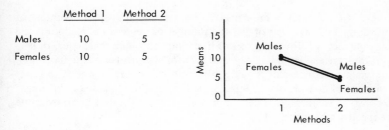

| | Method 1 | Method 2 |
|---|---|---|
| Males | 10 | 5 |
| Females | 10 | 5 |

**Figure III-11**
MEANS AND PLOTS OF A 2 × 2 FACTORIAL DESIGN SHOWING A POSSIBLE MAIN EFFECT FOR METHODS ONLY.

*measure* designs where the same individual (or a *matched* counterpart) appears in more than one treatment is also discussed in that chapter.

## Chi Square

Chi square ($\chi^2$) is used to test the significance between observed and "expected" or theoretical frequencies or counts of events, persons, or attributes. For example, a researcher may wish to compare the frequency or number of students attending elementary, junior, and senior high schools in a given district with the number of students expected on the basis of chance (in this case, the mean number of students attending the three types of schools) or on some other basis. Table III-6 provides fictitious data used to test the null hypothesis that the observed and expected frequencies differ by chance alone.

### TABLE III-6

Hypothetical Data Comparing the Number of Elementary, Junior, and Senior High Schools in a Given District

| | Elementary | Junior High | Senior High |
|---|---|---|---|
| Observed frequency | 200 | 150 | 100 |
| Expected frequency | 150 | 150 | 150 |
| Difference (observed − expected) | 50 | 0 | −50 |
| Differences squared | 2500 | 0 | 2500 |
| $\dfrac{\text{Differences squared}}{\text{Expected frequency}}$ | $\dfrac{2500}{150} = 16.67$ | $\dfrac{0}{150} = 0$ | $\dfrac{2500}{150} = 16.67$ |

$$\text{Total} = 450$$
$$\text{Mean} = \frac{450}{3} = 150$$

$$\chi^2 = \frac{\Sigma (fo - fe)^2}{fe} = 16.67 + 0 + 16.67 = 33.34$$

399

To test $H_0$, one enters a chi-square table with the appropriate number of degrees of freedom. For this type of $\chi^2$, the number of degrees of freedom is the number of schools minus 1. For 2 degrees of freedom, chi square must equal or surpass 5.99 for significance at the 0.05 level, and 9.21 for significance at the 0.01 level. Any elementary statistics text will provide minimum values of $\chi^2$ needed to reject $H_0$ for any number of degrees of freedom. Since the computed value of chi square is 33.34, the observed frequencies differ significantly (i.e., at the 0.01 level) from the frequencies expected by chance.

## $\chi^2$ as a Test of "Goodness of Fit" and "Independence"

If there is a single variable, chi square is said to be a test of "goodness of fit." It can be used to estimate the likelihood that the frequencies or observations correspond with values expected on the basis of chance. The data in Table III-6, for example, can be used as a test of goodness of fit. The number of degrees of freedom is the number of categories minus 1. As an example, if there is a 5-alternative multiple-choice item to which students respond, there would be 4 degrees of freedom (i.e., $5 - 1 = 4$); if there were 8 categories of favorableness to which women in a survey responded, the number of degrees of freedom would equal 7.

A second use of chi square is as a test of "independence." Tests of independence involve two sets of data that form $2 \times 2$ (read "two by two"), $2 \times 3$, $2 \times 4$, $3 \times 3$, $3 \times 4$, etc. tables. In these examples, the researcher asks whether or not the two sets of data are independent of one another. For example, are there differences between expected and observed numbers of men and women in their preferences to three political candidates? Or are there differences between high, average, and low income groups regarding recovery from four specified types of surgery? The first example involves a $2 \times 3$ table (men–women and each of the three candidates); the second involves a $3 \times 4$ table (three levels of income and four types of surgery).

## Determining Expected Values for Tests of Independence

Sometimes $\chi^2$ is determined from more than one basis of classification. Suppose that the number of students attending elementary, junior high, and senior high schools are also subdivided into males and females to form a $2 \times 3$ table. Again, $\chi^2$ is used to test the null hypothesis that the observed and expected values differ only by chance.

The expected or theoretical value for each cell is determined in the following way: 200 of the 450 students are males, and 250 of the 450 students are females. Thus, the probability of randomly selecting a male is $\frac{200}{450}$, and the probability of randomly selecting a female is $\frac{250}{450}$. Similarly, the numbers of elementary, junior, and senior high students are 200, 150, and 100, respectively. Thus, the probabilities of randomly selecting a student from these schools are $\frac{200}{450}$, $\frac{150}{450}$, and $\frac{100}{450}$. What is the probability of selecting by chance an elementary school pupil who is also a male?

This probability is found by multiplying the probability that a student is from an elementary school by the probability that a student is a male. The values for all combinations of schools and students are given below.

Probability of
Being a (an)

Elementary student $= \dfrac{200}{450} = 0.44$

Junior high student $= \dfrac{150}{450} = 0.33$

Senior high student $= \dfrac{100}{450} = 0.22$

Male student $\quad = \dfrac{200}{450} = 0.44$

Female student $\quad = \dfrac{200}{450} = 0.55$

| | | Observed | − | Expected | Diff. | Diff.$^2$ | Diff.$^2 \div$ Expected |
|---|---|---|---|---|---|---|---|
| Elementary and male | = 0.1936 | 80 | − | 87.12 | −7.12 | 50.69 | 0.582 |
| Junior high and male | = 0.1452 | 70 | − | 65.34 | 4.66 | 21.72 | 0.332 |
| Senior high and male | = 0.0968 | 50 | − | 43.56 | 6.44 | 41.47 | 0.952 |
| Elementary and female | = 0.2420 | 120 | − | 108.90 | 11.10 | 123.21 | 1.130 |
| Junior high and female | = 0.1815 | 80 | − | 81.675 | −1.675 | 2.81 | 0.034 |
| Senior high and female | = 0.1210 | 50 | − | 54.45 | −4.45 | 19.80 | 0.364 |

$$\chi^2 = 3.394$$

The probability of selecting a male elementary student by chance is 0.1936. This is the product of the probability of selecting a male by chance ($\frac{200}{450} = 0.44$) and the probability of selecting an elementary student by chance (which is also $\frac{200}{450}$ or 0.44). Converting 0.1936 to the *frequency* expected by chance requires multiplying 0.1936 by the total number of students, 450. For elementary males, this entails obtaining the product of 0.1936 × 450 or 87.12. To compute $\chi^2$ the value 87.12 has to be subtracted from the observed frequency of elementary males, 80, to yield the difference, −7.12. This value is squared ($-7.12^2 = 50.6944$) and divided by the expected or chance frequency ($50.69 \div 87.12 = 0.582$). This procedure is followed for the other cells in the table. Chi square is the sum of each difference squared and divided by its respective chance or expected value. For the example above, $\chi^2 = 3.394$.

To determine the significance of chi square, one must enter a chi-square table by using the appropriate number of degrees of freedom. For a double classification table, the degrees of freedom can be found by multiplying the number of rows minus 1 by the number of columns minus 1 [$df = (r-1)(c-1)$]. Because the example provides 2 rows (males and females) and 3 columns (elementary, junior, and senior high), the degrees of freedom are $(2-1)(3-1) = 2$. To reject $H_0$ at the 0.05 level requires $\chi^2 \geq 5.99$; at the 0.01 level, $\chi^2 \geq 9.21$. Since the computed value of $\chi^2 = 3.394$, one must conclude that the difference between observed and expected values for the number of males and females attending the three types of schools probably occurred as a result of chance.

## Assumptions for Chi Square

Chi square requires the use of frequencies or counts and is not appropriate for means. Chi square also assumes that the expected frequencies are larger than 5 and that each cell is independent of the others.[25] Chi square is not appropriate for determining if the number of individuals who are categorized in a pre-cell, for example, will also be categorized in a post-cell since pre–post differences are not independent.

Expected values of chi square in tests of goodness of fit can be any set of values hypothesized. Usually, it is obtained by using the mean frequency, but any set of predetermined values will do. Mendelian ratios (9: 3: 3: 1) or values predicted by the normal curve can also be used. The important point is to be sure that frequencies and not means are used for the observed data.

## Selected Supplementary Readings

1. ANDREWS, FRANK M., et al. *A Guide for Selecting Statistical Techniques for Analyzing Social Science Data.* Ann Arbor: Survey Research Center, Institute for Social Research, University of Michigan, 1974, 36 pp.

2. BRUNING, JAMES L., and KINTZ, B. L. *Computational Handbook of Statistics.* 2d ed. Glenview, Ill.: Scott, Foresman, 1977, 308 pp.

3. McCALL, ROBERT B. *Fundamental Statistics for Psychology.* 2d ed. New York: Harcourt, Brace & World, 1975, 406 pp.

4. CHASE, CLINTON I. *Elementary Statistical Procedures.* 2d ed. New York: McGraw-Hill Book Co., 1976, 277 pp.

5. COMREY, ANDREW L. *Elementary Statistics: A Problem Solving Approach.* Homewood, Ill.: Dorsey Press, 1975, 298 pp.

6. EDWARDS, ALLEN L. *Statistical Analysis.* 4th ed. New York: Holt, Rinehart and Winston, 1974 273 pp.

7. FERGUSON, GEORGE A. *Statistical Analysis in Psychology and Education.* 4th ed. New York: McGraw-Hill Book Co., 1976, 529 pp.

8. GLASS, GENE V, and STANLEY, JULIAN C. *Statistical Methods in Education and Psychology.* Englewood Cliffs, N.J.: Prentice-Hall, 1970, 596 pp.

[25]As the number of degrees of freedom increases, smaller expected values can be tolerated. With 1 degree of freedom, the minimum expected or chance value should be at least 5.

9. GUILFORD, J. P., and FRUCHTER, BENJAMIN. *Fundamental Statistics in Psychology and Education.* 6th ed. New York: McGraw-Hill Book Co., 1978, 545 pp.

10. HOPKINS, KENNETH D., and GLASS, GENE V. *Basic Statistics for the Behavioral Sciences.* Englewood Cliffs, N.J.: Prentice-Hall, 1978, 436 pp.

11. RUNYON, RICHARD P., and HABER, AUDREY. *Fundamentals of Behavioral Statistics.* 3d ed. Reading, Mass.: Addison-Wesley Publishing Co., 1976, 446 pp.

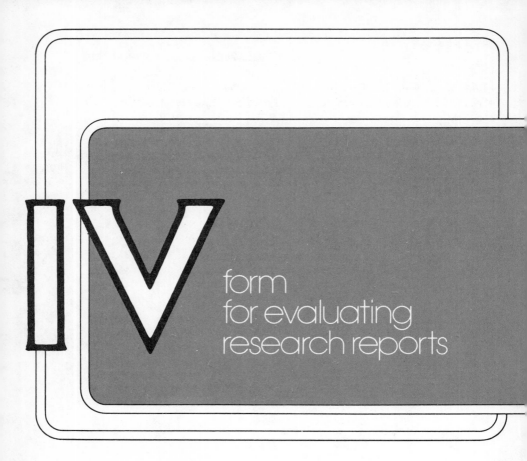

# IV

## form for evaluating research reports

### The Title

**1.** The dependent variables are clearly stated.
**2.** The independent variables are clearly stated.
**3.** Subject characteristics (age, grade, sex, race) are stated.
**4.** The relationships among dependent variables, independent variables, and subject characteristics are clear.

### Authorship

**1.** The person having primary responsibility is listed first.
**2.** All other authors have made important scientific contributions to the paper.
**3.** Degrees and titles are omitted.
**4.** Each author's institutional affiliation is reported.
**5.** Departmental affiliations are omitted.

404

## Problem

1. The reasons for conducting the study are clear.
2. The reasons for conducting the study are important.
3. The literature review shows how the study is related to previously conducted research.
4. Related theoretical positions are stated clearly and concisely.
5. The literature review points out methodological problems found in previously conducted research.
6. Methods for eliminating or reducing methodological problems are clearly stated.
7. Only relevant studies are referred to.
8. All important studies are included in the paper.
9. Studies are not listed without showing how they are related to one another.
10. The literature review is organized, and the organization is apparent to the reader.
11. Every source referred to has a reference in the bibliography.
12. The bibliography does not contain references not mentioned in the paper.
13. Assumptions are clarified.
14. Delimitations are specified.

## Hypotheses

1. All research hypotheses are in statement form.
2. All research hypotheses are clearly derived from the review of the literature.
3. All hypotheses are testable.
4. Research hypotheses are not confused with null hypotheses.
5. All ambiguous terms used in the hypotheses are defined operationally.

## Subjects

1. The population is defined.
2. The procedures used to draw samples are stated clearly.
3. Number of cases within each comparison group is specified.
4. Number of males and females in each comparison group is specified (if sex is relevant).
5. Means and standard deviations of subjects' ages or grades are reported for each comparison group (if these variables are relevant).
6. Social class characteristics and methods of measuring social class are included (if social class is relevant).
7. Ethnic, religious, racial backgrounds, and language difficulties (if any) of subjects are reported (if relevant).
8. A reasonable number of subjects was selected.
9. Names and any other identifying descriptions of subjects are omitted.
10. Method(s) used to select schools and/or classes are specified.
11. Generalized and ambiguous references (such as "typical middle-class community") are avoided or clarified with empirical evidence.

**12.** If subjects are matched, means and standard deviations on all matching variables of experimental and control groups are included.
**13.** Names of cooperating districts, schools, and teachers remain confidential.

## Apparatus or Materials

**1.** All materials and apparatus referred to are described by brand names and model numbers.
**2.** Homemade materials and apparatus are described in sufficient detail to allow other researchers to duplicate them.
**3.** The study uses standard apparatus and materials or the reason for changing is justified.

## Instruments

**1.** All standardized tests are reported by their correct title, form, level, and date of publication.
**2.** Appropriateness of test for subjects in study (reading level, difficulty level, clarity of questions, evidence of test bias, reasonableness of time limits, scoring objectivity, number of items, relevance and accuracy of reported norms, if any) is specified.
**3.** Evidence regarding reliability is presented for each age or grade level included in study.
**4.** Evidence of validity is presented for the specific purpose for which the instrument was designed.
**5.** Response mode is specified (true–false, matching, etc.).
**6.** If in multiple-choice format, number of options is reported.
**7.** Methods followed in constructing and selecting items are reported.

## Instructions to Experimental and Control Groups

**1.** Instructions are clear and complete for the maturational level of subjects.
**2.** Instructions are presented verbatim.

## Procedures

**1.** Characteristics of experimenters (race, sex, training) that might affect subjects' behavior are described.
**2.** Experimental treatment is described in sufficient detail to permit replication.
**3.** Control treatment is described in sufficient detail to permit replication.
**4.** Procedures have been approved by an appropriate institutional review committee to meet ethical standards.
**5.** Subjects and parents have given informed consent.
**6.** Subjects have not been coerced into participating.
**7.** Subjects face no physical or psychological stress or deception.
**8.** Provisions for anonymity and confidentiality have been made.

**9.** Procedures are directly related to the analysis of proposed hypotheses.
**10.** Number of subjects in each group who began study and later dropped out, if any, is reported.
**11.** Threats to internal validity have been eliminated (selection, history, maturation, testing, instrumentation, regression, and mortality).
**12.** Threats to external validity are controlled to a reasonable extent.

## Design

**1.** Pretests, if used, are entered into statistical analyses.
**2.** Assumptions underlying statistical tests of significance are met.
**3.** Level of significance required to reject each null hypothesis is specified.
**4.** Research hypotheses are converted to their null form (especially in longer reports, theses, and dissertations).
**5.** Statistical analyses are clearly related to research and null hypotheses.
**6.** Treatments are powerful and continued over reasonable periods of time.

## Results or Findings

**1.** Findings are presented in relation to each hypothesis.
**2.** Findings are described objectively and dispassionately.
**3.** Graphs and tables are numbered and referred to before they are presented in paper.
**4.** All graphs and tables are clearly labeled.
**5.** Standard ANOVA tables are presented, where appropriate.
**6.** Means and standard deviations of the dependent variable and the number of cases are presented for each group being compared.

## Discussion

**1.** The paper explains unanticipated findings.
**2.** The paper explains statistically nonsignificant findings.
**3.** Differences between statistical and practical significance are realized.
**4.** Findings are related to theory reported in the review of the literature.
**5.** Findings are related to the problem (reasons for conducting the study).
**6.** The importance of the findings is discussed.
**7.** Cautions and limitations of research findings are brought out.
**8.** Needed additional research is described.
**9.** Generalizations are restricted to similarly constituted persons, methods, and materials.

## References

**1.** Style is consistent from reference to reference.
**2.** Style is in a format acceptable to the institution or publishers.
**3.** References contain all sources referred to in document.
**4.** References are accurate and complete.

## Style

1. Slang and colloquial expressions are avoided.
2. The paper is clearly and logically organized.
3. Deadwood has been eliminated.
4. Sentence meaning is clear.
5. Transitional phrases guide the reader from sentence to sentence and paragraph to paragraph.
6. Redundancy is avoided.
7. Unnecessary prepositional phrases are avoided.
8. Trite expressions are avoided.
9. Grammatical rules are followed.
10. Spelling is correct.
11. Tenses are used correctly.
12. Abbreviations are appropriately used.
13. Measurements are reported in metric units.
14. Punctuation rules are followed.
15. Rules for capitalization are followed.
16. Sentences do not begin with numbers.
17. Numbers from *zero* to *nine* are spelled out unless they refer to statistical data.
18. Numbers larger than nine are presented as numerals.
19. Measurements, ages, percentages, arithmetic operations, ratios, exact values of money, scores, and scale values are reported in numerals whether they are below ten or not.
20. The manuscript is double spaced.
21. There are adequate margins on all sides of paper.
22. The manuscript is typed on white bond paper.
23. Typing and layouts are neat and in the proper format (correct headings and subheadings).
24. Manuscript is of appropriate length.
25. Quotations are appropriate and relevant.
26. The paper is interesting to read.

writing
the research
paper

V

Research is a shared adventure requiring communication among the members of the scientific enterprise. The purpose of research reports—whether they are master's theses, doctoral dissertations, or journal articles—is to convey ideas and information. The report allows other investigators to evaluate a study and, if desired, to replicate it on their own.

## Organization of the Research Report

The organization of research reports depends on such factors as institutional requirements, the permissible length of the document itself, and the type of research to be communicated (analytic, experimental, descriptive).

*Institutional Requirements.* Some departments, colleges, and universities have adopted certain stylistic and organizational principles for theses and dissertations. The University of Chicago Press, for example, publishes *A Manual of Style* 12th ed., rev. (1969) adhered to by many schools. Other schools may recommend or require formats suggested by Kate L. Turabian, *A Manual for Writers of Term Papers, Theses, and Dissertations*, 4th ed. (Chicago: University of Chicago Press, 1973); William G. Campbell and Stephen V. Ballou, *Form and Style: Theses, Reports, Term Papers*, 4th ed. (Boston: Houghton Mifflin Co., 1974), or the *Publication Manual of the American Psychological Association*, 2d ed. (Washington, D.C.: American Psychological Association, 1974), 136 pp. Before writing the research report, the student should determine which writing guides have been approved or are required.

*Document Length.* Because theses and dissertations are usually of unlimited length, they can include much more detail and supplementary information than would be possible with published reports. For example, a thesis or dissertation involving an empirical problem usually contains the following elements:

> Title
> Author
> Degree, school, and other preliminary information
> > (e.g., A Dissertation Presented to the FACULTY OF THE GRADUATE SCHOOL, UNIVERSITY OF WASHINGTON. In Partial Fulfillment of the Requirements for the Degree DOCTOR OF PHILOSOPHY in Education)
> Month and year in which degree is to be awarded
> Approval sheet and signatures of advisory committee
> Acknowledgements (optional)
> Table of Contents
> List of Tables
> List of Figures
> Abstract
> Chapter I: The Problem or Introduction
> Chapter II: Review of the Literature (or include this in Chapter I)
> Chapter III: Procedures or Methods
> Chapter IV: Findings or Results
> Chapter V: Summary, Conclusions, and Implications
> Bibliography or References
> Appendices

If the research report is to be published, the organization usually follows this format:

> Title
> Author
> Organizational Affiliation
> Abstract (not always required)
> Introduction or Problem
> Methods or Procedures
> Results or Findings

Discussion or Conclusions and Recommendations
References or Bibliography

Appendices containing raw data, copies of unpublished tests, and examples of materials used in the study should be included in theses or dissertations, but space restrictions do not permit their inclusion in published works such as journals. Supplementary materials can, however, be deposited with and ordered from ASIS/ NAPS (American Society for Information Science/National Auxiliary Publications Service), 40 Microfiche Publications, 305 East 46th Street, New York, N.Y. 10017.

*Type of Research.* The organizational outlines above can be used for descriptive and experimental studies. Nonempirical studies can be organized historically (i.e., sequentially or chronologically), by topic or subject, by cause and effect relationships, or by methods used to study the topic. When deriving mathematical relationships, the writer may want to organize the paper by discussing the importance of the topic, related formulas (and their assumptions), the assumptions made in the writer's derivations, the derivations themselves, the advantages and disadvantages in using the new formulas, and perhaps a numerical example.

## The Title

All research reports are titled for reference and identification purposes. A misleading or incomplete title can waste the time of other researchers trying to compile a bibliography of relevant studies. In addition, since indexing services often cross-list studies based on the words in a document's title, the author's responsibility is to construct a title that accurately reflects content. Too inclusive a title can be as misleading as one with picayunish detail.

One way to develop a title is to include a description of 1) the dependent variable, 2) the independent variable, 3) the subjects, and 4) their interrelationships. Consider the following title: "Spelling Achievement of Fourth-Grade Boys As a Function of Three Teacher Characteristics."

In this example, the dependent variable (spelling achievement) seems clear as does the nature of the subjects (fourth-grade boys). In addition, the title implies that an experiment has been performed in which three teacher characteristics act as independent variables. But a researcher cannot tell what these characteristics are without reading the article. The wording could be improved by including the word "Personality" ("Three Teacher *Personality* Characteristics") or, better yet, by indicating which teacher characteristics are being investigated (e.g., "As a Function of Teacher Empathy, Persuasiveness, and Internality").

## Authorship and Institutional Affiliation

In research articles, the author having primary responsibility for the paper is listed first. Only those persons who have made important scientific contributions to the paper should be listed as joint authors. Secretarial and clerical aid can be acknowledged in a footnote but are not granted authorship status. Degrees (MA, PhD) and titles (Dr., Professor) are omitted.

The institutional affiliation of each author is included in research papers. Departments within institutions, however, need not be specified.

# PARTS OF THE RESEARCH REPORT

## Abstract

Those journals that require an abstract usually restrict its length to 175 words. The abstract should be sufficiently detailed to permit readers to judge whether or not they care to read the entire article. The purpose of the study, methods used, subjects, instruments, type of research design, and findings should be included in the abstract.

## Introduction or Problem

The *Introduction* or *Problem* usually includes the following topics.

*Need for the Investigation.* Why is this study important? What contribution will it make? Will it contribute to theory? Will it help to resolve practical problems faced by teachers, administrators, or students? Will it clarify contradictory positions or opinions? Will it improve upon research designs of previous studies? Will it point out limitations of previous research?

*Review of Relevant Literature.* Show how the investigation relates to previously conducted research; point out related theories, opposing positions, methodological errors in earlier works; demonstrate how the problem has been studied by other persons and how your approach differs; if others have performed essentially the same study as you have, justify the need to conduct another study on the same topic.

The literature review is not a listing of studies tangentially or even closely related to the problem, nor is it an attempt to prove that the author has read all of the studies on a given topic. Rather, the review of the literature is selective, organized, and should demonstrate how the present study will build upon others' contributions. It should stress important theoretical positions, relevant major methods, and essential conclusions.

The review of the literature becomes a mere listing of studies if the author fails to point out the contributions or values of the cited studies to the present investigation. Listings often take the following form: "Johnson (1969) found. . . . Billingsly (1972) found . . . , etc." Each study cited should help clarify the relationships between that study and the present one.

The first draft of the review of the literature is often written before the study is actually conducted. This has the advantage of forcing the researcher into considering whether or not the proposed investigation is worth pursuing and may also suggest which approaches or methods may be useful.

*Research Hypotheses.* Research hypotheses should be written in statement form expressing a definite expectation derived from the review of the literature. Hypotheses are not testable if they are expressed as questions.

Sometimes it may appear that the literature is mute on a given topic when in fact the student may not have considered looking in alternative sources. For example, one student proposed a study that involved the training of persons working in sheltered workshops. The proposal was to modify the training environments to more closely approximate the actual conditions of work. The student had searched through the literature on such topics as retardation, sheltered workshops, environments, etc., with no luck. However, when it was suggested that she study the literature on transfer of training and generalization, she was able to find numerous studies and theoretical positions that helped to propose meaningful hypotheses.

*Definition of Terms.* All ambiguous terms used in the hypotheses should be defined operationally. It is not always necessary to devote a special section to the definition of terms. One can, for example, define each ambiguous term following its first presentation. Another possibility is to replace vague terms by more specific referents. Instead of referring to poor adjustment, it might be clearer to talk about high (or low) scores on some specific adjustment inventory.

## Procedures or Methods

The section on procedures will differ depending on the type of study. Empirical studies commonly contain the following topics.

*Subjects.* Describe the characteristics of the population and the method used to draw samples from this population. If relevant, provide tables showing the precision or accuracy of matching experimental and control $Ss$. Include means, standard deviations, and number of cases (standard errors of means are also helpful). If $Ss$ have been assigned randomly to various groups without matching, inform the readers how randomization was accomplished. If an ANCOVA was used to equate $Ss$, describe the covariate means, standard deviations, and the correlation of the covariate with the dependent variable. Always include the number of cases in each comparison group. Describe the similarities and differences between $Ss$ in each treatment. Sufficient detail should be included to allow for replication. Quantify descriptive statements wherever possible. For example, rather than report that 200 college students participated in the study, it would be of greater use also to indicate their year in school, sex distributions, majors, whether or not $Ss$ volunteered or were required to participate, grade point average, and the like.

The researcher is obligated both morally and legally to protect the subject's anonymity and confidentiality. No information that could identify a research participant should be included in a research report. In this matter, faculty have the same rights as students and should not be identifiable in the report unless they agree in writing. Similarly, cooperating schools should not be identified by name unless formal permission to do so is obtained from district superintendents or their authorized personnel.

*Apparatus or Materials.* Commonly used apparatus or materials can be referred to briefly in the research report by describing brand names and model numbers. Unconventional materials or apparatus should be described in greater detail particularly if they might affect student performance. All custom-made equipment should be described in sufficient detail to permit readers to construct the same instruments. Blueprints, drawings, and photographs can be helpful in this regard.

Educational materials are of almost unlimited scope. They range from books and learning aids to desks, tables, learning centers, computer consoles, tests, audio-visual equipment, etc. Whenever possible, the use of equipment and materials should be standardized so their effects can be kept constant in similar studies.

*Instruments.* All tests, interview or questionnaire protocols, and observation records should be described in detail. Reliability and validity data should also be presented for the sample of *Ss* participating in the study. The principles and methods used to construct instruments should be described. The rationale for any elimination of items should be described.

*Instructions.* All instructions to experimental and control *Ss* should be reported verbatim if they constitute an experimental treatment. Standardized test instructions, if used verbatim, need not be reported. Any modifications, of course, must be included in the research report.

*Sequence of Activities.* The replication of any study requires knowledge of the sequence of activities followed by the experimenters. How were *Ss* approached to participate in the study? Were follow-up calls made to persuade *Ss* to participate? How many *Ss* failed to show up? How were experimental treatments administered? Under what conditions were treatments administered? On what basis were groups formed? How were control conditions applied?

*Type of Design.* Let the reader know the type of design employed in the study (*ex post facto*, longitudinal, randomized posttest only, etc.). What statistical analyses were used to test each hypothesis? To what extent were all statistical assumptions met? Be careful to specify which variables were compared and how they were compared. Convert all research hypotheses to their null form if space permits. Specify the level of significance required to reject the null hypothesis.

## Results or Findings

The section on *Results* or *Findings* objectively describes what the experimenter found with regard to each hypothesis. Data can be presented in tables or figures (graphs, lines, charts), but to avoid confusion, they are always referred to or introduced before they are presented.

Results or findings should be presented whether they support *E's* hypotheses or not. Although the explanation of findings is not in this section, the writer has to make sure that all data required in the section on *Discussions* (sometimes called *Summary, Conclusions, and Implications*) are included in the findings.

## Discussion

The last section of the research report permits the writer to *interpret* the study as a whole. It is designed to answer such questions as: Were each of the hypotheses supported at the required significance level? How will you explain contradictory or nonsignificant results? How do these findings fit in with those published by other researchers and referred to in the review of the literature? What exceptions to general principles have been noted in this study? What evidence is there to support or reject opposing points of view? What difference did the study make? Did it contribute to understanding or improving education as the writer argued it would when *The Problem* was discussed? What other studies should be conducted to help resolve the problem?

### References or Bibliography

The bibliography contains only those sources specifically referred to in the text; it omits sources examined but not used by the investigator.

Almost all style manuals provide detailed information on how to prepare a bibliography. The three most important rules are 1) provide enough information to permit the reader to locate the source, 2) be consistent in the way sources are cited, and 3) be accurate. Because different schools, departments, and journals may have their own bibliographical style, it would be wise to check recent publications of these sources and to follow their example.

## ELEMENTS OF STYLE

The research report is a formal document that does not permit colloquial or slang expressions. Its goal is accurate and concise communication; anything that interferes with this goal is to be avoided.

Effective writing takes time. Thoughts must be organized, revised, and edited to present a coherent flow of ideas. The reader has to be guided from one point to the next without being pushed, harangued, talked down to, or—perhaps worse—confused by a writer more interested in completing the report than in communicating with an intended audience.

### Conciseness

Long, rambling sentences obscure the author's purpose and try the patience of busy readers. Consider the following example:

In order to study the area of educational administration, it is evident that today's schools should be examined personally with reference to or in light of modern organizational theory. With a view to better understanding educational administration, by and large what is necessary is that the administrator be familiar with general theoretical principles having wide relevance and an acquaintance with practical leadership skills.

First, eliminate deadwood, those words and expressions that do not contribute to meaning.

To study educational administration, schools should be examined personally with reference to organizational theory. The administrator [should] be familiar with [theory] and [possess] leadership skills.

Second, ask yourself if the meaning is clear. In what way is the study of educational administration related to the personal examination of schools? How does one "examine schools personally with reference to organizational theory?" What theory should the administrator "be familiar with" and what is the relationship between leadership and the rest of the paragraph? What the writer meant was: "The study of educational administration requires an understanding of organizational theory as well as practical administrative experience."

Redundancy violates the principle of economy in writing. A "mutual discussion" is redundant because all discussions are "mutual." Other redundancies include "true facts," "students in schools," and "classroom teachers."

Prepositional phrases tend to increase verbosity. Try to eliminate or substitute for such expressions as *in light of, in terms of, in order to, in favor of, in the neighborhood of, in the area of, on the grounds of, on the basis of, for the purpose of, with regard to, with reference to, with a view to, with the result that,* etc.

Careful and concise writers also avoid beginning sentences with *there are, there were, there is.* For example, "There were too many students in the room" can easily be changed to the more direct sentence, "Too many students were in the room."

Certain words have been used so often that they have become trite and imprecise. The word *case,* for example, can usually be omitted or replaced by a more specific term. "In most cases, the woodwinds were delightful" could mean that *generally* they were delightful or that they were delightful as long as they were crated. When one remembers that *case* may be used to refer to a patient, a legal suit, an instance, an example, a situation, support for an argument, and the like, the word loses much of its clarity.

Other words that should be used carefully include *prove, cause, determine,* and *influence. Prove* is usually reserved for mathematical and other deductive proofs. *Cause* should not be confused with other types of functional relationships. *Determine* can mean *cause, control,* or *affect* and therefore should be used only if its meaning will be clear from context. *Influence* is usually limited to an effect on persons.

Generally, simpler and more concrete words are preferred to the more complex and abstract. *Teacher* is clearer than *school personnel,* and *test score* is preferred to *knowledge level.*

Unfortunately, certain terms are widely (but incorrectly) used in education. *Conference,* for example, is a noun and not a verb. One may *confer* but not *conference.* Reports may be *completed* but not *finalized.* Students may show *enthusiasm* but are not *enthused.*

Some words may sound as if they could be used as synonyms, when, in fact, they have different meanings. *Percent* (or the symbol %), for example, must be used with a number (i.e., use either *10 percent* or *10%*); *percentage* is used with an adjective (such as a *small percentage*) or when no number is specified (e.g., *the percentage was unknown*). The expression "some percentage of students" is redundant and should be written as simply "some students."

## Grammar

Sometimes errors of number appear in research reports:

*Each, every,* and *everyone* are singular and require a singular verb.
*Datum* is singular; *data* requires a plural verb ending.
*Curriculum* is singular; *curricula* is plural.
*Curriculum vitae* is singular; *curricula vitae* is plural (the term *résumé* may be simpler to use).
*Analysis* is singular; *analyses* is plural.
*Criterion* is singular; *criteria* is plural.
*Phenomenon* is singular; *phenomena* is plural.

## Tenses

*The present tense is used* to report well-accepted generalizations that apply to current situations:

"Developmental data *can be* analyzed cross-sectionally and longitudinally."

and to refer to the presentation of data:

"Table 1 *shows* the means and standard deviations of posttest data for the experimental and control groups."

*The past tense is used* to report research findings:

"The experimental group *obtained* a mean of 12.67."

to specify findings reported by others:

"Allington (1976) *found* that. . . ."

and to report one's own conclusions:

"Sixth graders *performed* at a higher level than did the fifth graders."

Use the past and present tenses in discussing findings:

"Although the data *are* not unequivocal, they *support* the evidence *reported* by Smith (1974).

## Abbreviations

Abbreviations should be used sparingly and only if they are commonly understood or defined in the research paper. Such abbreviations as IQ, ESP, and YMCA need not be defined in the paper since they are commonly understood. Other abbreviations should be spelled out the first time they appear in the report (e.g., "The Initial Teaching Alphabet (ITA)"). Subsequently, the abbreviation may be used without definition. Abbreviations using capital letters appear without periods. Periods do, however, separate letters that refer to initials (e.g., B. F. Skinner).

Currently, journals of the American Psychological Association (APA) do not use the abbreviations *S* and *E* for subject and experimenter, but this practice is not commonly followed in educational journals. APA[1] has argued that it is often clearer to refer to generic terms such as *children*, *rats*, or *teachers*.

Statistical abbreviations are underlined if they are to appear in italic print: *df*, *t*-test, *F* ratio, *N*. Greek letters and subscripts are not italicized: $\sigma$, $SS_\omega$.

Commonly used Latin abbreviations are presented with lowercase letters:

| | |
|---|---|
| ca. | (about) |
| cf. | (compare) |
| et al. | (and others) |
| etc. | (and so forth) |
| i.e. | (that is) |
| ibid. | (in the same place) |
| p. | (page) |
| pp. | (pages) |
| viz. | (namely) |
| vs. | (versus) |

The trend is to report all measurements in metric units. Some common metric conversions are provided in Table V-1.

### TABLE V-1

### Metric Conversions

| To Convert: | Multiply U.S. Measures by: |
|---|---|
| Inches to meters (in. to m.) | .0254 |
| Feet to meters (ft. to m.) | .3048 |
| Yards to meters (yd. to m.) | .9144 |
| Miles to kilometers (mi. to km.) | 1.609 |
| Ounces to grams (oz. to g.) | 28.35 |
| Pounds to kilograms (lb. to kg.) | .4536 |
| Gallons to liters (gal. to l.) | 3.785 |
| Quarts to liters (qt. to l.) | .946 |

[1] American Psychological Association, *Publication Manual of the American Psychological Association*, 2d ed. (Washington, D.C.: American Psychological Association, 1974), p. 35.

418

Kilometers and kilograms consist of 1000 meters and 1000 grams, respectively. One mile, for example, is equivalent to 1609 meters or 1.609 kilometers. To convert meters to kilometers, divide meters by 1000. Because centimeters are $\frac{1}{100}$ of meter, multiply meters by 100 to find the number of centimeters (thus, there are 160,900 centimeters in a mile). Millimeters are found by multiplying meters by 1000.

To convert degrees Fahrenheit (°F) to degrees Celsius (°C), subtract 32° from °F, and then multiply by $\frac{5}{9}$. For example, 32°F = 0°C, and 65°F is 18.33°C.

## Spelling

Dictionaries permit a choice in the spelling of some words. Use the preferred spelling, which is almost always listed first. *Webster's Third New International Dictionary* is considered authoritative and comprehensive; when in doubt, consult that source.

The American Psychological Association's *Publication Manual*[2] lists a number of principles for hyphenation:

*1.* Hyphens should be used only if they serve a purpose. Little is gained by hyphenating perfectly clear expressions such as *factor analytic methods.*

*2.* Hyphens can change the meaning of words as in the sentence, "The man re-covered the book" (covered the book again) and "The man recovered the book" (the man regained the book).

*3.* Compound adjectives that precede the noun normally require hyphenation (*a chi-square test*), but the hyphen is dropped when the adjective follows the verb (*The best test would be a chi square*). *The use of chi square* shows the same word as a noun.

*4.* Except to avoid awkwardness of expression or confusion, prefixes should be written without hyphens as in *posttest* or *multitrait*. All words beginning with *self,* as in *self-conscious,* are hyphenated.

*5.* Use hyphens if there are two or more terms that modify the same noun as in *30-, 40-, and 50-minute delays.*

*6.* Compound numbers from *twenty-one* to *ninety-nine* are hyphenated.

*7.* Compounds that begin with a number should be hyphenated: 5-point scale, two *15-minute* sessions.

## Capitalization

Proper nouns are capitalized even though they are used generically: *Xerox, Plexiglas, Coke.* Also capitalized are the names of factors derived from factor analytic studies: *Ascendance, Introversion,* etc. Use capitals for names of tables, figures, and chapters when they appear in the text, as *Table 3, Figure 8, Chapter 12.*

## Use of Numbers

If possible, avoid beginning sentences with a number. If a number must begin a sentence, spell it out: "*Three hundred twenty-four* students were enrolled."

[2]American Psychological Association, pp. 72–75.

Cardinal numbers from *zero* through *nine*, and ordinal numbers from *first* through *ninth* should be spelled out unless they refer to statistical data ($r = +0.37$, $\bar{X} = 4.6$); numbers greater than *nine* appear as numerals. For example: *four* lists, *ninth* chapter, *10* lists, *10th* chapter, $N = 3$. Centiles, however, are always expressed in figures: *8th* percentile, *34th* percentile, percentile of *25*.

In general, avoid roman numerals except when custom requires their use: *Type I error; Factor III.* In all other instances, use arabic numerals: Table 1, Figure 5, Volume 4, Experiment 2. The *Publication Manual* of the American Psychological Association (1974) suggests that arabic numerals be used in the following circumstances even if they refer to numbers below 10:

| | |
|---|---|
| Measurements: | students received 2 mg. of drug $X$ |
| Ages: | varied in age from 6 to 7 years |
| Percentages: | received 6% rebate (or 6 percent) |
| Math operations: | divided by 2 (or $\div$ 2) |
| Ratios: | 2:1 |
| Fractions or decimals: | $4\frac{1}{2}$-year-old, 3.67 m. |
| Exact values of money: | who received \$5 an hour |
| Scores: | a score of 37 |
| Scale values: | a 5-point scale |

## Preparing the Research Report

All manuscripts (except final copies of theses and dissertations) should be double spaced throughout including footnotes, tables, titles, and references. Footnotes and references, however, are single spaced in the final copy of theses and dissertations.

*Paper.* Many colleges and universities have rules regarding the quality of paper to be used for theses and dissertations (usually 100 percent rag and a minimum weight of 16 pounds). For research reports submitted to journals, white bond paper is satisfactory. Do not use onionskin, or coated (erasable) paper since it tears easily, smudges, and is difficult to edit. All paper should be standard size ($8\frac{1}{2}$-by-11 inches).

*Typing.* All manuscripts must be typed on only one side of each sheet, with a 1- to $1\frac{1}{2}$-inch margin on all sides of the text. Use standard type (pica or elite) and avoid manuscript, italic, and other difficult-to-read styles. Corrections should be kept to a minimum and should not be easily detected. Most schools will not permit noticeable typographical errors, but journals will usually accept minor corrections if they are made neatly. Use black ribbons only.

Paragraph openings are indented five spaces. Hyphens are typed without spaces (cross-sectional), except in certain cases (a 5- or 6-point difference); but minus signs are typed with a space preceding and following the hyphen ($5 - 2$), unless a negative number is indicated ($-1.05$); a dash is typed as two successive hyphens, with no spaces.

*Quotes.* Unless a quotation is necessary, it should be omitted. Short quotations are set off by quotation marks with the page number of the original source in parentheses at the end of the sentence: Jones (1975) reported, "Fewer than 1% . . . remained" (p. 15); *or* The investigator reported, "Fewer than 1% . . . remained" (Jones, 1975, p. 15).

Quotations requiring three or more lines of type should appear without quotation marks. The entire quote (and not just the first line) should be indented five spaces from the left margin; the page reference follows the period.

Jones (1975) concluded:

> Although the difference between the experimental and control groups was statistically significant, a difference of only 0.7 points is hardly of practical importance. (pp. 25–26)

Quotations must always credit the author; failure to do so is plagiaristic, unethical, and possibly illegal. Paraphrases are not quotations, but if the material is recognizably someone else's, it may be treated as plagiarism by the copyright holder. Ordinarily, it is permissible to quote a small portion (up to 250 words) of a textbook without obtaining permission from the copyright holder if the source is credited. But poetry (of any length), photographs, illustrations, charts, letters, tables, music, speeches, newspaper articles, cartoons, and material from books written for the general public (i.e., not textbooks) should never be used without obtaining written permission of the copyright holder.[3]

*Headings and Subdivisions.* Use headings and subdivisions to show how the report is organized. For research papers other than theses and dissertations (which are organized into chapters), use the following format for main headings, side headings, and paragraph headings:

# METHOD (MAIN HEADING)

## Subjects (Side Heading)

Paragraph⎱ *Population.* The population was defined as. . . .
headings  ⎰ *Sample.* The sample consisted of. . . .

## Apparatus and Materials (Side heading)

All headings are underlined and begin with capital letters. Main and side headings are typed without periods and placed on lines by themselves. Paragraph headings, in contrast, are typed on the same line as the first sentence of the paragraph and are followed by periods. If more than one word is used in paragraph headings, only the first word is capitalized. All main words are capitalized in main and side headings.

[3] *Prentice-Hall Author's Guide* (Englewood Cliffs, N.J.: Prentice-Hall, 1962), pp.10–12.

*Tables.* Each table is typed on a separate page and is referred to in the text before it is presented. Although the table must be complete enough so that it can be understood, the important points should be summarized in the text.

All tables are numbered (Table 1, Table 2, etc.) and given titles. The most important elements in the table must appear in the title (see Table V-2).

## TABLE V-2

Means and Standard Deviations of Experimental and Control Children in Grades 7–8 on the Criterion Measure

| | | Grades | | | |
| | | 7 | | 8 | |
| GROUP | $N$ | $\bar{X}$ | $s$ | $\bar{X}$ | $s$ |
|---|---|---|---|---|---|
| Experimental | | | | | |
|   Males | 36 | 36.4 | 4.6 | 41.3 | 5.1 |
|   Females | 38 | 37.1 | 4.4 | 40.8 | 5.2 |
| Control | | | | | |
|   Males | 35 | 31.3 | 4.7 | 35.8 | 4.5 |
|   Females | 39 | 31.4 | 4.4 | 35.6 | 4.3 |

All columns and rows in the table must have headings. Horizontal lines may be included to separate the title from column headings; vertical lines should be avoided since they tend to clutter the table.

*Figures.* Figures and graphs are expensive to reproduce and, for that reason, should be used sparingly. Because tables usually provide more accurate data than do figures, they are usually preferred unless the intent is to depict trends or relationships more easily understood by a graph.

Figures, drawings, and photographs are best prepared by professionals. Most universities have copy or printing centers that prepare accurate reproductions, but art and engineering stores do carry stencils and black india ink for hand lettering.

Figures should be numbered consecutively (with arabic numerals). The word *Figure*, followed by a number and a period (e.g., Figure 1.), is placed under the display. The caption, like the title of a table, must clearly describe whatever the figure is attempting to show. Explanations of the figure (in parentheses) follow the caption. Be sure that axes are labeled and relationships shown without exaggeration.

library sources
useful
in educational
research

VI

## Indexes

*1*. **Bibliographical Index:** Contains lists of sources that contain extensive bibliographies.

*2*. **Public Affairs Information Service Index:** Published weekly since 1915 with an annual cumulation; contains current information throughout the world with many articles pertaining to education.

*3*. **Social Science Index:** Since 1916, a quarterly index of some 200 periodicals. Prior to 1975, it was known as the *Social Sciences and Humanities Index*.

*4*. **Humanities Index:** This is the second index that developed out of the *Social Sciences and Humanities Index*.

---

[1] *Resources in Education* (RIE), *Current Index to Journals in Education* (CIJE), and the *Education Index* have been discussed in Chapter 3.

*5.* **Social Science Citation Index:** Lists authors who have been quoted in a book, footnote, or bibliography.

*6.* **State Education Journal Index:** Annotates state education journals by subject.

*7.* **United States Government Publications Monthly Catalog:** This is the only index for government publications. It has an excellent annual subject index.

*8.* **The Index to Periodicals by and about Negroes:** Indexes by author and subject and includes book reviews, poems, creative works, etc. In 1974, The Index to Periodicals by and about Blacks superseded the previous index.

*9.* **Imprints Pre-1956:** Published by the Library of Congress, it is estimated to be an 800-volume work when completed; will enable one to look up any book published before 1956 and held in major libraries of the United States. Main entries are listed.

*10.* **Library of Congress Catalog. Books: Subject:** A multivolume set of books with reproduced subject cards of the Library of Congress and other American libraries participating in its cooperative cataloging program.

*11.* **Business Education Index:** Published annually; indexes articles from selected periodicals and yearbooks.

## ERIC Clearinghouse Publications

*1.* **AIM/ARM (Abstracts of Instructional Materials in Vocational and Technical Education and Abstracts of Research and Related Materials in Vocational and Technical Education):** Published by Ohio State University's Clearinghouse since 1967. Contains résumés organized under topical headings; abstracts available by computer search.

*2.* **ERIC Clearinghouse on Early Childhood Education:** Since 1973, has processed all documents on childhood education (published at University of Illinois); since 1974, published *Research Relating to Children*, formerly published by U.S. Children's Bureau.

*3.* Miscellaneous bibliographies have been published in book form on such topics as *Migrant Education, Indian Children, Mexican-American Education, Reading, Educational Administration*, and *Early Childhood Education*.

## Abstracts

*1.* **Research Studies in Education:** Published annually since 1928. Contains a classified and annotated list of doctoral dissertations and, recently, a methods bibliography.

*2.* **Psychological Abstracts:** Since 1927, an excellent source for anyone interested in a psychological problem. Published monthly, these abstracts provide a topic and author index. Three-year cumulative indexes are available. A subject search is also available by computer.

*3.* **Poverty and Human Resources Abstracts and Survey of Current Literature:** Published monthly since 1966; contains abstracts, feature articles, and special analyses of current problems.

*4.* **Rehabilitation Literature:** Annotates periodical articles, pamphlets, and books relating to rehabilitation under many subject entries monthly since 1950.

*5.* **Child Development Abstracts and Bibliography:** Published three times a year since 1927+; abstracts 140 journals and selected books in biology, psychology, education, medicine, and public health. It contains author and subject indexes.

*6.* **Crime and Delinquency Abstracts and Current Projects: An International Bibliography:** Published bimonthly 1963 to 1972; abstracts scientific and professional literature and includes accounts of ongoing research projects.

*7.* **Sociology of Education Abstracts:** Published bimonthly since 1965 for those interested in theory and methods in the social sciences. Also included are education for vocations and education for the disavantaged.

*8.* **Educational Administration Abstracts:** Published three times a year since 1965; abstracts from almost 100 journals and related areas from the United States, England, France, and Australia.

*9.* **Dissertation Abstracts International:** Provides brief résumés of doctoral dissertations from nearly all colleges and universities offering this degree. Master's theses, if available or referenced at all, are sometimes loaned to students through interlibrary loan arrangements. Doctoral dissertations can be bought either on microfilm or on hard copy from University Microfilm, Ann Arbor, Michigan.

*10.* **Abstracts for Social Workers:** Published quarterly; covers 200 journals in social work and related sciences and professions. It contains author and subject indexes.

*11.* **American Educational Research Association Annual Meeting Abstracts of Papers and Symposia:** Lists paper sessions and symposia presented at annual meetings since 1970.

*12.* **College Student Personnel Abstracts:** Published quarterly; abstracts articles, proceedings, and books from over 100 journals since 1965.

*13.* **Language Teaching Abstracts:** Published quarterly since 1968; summarizes articles in psychology, linguistics, language studies, teaching, and methodology and technology.

*14.* **Mental Retardation Abstracts:** Published quarterly since 1964; covers international literature on mental retardation.

*15.* **Exceptional Child Education Resources:** Formerly titled "Exceptional Child Education Abstracts." Includes current publications, dissertations, and media materials; published quarterly.

## Bibliographies

*1.* Morrow, William R. **Behavior Therapy Bibliography** (1950–1969): Annotates and indexes published sources according to type of experiment, setting variables, subject variables, form of target behaviors or behavior deficits, and type of modification procedures.

*2.* Tyler, Louise. **A Selected Guide to Curriculum Literature** (1970): Analyzes and critiques selected curriculum material.

*3.* Davis, Bonnie M., comp. **A Guide to Information Sources for Reading:** Lists bibliographies, published reviews at all levels, abstracts and indexes publications, journals, conference proceedings, and general and related information sources.

*4.* **Britannica Review of Foreign Language Education:** Sponsored by the American Council on the Teaching of Foreign Languages, it is an excellent source of information on this general topic. It is published irregularly by different editors. Bibliographies and indexes are included. *The ACTFL Review of Foreign Language Education* is the new title that continues the series through 1975.

*5.* Monroe, Walter Scott, and Shores, Louis. **Bibliographies and Summaries in Education:** An annotated catalog and important historical source of over 4000 bibliographies published 1910–1935.

## Book Trade Catalogs

*1.* **Books in Print** provides the researcher with a list of all books currently available from different publishers arranged by author and title.

*2.* **A Subject Guide to Books in Print** makes it possible to locate books currently available on any given topic.

*3.* **Forthcoming Books in Print** has an author and subject guide and indicates books that have been accepted for publication.

*4.* The **Publishers' Trade List Annual** (PTLA) provides alphabetical listings of major publishers' catalogs. The PTLA is particularly useful in finding the authors and titles of books in series such as those published by Teachers College, Columbia University.

*5.* The **Cumulative Book Index** (CBI) appears monthly and lists newly published books.

*6.* The **Union List of Serials in Libraries of the United States and Canada**, 3d ed. (1965) provides a list of periodicals and serials held by libraries in the United States and Canada, arranged alphabetically by title or main entry. It is particularly useful in helping to locate a periodical not locally available. There are also supplementary volumes, *New Serial Titles, 1950–1974*, and quarterly supplements, which also provide listings held geographically. *New Serial Titles 1950–1974 Subject Guide* is also available, thus making it possible to look under a topic to locate holdings of various libraries.

*7.* The National Information Center for Educational Media has *Subject Indexes* listed for many types of media, vol. 1 (1971+).

*8.* The U.S. Library of Congress **Catalog of Motion Pictures and Filmstrips** (1963 to date) has the most complete catalog available of films and filmstrips.

*9.* The U.S. Library of Congress **Catalog of Music and Phonograph Records** (1963 to date) is also a useful source of information.

index

Lexical definitions, 69-70, 72
Library, use of, 49-51, 423-26
Likert scale, 249-50, 255, 256, 260, 290
Limited-response question, 235
Lindquist, E. F., 123, 124, 317
Lindzey, Gardner, 294
Linguistic research, 17
*Literary Digest* poll, 179-80, 183
Literature, and data retrieval, 18
Literature, review of, 40, 58;
  sources of information, 51-52;
  use of library, 49-51;
  uniform bibliographical card system,
    54-56;
  writing, 52-54
Logic, 4-5;
  and hypothesis, 62
*Logic of Modern Physics, The,* 70
Longitudinal approach, 98-100, 108


Machine scoring answer sheets, 315-18
Machover Draw-a-Person Test, 283-84
McNemar, Quinn, 203
Maier, N.R.F., 8-9
Maier's law, 8
Manchly, John, 330
Mander, A.E., 3
Mark I computer, 330
Marks, Eli S., 203
Mark-sense cards, 319-20
Massachusetts Institute of Technology, 331
Massilas, Byron G., 47
Mathematical reasoning, 5
Mathematical research, 17
Mathematics, new, 23-24
Maturation, of experiment subjects, 126, 146
May, Mark A., 102, 277
Mead, Margaret, 104-105
Mean, 371-72
Measurement: as change agent, 270, 278;
  reliability. *See* Reliability coefficients;
  repeated, 133-38, 147;
  validity of, 227-28
Measurement Research Center, 317
Measures, unobtrusive, 269-73, 278-79;
  and observation, 273-78, 279
Median, 372-73
Meehl, Paul E., 80
Memory, computer, 332-33
Memory: tests of, 287-89; theories of, 7-8
Mencken, H. L., 31
*Mental Measurements Yearbooks,* 205-206
Mercury Theatre, 48-49
Methods, research: and contradictory
    findings, 42-43;
  faulty, 43-44;
  and research purpose, 40-41;
  uncritical acceptance of, 31-34, 36
Miles, Mathew B., 38
Milgram, Stanley, 276
Mill, John Stuart, 86-87

*Minnesota Multiphasic Personality
    Inventory,* 224
Misinformation, control and reduction of, 6
Misperception test, 288-89
Mixed model, 166, 175
Models, 12;
  and factorial designs, 166, 174-75;
  and theory construction, 10-11
Modification, 21
Moore School of Electrical Engineering, 330
Moral judgement tests, 289-90
Moreno, J. L., 291
Morgan, John J. B., 286-87
Morphett, Mabel V., 32
Mortality, experimental: and internal
    validity, 127, 147
Morton, James T., 286-87
Mosteller, Frederick, 239
Motivation, and interview, 233
Multiple correlation, 95, 108
Multiple hypotheses, 63-64, 72
Multiple treatment interference, 143, 148
Multiple-variable prediction, 93-95
Murdock, George P., 105
Murray, H. A., 290

Nagel, Ernest, 15
National Education Association, 2
Naturalistic observation, 100-103, 108-109
Neel, Ann Filinger, 67-69
New Math, 23-24
Newton, Issac, 64
New York *Evening Mail,* 31
No-failure grading policy, 24
Nominal scale, 248
Nomograph, 324-26
Nomothetic approach, 77, 106
Nonequivalent control group design, 159-60,
    173, 174
Note-taking, skills, 54-57
Novelty effects, 143, 148
Null hypothesis, 380-81

Objectivity, in interview, 238-42
Observation: contrived, 275-78;
  in empiricism, 6-7;
  and hypothesis, 62;
  naturalistic, 100-103;
  simple, 273-75;
  situational, 102-103, 109
Observational set, 273
Observer, participant, 275
One-group pretest-posttest design, 153-54,
    172, 173
One-shot case study, 153, 172, 173
Operational definitions, 70-71, 73
Operationalism, 70, 73
Opinion, research to resolve conflicting,
    45-46
Optical scanning machine scoring system, 318
Ordinal interactions, 169
Ordinal scale, 248, 249-52

Organismic variable, 117, 146
Organizations, and factor analysis, 86
Osgood, Charles E., 297-300
Output, computer, 333-34

Parameter, 371, 386
Parry, Hugh J., 234, 242
Parsimony, law of, 10, 12, 64, 72
Parten, Mildred B., 267
Partial correlation coefficient, 88-89, 107
Pascal, Blaise, 329
Payne, Stanley L., 238
Peatman, John Gray, 183
Perception, tests of, 287-89
Peterson, John, 42
Philosophical analyses, 17
Piaget, Jean, 77, 101
Platt, John R., 75
Politz, Alfred, 203
Population: defined, 180;
   homogeneity of, 197, 199, 200;
   in statistics, 371;
   validity, 141, 148
Posttest-only control group design, 159, 173, 174
Posttest sensitization, 144, 148
Practice, and theory, 28-31, 36
Pragmatism, 28
Prediction studies, 89-97, 107-108
Predictive validity, 220, 222, 228
Prejudice. See Bias
Pretest-posttest control group design with randomization, 157-58, 173, 174
Pretest sensitization, 144, 148
Preyer, William, 101
Problem, research: criteria used to select, 47-49;
   defined, 40-41;
   and multiple hypotheses, 63, 74;
   types of, 41-47
Program, computer, 338-39
Programs, educational, 21-22
Progress, American view of, 16
Projective techniques, 283-85
PROJECT TALENT, 45, 188-89
Proofs, mathematical, 4-5
Psychoanalytic theory, 7-8
Punched card, EDP, 321-23
Purpose, research, 40-41
*Pygmalion in the Classroom,* 32n, 33-34, 36

Q-sort technique, 294-96
Questionnaire, 244, 262;
   advantages, 244-45, 262;
   arrangement of items, 255-56, 263-64;
   classification by form, 256-57, 264;
   cover letter, 258-59, 264;
   disadvantages of, 245-46, 262-63;
   form of items, 248-55, 263;
   item writing, 257-58, 264;
   preliminary run, 258, 264;

Questionnaire *(cont.):*
   reliability of measurements obtained from, 259-60, 264;
   use of, 246-48;
   validity of, 260-61, 264-65;
   work table, 246-48, 263. *See also* Interview

Rand Corporation, 183
Randomization, 118-19, 146;
   and equating experimental group with control group, 128-29, 139, 147;
   and pretest-posttest control group design, 157-58, 173
Randomized-block design, 138n
Random model, 166, 175
Random number, 184, 185, 191
Random sampling: simple, 183-85, 199;
   stratified, 183, 185-90, 199
Rationalism, 4-5, 11
Ratio scale, 248
Reactive arrangement, 142, 148
Record: episodic, 272-73;
   private, 273;
   running, 272
Regression, linearity of, 89, 107
Regression, statistical: and internal experiment validity, 126-27, 147
Regression line, 91n
Reliability, 206-208, 226;
   interobserver, 239;
   interview, 238-42;
   of measurements from questionnaires, 259-60
Reliability coefficient: assumptions about, 213-15, 227;
   equivalence, 209-211, 227;
   and group variability, 215-16, 227;
   internal consistency, 211-13, 27;
   and level of difficulty, 218-19, 227;
   and number of items, 216-18, 227;
   required magnitudes of, 219;
   stability, 208-209, 226;
   stability and equivalence, 209-211, 227;
   types of, 208-215
Replication, of research events, 48-49
Report, research: form for evaluating, 404-408;
   parts of, 412-15;
   style, 415-22;
   writing, 409-412
Reproducibility index, 252
*Resources in Education* (RIE), 52
Results, and evaluation, 20-21
Revelation, 4, 11
Revie, V. A., 295-96
Rice, J. M., 2
Richardson, Stephen A., 235
RIE, 52
Role selection, 270-78
Rorschach test, 283, 284
Rosenthal, Robert, 32-34

Ross, Mina, 15
Rowntree, B. Seebohm, 194-95, 200
Russell, David H., 304

Salk, Jonas, 23
Sample survey, as descriptive research, 80, 107
Sampling, 179-80, 199-200;
  accuracy, 194-96, 200;
  area, 183, 192-93, 199;
  biased sample, 182;
  characteristics of sample, 180-81;
  cluster, 183, 192-93, 199;
  cost of, 196-97, 198, 200;
  defined, 180;
  distribution, 378;
  episode, 101, 108-109;
  homogeneity of population, 197, 199, 200;
  random, 180;
  representative, 180;
  selecting samples, 181-83;
  simple random, 183-85, 199;
  size of sample, 193-94, 200;
  stratified random, 183, 185-90, 199;
  systematic, 183, 190-92, 199;
  time, 101-102, 109;
  unbiased sample, 182-83
Samuels, S. Jay, 66
Sax, Gilbert, 44, 45-46
Scalogram technique, 251-52
Schafer, Roy, 183
Scheffé, H., 392
Science, 5-11
Score. See Measurement
Seeman, Melvin, 289-90
Selection, and validity, 125, 146
Semantic differential, 296-301
Sensitivity, experimental, 119-25, 146
Sensitization, 144, 148
Seperate-sample pretest-posttest design, 160-62, 173, 174
Serendipity, 65, 72
Sheldon, M. Stephen, 295
Shinn, Milicent W., 101
Sidman, Murray, 65
Significance, statistical vs. practical, 386-87
Significance level, 381
Simmons, Willard, 203
Simple random sampling, 183-85
Simplicity, of theory, 10, 12
Simulation, of experiment by computer, 328
Single group experimental design, 152, 172;
  equivalent materials design, 156, 173, 174;
  equivalent time-sampling design, 155-56, 173, 174;
  one-group pretest-posttest design, 153-54, 172, 173;
  one-shot case study, 153, 172, 173;
  time-series experiment, 154-55, 173, 174
Single-variable prediction, 89-93, 107-108
Situational observations, 102-103, 109

Situational test, 277
Slonim, Morris James, 203
Smith, B. B., 183
Smith, C. E., 290
Smith, Frederick R., 47
Snedecor, George S., 183
Sociometry, 291-94
Solomon, Richard L., 159
Solomon four-group design, 158-59, 173, 174
Sorenson, A. Garth, 295
Spearman, Charles, 85
Spearman-Brown formula, 216-17, 242;
  nomograph for, 325, 326
Spiral-omnibus, form of item arrangement, 212
Split-half formula, 211-13
Spranger, 273
Spurious index correlation, 87-88
Squares, sum of, 373;
  between methods, 393-94;
  between-sexes, 394
Stability and equivalence coefficients, 208, 210-11, 227
Stability coefficients, 208-209, 226
Standard deviation, 374-75
Standard error of the mean, 378-79
*Standards for Educational and Psychlogical Tests,* 207-208, 220
Stanfor-Binet Intelligence Scale, 70, 223
Stanley, Julian C., 45, 152, 154, 156-57, 158, 164, 172
State University of Iowa, 317
Static-group comparison, 156-57, 173, 174
Statistical inference, 182, 377-87
*Statistical Package for the Social Sciences,* 335
Statistical reasoning, 370-71
Statistics: descriptive, 371-77;
  research to correct inappropriate use of, 44-45. *See also specific entries e.g.* Squares, sum of
Stephenson, William, 294
Stereotypes, 4. *See also* Bias
Stevens, S.S., 248
Storage, computer, 332-33
Strata, 185-86
Stress interview, 235
Suci, George J., 299
Sudman, Seymour, 202
Suppes, Patrick, 15
Syllogism, 5, 286-87
Syllogistic reasoning tests, 286-87
Systematic sampling, 190-92, 199-200

Tables, computational, 324
Tape, audio: and contrived observation, 278
Teacher-pupil ratio, 22
Teachers, and educational research, 27-28, 36
Terman, Lewis M., 51
Terms, definition of, 69-71, 72-73
Test Analysis Form, 205

Test revision, and factor analysis, 85-86
Tests, 204-205, 226;
　criterion contamination, 225, 228;
　cross validation, 225-26, 228;
　and internal experiment validity, 126, 147;
　selecting, 205-206, 226.
　　*See also* Measurement; Reliability;
　　Reliability coefficients; *names and types*
　　*of specific tests. e.g.:* Rorschach test;
　　Projective techniques
Tests of General Ability (TOGA), 33-34
Textbooks, 51-52
Thematic Apperception Test, 283, 284
Theory, 5;
　construction, 7-8, 12;
　and cross-cultural study, 104;
　defined, 7;
　development of, 42;
　and facts, 8-10, 12;
　and empirical investigations, 41-42;
　models, 10-11, 12;
　research to clarify or validate, 41-42;
　simplicity of, 10, 12
*Thesaurus of ERIC Descriptors,* 52
Thorndike, Robert L., 33-34
*Three Princes of Serendip, The,* 65
Thurstone, L. L., 253
Thurstone scale, 253-54, 255, 260, 290
*Time,* 246
Time, interaction with treatment, 145, 148-49
Time sampling, 101-102, 109
Time-sampling, equivalent, 155-56, 173, 174
Time-series experiment, 154-55, 173, 174
Timing instruments, 278
Traces, physical, 271
Training: in educational research, 27-28, 36,
　48, 57;
　of interviewers, 233-34
Travers, R.M.W., 52
Treatment, experimental, 21-22;
　and history, 144-45, 148;
　interaction, 141, 148;
　and sensitivity, 125, 146;
　and time, 145, 148-49
Tukey, John W., 392
Tylor, Edward B., 104
*Types of Men,* 273

UICSM, 22-23
Uncritical acceptance, of research findings,
　31-34, 36
Underachievement, 42-43
UNESCO, 161
Uniform bibliographical card system, 54-55,
　58
Uniqueness, as criteria of research problem,
　48-49, 57

United Nations, 161
U.S. Office of Education, 76;
　Cooperative Research Branch, 45
U.S. Office of Strategic Services, 277
University Microfilms, 328
University of Illinois, 22-23, 331
University of Pennsylvania, 330-31
University of Pittsburgh, 45
Unobtrusive measures, 269-73, 278-79;
　and observation, 273-78, 279

Validity: external, 125-27, 140-45, 146,
　148-49;
　interview, 238-42;
　of measurements, 221-26, 227-28;
　population, 141, 148;
　of questionnaire, 260-61
Van Dalen, D. B., 9
Variables: adjusting, 130, 147;
　in crosscultural studies, 105;
　dependent, 117, 118, 146;
　dependent, measurement of, 145, 148;
　in experimental research, 116-18. 146;
　extraneous, 118, 146;
　extraneous, control of, 125-27, 146;
　independent, 117, 118, 146;
　independent, describing, 142-43, 148;
　intervening, 71, 73;
　in prediction studies, 89-97;
　treatment, 21-22, 35
Variance, analysis of: factorial experiments,
　392-402;
　one-way randomized groups, 387-92
Verification, 6, 12
Visual perception test, 288

Walberg, Herbert J., 144
Walpole, Horace, 65
Washburne, C., 32
Watson, G. B., 286, 289
Webb, Eugene, 50, 271, 273
Wechsler Adult Intelligence Scale, 70, 223
Welch, Wayne W., 144
Western Electric Corporation, 142
Whirlwind I computer, 331
White, Mary Alice, 203
Whiting, John W. M., 104, 106
Willover, Donald, 75
Wittrock, M. C., 297
Wolff, H. A., 290
Work table, questionnaire, 246-48

Yale University, 276
York, England, 194